INTERPRETING THE PARABLES

CRAIG L. BLOMBERG

INTERVARSITY PRESS
DOWNERS GROVE, ILLINOIS 60515

InterVarsity Press is the book-publishing division of InterVarsity Christian Fellowship, a student movement active on campus at hundreds of universities, colleges and schools of nursing. For information about local and regional activities, write Public Relations Dept., InterVarsity Christian Fellowship, 6400 Schroeder Rd., P.O. Box 7895, Madison, WI 53707-7895.

Cover illustration: Roberta Polfus

ISBN 0-8308-1271-7

Printed in the United States of America ∞

Library of Congress Cataloging-in-Publication Data

Blomberg, Craig.
    Interpreting the parables / Craig L. Blomberg.
      p.   cm.
    Includes bibliographical references.
    ISBN 0-8308-1271-7
    1. Jesus Christ—Parables.   I. Title.
  BT375.2.B54   1990
  226'.806—dc20   89-38811
                                               CIP

---

21 20 19 18 17 16 15 14 13 12
13 12 11 10 09 08 07 06 05 04

Abbreviations of Periodicals

ASTI	*Annual of the Swedish Theological Institute*
ATR	*Anglican Theological Review*
BeO	*Bibbia e oriente*
Bib	*Biblica*
BJRL	*Bulletin of the John Rylands Library of the University of Manchester*
BSac	*Bibliotheca Sacra*
BT	*Bible Translator*
BTB	*Biblical Theology Bulletin*
BZ	*Biblische Zeitschrift*
CBQ	*Catholic Biblical Quarterly*
ChQ	*Church Quarterly*
CSR	*Christian Scholars' Review*
CTM	*Concordia Theological Monthly*
CTQ	*Concordia Theological Quarterly*
EQ	*Evangelical Quarterly*
EstBib	*Estudios bíblicos*
ETL	*Ephemerides theologicae lovanienses*
ETR	*Études theologiques et religieuses*
EvTh	*Evangelische Theologie*
ExpT	*Expository Times*
Greg	*Gregorianum*
GTJ	*Grace Theological Journal*
HeyJ	*Heythrop Journal*
HTR	*Harvard Theological Review*
Int	*Interpretation*
JAAR	*Journal of the American Academy of Religion*
JAC	*Jahrbuch für Antike und Christentum*
JBL	*Journal of Biblical Literature*
JETS	*Journal of the Evangelical Theological Society*

JJS	*Journal of Jewish Studies*
JR	*Journal of Religion*
JSJ	*Journal for the Study of Judaism*
JSNT	*Journal for the Study of the New Testament*
JTS	*Journal of Theological Studies*
LingBib	*Linguistica Biblica*
NovT	*Novum Testamentum*
NRT	*Nouvelle revue theologique*
NTS	*New Testament Studies*
PRS	*Perspectives in Religious Studies*
RB	*Revue biblique*
RestQ	*Restoration Quarterly*
RevQ	*Revue de Qumran*
RSR	*Recherches de science religieuse*
SJT	*Scottish Journal of Theology*
ST	*Studia Theologica*
STK	*Svensk Teologisk Kvartalskrift*
Theol	*Theology*
TheolBeitr	*Theologische Beiträge*
ThRu	*Theologische Rundschau*
TrinJ	*Trinity Journal*
TS	*Theological Studies*
TToday	*Theology Today*
TU	*Texte und Untersuchungen*
TynB	*Tyndale Bulletin*
TZ	*Theologische Zeitschrift*
USQR	*Union Seminary Quarterly Review*
VC	*Vigiliae christianae*
VF	*Verkündigung und Forschung*
VoxEvang	*Vox Evangelica*
WTJ	*Westminster Theological Journal*
ZNW	*Zeitschrift für die neutestamentliche Wissenschaft*
ZTK	*Zeitschrift für Theologie und Kirche*

Preface

This book has led a checkered life. Some of the research for it took place as I was writing a doctoral dissertation on the tradition history of the parables found in the central section of Luke's Gospel.[1] Much study occurred as I began to prepare a manuscript for another publisher on the parables and modern literary criticism. That project was abruptly halted when the publisher suddenly decided to close down virtually all of its academic books division. Occasionally, I have relied on the research for my recent book, *The Historical Reliability of the Gospels* (Leicester and Downers Grove: IVP, 1987), to support various points. And of course much fresh work has gone into the preparation of this study in its current form.

I hope the result is that this book has a little something to offer just about all serious readers. The footnotes interact with a sizable

---

[1]Craig L. Blomberg, "The Tradition History of the Parables Peculiar to Luke's Central Section" (Ph.D. diss., Aberdeen, 1982).

amount of recent scholarship on the parables, both in the United States and in Europe, and may point other researchers to the most significant current literature. The text, however, is intended to be read with profit not just by scholars, but by pastors, students and educated laypeople. Part two sets forth most succinctly my conclusions concerning the main lessons of each of the parables; *readers who wish to avoid the theoretical detail of part one may choose to turn immediately to the second half of the book.* But because my interpretations rely on a "minority report" concerning parable interpretation, I have spent a fair amount of time justifying my method in the first half of the volume. As a result, my format closely resembles that of Joachim Jeremias's famous study of the parables,[2] though I do not pretend to have written the classic which he did.

Readers who wish to consult a much more simplified presentation of the parables' message should turn first of all to David Wenham, *The Parables of Jesus* (London: Hodder & Stoughton; Downers Grove: InterVarsity Press, 1989). From the portions of his manuscript which he kindly shared with me prior to its publication, I feel confident in predicting that it will become the best work available at the popular level. It is based on all the finest scholarship, yet it is presented in a readable and engaging way that should illuminate even those readers who have very little familiarity with Scripture. My one regret is that I did not see Wenham's work in time to incorporate references to it throughout the rest of this book.

In addition to Dr. Wenham, seven other individuals read and commented on the entire manuscript, making immeasurable contributions to this volume. These, to whom I express my heartfelt thanks, include Prof. I. H. Marshall, Dr. Robert H. Stein, Dr. John W. Sider, Dr. Stanley E. Porter, Mr. James Hoover, Mrs. Alice Mathews and my wife, Fran, who has helped in numerous other ways throughout every stage of the project. Others, who read and critiqued sizable portions of the book in various stages, include Dr. Mary Ann Beavis, Dr. Kevin J. Vanhoozer, Dr. Elsie Holmes, Mr. Paul Franklin and Mr. Dennis Stamps. To all of these people I am most grateful.

---

[2]Joachim Jeremias, *The Parables of Jesus* (London: SCM; Philadelphia: Westminster, 1972 [Germ. orig. 1947]).

Two additional people deserve mention. Of the past ten years, I have spent only five gainfully employed with a full-time salary. Three others were occupied with doctoral studies, one was a year's leave of absence from a teaching position in order to research and write my previous book, and one involved an adjunct professorship. Without the love and generous financial support of my parents throughout that entire decade, I could not have lived as I did. Inasmuch as my study of the parables occupied a considerable portion of my attention off and on during all ten of those years, it is fitting that I dedicate this book to my father and mother, Mr. John W. Blomberg and Mrs. Eleanor M. Blomberg.

1
Introduction

ANY WELL-STOCKED RELIGIOUS BOOK STORE IS LIKELY TO CARRY several different kinds of books about the parables of Jesus. Some will probably reflect popular exposition and preaching, a few will be among the standard textbooks used in college or seminary courses that deal with the teaching of Jesus, and a few more technical monographs might appear as well. In fact, in this century, more studies of the parables have been produced than those for any other section of comparable length in the Bible.[1] So any new work, especially one of book-length like this one, might well be expected to justify its existence in some detail. There are at least two main reasons for this book. The first may be explained quite simply; the second will require some elaboration.

The simpler reason is that whenever an area of research generates as many studies as the parables have, a majority of Bible readers are unlikely ever to know of most of them, much less understand their contributions and significance. In

---

[1]See Warren S. Kissinger, *The Parables of Jesus: A History of Interpretation and Bibliography* (Metuchen, N.J.; London: Scarecrow, 1979), pp. 231-415.

conservative circles, the gap between scholar and student is often particularly acute, since only recently have a few good texts on the parables appeared which take account of the flood of recent research.[2] In churches, pastors and teachers often continue to recommend the standard works of a generation or more ago. Quite frankly, many of these older works are painfully out-of-date and methodologically inadequate in many respects, even if they do contain numerous helpful devotional insights.[3]

Contemporary expositions of the parables are often equally at sea; recent works by some of America's most respected preachers tend to vary greatly in quality. Some lack a clear method of interpretation, while others inconsistently implement the methods they outline. The desire to preach at length on a short passage usually results in overinterpretation.[4] This volume, therefore, brings a state-of-the-art report on parable scholarship in a form which is intended to be useful as an update for pastors and scholars, a basic textbook for students in colleges and seminaries, and an introduction to the field for the layperson willing to wrestle in some detail with scholarly concerns.

This book, however, also defends a thesis. *This is the second reason for its publication: there are good reasons to believe that in important ways the dominant approaches of the twentieth century to the interpretation of the parables are misguided and require rethinking.* This is a bold claim, but it is one which I not only defend but which a growing number of studies of the parables are echoing. Yet across almost all theological traditions, these developments are virtually unknown among pastors and laypeople. Even many academics seem unaware of the new trend, unless they have kept close watch on developments within this par-

---

[2]Esp. helpful are Kenneth E. Bailey, *Poet and Peasant: A Literary-Cultural Approach to the Parables in Luke* (Grand Rapids: Eerdmans, 1976); idem, *Through Peasant Eyes: More Lucan Parables* (Grand Rapids: Eerdmans, 1980); Simon J. Kistemaker, *The Parables of Jesus* (Grand Rapids: Baker, 1980); and Robert H. Stein, *An Introduction to the Parables of Jesus* (Philadelphia: Westminster, 1981; Exeter: Paternoster, 1982).

[3]Common examples include Richard C. Trench, *Notes on the Parables of Our Lord* (London: Macmillan, 1870; New York: Appleton, 1873); A. B. Bruce, *The Parabolic Teaching of Christ* (London: Hodder & Stoughton, 1882; New York: Armstrong, 1883); G. Campbell Morgan, *The Parables and Metaphors of Our Lord* (New York: Revell, 1943; London: Marshall, Morgan & Scott, 1944).

[4]E.g., James M. Boice, *The Parables of Jesus* (Chicago: Moody, 1983); David A. Hubbard, *Parables Jesus Told* (Downers Grove: IVP, 1981); J. Dwight Pentecost, *The Parables of Jesus* (Grand Rapids: Zondervan, 1982); Lloyd J. Ogilvie, *Autobiography of God* (Ventura, Calif.: Regal, 1979). Better than most in not succumbing to this temptation are D. Stuart Briscoe, *Patterns for Power* (Ventura, Calif.: Regal, 1979); and Earl F. Palmer, *Laughter in Heaven* (Waco, Tex.: Word, 1987).

ticular arena of New Testament scholarship.

A major development in current American biblical scholarship is the ongoing work of the "Jesus Seminar." This group of over two hundred professors and pastors is attempting to rank all of the teachings of Jesus in the Gospels and other early Christian litera- ture according to the degree of probability that he actually spoke any given saying attributed to him. This group is also concerned about disseminating its findings to the American public at large and to date has received widespread coverage in the popular press. The first portion of the Gospels on which the seminar has completed its work is the parables. Yet the published version of its conclusions betrays not one hint of interaction with or even awareness of the numerous studies which support the findings of this book.[5] So this book hopes to make a fresh contribution to the interpretation of the parables as well as to survey the contemporary scholarly scene.

1.1 The Scholarly Consensus

How do the majority of scholars approach the exegesis of Jesus' parables?[6] The typical New Testament survey or hermeneutics textbook[7] will likely contain many or all of the following assertions.

1. Throughout the history of the church, most Christians interpreted the parables as allegories. That is, interpreters assumed that many of the individual characters or objects in the parables stood for something other than themselves—spiritual counterparts which enabled the story to be read at two levels. A parable was not just a story about human activity but also a narrative of "heavenly reality."

To take perhaps the most famous parable of all as an example, the story of the prodigal son (Lk 15:11-32) was viewed not simply as a poignant drama of a Jewish father's remarkable forgiveness for

---

[5]Robert W. Funk, Bernard B. Scott, James R. Butts, *The Parables of Jesus: Red Letter Edition* (Sonoma, Calif.: Polebridge, 1988).

[6]By far the best book available summarizing and somewhat popularizing a middle-of-the-road approach to parable scholarship, with considerable discussion of each major parable, is Herman Hendrickx, *The Parables of Jesus* (London: Geoffrey Chapman; San Francisco: Harper & Row, 1986). But Hendrickx offers only a very brief methodological introduction.

[7]Compare, e.g., A. Berkeley Mickelsen, *Interpreting the Bible* (Grand Rapids: Eerdmans, 1963), pp. 212-30; Gordon D. Fee and Douglas Stuart, *How to Read the Bible for All Its Worth* (Grand Rapids: Zondervan, 1982; London: Scripture Union, 1983), pp. 123-34; Joseph B. Tyson, *The New Testament and Early Christianity* (New York & London: Macmillan, 1984), pp. 223-25; Norman Perrin, *The New Testament: An Introduction*, rev. ed. by Dennis C. Duling (New York & London: Harcourt, Brace, Jovanovich, 1982), pp. 415-20.

his wayward son. Rather it was assumed that a series of one-to-one correspondences could be set up so that the father stood for God, the prodigal for any sinner running away from God, and the older brother for the hardhearted Pharisee. Usually the number of correspondences was extended. The ring which the father gave the prodigal might represent Christian baptism, and the banquet could easily be associated with the Lord's Supper.[8] The robe which the newly returned son put on could reflect immortality; and the shoes, God's preparation for journeying to heaven.[9] One by one most all of the details were explained, and the spiritual significance of the story was determined.

2. Modern scholarship has rightly rejected allegorical interpretation in favor of an approach which sees each parable as making only one main point. Down through the centuries, the artificial and arbitrary nature of the elaborate type of allegorization illustrated above became progressively clearer. A careful comparison of older expositors shows that they often did not agree on what each of the details in a given parable represented. To return to the example of the prodigal's robe, in addition to immortality it was interpreted as standing for sinlessness, spiritual gifts, the imputation of Christ's righteousness, or the sanctity of the soul.[10]

Clearly all of these views recognized that the father gave the robe to the prodigal to indicate his restoration to the family. But it was impossible to agree on how to match the robe with one particular aspect of a new Christian's relationship with his heavenly Father. Presumably the lesson to be learned is that the robe is not meant to be allegorized. In fact even to view the father as directly standing for God is now widely held to be inappropriate. After all, God himself seems to be referred to in the parable as a separate character, however indirectly, when the prodigal speaks of sinning against his father *and against heaven* (vv. 18, 21). So instead of allegorizing individual details, one must seek to encapsulate the story's message under one overarching theme, for example, "the boundless

---

[8]Tertullian *On Modesty* 9.

[9]Clement of Alexandria *Fragments* (from Macarius Chrysocephalus) 11.

[10]Tertullian *On Modesty* 9; John Calvin, *A Harmony of the Gospels Matthew, Mark and Luke*, ed. David W. & Thomas F. Torrance, vol. 2 (Edinburgh: St. Andrew; Grand Rapids: Eerdmans, 1972), p. 224; and for the last two views, Trench, *Parables*, p. 406.

joy of God's forgiveness."[11]

3. *Nevertheless, the parables as they appear in the Gospels do have a few undeniably allegorical elements, but these are the exception and not the rule.* One frequently cited example is the narrative of the wicked tenants (Mk 12:1-12 pars.).[12] The plot, in which the landlord's tenants beat and kill his servants, and finally kill his son in hopes of obtaining full control of the vineyard, so closely matches the history of Israel's leaders' antagonism to God's prophets, and finally to Christ, that most commentators admit that the parable as it stands is allegorical. But for this reason many scholars deny that Jesus ever spoke this particular parable, or at least not in the form in which it now appears.[13] The presumption is still that parable and allegory are strikingly different forms of speech, and allegory is usually regarded as aesthetically inferior. Thus, as an expert in telling parables, Jesus had no need or use for allegory. Other scholars are more willing to admit that the dichotomy is not so great, and that Jesus may have on occasion employed allegory.[14] But the allegorical parable still remains the exception, not the norm.

The problem with all that has been summarized so far comes to a head most clearly when one examines the only two parables for which Jesus himself supplied a detailed interpretation—the sower (Mk 4:3-9, 13-20 pars.) and the wheat and tares (Mt 13:24-30, 36-43). In each of these interpretations, almost all the major details of the parables are explained by means of a series of one-to-one correspondences. The seed is the Word of God, the four soils are four kinds of people, the birds represent Satan, the thorns stand for the cares of this life, and so on. Yet this is precisely the allegorical approach of the pre-modern era which has so roundly been rejected!

4. *Thus the occasional explicit interpretations of parables in the Gospels are additional exceptions to Jesus' usual practice, and they too are not to be taken as normative.* At this point all but the most conservative commentators

---

[11]Adolf Jülicher, *Die Gleichnisreden Jesu,* vol. 2 (Freiburg: Mohr, 1899), p. 362.

[12]The abbreviation par(s). will be used for "and parallel(s)."

[13]E.g., J. D. Crossan, "The Parable of the Wicked Husbandmen," *JBL* 90 (1971): 451-65; Werner G. Kümmel, "Das Gleichnis von den bösen Weingärtnern (Mark. 12, 1-9)," in *Heilsgeschehen und Geschichte* (Marburg: Elwert, 1965), pp. 207-17.

[14]E.g., C. E. B. Cranfield, *The Gospel according to St. Mark* (Cambridge: University Press, 1977), pp. 367-68; A. M. Hunter, *Interpreting the Parables* (London: SCM; Philadelphia: Westminster, 1960), p. 87; Ralph P. Martin, *New Testament Foundations,* vol. 1 (Grand Rapids: Eerdmans, 1975; Exeter: Paternoster, 1985), pp. 299-305.

agree that the interpretations for these parables are simply not authentic. They were supplied by the early church or perhaps even the Gospel writers themselves. The true meaning of a parable like that of the sower is to be found in a general principle such as this: "In spite of every failure and opposition, from hopeless beginnings, God brings forth the triumphant end which he had promised."[15] Those few scholars who do accept that the interpretations found in the Gospels reflect what Jesus actually said nevertheless insist that this type of interpretation is exceptional.[16] The very fact that Jesus left most of his parables without such interpretation proves that they are to be taken less elaborately.

5. Apart from this small amount of allegory, most of the parables and most parts of each parable are among the most indisputably authentic sayings of Jesus in the Gospels. Most Gospel critics regularly differentiate between sayings ascribed to Jesus which they can with a fair degree of probability accept as genuinely his and those which they believe came from a later source. The most prominent criteria which they use to make such distinctions include "dissimilarity" (that which marks Jesus off as different from both the Judaism of his day and from the early church could have come from no one else), "multiple attestation" (that which occurs in several Gospels or in several different Gospel sources is more likely authentic than that which is singly attested), and "coherence" (that which fits in with material authenticated by other criteria may also be accepted).[17]

The authentic "core" of the Gospels lies in Jesus' teaching about the kingdom of God entering history by means of his ministry, a theme which well satisfies all the criteria.[18] Because many of the parables form the heart of Jesus' teaching about the kingdom, they

---

[15]Joachim Jeremias, *The Parables of Jesus* (London: SCM; Philadelphia: Westminster, 1972 [Germ. orig. 1947]), p. 150.

[16]John C. Purdy, *Parables at Work* (Philadelphia: Westminster, 1985), p. 93, puts it this way, commenting on the parable of the tares: "So just this once we have permission to read the parable as an allegory." Cf. Kistemaker, *Parables*, p. xv; Stein, *Parables*, p. 56; Walter M. Dunnett, *The Interpretation of Holy Scripture* (Nashville: Thomas Nelson, 1984), p. 113.

[17]For a judicious use of these and other criteria see esp. Robert H. Stein, "The 'Criteria' for Authenticity," in *Gospel Perspectives*, vol. 1, ed. R. T. France and David Wenham (Sheffield: JSOT, 1980), pp. 225-63. Cf. Stewart C. Goetz and Craig L. Blomberg, "The Burden of Proof," *JSNT* 11 (1981): 39-63.

[18]On which see esp. George E. Ladd, *The Presence of the Future* (Grand Rapids: Eerdmans, 1974; London: SPCK, 1980); Bruce D. Chilton, *God in Strength: Jesus' Announcement of the Kingdom* (Freistadt: F. Plöchl, 1979; Sheffield: JSOT, 1987); G. R. Beasley-Murray, *Jesus and the Kingdom of God* (Grand Rapids: Eerdmans; Exeter: Paternoster, 1986).

too (by "coherence") are widely held to be authentic. Moreover, virtually no one in the early church taught by means of parables, and rabbinic parables served primarily to illustrate or expound the Law instead of teaching fresh insights about God's ways with humanity. So the parables of Jesus satisfy the "dissimilarity" criterion. They are also multiply attested. Parables occur in all of the Synoptic Gospels and in all of the layers into which the Gospels are usually separated (the triple tradition of passages common to Matthew, Mark and Luke; the double tradition of material common to Matthew and Luke; and the peculiarly Lukan and peculiarly Matthean traditions).[19]

There are a few features of the parables which are usually attributed to later stages of tradition. But these can generally be identified by discerning the "laws of transformation" which the oral tradition of Jesus' sayings underwent prior to the writing of the Gospels, or by observing patterns of "redaction"—the ways in which the Gospel writers themselves shaped the material they inherited. The disciplines of form criticism and redaction criticism have grown up among students of the Gospels primarily to detect these kinds of changes on a more widespread basis, so that it is not too difficult to apply their insights in the particular case of the parables.

1.2 The Minority Report

These five common hermeneutical rules which comprise the scholarly consensus are somewhat selective, but they suffice to illustrate the main issues. It is at least curious that the upshot of twentieth-century scholarship is to declare the vast majority of all previous nineteen centuries of Christian interpretation in error. Slightly more disconcerting is the belief that viewing the parables as allegories is the most illegitimate method for interpreting them. After all, this is the only method which the Gospel writers themselves ever portray Jesus as using, even if he used it only occasionally.

---

[19]For a more detailed summary of arguments for the authenticity of the parables see Philip B. Payne, "The Authenticity of the Parables of Jesus," in *Gospel Perspectives*, vol. 2, ed. R. T. France and David Wenham (Sheffield: JSOT, 1981), pp. 329-44. Cf. also B. B. Scott, "Essaying the Rock: The Authenticity of the Jesus Parable Tradition," *Forum* 2.3 (1986): 3-53, who emphasizes that the burden of proof rests with the skeptic for the corpus of Jesus' parables, though he is unnecessarily generous with how much he assigns to redaction rather than tradition.

More puzzling still is the inability of these rules to account readily for the enigmatic comments attributed to Jesus in Mark 4:11-12 pars., in which he explains to his disciples his purpose for teaching in parables: "the secret of the kingdom of God has been given to you. But to those on the outside everything is said in parables so that, 'they may be ever seeing but never perceiving, and ever hearing but never understanding; otherwise they might turn and be forgiven!' " Understandably, these words are also widely held to be inauthentic.[20] Jesus' parables, according to the generally held principles of interpretation, are intended to reveal and not to conceal. Moreover, this list of rules fails to address a number of other questions which will arise in the course of this study. Not surprisingly, more and more commentators are beginning to question the consensus.

Although they may differ widely on other aspects of parable interpretation, a minority of interpreters from a broad spectrum of theological traditions are increasingly willing to affirm a different set of statements from those listed above.[21]

1. *The parables, as they stand in the Gospels, are much more allegorical than is usually acknowledged.* This does not mean that all the elaborate interpretations of previous commentators are correct. Rather, the problem of older interpretations is not their allegorical nature per se, but the *extent* to which they allegorized and the *specific* meanings which they often gave to certain details in the narratives. We may argue, for instance, that the prodigal's robe *is not* meant to stand for any specific part of one's spiritual life, whereas the Father *is* meant to symbolize God. Allegorizing one detail does not commit an interpreter to allegorizing all of the details. One of the key problems with modern biblical criticism has been a wholesale misunderstanding and misrepresentation of standard literary theory, as if all or most of the details of a story had to disclose double meanings in order for it to be allegorical.

---

[20]E.g., Hugh Anderson, *The Gospel of Mark* (London: Oliphants, 1976; Grand Rapids: Eerdmans, 1981), p. 130; Heikki Räisänen, *Die Parabeltheorie im Markusevangelium* (Helsinki: Finnischen Exegetischen Gesellschaft, 1973), pp. 111-12; Rudolf Pesch, *Das Markusevangelium,* vol. 1 (Freiburg: Herder, 1976), p. 238.

[21]See esp. Madeleine Boucher, *The Mysterious Parable* (Washington: Catholic Biblical Association of America, 1977); Hans-Josef Klauck, *Allegorie und Allegorese in synoptischen Gleichnistexten* (Münster: Aschendorff, 1978); John W. Sider, "Proportional Analogy in the Gospel Parables," *NTS* 31 (1985): 1-23.

2. If the parables are fairly uniformly allegorical in nature, then they are likely to be either even more entirely authentic than the consensus admits or much more inauthentic. By accepting the possibility that Jesus himself employed allegory, the critic discards a major criterion for dividing the parables into authentic and inauthentic bits and pieces. A growing tendency has been to assume greater inauthenticity,[22] but this study will argue for greater authenticity. Jesus' teaching about the purpose for parables will then also fit in with his method of interpretation more easily; parts of them are not as self-explanatory as others and perhaps, from one angle, intentionally cryptic. Neither do the interpretations of the sower and of the wheat and tares stand out as quite so exceptional, although many of the other parables have fewer allegorical elements. But the distinction will resemble that of points on a continuum more than a radical dichotomy. Other arguments for the inauthenticity of portions of the parables, based largely on form and redaction criticism, have also been challenged.

3. Many parables probably make more than one main point. Beyond this, little agreement exists, and it is easy to swing too far back in the direction of deriving too many points from a passage. One noted writer has recently argued for seeing a "theological cluster" of points for each passage, and in his exposition these may number as many as ten.[23] Devotees of newer movements in literary criticism like to speak of "polyvalence" where the number of meanings or lessons drawn from a text may be endless! Without going to these extremes, however, one does have to be willing to look for multiple points in a parable. One of the major theses to be defended in this book is that a majority of the parables make exactly three main points.

1.3 Newest Developments
A variety of recent literary and hermeneutical schools of thought call into question both of the main approaches surveyed above.

---

[22]E.g., M. D. Goulder, *The Evangelists' Calendar* (London: SPCK, 1978); John Drury, *The Parables in the Gospels* (London: SPCK; New York: Crossroad, 1985). John R. Donahue, *The Gospel in Parable* (Philadelphia: Fortress, 1988), p. 4, is more agnostic about the parables' original meanings but still prefers to concentrate only on their meanings in the evangelists' contexts.

[23]Bailey, *Eyes*, pp. xxi-xxiii; cf. pp. 111-12.

These schools allege that the parables are neither simple stories drawn from everyday life meant to illustrate one particular religious truth nor allegories in which numerous details stand for distinct spiritual counterparts. Rather they are metaphors, which, among other things, means that they cannot be paraphrased in propositional language or reduced to a certain number of points at all.

The most extensive commentary on the parables of Jesus to appear in half a century reflects this perspective. B. B. Scott's 1989 study, *Hear Then the Parable*, represents the approach of the Society of Biblical Literature's parables study group which first began publishing its discussions in the mid-1970s. Scott, like most in the SBL group, believes not only that it is impossible ever to state the meaning of a parable but also that (a) the parables do not point to an apocalyptic kingdom of God; (b) they regularly subvert conventional religion and morality, employing irony, parody and burlesque imagery; (c) they were uniformly misunderstood by the Synoptic evangelists, who almost entirely obscured their significance through their redactional activity; (d) they are often at least as well represented in the Gospel of Thomas as in the canonical gospels; and (e) the quest for the most original version of any given parable is misguided from the outset, because oral storytellers varied their narratives with every performance.[24] Scott's insights range from the indispensable to the highly improbable. So it is clear that there is still much work to be done in trying to sift the wheat from the chaff among recent parable scholarship.

1.4 The Scope and Outline of This Book

This volume falls into two relatively evenly balanced parts. Part one discusses the theories of interpreting the parables and evaluates their relative merits. Part two applies the conclusions of part one to a brief discussion of each of the principal parables of the Gospels. Each part contains four chapters followed by a brief summary of results. Chapter two begins by focusing more closely on the debate about the difference between parable and allegory. What reasons

---

[24]Bernard B. Scott, *Hear Then the Parable* (Minneapolis: Fortress, 1989). Scott's most important precursors were Dan O. Via, Jr., Robert W. Funk, and J. D. Crossan, all of whose numerous works on the parables regularly appear in the notes throughout the chapters ahead.

have the modern consensus and "minority report" given for their conflicting views, and how well do the reasons stand up to close scrutiny? What insights do studies of literary criticism, in general, and of the large volume of rabbinic parables, in particular, disclose? Chapter two concludes that *given proper definition* the parables may and ought to be termed allegories, but that this in no way requires a return to the more arbitrary exegesis which often characterized past generations.

Chapter three investigates the contributions of form criticism to the study of the parables. After a brief examination of the strengths and weaknesses of the discipline as a whole and of some important principles for interpretation which emerge, more detailed scrutiny is given to the so-called laws of transformation which supposedly characterized the period of oral tradition of Jesus' teachings prior to the writing of the Gospels. This chapter determines that these laws need substantial modification, and it concludes by suggesting a quite different model for the tradition history of the parables.

Chapter four turns to redaction criticism, with its emphasis on the important differences between parallel accounts of the same stories in different Gospels. Nuances of meaning do vary from one account to the next, and the interpretation of a parable in one Gospel will not necessarily be identical in every respect to its interpretation in a different Gospel. Each evangelist had distinctive themes he wanted to highlight and contemporary expositors dare not miss these. Nevertheless, those views are rejected which allege that these differences are so great that one must speak of outright contradictions or of incompatible theologies. The upshot of chapters two through four combined, then, is that one may actually view the parables of Jesus as both allegorical and authentic.

Chapter five rounds out the theoretical discussion by surveying the three newest literary and hermeneutical methods and the challenges they pose to the preliminary conclusions just posited. The *new hermeneutic* denies that narrative writing may be interpreted in any non-narrative fashion without doing violence to the original meaning of the narrator. Therefore it is inappropriate to boil the parables down into *any* number of "main points." *Structuralism* denies that the most important meaning of a passage may be determined from the superficial features of the text. Instead interpreters must seek a more hidden level of meaning by analyzing the passage's *deep structure*. *Poststructuralism* denies that the meaning of a text is fixed either in the author's original intention or in the actual meaning of the words of a text, but is limited only by the creativity of a text's readers or hearers and the interpretive conventions of the communities to which they belong. Each of these three movements offers a few important interpretive insights which should be embraced, but in general their value has been overestimated. Neither the allegorical nor the authentic nature of the parables is impugned by any of them.

Chapters six through eight form the bulk of part two. These three chapters illustrate the principles of interpretation with which the summary of part one concludes, by means of a brief analysis of each of the major parables of Jesus. No attempt is made to produce a full-fledged commentary or detailed exegesis for each passage. There are plenty of reliable sources which adequately summarize the most basic historical background of the parables' imagery, the meaning of key Greek terms or phrases, and the function of a given passage in the overall outline of the Gospel in which it appears.[25] Rather, attention is concentrated on major interpretive controversies and conclusions, along with those features of exegesis which directly result from the distinctive method espoused here. As a result, questions about the authenticity and the allegorical nature of each passage receive special attention.

A division according to form or structure is adopted, by which the parables are classified into three main categories, one per chapter. Chapter six presents *simple three-point* parables, the most common form found in the Gospels. These are parables which contain three main characters, one who functions as a ruler or authority figure and two subordinates, one good and one bad, who illustrate contrasting patterns of responses to their master. Chapter seven surveys *complex three-point* parables. These are passages in which more

---

[25]In addition to the works cited above in nn. 2 and 14, see esp. the major commentaries on Matthew by D. A. Carson (*Matthew*, in The Expositor's Bible Commentary, ed. Frank E. Gaebelein, vol. 8 [Grand Rapids: Zondervan, 1984]) and David Hill (*The Gospel of Matthew* [London: Oliphants, 1972; Grand Rapids: Eerdmans, 1981]); on Mark by William L. Lane (*The Gospel according to Mark* [Grand Rapids: Eerdmans, 1974; London: Marshall, Morgan & Scott, 1975]) and Robert A. Guelich, *Mark 1—8:26* (Dallas: Word, 1989); on Luke by I. Howard Marshall (*The Gospel of Luke* [Exeter: Paternoster; Grand Rapids: Eerdmans, 1978]) and Joseph A. Fitzmyer (*The Gospel according to Luke*, 2 vols. [Garden City: Doubleday, 1981-85]).

than three characters appear, but which ultimately reflect the same structure as the simple triadic model, as well as those which have only three characters but with roles different from those of the paradigm of chapter six. Chapter eight, finally, considers *two-point* and *one-point* parables, passages with fewer key characters or elements, from which should be derived only two or one rather than three main points.

Chapter nine closes the volume by examining what implications the messages of the parables have for understanding their speaker and his teaching more generally. In other words, what do the parables contribute to an understanding of the kingdom of God and to Christology? Is the kingdom present or future? Is it a reign or a realm? Does it involve social action or personal conversion? How does it relate to Israel and the church? Do the parables support the view, as might superficially seem to be the case, that Jesus was simply a great human teacher? Or are there implicit (or even explicit) indications that his parables support Christian belief in Jesus' deity?

This rather substantial agenda may seem quite imposing when one considers that Jesus apparently first taught in parables to unlettered Galilean peasants in order to make clear his understanding of the kingdom of God. Yet, as even the pages of the Gospels record, many, often including his own disciples, failed to understand him. A perusal of subsequent commentators shows that confusion has persisted ever since. Even today, when one may speak of a consensus of twentieth-century principles of interpreting the parables, there is not nearly as much agreement when those principles are applied in the exegesis of specific passages. So perhaps the issues are more complex than they first appear. It is the sincere hope and goal of this study, however, that after working through some fairly complicated questions, simple principles may re-emerge which will make the modern reader's task easier in recovering the true meaning of these portions of God's Word.

Part I
Methods & Controversies in Interpreting the Parables

2

Parable
&Allegory

WHO DOES THE GOOD SAMARITAN REPRESENT—ONE'S NEIGH-
bor, one's enemy, Christ? Does the prodigal son's older brother
stand for the Pharisees? Are Jesus' disciples really to imitate the
unjust steward who deceived his master by lowering his debtors'
bills? Does the servant who is wounded in the head in Mark's version of the parable of the wicked tenants symbolize John the Baptist? What is the significance of the oil which the five wise maidens
tell the five foolish ones they cannot transfer to their torches?
These and many similar questions that confront readers of Jesus'
parables plunge them instantly into the most significant issue in the
history of their interpretation. To what extent, if at all, are the
parables allegories? That is to ask, does each detail in the "earthly"
picture stand for some "heavenly" counterpart? Do any? If so,
which ones, and how do we determine their proper referents?

2.1 The Current Debate: Two Main Approaches
2.1.1 Parable vs. Allegory
As noted in the introduction, the dominant stance of twentieth-

century parable scholarship has been to differentiate sharply between parables and allegories. Parables, it is stressed, revolve around one main point of comparison between the activity in the story and Jesus' understanding of the kingdom of God, and thus they teach one primary lesson. Subordinate details are significant only to the extent that they fit in with and reinforce the central emphasis. Allegories, on the other hand, are more complex stories which require numerous details in them to be "decoded." The classic example which is often cited is John Bunyan's *Pilgrim's Progress*, in which one recognizes that the story of Christian's journey stands for the spiritual pilgrimage which every follower of Christ must make. The various places to which he travels then correspond to different kinds of religious experiences. Bunyan gives them specific labels so that everyone may understand: the Slough of Despond, the Hill of Difficulty, the Valley of Humiliation, and the like. The developments which led to the establishment of this dichotomy between parables and allegories have been explained repeatedly and at length,[1] so this discussion will limit itself to the most significant reasons given to support the distinction.

1. *The allegorical method of interpretation emerged early in the history of the church as a result of the influence of Greek philosophy, and was applied widely to all portions of Scripture as a substitute for a more legitimate, literal reading of the text.* The rationale for allegorizing often seemed praiseworthy. The church fathers wished to derive additional meaning from the text beyond that which a more straightforward reading would elicit, especially in narratives where there seemed to be few explicit lessons or where characters' actions seemed morally suspect. The parables proved particularly ripe for allegorizing, because the Gospels themselves describe Jesus deciphering each of the details of the parables of the sower (Mk 4:13-20 pars.) and of the wheat and tares (Mt 13:36-43). It was only natural to assume that the other parables which he did not explain should be interpreted similarly. After all, he had seemed to imply that his teaching would be confusing unless one understood "the secret" of God's kingdom (Mk 4:11 pars.). And

---

[1]A detailed history of interpretation appears in Warren S. Kissinger, *The Parables of Jesus: A History of Interpretation and Bibliography* (Metuchen, N.J; London: Scarecrow, 1979), pp. 1-230. More briefly, see Hans Weder, *Die Gleichnisse Jesu als Metaphern* (Göttingen: Vandenhoeck & Ruprecht, 1978), pp. 11-57; Robert H. Stein, *An Introduction to the Parables of Jesus* (Philadelphia: Westminster, 1981; Exeter: Paternoster, 1982), pp. 42-71.

did he not go on explicitly to say that understanding the parable of the sower was the key to understanding all the parables (Mk 4:13)?

St. Augustine provided the classic example of ancient allegorizing with his interpretation of the parable of the good Samaritan (Lk 10:30-37): the wounded man stands for Adam; Jerusalem, the heavenly city from which he has fallen; the thieves, the devil who deprives Adam of his immortality; the priest and Levite, the Old Testament Law which could save no one; the Samaritan who binds the man's wounds, Christ who forgives sin; the inn, the church; and the innkeeper, the apostle Paul![2] Some lesser-known but equally imaginative examples include Irenaeus's treatment of the laborers in the vineyard (Mt 20:1-16)—the parable depicts those who have been saved at different periods of world history, while the denarius with which each was rewarded, engraved with the royal image, stands for God's royal son and the immortality he conveys.[3] Or again, Gregory the Great explains the farmer's threefold coming to the barren fig tree in search of fruit (Lk 13:6-9) as God's bestowing humanity with reason, law and grace, respectively.[4]

For nearly nineteen centuries this approach persisted. Periodic voices called for a halt. Chrysostom, Aquinas and Calvin are noteworthy examples from the patristic, medieval and Reformation periods, respectively, but even they were unable consistently to avoid allegory in their own exegesis. Even as recently as the late 1800s, Archbishop Trench, in his classic *Notes on the Parables of Our Lord*, could claim that the expositor should assume a meaning behind every detail in the text without good evidence to the contrary.[5]

Two main problems with this kind of approach, however, were becoming increasingly obvious. First, rarely did two expositors agree on what every detail in a particular passage stood for, given the many different ways they might frame a moderately plausible interpretation. Second, some of the meanings attributed to details in the parables were clearly anachronistic. That is, they reflected

---

[2]*Quaest. Evang.* II, 19.

[3]*Adv. Haer.* IV, 36:7.

[4]*Homilia* XXXI.

[5]Richard C. Trench, *Notes on the Parables of Our Lord* (London: Macmillan, 1870; New York: Appleton, 1873), p. 37. Equally adamant in this respect were C. G. Lang, *Thoughts on Some of the Parables of Jesus* (New York: Dutton, 1905; London: Pitman & Sons, 1906); and Ada R. Habershon, *The Study of the Parables* (London: Nisbet; New York: Charles Cook, 1904).

understandings of Christian doctrine which dated from a time later than Jesus' own ministry. No one in his original audience, for example, could ever have been expected to associate the Samaritan's innkeeper with the apostle Paul!

2. *The allegorical method ignores the realism, clarity and simplicity of the parables.* The scholar, at the turn of this century, who almost singlehandedly demolished the allegorical interpretation of the parables, was the German liberal Adolf Jülicher. His two massive volumes argued at great length that each parable briefly and concisely reflected true-to-life conditions of first-century Palestine, sharply contrasting with the artificiality of most allegories which made sense only when properly decoded. Jülicher based this contrast on the classic, Aristotelian distinction between simile and metaphor. While both are figures of speech comparing two things which seem to be "like" each other in some way, the simile is much more self-explanatory, because it explicitly uses a word such as *like* or *as* to make the nature of the comparison clear. The parables are nothing more than extended similes ("the kingdom of God is like . . .") and therefore far removed from the mysterious world of allegory. Jesus' parables thus also differ markedly from the allegorical stories of the rabbis (usually also termed parables) as "the fresh air of the fields" differs from "the dust of the study."[6]

Jülicher went on to deny the possibility of Jesus composing intermediate forms—part simple comparison and part allegory. Where undeniably allegorical details do appear in the Gospel parables, they may not be accepted as authentic. What details Jesus did originally include merely gave the parables life and vividness and reinforced the single lesson which he wanted to teach. For Jülicher these lessons were often fairly bland generalizations in keeping with the old liberal view of the kingdom of God as being ushered in through the efforts of Christians. For example, the parable of the talents (Mt 25:14-30) commended faithfulness with everything with which one is entrusted. The story of the unjust steward (Lk 16:1-13) encouraged the prudent use of the present to ensure a happy future. And the example of the rich man and Lazarus (Lk 16:19-31) illustrated

---

[6]Adolf Jülicher, *Die Gleichnisreden Jesu,* vol. 1 (Freiburg: Mohr, 1899), pp. 169-73. On simile vs. metaphor and parable vs. allegory, see esp. pp. 52-58. The lack of any English translation of this work is one of the strangest omissions in modern biblical scholarship.

the need to avoid a life of wanton wealth and pleasure.[7] Most commentators have since rejected Jülicher's "moralizing" summaries in favor of more specific lessons concerning God's bringing the kingdom, but they agree that their goal is to epitomize the message of each parable in a single proposition.

3. *Traces of allegory which do occur in the Gospel parables can be attributed to the early church's imposition of the motif of the "Messianic secret" onto the Jesus tradition.* At first glance it would seem quite arbitrary for Jülicher simply to have denied the evidence of the Gospels which ran contrary to his understanding of the parables. But William Wrede soon proposed an explanation of how a large portion of the clear, simple teaching of Jesus became mixed together with esoteric explanation and shrouded in mystery. Wrede's theory has remained widely influential ever since.

In short, Wrede's thesis is this: Jesus himself never claimed to be more than a man, but after his death his disciples soon came to believe in him as Messiah and God's Son. Obviously, they could not tell their contemporaries that Jesus had ever publicly used either of these titles, because others who had heard him preach would know better. So they told of how Jesus taught certain things privately to his disciples which he concealed from the public, including allegorical interpretations of his parables. It was in this context, they alleged, that he revealed his more exalted views of himself. This Messianic-secret theme runs throughout the Gospels, especially in Mark, and may account for why Jesus consistently tells people not to disclose his identity. It also gives a plausible explanation of Jesus' purpose for speaking in parables in the first place (according to Mk 4:11-12).[8]

4. *Studies of the transmission of oral tradition demonstrated a tendency for parables to be allegorized as their original contexts were soon forgotten.* The rise of form criticism bolstered Jülicher further. Rudolf Bultmann drew on studies of ancient oral folklore and proposed relatively fixed laws of transmission, which among other things described the process of converting a simple parable into a complex allegory as it was told

---

[7]Ibid., vol. 2, pp. 472-95, 495-514, 617-41.

[8]William Wrede, *Das Messiasgeheimnis in den Evangelien* (Göttingen: Vandenhoeck & Ruprecht, 1901). Wrede was translated into English only in 1971—as *The Messianic Secret* (London: J. Clarke, 1971).

and retold.[9] These "laws" were refined and elaborated by Joachim Jeremias, whose work will be discussed in detail in chapter three.

Jeremias, following the pioneering work of C. H. Dodd, rejected Jülicher's universalizing interpretations of the parables in favor of ones which anchored them firmly in specific, historical situations in the life of Jesus.[10] These situations generally revolved around Jesus' proclamation of mercy for sinners and his call to Israel to repent in light of God's impending judgment. Dodd understood Jesus' teaching to reflect "realized eschatology"—the kingdom of God as already present in his ministry—while Jeremias preferred the more precise description of "eschatology in the process of being realized." Both agreed that the parables were the primary medium of this message, and Jeremias's insights into the customs of first-century Palestinian life enriched his exegesis to such an extent that his work is still a standard textbook. But form critics remained as adamantly anti-allegorical as Jülicher, even if the main point they found for each parable was more specific than that which Jülicher had identified.

5. *Allegory is an inferior form of rhetoric, unworthy of Jesus, who instead was master of the metaphor.* A third early form critic who wrote extensively on the parables was A. T. Cadoux. Although his exegesis has not proved as influential as that of Dodd or Jeremias, he did make one claim which has commanded nearly universal assent. Cadoux rejected the authenticity of all of the brief conclusions or applications with which most of the parables end, stressing that "the speaker who needs to interpret his parables is not master of his method."[11] Dodd discloses a similar value judgment in his definition of a parable, which many still employ: "a metaphor or simile drawn from nature or common life, arresting the hearer by its vividness or strangeness, and leaving the mind in sufficient doubt about its

---

[9]Rudolf Bultmann, *The History of the Synoptic Tradition* (Oxford: Blackwell; New York: Harper & Row, 1963 [Germ. orig. 1921]), pp. 166-205. Bultmann frequently drew on the work of Heinrich Weinel, *Die Gleichnisse Jesu* (Leipzig: Teubner, 1910), who was one of Jülicher's most ardent defenders. The other most well-known "founder" of Gospel form criticism, Martin Dibelius, *From Tradition to Gospel* (Cambridge: J. Clarke, 1934; New York: Scribner's, 1935 [Germ. orig. 1919]), pp. 254-57, was more ambivalent about the possibility of Jesus having used a limited amount of allegory in his parables.

[10]Joachim Jeremias, *Die Gleichnisse Jesu* (Zürich: Zwingli, 1947) [the standard English edition is *The Parables of Jesus* (London: SCM; Philadelphia: Westminster, 1972)]; C. H. Dodd, *The Parables of the Kingdom* (London: Nisbet, 1935; New York: Scribner's, 1936).

[11]A. T. Cadoux, *The Parables of Jesus: Their Art and Use* (London: J. Clarke, 1930; New York: Macmillan, 1931), p. 19.

precise application to tease it into active thought."[12] To spell out a specific application closes the door to numerous other legitimate uses of the parable and is more likely the type of addition which someone would have made later in the church's history. Examples of such applications include "Go and do likewise" (Lk 10:37), "So the last will be first; and the first, last" (Mt 20:16), and "in the same way there will be more rejoicing in heaven over one sinner who repents than over ninety-nine righteous persons who need no repentance" (Lk 15:7).

Although they did not phrase it in so many terms, what Cadoux and Dodd were anticipating was the more recent distinction between metaphor and allegory. Because an allegory encodes a relatively static series of comparisons which its author wishes to communicate, its interpretation is not nearly as open-ended as that of a metaphorical story, which juxtaposes two basically dissimilar objects (e.g., the kingdom of God and a mustard seed),[13] and in which the possible lines of comparison are not as clear or limited. Jesus as a master teacher would not have spelled things out so simplistically.[14]

The modern view of metaphor (see also chapter six) goes even further, arguing that it is impossible to summarize the meaning of a parable, when viewed as a metaphor, in either one or several points. Instead all one can do is describe the impact which it creates. Thus the parable of the ten virgins *predicts* the need for readiness for the advent of God's kingdom, the mustard seed *promises* the kingdom's surprisingly wide influence despite small beginnings, and the barren fig tree *warns* that a time will come when it is too late for repentance. Note that the verbs in each of these clauses describe the action accomplished by the parable rather than summarizing a lesson taught.

---

[12]Dodd, *Parables*, p. 16. On the influence of this definition in subsequent parable research, see Robert W. Funk, *Language, Hermeneutic and Word of God* (New York: Harper & Row, 1966), pp. 133-62; John R. Donahue, *The Gospel in Parable* (Philadelphia: Fortress, 1988), pp. 5-20.

[13]One needs to realize that literary critics use the term *metaphor* in numerous ways. Jülicher referred to the narrow sense of metaphor as contrasting with simile (i.e., the comparison of two objects without a specific comparative word—e.g., "the sea was glass" instead of "the sea sparkled like glass"). Here the reference is to the broader sense of any figure of speech which compares fundamentally dissimilar objects.

[14]Gerhard Sellin surveys much of this recent scholarship and concludes dogmatically that allegory is feeble and limited, and cannot stand on its own, always requiring "translation" of its symbols into the hidden truth implied. Thus he concludes it "has no more place today in literature" ("Allegorie und 'Gleichnis'," *ZTK* 75 [1978]:311).

In the opinion of the current consensus, the era of confusing parable and allegory has thus vanished forever. Questions about what particular details "stand for," such as those with which this chapter began, are simply misguided from the outset. The consensus is all the more weighty inasmuch as it comprises interpreters of virtually all theological persuasions.[15]

2.1.2 Parable as Allegory

Despite this consensus, another strand of parable interpretation, which has been mostly ignored but never refuted, has woven itself throughout this century's scholarship.[16] It affirms that to varying extents the parables may be considered allegories and that each of the previous arguments to the contrary fails to convince. The first five claims presented below contest the five points discussed above, and then four additional affirmations suggest further rationale for the pro-allegorical perspective.

1. *More important than the Greek background of allegorical interpretation in general is the specific Hebrew background of allegorical parables.* Almost as soon as Jülicher's work appeared, major dissenters protested. Christian Bugge argued that Old Testament and rabbinic literature rather than Aristotle provide the background for interpreting Jesus' use of parables. In Hebrew the word *mashal* (often translated as παραβολή in the Greek Bible [= English "parable"]) is used for all types of figurative speech—proverbs, riddles, taunts, simple comparisons and complex allegories. So it is arbitrary to restrict Jesus' use of parables to the patterns of Greek rhetoric, because he used the language and thought forms of Aramaic, a Semitic language very similar to Hebrew.[17]

---

[15]See esp. the survey of research since Jeremias in Norman Perrin, *Jesus and the Language of the Kingdom* (Philadelphia: Fortress; London: SCM, 1976); Perrin's own views are best summarized on p. 6. Cf. also C. F. Evans, *Parable and Dogma* (London: Athlone, 1977); J. Ramsey Michaels, *Servant and Son: Jesus in Parable and Gospel* (Atlanta: John Knox, 1981); Sallie M. TeSelle, *Speaking in Parables: A Study in Metaphor and Theology* (Philadelphia: Fortress; London: SCM, 1975).

[16]John Drury, "Origins of Mark's Parables," in *Ways of Reading the Bible*, ed. Michael Wadsworth (Brighton: Harvester; Totowa, N.J.: Barnes & Noble, 1981), pp. 172-73, suggests three reasons for this: (a) the allegorical approach of the past was clearly abused, (b) Dodd's clarity, churchmanship and concern for relevance won him many followers in the English-speaking world and (c) most of the opposition to the consensus has appeared in less widely known sources.

[17]Christian A. Bugge, *Die Haupt-Parabeln Jesu* (Giessen: J. Ricker'sche Verlagsbuchhandlung, 1903). Cf. the similar reactions of Julius Wellhausen, *Das Evangelium Marci* (Berlin: Georg Reimer, 1903), pp. 30-31; and M.-J. Lagrange, "La parabole en dehors de l'évangile," *RB* 6 (1909):198-212, 342-67.

Paul Fiebig supported Bugge with two books in which he compiled a large number of rabbinic parables, highlighting their allegorical nature, and, contra Jülicher, demonstrating that a mixture of parable and allegory was both common and well-liked in ancient Judaism. Due to numerous parallels in structure and form, it was not fair to oppose the parables of the rabbis so diametrically to those of Jesus, and it was logical to assume that both sets of texts should be interpreted in reasonably similar fashion.[18]

Fiebig also emphasized the presence of a large number of "standard metaphors" (most notably the king standing for God) which were so frequently used by the rabbis that Jesus' audiences almost certainly would have interpreted them in fairly conventional ways. More recent studies have surveyed the imagery of various Old Testament and intertestamental texts and expanded the list of stock symbols which would have had relatively fixed meanings in Jesus' day. Among the most important for interpreting Jesus' parables are: a father, king, judge or shepherd for God; a vineyard, vine or sheep for God's people; an enemy for the devil; a harvest or grape-gathering for the final judgment; and a wedding, feast or festal clothing for the Messianic banquet in the age to come.[19]

2. Rhetorically, the Aristotelian distinction between simile and metaphor is greatly exaggerated. Not only did Jülicher underestimate the importance of the Hebrew background to the parables, he also overestimated the difference between allegorical and non-allegorical forms of writing or speaking within the Greco-Roman world. Another turn-of-the-century scholar, the French Catholic Denis Buzy, demonstrated that in the first century Aristotle was not viewed as the only or even the most respected authority on rhetoric. Had Jülicher, for example, read the influential Latin orator Quintilian, he would have seen the opinion expressed that pure forms (simple comparisons with only one main point or allegories so detailed that every point stands for something) are quite rare and that mixed forms (where some but not all of the details point to a second level of

---

[18]Paul Fiebig, *Altjüdische Gleichnisse und die Gleichnisse Jesu* (Tübingen: Mohr, 1904); idem, *Die Gleichnisreden Jesu im Lichte der rabbinischen Gleichnisse des neutestamentlichen Zeitalters* (Tübingen: Mohr, 1912). A somewhat later English counterpart of sorts was W. O. E. Oesterley, *The Gospel Parables in the Light of Their Jewish Background* (London: SPCK; New York: Macmillan, 1936).

[19]Gustav Stählin, "Das Bild der Witwe," *JAC* 17 (1974):7. Cf. Robert M. Johnston and Harvey K. McArthur, *They Also Taught in Parables* (Grand Rapids: Zondervan, forthcoming).

meaning) are in fact the most artistic type of figurative discourse.[20]

Later another French Catholic, Maxime Hermaniuk, produced an even more prodigious volume, although it was overshadowed by Jeremias's work which appeared in the same year. Hermaniuk analyzed parabolic-like narratives in the Old Testament, apocrypha, rabbinic literature, New Testament and several second-century Christian writings. He agreed that from both Jewish and Greco-Roman perspectives, parables were seen as extended comparisons or similes, while allegories were extended metaphors (where the comparisons are left implicit). But he stressed that the difference in meaning (though not in impact) between simile and metaphor is negligible once the points of comparisons are recognized.[21] Hermaniuk also discussed Quintilian at length, reaffirming that the most artistic and effective type of parable combines details which clearly stand for something other than themselves, those which only add life and color to the portrait, and others which are susceptible of either interpretation.[22]

Various studies of more recent vintage have claimed to corroborate Buzy and Hermaniuk from the standpoint of modern literary criticism. E. J. Tinsley, for example, argues that biblical scholars have consistently misunderstood the nature of allegory as an arbitrary or artificial device, although he admits that poorly constructed allegories deserve this criticism. But carefully composed allegories integrate their details in both the realistic and the symbolic worlds which they depict. Augustine's method was actually better than Jülicher's; Augustine simply deciphered too many of the details and used the wrong code. In short, "the main question therefore would seem to be not whether any or many of the parables of Jesus are allegorical or not, but *what they are allegories of.*"[23] Tinsley strengthens this argument in a subsequent article by citing Graham Hough's discussion of the "allegorical circle" (see diagram).

⎯⎯⎯⎯⎯⎯⎯⎯⎯⎯⎯

[20]Denis Buzy, *Introduction aux paraboles évangéliques* (Paris: Gabalda, 1912), esp. pp. 170-81. Cf. Quintilian *Inst. orat.* VIII, 6, 4.9.

[21]Thus in the example in n. 13 above, the essential meaning of "the sea was glass" and "the sea sparkled like glass" would be the same.

[22]Maxime Hermaniuk, *La parabole évangélique* (Paris: Desclée; Louvain: Bibliotheca Alfonsiana, 1947), esp. pp. 35-61.

[23]E. J. Tinsley, "Parable, Allegory and Mysticism," in *Vindications,* ed. Anthony Hanson (London: SCM; New York: Morehouse-Barlow, 1966), p. 179.

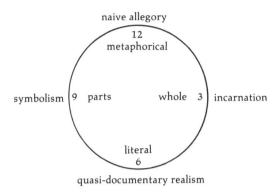

Hough differentiates between *naive allegory* and *quasi-documentary realism* as two opposite types of prose fiction (at 12 o'clock and 6 o'clock on his circle). In the former, the metaphorical meaning dominates; in the latter, the literal meaning prevails. Halfway in between are *incarnation* (3 o'clock) and *symbolism* (9 o'clock), in which the literal and metaphorical levels are evenly balanced. In an incarnational narrative, meaning derives from the entire story considered as a whole; in a symbolic narrative, from a particular part (the symbol), which is given extra attention. Tinsley views the most famous of Jesus' parables as examples of Hough's incarnational narratives.[24] Not every detail in them points to a second level of meaning, but some do, and this suffices to qualify them for the label *allegory*.

3. *Both the Messianic secret motif and the enigmatic purposes attributed to Jesus for speaking in parables may be explained better than by Wrede's hypothesis.* Many of the writings in the New Testament apocrypha claim to be secret revelations by Jesus to one or more of his disciples, yet these claims were widely rejected by the early church. This suggests that the strategy outlined by Wrede could not have succeeded even if it had been tried. More plausible are the explanations that Jesus sometimes enjoined secrecy concerning his identity because (a) many Jews were looking for a different type of Messiah from that which Jesus understood his mission to involve (i.e., a nationalistic or mil-

---

[24]E. J. Tinsley, "Parable and Allegory: Some Literary Criteria for the Interpretation of the Parables of Christ," *ChQ* 3 (1970):32-39; Graham Hough, "The Allegorical Circle," *Critical Quarterly* 3 (1961):199-209. Northrop Frye, *Anatomy of Criticism* (Princeton: University Press; London: Oxford University Press, 1957), p. 91, speaks of a "sliding scale" rather than a circle, but makes the identical point. Cf. also Leland Ryken, *How to Read the Bible as Literature* (Grand Rapids: Zondervan, 1984), pp. 139-53, 199-203.

itary ruler rather than a suffering servant)[25] and/or (b) it was inappropriate for him to make detailed claims about his identity until after his crucifixion and resurrection, which served to corroborate those claims.[26]

But even if Wrede's scenario were accepted, it would not be clear that the role of the parables as in some sense concealing truth necessarily formed part of the Messianic secret. There is nothing *explicitly* Christological in the teaching of the parables, and their mysteriousness seems to involve a different issue altogether—how to interpret specific details in each text.[27] Some have tried to deny this mysteriousness by explaining the apparent purpose clause of Mark 4:12 ("in order that seeing they might not perceive . . .") as really a result clause (as some think Matthew may have, substituting "so that" for "in order that"—Mt 13:13)[28] or as simply an abbreviation for an introduction to the Old Testament quotation (cf. Is 6:9)—i.e., equaling "in order that the following passage might be fulfilled."[29]

But the first of these explanations requires translating ἵνα ("in order that") in a relatively unusual manner, while the second simply shifts attention to the significance of the Old Testament text—in what sense was it fulfilled if it was neither the purpose nor the result of Jesus' preaching? It is better to take the ἵνα in its usual sense of purpose, and seek a different explanation for how one of Jesus' motives for speaking in parables could be to conceal. The key seems to lie in the meaning of the words "understand" and "perceive." Hans-Josef Klauck perhaps expresses it best when he speaks of those who are "outside" the kingdom:

> They understand the provocative claim of the parables very well, but they are not prepared to accept it. For Mark, Jesus' speaking

---

[25]See esp. James D. G. Dunn, "The Messianic Secret in Mark," *TynB* 21 (1970):92-117.

[26]See esp. Richard N. Longenecker, *The Christology of Early Jewish Christianity* (London: SCM; Naperville: Allenson, 1970), pp. 71-74.

[27]See in detail Heikki Räisänen, *Die Parabeltheorie im Markusevangelium* (Helsinki: Finnischen Exegetischen Gesellschaft, 1973); idem, *Das "Messiasgeheimnis" im Markusevangelium* (Helsinki: Finnischen Exegetischen Gesellschaft, 1976). Jonathan Bishop, "*Parabole* and *Parrhesia* in Mark," *Int* 40 (1986):39-52, sees both the parable theory and the Messianic secret as specific examples of Mark's broader practice of alternating between "mystery" and "interpretation" in his narrative.

[28]See esp. T. W. Manson, *The Teaching of Jesus* (Cambridge: University Press, 1939), pp. 76-80. Cf. C. S. Mann, *Mark* (Garden City: Doubleday, 1986), p. 264.

[29]E.g., Jeremias, *Parables*, p. 17; William L. Lane, *The Gospel according to Mark* (Grand Rapids: Eerdmans, 1974; London: Marshall, Morgan & Scott, 1975), p. 19.

in parables is not a riddle as such. What is perplexing is the behavior that it calls forth—that man can see salvation personified and nevertheless not come to conversion and belief.[30] This position squares with the use of "perceive" and "understand" elsewhere in Scripture.[31] It accounts for the fact that even Christ's enemies apparently understood his parables at a cognitive level (cf. esp. Mk 12:12 pars.). And it fits the nature of his preaching more generally. Jesus regularly called men and women to a point of radical decision—either to draw closer to him in discipleship or to make clear their rejection of him and in that sense actually be repelled (cf. Mt 12:33-35 par., Mk 9:40, Lk 11:23 par., Mk 3:6 pars.).

4. *The tendency of oral tradition increasingly to allegorize simple stories is counterbalanced by the even more common tendency to abbreviate and "de-allegorize" them.* The rise of form criticism also met with serious objections which will be discussed in more detail in chapter three. Perhaps the most important observation to make here is that even one of the pioneer form critics, Vincent Taylor, pointed out that fairly detailed narratives (like many of the parables) tended to be abbreviated as they were passed along by word of mouth, rather than expanded and allegorized as Bultmann had claimed.[32] More recently J. A. Baird has observed that over two-thirds of the parables which Jesus explained, however briefly, were addressed to his disciples, while most of those left unexplained were addressed to his opponents. This pattern fits in with Jesus' desire to make his teaching in some sense clearer to insiders than to outsiders. Such consistency and restraint, Baird concludes, was unlikely to have been the product of a Christian tradition which felt free to allegorize the parables indiscriminately.[33]

5. *Far from being an inferior art form, avoided by the master teacher, allegorical interpretation is an inevitable method of explaining the parables, which even those who deny it in theory cannot avoid in practice.* Fiebig's and Buzy's

---

[30]Hans-Josef Kauck, *Allegorie und Allegorese in synoptischen Gleichnistexten* (Münster: Aschendorff, 1978), p. 251.

[31]Cf. J. Goetzmann, "σύνεσις," *The New International Dictionary of New Testament Theology*, ed. Colin Brown, 3 vols. (Grand Rapids: Zondervan, 1975-78), 3:130-33.

[32]Vincent Taylor, *The Formation of the Gospel Tradition* (London: Macmillan, 1933), esp. Appendix B, pp. 202-9.

[33]J. Arthur Baird, "A Pragmatic Approach to Parable Exegesis: Some New Evidence on Mark 4:11, 33-34," *JBL* 76 (1957): 201-7. Cf. Raymond E. Brown, "Parable and Allegory Reconsidered," *NovT* 5 (1962):36-45.

studies already had pointed out that, from Quintilian on, many felt allegory to be an aesthetically satisfying form of rhetoric or literature. Matthew Black later noted that even as anti-allegorical an interpreter as Dodd could not avoid allegory despite his disclaimers. In his exposition of the parable of the wicked tenants, for example, Dodd winds up conceding that the natural meaning which Jesus most likely intended is that the vineyard is Israel; the tenants, the Jewish leaders; the servants, the prophets; and the son, Jesus.[34]

The same could be said of most other works from the "consensus perspective." To go back to the story of the prodigal son, even Jeremias, who at first denies that the father stands for God, then concedes that "some of the expressions used are meant to reveal that in his love he is an image of God."[35] The problem remains precisely that which Tinsley pinpointed: it is not that no elements in the parables stand for things other than themselves; it is a question of how many do so and to what they refer. The error of premodern interpreters lay in overzealous and anachronistic use of allegory, not in the method per se.

Despite all of the criticisms of the Jülicher-Jeremias tradition just noted, until quite recently few scholars were willing to say more than that there must be a little more allegory in the parables than has commonly been recognized. And the "one main point" rule for interpretation has remained virtually inviolate. Within the last decade, however, several scholars with cross-disciplinary expertise in Western literature and biblical studies have moved well beyond this position, affirming that most of the major narrative parables of Jesus are, by every standard literary definition of the word, genuine allegories.[36] These affirmations rely on four additional key principles.

6. *It is not multiple points of comparison which make a narrative an allegory; any narrative with both a literal and a metaphorical meaning is in essence allegorical.* The primary advocate of this assertion is Madeleine Boucher, who earned an M.A. in English literature at Harvard before

---

[34]Matthew Black, "The Parables as Allegory," *BJRL* 42 (1960):273-87; cf. Dodd, *Parables,* pp. 124-32.

[35]Jeremias, *Parables,* p. 128. Cf. Stein, *Parables,* p. 118.

[36]Madeleine Boucher, *The Mysterious Parable* (Washington: Catholic Biblical Association of America, 1977); Klauck, *Allegorie;* John Sider, "Proportional Analogy in the Gospel Parables," *NTS* 31 (1985):1-23.

proceeding to doctoral work in biblical studies. Boucher observes that for most literary critics there are only two "modes" of meaning—*literal* and *tropical* (pronounced with a long *o*—that which is popularly called "figurative"). Some examples of tropes include circumlocution (a "roundabout" way of speaking), metaphor, synecdoche (the substitution of the part for the whole), metonymy (the substitution of one thing for something else closely associated) and irony. Any one of these tropes may be developed into a full-fledged narrative; when a metaphor is thus developed, allegory results. Allegory is "nothing more and nothing less than *an extended metaphor in narratory form* (the term *narratory* here being used to include both dramatic and narrative works, that is, all works which tell a story)."[37]

Boucher further argues that allegory is a device of meaning, not a literary form or genre. So a parable may be an allegory even if its constituent elements do not involve separate metaphors, so long as the overall point of the parable transcends its literal meaning (e.g., the story is about the kingdom of God rather than just, say, farming, fishing or banqueting). The only types of parables that are not allegories, then, are either those that are so short that they are just simple comparisons rather than full-fledged narratives, or those that are extended synecdoches rather than extended metaphors, as in the parable of the rich fool or of the Pharisee and publican, where the main characters are representative of an entire class of *similar* people.

As for Jesus' purpose in speaking in parables, since he wanted to win his audiences over to his point of view, he had to be intelligible to them. Nevertheless, they could have found his meaning "mysterious," since many may have been either unable or unwilling to identify the proper spiritual equivalents for Jesus' down-to-earth metaphors.[38]

7. Identifying a narrative as an allegory is a far cry from imposing an allegorical interpretation on a passage which was never intended to contain a second level of meaning. By far the most ambitious and erudite of the

---

[37]Boucher, *Parable*, pp. 20-21. Cf. the cautious endorsements of Boucher by Mary A. Tolbert, *Perspectives on the Parables* (Philadelphia: Fortress, 1979), p. 28; and G. B. Caird, *The Language and Imagery of the Bible* (London: Duckworth; Philadelphia: Westminster, 1980), pp. 160-67.

[38]Cf. Boucher's further volume which both popularizes and adds additional exegetical examples for her thesis: *The Parables* (Wilmington: Glazier; Dublin: Veritas, 1981).

recent works on parable and allegory, Hans-Josef Klauck's Ph.D. dissertation ties together most of the studies previously mentioned in this section, ranging widely across the fields of biblical and literary criticism. Klauck concludes that important distinctions must be made between what he calls "allegory" (*Allegorie*), a rhetorical device applicable to many literary genres which gives a symbolic dimension to a text; "allegorizing" (*Allegorese*), which ascribes to a text hidden, often anachronistic meanings which its author never intended; and "allegorization" (*Allegorisierung*), the allegorizing expansion and embellishment of a text which originally was already an allegory in simpler form.[39] Turning to Jesus' parables, Klauck concludes that many of them are "allegories," some may have undergone a little "allegorization" (a necessary interpretive device, in his opinion, to make the texts relevant for each new generation of Christians), but that "allegorizing" per se, so typical of the pre-Jülicher era, is never justified.

The difference, therefore, between texts as apparently dissimilar as the parable of the prodigal son and *Pilgrim's Progress* is not that the latter is an allegory while the former is not. Instead, Klauck, like Tinsley, prefers to speak of an allegorical continuum with opposite extremes which he entitles "naive realism" and "naive picture-writing" (*Bilderschrift*).[40] Bunyan's would be closer to the latter extreme and the prodigal son closer to the former. Moreover, one cannot rule out any of the Gospel parables or interpretations as inauthentic due to the presence of "allegory," only if there is "allegorizing." The intermediate process of "allegorization" Klauck believes can explain some of the differences reflected in a comparison of Synoptic parallels, since it is a demonstrable tendency of oral tradition.

In a recent review article, Charles Carlston has labeled Klauck's work "the most learned study of the parables in any language since Jülicher."[41] If Klauck is right, then the parables are not the vehicle for Jülicher's universal truths, nor limited to Jeremias's situation-specific main points, nor even the untranslatable metaphors of the

---

[39]Klauck, *Allegorie*, p. 91.

[40]Ibid., p. 354.

[41]Charles E. Carlston, "Parable and Allegory Revisited: An Interpretive Review," *CBQ* 43 (1981):242. Cf. the reviews by J. Dupont, *Bib* 60 (1979): 435-38; and H. Merklein, *BZ* 24 (1980):133-35.

new hermeneutic and more recent movements. Rather they are "rhetorical allegories" in the tradition of Quintilian, Buzy and Hermaniuk, which require at least some deciphering in order to interpret them in accordance with Jesus' original intent.[42]

8. *The presence of mysterious and unusual details in the parables, pointing to an additional level of meaning, is much more widespread than has usually been realized.* The scholar who has championed this view more than any other is John Drury, who has highlighted the rich tradition in Hebrew narrative of the dark or enigmatic saying. Drury has pointed out numerous potential but subtle allusions in the parables to various Old Testament texts not usually discussed as background for these stories. He has also repeatedly shown how the interpretations, contexts and concluding generalizations which the evangelists provide fit the parables quite adequately. But he still believes, on form- and redaction-critical grounds, that this framing material cannot accurately reflect the original messages of Jesus, so he believes that the parables en masse are creations of the early church or the Gospel writers.[43]

Other studies have avoided these conclusions about inauthenticity while at the same time confirming that the parables regularly contain not only common, down-to-earth portraits of Jewish village life but also "extravagant"[44] and unrealistic features which point to more than one level of meaning. The ridiculous and implausible excuses of the invited guests in the parable of the great supper (Lk 14:18-20), the enormous size of the mustard plant which could provide shade for perching birds (Mk 4:32 pars.) and the inexplicable hiring practice of the owner in the parable of the vineyard laborers (Mt 20:1-16) all aptly illustrate this propensity for "atypical features."[45] But although these features appear implausible as de-

---

[42]Klauck, *Allegorie*, pp. 112, 146.

[43]John Drury, "The Sower, the Vineyard, and the Place of Allegory in the Interpretation of Mark's Parables," *JTS* 24 (1973):367-79, originally left the question of authenticity open, but after a critique of his work by John Bowker, "Mystery and Parable: Mark iv. 1-20," *JTS* 25 (1974): 300-17, he adopted his more radical stance. See Drury, "Origins," p. 186; p. 188, n. 19; and now esp. idem, *The Parables in the Gospels* (London: SPCK; New York: Crossroad, 1985).

[44]This is the term regularly used by Paul Ricoeur, "Biblical Hermeneutics," *Semeia* 4 (1975): esp. 114-18, although he eschews an explicit identification of the parables with allegory. Frederick H. Borsch, *Many Things in Parables: Extravagant Stories of New Community* (Philadelphia: Fortress, 1988), pp. 14-15, makes much of this feature and is more open to allegory than many without endorsing the detailed type of allegorical approach advocated here.

[45]Cf. esp. Norman A. Huffman, "Atypical Features in the Parables of Jesus," *JBL* 97 (1978):207-20.

scriptions of normal events, they make excellent sense when interpreted allegorically as standing for various spiritual truths.

9. *The parables are best viewed as "proportional analogies" which can be
expressed by means of a series of equations of the form "A is to B as a is to b
with respect to x."*[46] John Sider, a professor of English at Westmont
College in California, agrees that παραβολή must be viewed as representing a wider variety of figures of speech than have usually
been associated with the term. Consider, for example, Luke's use of
it for the very short proverb, "Physician, heal yourself" (Lk 4:23). But
Sider denies that its semantic range is as broad as that of *mashal*.

In every instance in which παραβολή appears in the Gospels, an
"analogy" is involved, either of "equation" or "example." An equation
relates "a particular vehicle to a particular tenor, by way of some
common feature which is viewed as the subject of a general class."
An "example" relates "a vehicle consisting of some particular instance to a tenor which is the general class."[47] By vehicle and tenor,
Sider is referring, respectively, to the story line of the parable and the
meaning intended by that story. Sider's "equation" resembles
Boucher's "extended metaphor," while his "example" improves on her
"extended synecdoche," since exemplary characters in the parables
(for example, the rich man and Lazarus) are not really parts of some
larger whole but examples of a particular category of people.

The correct interpretation of a parable, in either case, requires a
recognition of the fact that certain elements in the parable are being
compared to certain spiritual realities as in an analogy, with respect
to one or more specific characteristics. For example, the parable of
the unjust judge (Lk 18:1-7) compares (A) God to (B) his elect as (a)
the judge to (b) the woman, with respect to (x) the fact of vindication despite its appearance of delay. The parable of the householder and the thief compares the disciples to the coming of the Son
of man as the householder to the coming of the thief with respect
to readiness for the unexpected. And there are usually several of
these comparisons or contrasts in each parable. Parables that Jesus
in some way explains merely make more explicit the kind of com-

---

[46]Interestingly, Jülicher himself noted this *(Gleichnisreden,* vol. 1, pp. 69-70) but did not develop
it to its logical conclusions.

[47]John W. Sider, "The Meaning of *Parabole* in the Usage of the Synoptic Evangelists," *Bib* 62
(1981):460.

parisons that Jesus intended in those left unexplained. Thus because of the presence of multiple analogies, the longer "story parables really are 'allegorical' after all." In fact, Sider claims that stories making only one main point, as Jülicher supposed the parables to be, exist "nowhere in the Gospels" and "it could be hard to find them anywhere in literature"![48]

2.2 Evaluating the Debate

How ought we to assess these rather diametrically opposite approaches in the history of the debate about parable and allegory?[49] To begin with, it is important to note one point on which virtually everyone is agreed. The days of anachronistic, allegorizing interpretation must remain in the past. For this, commentators remain forever in Jülicher's debt. Indeed, part of the debate is simply a semantic one involving the meaning of allegory. Many scholars who reject the term nevertheless recognize stock symbols in almost all of the parables, which "stand for" something other than themselves and would have been well known to Jesus' original audiences. Yet the other "side" replies that this is precisely what allegory usually involves. Moreover, almost all commentators who actually expound a selection of the parables wind up with some allegorical interpretations, as the anti-Jülicher tradition defines them, regardless of what they may say about their method.

But these commentators might simply acknowledge their inconsistency and work harder at avoiding it.[50] The controversy involves more than definitions; it involves key issues in literary criticism and comparative religions. Even scholars who agree on the definition of allegory are divided over its function, value and legitimacy. This in

---

[48]Idem, "Proportional Analogy," p. 22.

[49]Reactions among studies of the parables recent enough to be able to reflect on some of the latest developments in the debate are understandably mixed. At one extreme, B. B. Scott, *Jesus, Symbol-Maker for the Kingdom* (Philadelphia: Fortress, 1981) p. 58, n. 1, admits that *parable* is used by biblical scholars in a "technical" way contrary to standard usage (as defined even by the Oxford English Dictionary) but otherwise ignores the issue altogether. At the opposite extreme, the evangelical literary critic Leland Ryken, *Words of Life: A Literary Introduction to the New Testament* (Grand Rapids: Baker, 1987), pp. 65-67, forthrightly accepts the equation of parable with allegory. Most simply continue to admit that a larger than normally accepted allegorical element in the parables probably exists, but their exegesis shows little impact from this concession.

[50]J. D. Crossan, *In Parables: The Challenge of the Historical Jesus* (New York and London: Harper & Row, 1973), p. xv, is more straightforward than most about the contradiction of expounding parables which are believed to be untranslatable into nonmetaphorical or propositional idiom: "the ultimate function of such exegesis is to render itself unnecessary"!

turn influences their judgments concerning whether Jesus would have actually used it, which determines their position on the authenticity of the undeniably allegorical parts of the parables or their interpretations as the Gospels present them.

C. S. Lewis's famous mistrust of biblical scholars' appreciation of literary devices, structure and quality enters in here as well.[51] Most biblical scholars have simply never taken the time to study these topics sufficiently to make their literary judgments persuasive. That the leading exponents of the pro-allegorical position prove the exception to this rule gives their position a priori greater attractiveness. But even Boucher, Klauck and Sider interact in only a limited way with secular literary critics; clearly there is room for more comparative study here. For example, one issue to which no one supporting an allegorical interpretation of the parables has to date given more than a passing aside is the question of how to determine which and how many details in a given parable "stand for" something or someone other than themselves.

Regarding parallels to Jesus' parables in other ancient religious traditions, there seems to be agreement that there are only two main options. Either Jesus' parables are largely unique and without parallel or the corpus of rabbinic parables provides the most promising material for comparative study. The only really close biblical parallel is Nathan's story of the ewe lamb (2 Sam 12:1-10)—and it, incidentally, is given at least a partially allegorical explanation (the rich man represents David, the poor man is Uriah, and the sheep stands for Bathsheba). Apart from the parables of the rabbis, no other group of relatively close parallels to Jesus' parables of any significant size exists.[52]

---

[51]C. S. Lewis, "Modern Theology and Biblical Criticism," in *Christian Reflections*, ed. Walter Hooper (Grand Rapids: Eerdmans, 1967), pp. 152-66 (= "Fern-Seed and Elephants," in *Fern-Seed and Elephants and Other Essays on Christianity*, ed. Walter Hooper [London: Collins, 1975], pp.104-25).

[52]It is generally agreed that, besides 2 Sam 12:1-10, few other Old Testament and intertestamental *meshalim* closely parallel Jesus' parables and probably none is structurally identical. See esp. Birger Gerhardsson, "The Narrative Meshalim in the Synoptic Gospels," *NTS* 34 (1988):339-63. Interestingly, even the moderately close parallels are usually at least partially allegorical. Cf. Judg 9:7-15; 2 Sam 14:1-17; 1 Kings 20:39-42; 2 Kings 4:9-10; Is 5:1-7; Jer 13:12-14; Ezek 17:1-15; and several of the Similitudes of Enoch. For a thorough discussion of non-rabbinic, pre-New Testament parable-like material of antiquity, see Klauck, *Allegorie*, pp. 32-115; cf. Drury, *Parables*, pp. 7-38. On Enoch in particular, see David W. Suter, *Tradition and Composition in the Parables of Enoch* (Missoula: Scholars, 1979); idem, "Masal in the Similitudes of Enoch," *JBL* 100 (1981):193-212. The primary source of post-New Testament Christian "parables" is the quite distinct collection of "visions" in the Shepherd of Hermas, on which see David Hellholm, *Das Visionenbuch des Hermas als Apokalypse*, vol. 1 (Lund: Gleerup, 1980).

But working with the rabbinic literature has proved even more daunting than mastering the basics of literary criticism for students trained primarily in New Testament studies. Over 2,000 rabbinic parables exist, they are scattered throughout a wide variety of writings spanning several centuries (none demonstrably pre-Christian), and translations of the Hebrew into modern European languages until recently have been sometimes inaccessible or non-existent. This situation, however, has been dramatically altered since the dissertation of Robert M. Johnston, who collected the 325 parables either attributed to Tannaim (the rabbis of the first three centuries of the Christian era) or found in Jewish writings of that period, provided translations for all of them and even offered a rudimentary commentary on them.[53] The rest of this chapter, therefore, will survey some of the insights first of modern literary criticism and then of the ancient Tannaitic *mashal* to see if further progress can be made on the question of parable and allegory.

2.2.1 Contemporary Literary Criticism

Valid generalizations about what all literary critics believe prove as elusive as stating what all biblical scholars affirm. Many different schools of thought abound, especially with the advent in recent years of several radically new approaches to the interpretation of literature. But the following principles are fairly widely held and suggest helpful insights which students of the parables should take into account.

1. *The disjunction between allegory and parable by many biblical critics is closely paralleled by the older disjunction between allegory and symbol by many literary critics, a disjunction now widely recognized to be invalid.* The nineteenth-century school of thought known as Romanticism, led by Goethe in Germany and Coleridge in England, resoundingly rejected allegory as an artificial and outmoded form of literature. In its place Romantics exalted symbolism. Symbolism referred to the use of verbal and visual images which did not simply stand for something other than themselves, but which actually suggested more than one meaning within themselves.

---

[53]Robert M. Johnston, "Parabolic Interpretations Attributed to Tannaim" (Ph.D. diss., Hartford Seminary Foundation, 1978). A selection of these now appears in Johnston and McArthur, *Parables*.

A cross, for example, might appear as an entirely natural element in the story line of a given piece of fiction, while at the same time evoking memories of the crucifixion of Jesus and disclosing a deeper meaning in the plot as well. In American literature one thinks, for example, of the role played by the inescapable "A" (for adulteress) sewn onto Hester Prynne's dress in Hawthorne's *The Scarlet Letter*, or of the great white whale which obsesses the central characters in Melville's *Moby Dick*. The Romantics considered stories built around such symbols more aesthetically pleasing and artistically elegant than the type of personification of abstract concepts so familiar from an allegory such as Spenser's *Faerie Queene*.

The problem with this disjunction between allegory and symbolism, however, and one not widely admitted until about thirty years ago, was that it rested on what philosophers call a category mistake (comparing or contrasting two things which do not really belong to the same class or group). Allegory, as classically defined, is a manner of speaking in which two or more levels of meaning are intended (and often also used to refer to an entire work which employs allegorical discourse), while a symbol refers to a specific element within a story which functions as a key to unlock additional levels of meaning. Although they can exist without one another, allegories usually contain numerous symbols, and symbolic writing may easily turn into allegory.[54]

The Romantics' theory was further flawed in that it rested on the arbitrary assertion that the highest aim of all art ought to be the representation of the general by the specific (rather than the substitution of one specific for another as in allegory).[55] One cannot help but think of Jülicher's similar assertion that the parables of Jesus could make only one very general point. By moving away from a generalizing summary of a parable's meaning to the very situation-specific approach of Dodd and Jeremias, interpreters of the parables, without realizing it, already approached the border of allegorical interpretation.

---

[54]The origin of the problem is nicely summarized in John A. Hodgson, "Transcendental Tropes: Coleridge's Rhetoric of Allegory and Symbol," in *Allegory, Myth, and Symbol*, ed. Morton W. Bloomfield (Cambridge, Mass., and London: Harvard University Press, 1981), pp. 273-92; the major impetus for the critique of the Romantics' position on allegory came from Frye, *Anatomy*.
[55]Charles Hayes, "Symbol and Allegory: A Problem in Literary Theory," *Germanic Review* 44 (1969):276.

2. The views that allegory is equivalent to metaphor extended to narrative, and that it may contain many or few points of comparison, are widely acknowledged. The following definitions are fairly technical, but they serve to illustrate the different ways in which this definition of allegory may be expressed. For Michael Murrin, allegory is a specific kind of analogy in which the author "expresses a truth he has received in contemplation through the medium of tropological figures."[56] Beatrice Batson explains more specifically:

> Allegory . . . may be perceived then as the embodiment of beliefs in concrete form. It is a work in which the author imitates external actualities and at the same time suggests the significance of such imitations by *extending a central metaphor* and by showing additional analogies.[57] [italics mine]

More technical still is the definition of Gayatri Spivak: "the setting up of a double structure, one component of which is a metasemantic system of significance corresponding to the other component—a system of signs present in the text itself."[58] In other words, when certain details in a narrative stand for something other than themselves or point to a second level of meaning, allegory is present.

A related point, which is rarely disputed, involves the spectrum or continuum of various degrees of allegorical writing which may be found in any given work. Though not always expressed in as much detail as Graham Hough's "allegorical circle" (see above, p. 39), most recent studies emphasize that some allegories have a greater percentage of details with metaphorical referents than others. Many would argue that the best allegories are quite realistic as pieces of fiction in their own right, and that part of their artistry is leaving their audiences in doubt about just which details are supposed to have a double meaning.[59]

---

[56]Michael Murrin, *The Veil of Allegory* (Chicago and London: University of Chicago Press, 1969), p.70. This would allow for the constituent elements of the allegory not only to be metaphors but other figures of speech as well, e.g., metonymy. The use of metonymy in allegory is stressed by Holly W. Boucher, "Metonymy in Typology and Allegory, with a Consideration of Dante's Comedy," in *Allegory*, ed. Bloomfield, p. 130.

[57]E. Beatrice Batson, *John Bunyan: Allegory and Imagination* (Totowa, N.J.: Barnes & Noble; London: Croom Helm, 1984), p. 29.

[58]Gayatri C. Spivak, "Thoughts on the Principle of Allegory," *Genre* 5 (1972):348.

[59]Angus Fletcher, *Allegory: The Theory of a Symbolic Mode* (Ithaca and London: Cornell, 1964), p. 7; Edwin Honig, *Dark Conceit: The Making of Allegory* (Evanston: Northwestern; London: Faber & Faber, 1959) pp. 5, 93; Frye, *Anatomy*, p. 91.

In fact, in any lengthy allegory a sizable majority of the details do not have double meanings; only a few key elements do. For example, at the end of C. S. Lewis's *The Lion, the Witch and the Wardrobe*, critics recognize symbolic meaning in Aslan's death and resurrection, but not to the stone table, the shaving of Aslan and the mice who gnaw through the ropes which bind him.[60] Jülicher's emphasis on the realism of parables contrasting with the artificiality of allegories, echoed by virtually all of his successors, finds precious little support in contemporary literary criticism. There is a fine blend of the realistic and the extraordinary both in the parables and in the best allegories.

3. There is still a fairly widespread popular denigration of the aesthetics of allegory, but it is unwarranted. While a one-to-one correspondence between all the details of allegories and their metaphorical counterparts cannot be expected, the meaning which can be communicated is by nature limited. Unlike some, primarily modernist, modes of discourse, allegories are not entirely open-ended. Certain key elements may convey more than one "secondary" sense, but the overall structure of the story as a "twice-told tale" prevents derivative meanings from being multiplied indefinitely.

In Northrop Frye's opinion, this is probably a major reason why modern secular and biblical critics alike have demeaned allegorical discourse: "The commenting critic is often prejudiced against allegory without knowing the real reason, which is that continuous allegory prescribes the direction of his commentary, and so restricts its freedom."[61] It is not as easy to impose convincingly some of the various modern fashions of interpretation (e.g., psychoanalytic, Marxist, feminist) on texts whose meaning is relatively straightforward.

In addition, allegories frequently exhibit a simplicity which is disarming. Once the key to the second level of meaning is grasped, it is often relatively easy and enjoyable to discern the correct interpretation throughout. Certainly that is true for the basic contours of a work like *Pilgrim's Progress*. So it is not fair to contrast the simplicity of the parables with allegedly complicated allegories. Le-

---

[60]Ryken, *How to Read the Bible*, pp. 199-200.
[61]Frye, *Anatomy*, p. 90.

land Ryken in fact argues precisely the reverse:

> The academic world has surrounded the parables with so many
> intricate rules for interpreting them that ordinary people have
> become convinced that they had best leave the parables to the
> specialist. It is time to give the parables back to the group to
> which Jesus originally told them—ordinary people. Viewing the
> parables as allegorical would be a step in the right direction, since
> simple allegory has usually struck ordinary people as being acces-
> sible.[62]

Yet, at the same time, the meaning of allegories is not exhausted
as easily as some commentators might think. Gay Clifford explains:
"Writers of allegory conceive of truth as in some degree hermetic,
too complex to be rendered in baldly prescriptive or descriptive
language."[63] And because one can never be sure just how many of
the subordinate details in a narrative are meant to carry extra
freight, there is always an elusiveness to allegory to entice the
curious. The first reading of an allegory like Orwell's *Animal Farm*
aptly illustrates this ambiguity.

The clichés "all animals are comrades" and "all animals are equal"
(with the eventual addition "but some animals are more equal than
others") immediately conjure up the specter of Soviet Communism.
But do the two pigs, Snowball and Napoleon, represent specific
Soviet leaders? Or is the entire novel in fact an allegory about
totalitarianism more generally? If Orwell had not specifically answered these questions elsewhere, critics would probably be hard
pressed to reach a consensus. Similar ambiguities face the reader of
Christ's parables, especially when Jesus did not spell out in detail
what he meant.

4. *The purposes of allegory closely match both the revelatory and the esoteric
purposes for which Christ, according to Mark 4:11-12, spoke in parables.*
Contemporary analysis largely agrees that there are at least three
primary functions of allegory: (a) to illustrate a viewpoint in an
artistic and educational way, (b) to keep its message from being
immediately clear to all its hearers or readers without further reflection, and (c) to win over its audience to accept a particular set

---

[62]Ryken, *How to Read the Bible*, p. 203.

[63]Gay Clifford, *The Transformations of Allegory* (London and Boston: Routledge & Kegan Paul,
1974), p. 53.

of beliefs or act in a certain way. At first glance (a) and (b) can seem contradictory, but in fact they complement one another in service of (c).

A speaker or writer who has a viewpoint he wishes his audience to accept that it does not currently hold will seldom succeed by means of a straightforward explanation of his position. Rather he has to think of some innocuous method of introducing the subject, while at the same time challenging his listeners to think of it in a new way. A carefully constructed allegory may well accomplish what its nonmetaphorical, propositional counterpart never could. As Michael Murrin explains, "the audience of the allegorist did not encounter truth in so uncompromising a manner. Since it was concealed from them, at least initially, they could gradually move closer and closer to it."[64]

An excellent example is Golding's *Lord of the Flies.* Those who believe that individuals are by nature good and that it is society which corrupts them are not likely to abandon their convictions as a result of a direct challenge to their world view. But they may be drawn into an alternate world view through the experience of the boys on the island, who ultimately reveal their evil character even when divorced from civilization. Of course the allegorist's strategy does not guarantee success. There are thus two ways in which allegory can conceal even as it tends to reveal. In the first case, a person may simply fail to grasp the meaning of one or more of an allegory's constituent metaphors; in the second, while recognizing the meaning of an allegory, he may reject its appeal to bring about some kind of transformation in his life.[65]

The similarity between this literary analysis of allegory and the Gospels' treatment of Jesus' parables staggers one accustomed to thinking of parable and allegory as opposites. We no longer have to choose between a Jesus who uses parables to clarify and a Mark who misinterprets their meaning as obfuscatory. Both clarity and concealment go hand in hand as Jesus seeks a creative and disarming way to revolutionize his audiences' thinking about the kingdom of God, especially in relation to the Judaism of his day.

---

[64]Murrin, *Allegory*, p. 42; cf. Fletcher, *Allegory*, pp. 23, 82, 330-31.
[65]Fletcher, *Allegory*, p. 359; Clifford, *Allegory*, p. 29.

Sometimes they fail to understand his meaning because they don't know what certain imagery stands for, but more often they very clearly perceive his meaning but are not prepared to accept it. Mark 12:12 pars. point this out clearly as the authorities recognize that Jesus told the parable of the wicked tenants against them. But because they are unwilling to change their ways, they merely redouble their efforts to destroy him. Murrin, in passing, actually applies his discussion of allegory to the Gospels and declares of the apparent purpose clause in Mark 4:12 that "this paradox cannot be explained away" and that "the allegorist had for his end the same general objectives which the prophet had: the moral reform of the multitude and the proclamation of truth."[66]

Of course this is precisely what many conservative biblical scholars have been saying all along (recall also Klauck's explanation, above, pp. 40-41). Jesus' preaching deliberately led people, at first gently but then inexorably, to a point of decision—either to follow or to reject him, and from his perspective those who rejected him did not really understand either who he was or what were the consequences of their actions.[67] Or in the words of T. F. Torrance, "the Kingdom of God comes into the midst and throws a man into the crisis of decision, and yet by its veiled form the Word of the Kingdom holds man at arm's length away in order to give him room and time for personal decision." Again, "Jesus deliberately concealed the Word in parable lest men against their will should be forced to acknowledge the Kingdom, and yet He allowed them enough light to convict them and to convince them."[68] So, too, literary criticism has now provided enough light to uphold the authenticity of Mark 4:11-12 in its present context; yet many skeptics "see but do not perceive."

5. *The key to interpreting most allegories lies in recognizing what a small handful of characters, actions or symbols stand for and fitting the rest of the story in with them.* The classic, medieval allegory employed personification

[66]Murrin, *Allegory*, pp. 32, 39.

[67]J. R. Kirkland, "The Earliest Understanding of Jesus' Use of Parables: Mark IV, 10-12 in Context," *NovT* 19 (1977):1-21. For similar conclusions at the redactional level, cf. Craig A. Evans, "The Function of Isaiah 6:9-10 in Mark and John," *NovT* 24 (1982):124-38; Frank E. Eakin, Jr., "Spiritual Obduracy and Parable Purpose," in *The Use of the Old Testament in the New*, ed. J. Efird (Durham, N.C.: Duke University, 1972), pp. 87-109.

[68]T. F. Torrance, "A Study in New Testament Communication," *SJT* 3 (1950):304-5.

to make clear the main points of comparison. Thus in the *Faerie Queene*, the lady Lucifera, who symbolizes pride, could be drawn in her carriage by horses with riders named Idleness, Gluttony, Avarice and the like. In Lewis's modern-day Chronicles of Narnia, characters are not named for virtues, but the lion Aslan certainly takes on human (and Godlike) qualities so that readers recognize him as a Christ-figure. Other writers of allegories use puns or wordplays or unrealistic actions designed to alert the reader to multiple meanings. In many cases the protagonist unravels the allegory's mystery. Once we recognize who or what he stands for, then subordinate characters who either help or oppose him can be identified.

After the more obvious identifications, however, come details which regularly remain ambiguous. Edwin Honig terms these "allegorical wavers."[69] They form part of the artistry of a good allegory, and many times even the author himself does not consciously realize how many details fit naturally into the two parallel story lines. A number of students of allegory are accepting the common-sense tradition resurrected by E. D. Hirsch that the meaning of a piece of literature depends on the author's original intention,[70] but at this point they often add an important qualification. Since "the language of allegory makes relationships significant by extending the original identities of which they are composed with as many clusters of meaning as the traffic of the dominant idea will bear,"[71] perhaps a better criterion for valid interpretation is *both* that meaning which the author intended *and* that which readily coheres with what he did intend.

This of course is entirely different from "allegorizing" or "allegoresis," which is interpreting a text as allegory which was never intended in that way at all. But it is similar to Klauck's "allegorization" and may be viewed as a legitimate process. It is the type of interpretation of a work which one could imagine presenting to its author and having him reply, "Oh, I hadn't quite thought it all through that far, but now that you point it out I wholeheartedly

---

[69]Honig, *Conceit*, p. 129.

[70]E. D. Hirsch, *Validity in Interpretation* (New Haven and London: Yale, 1967); idem, *The Aims of Interpretation* (Chicago and London: Univ. of Chicago Press, 1976). Cf. esp. Peter Berek, "Interpretation, Allegory, and Allegoresis," *College English* 40 (1978):117-32; Joseph A. Mazzeo, "Allegorical Interpretation and History," *Comparative Literature* 30 (1978):13.

[71]Honig, *Conceit*, p. 114.

agree; it certainly fits in with everything I was trying to say."[72]

6. *The result of all of the above is that many literary critics readily appeal to the parables of Jesus as a prime illustration of allegory.* A text like Leland Ryken's *The Literature of the Bible* begins its chapter on parables with the unequivocal affirmation that "the parables of Jesus belong to the literary family known as allegory."[73] Following Northrop Frye's classic discussion,[74] Ryken would distinguish between "naive allegory"—parables like the sower or the wicked tenants, where virtually all details stand for something—and "realistic allegory"—parables like the good Samaritan or the prodigal son, where many details have no secondary meaning.

The studies surveyed here, however, offer no support for the notion that the interpretations attributed to Jesus for some of his parables, whether long or short, are the sign of the early church misunderstanding the nature of his teaching. Instead, they represent a natural and legitimate method for him to clarify his meaning. Philip Rollinson puts it even more absolutely: "The parabolic story, then, is only parabolic if it is linked with some application, explicit or implied. This application may be vague, general, or highly detailed and precise, but there must be some analogous application indicated."[75] A final testimony deserves somewhat fuller citation. Using somewhat more technical language, Charles Hayes declares:

> Whenever a sequence of interconnected motifs is so constructed that central features of the concrete fictive reality acquire a distinctly metaphysical frame of reference, and not just by virtue of the work's theme or the general nature of its characters' experiences but because certain motifs engender a sharp, perceptible duality of perspectives; whenever the facts presented are "likened unto" something else, *as in the Biblical parables,* so that a figurative language comes into use and the factual gains a dimension of pervasive extrinsic meaning—whenever a work is so

---

[72]An analogous situation in which even very conservative biblical critics often use this type of principle is with the New Testament's use of the Old. See, e.g., D. A. Carson, "Matthew," in *The Expositor's Bible Commentary,* ed. Frank E. Gaebelein, vol. 8 (Grand Rapids: Zondervan, 1984), p. 92, commenting on the use of Hos 11:1 in Mt 2:15.

[73]Leland Ryken, *The Literature of the Bible* (Grand Rapids: Zondervan, 1974), p. 301.

[74]Frye, *Anatomy,* pp. 89-92.

[75]Philip Rollinson, *Classical Theories of Allegory and Christian Culture* (Pittsburgh: Duquesne; Brighton: Harvester, 1981), pp. 40-41. Cf. John MacQueen, *Allegory* (London: Methuen; New York: Harper & Row, 1970), pp. 24-25.

structured *it cannot be anything except allegory.*[76] [italics mine]
What a complete contrast with the Jülicherian legacy that has dominated this century's parable scholarship!

2.2.2 The Rabbinic Parables
Since the anti-allegorical school of parable interpretation has regularly appealed to modern literary criticism for support, the previous survey fills a crucial gap in the defense of the pro-allegorical view. But ultimately it is not as important how modern critics, literary or biblical, view the parables as how people in Jesus' own day understood them. As already noted, the only close analogy from the ancient world is the corpus of rabbinic parables. But even here there is a lively debate over the relevance of these stories for the interpretation of Jesus' teaching.

To begin with, almost none of the rabbinic parables can be dated as early as the first half of the first century. The examples surveyed are largely second- or third-century compositions. Christian commentators since Jülicher, moreover, have regularly endorsed his verdict that the rabbinic parables are an inferior variety of that form of teaching which only Jesus truly mastered.[77] But this affirmation is usually accompanied by only a brief sample of prooftexts. A more careful reading of all the 325 Tannaitic[78] parables which have been preserved makes this verdict hard to sustain. There are crucial differences between the parables of Jesus and those of the rabbis, but the similarities seem to outweigh the differences.

---

[76]Hayes, "Symbol and Allegory," p. 284.

[77]E.g., Jeremias, *Parables*, p. 12; A. M. Hunter, *Interpreting the Parables* (London: SCM; Philadelphia: Westminster, 1960), p. 116; G. V. Jones, *The Art and Truth of the Parables* (London: SPCK, 1964), p. 79; Peter R. Jones, *The Teaching of the Parables* (Nashville: Broadman, 1982), p. 36. For a brief survey of the most important scholarship of the past century on the rabbinic parables, see Clemens Thoma, "Prolegomena zu einer Übersetzung und Kommentierung der rabbinischen Gleichnisse," *TZ* 38 (1982):514-31.

[78]On the general (though by no means absolute) reliability of the attributions to a given rabbi during the earliest centuries of the Christian era, see Johnston, "Interpretations," pp. 136-38, and cf. b.Yeb. 97a, Aboth 6:6, Midr. Rab. on Eccl. II.15, 5. Cf. even Jacob Neusner, *The Rabbinic Traditions about the Pharisees Before 70*, vol. 3 (Leiden: Brill, 1971), p. 181, who has spearheaded a movement among Jewish scholars to treat the rabbinic literature with at least as much skepticism as the higher-critical tradition of biblical interpretation: "I assume that later masters [i.e., from the post-70 A.D. period, to which six of the seven generations of Tannaim and the vast majority of Tannaitic parables belong] commonly tried to assign sayings to the man who said them, not to some earlier and more prestigious authority" (though note his vacillation on p. 182). The fact that approximately half of the Tannaitic parables were left unassigned to any rabbi seems to bear out this assumption.

As for dating, since the form and structure of the rabbinic texts remained relatively constant for nearly half a millennium (from the second to the sixth centuries), it seems unlikely that first-century teachers would have employed drastically different methods of illustration or debate. Modern studies of Israel's history have emphasized that the destruction of Jerusalem in A.D. 70 required Jewish survivors radically to reassess certain key *beliefs and attitudes* in their religion, but what evidence remains suggests that *forms* of teaching or rhetoric (such as a parable) remained remarkably stable.[79] Thus Norman Perrin, while inconsistently rejecting any allegorical interpretation of Jesus' parables, nevertheless recognized the rabbinic parables as their closest parallel in "literary form and function."[80] Ironically, B. B. Scott, like many in the SBL parables seminar, completely inverts the significance of the data. Scott is prepared to use numerous rabbinic texts from as late as the ninth century to illuminate first-century belief, but he refuses to consider the consistently allegorical parables of the rabbis from even as early as the second century as having any bearing on the form of Jesus' parables.[81]

The reason that almost no first-century Jewish parables have been preserved is simply that so little first-century Jewish literature of any kind has been preserved, and almost nothing from the Pharisaic party from which the post-A.D. 70 rabbis almost exclusively emerged. So just as Jesus obviously invested other well-established forms of speaking (e.g., proverb, hyperbole or prophecy) with distinctive content, he most likely adopted a well-known method of instruction when he spoke in parables. The difference lay in his message and his authority (cf., e.g., Mt 7:28-29). The following observations about the similarities and differences between the parables of Jesus and those of the earliest rabbis support these claims.

2.2.2.1 Similarities with the Parables of Jesus

1. The Rabbinic parables almost always begin with an introductory formula which parallels those found in the Gospels. By far the most common is

---

[79]See esp Rainer Riesner, *Jesus als Lehrer* (Tübingen: Mohr, 1981). pp. 97-245.
[80]Perrin, *Jesus*, pp. 95-96.
[81]Bernard B. Scott, *Hear Then the Parable* (Minneapolis: Fortress, 1989).

some, often abbreviated, form of the saying: "A parable—to what may it be compared? It is like the case of . . ." (cf., e.g., Mt 11:16). Occasionally, however, they will begin with a simple reference to one of the characters in the story (often the main one) as "a certain man" or "a king of flesh and blood." Fiebig saw these as equivalent to the Greek expressions ἄνθρωπός τις ("a certain man") and ἄνθρωπος βασιλεύς ("a man, a king"),[82] often introducing Gospel parables as, for example, in Matthew 18:23 and Luke 16:1. A few rabbinic parables, however, begin with the unparalleled phrase "in the custom of the world" and draw their spiritual point from a comparison with what is taken for granted in human affairs.

2. *Often the logic of this last category of parable is "from the lesser to the greater."* That is to say the passage argues that "if such-and-such is true with men, how much more so with God." This "from the lesser to the greater" logic (Latin: *a fortiori*; Hebrew: *qal-wa-homer*) is common in the Gospel parables (e.g., Lk 11:13) and is often tipped off by a distinctive introduction. Especially in Luke, Jesus frequently precedes a parable with the rhetorical question "Which of you . . . [would do a certain thing]?" in which the obvious answer is "no one" (e.g., Lk 11:5, 9). The conclusion then follows—how much more should such behavior not be expected of God. In a few cases, however, the logic is reversed with positive affirmations implied. If something holds true even in the secular sphere, how much more must it apply to the spiritual realm. Consider Jesus' parable of the lost coin with its remarkable parallel attributed to R. Phineas b. Jair:

> Or what woman having ten drachmas, if she loses one drachma, does not surely light a lamp, sweep the house, and search carefully until she finds it? And having found it she calls together her friends and neighbors saying, "Rejoice with me, for I have found the drachma which I lost." Thus, I say to you, there is joy in the presence of the angels of God over one sinner repenting. (Lk 15:8-10)

> If a man loses a *sela'* or an *obol* [a small coin] in his house, he lights lamp after lamp, wick after wick, till he finds it. Now does it not stand to reason: if for these things which are only ephemeral and of this world a man will light so many lamps and lights

[82]Fiebig, *Altjüdische Gleichnisse*, p. 84.

till he finds where they are hidden, for the words of the Torah which are the life both of this world and of the next world, ought you not to search as for hidden treasures? (Midrash Rabbah on Song of Songs 1.1, 9).[83]

The logic is in each case incontrovertible.

3. *The length and structure of the rabbinic parables also resemble those of the parables of Jesus.* Both groups of parables are generally quite short, with occasional lengthier exceptions. They usually contain only two or three main characters, though some have as few as one or as many as four. The rabbis, like Jesus, regularly contrasted the good behavior of the wise with the wicked behavior of the foolish. Occasionally the parallelism between the parts of the parable dealing with these characters is virtually exact, except for the specific behavior contrasted. Compare, for example, Jesus' contrast between the man who built his house on the rock and the one who built his on sand (Mt 7:24-27/Lk 6:47-49) with the parable of R. Eleazar b. Azariah:

He whose wisdom is more abundant than his works, to what is he like? To a tree whose branches are abundant but whose roots are few; and the wind comes and uproots it and overturns it. . . . But he whose works are more abundant than his wisdom, to what is he like? To a tree whose branches are few but whose roots are many; so that even if all the winds in the world come and blow against it, it cannot be stirred from its place. (Aboth 3:18)[84]

This type of parallelism not only contributed to an aesthetically pleasing story and to a sharply delineated contrast, but it also made for easy memorization and reliable transmission as the parables were passed along by word of mouth. In a detailed study of the structural patterns of Jesus' and the rabbis' parables, Raymond Pautrel concluded that both lent themselves to quite accurate preservation during the period of oral tradition before they were first written down.[85]

4. *The parables of Jesus and the rabbis further share common topics and imagery.* Kings and their courts, banquets and weddings, farmers and

---

[83]Trans. Maurice Simon, in *Midrash Rabbah*, vol. 4, sec. 5, ed. H. Freedman & Maurice Simon (London: Soncino, 1977), p. 11.

[84]Trans. Herbert Danby, *The Mishnah* (London: Oxford University Press, 1933), p. 452.

[85]Raymond Pautrel, "Les canons du mashal rabbinique," *RSR* 26 (1936):6-45; 28 (1938):264-81. Cf. Fiebig, *Gleichnisreden*, pp. 222-78; and, more generally, Joseph M. Baumgarten, "Form Criticism and the Oral Law," *JSJ* 5 (1974):34-40. See also below, chaps. 3-4.

their hired help, landlords and their tenants, fishermen, merchants, and debtors all appear regularly in both bodies of literature to illustrate the dealings of God with his people. Despite the claims of those committed in advance to demonstrating for every facet the superiority of Jesus' parables to those of the rabbis, neither corpus is significantly more or less realistic than the other in the portraits sketched.

Asher Feldman demonstrated this point with respect to the agricultural and pastoral imagery in rabbinic parables and similes.[86] In a monumental study, Ignaz Ziegler did the same for over 900 of the metaphorical sayings dealing with kings, showing the great detail with which they accurately reflected life under the Roman emperors.[87] And the less realistic portions do not distinguish the rabbis from Jesus; as already noted, Jesus' parables also contain many "atypical" features (see above, p. 45). With both groups of writings, unusual details often disclose the metaphorical or allegorical significance of the narratives.

In some instances, the actual details of a Tannaitic parable so closely match the imagery of one of Christ's parables that it is virtually impossible to argue for any qualitative difference between them, to say nothing of a generic distinction. One is even forced to ask if there is not some literary connection. If direct borrowing is precluded because of considerations of time and place of origin, then at least evidence is furnished for a common stock of popular stories whose details were modified by individual teachers to suit their own purposes.[88] The following are only three of a large number of striking parallels that can be adduced:

> Another explanation: "Thou wilt return to the Lord thy God." R. Samuel Pargrita said in the name of R. Meir: This can be compared to the son of a king who took to evil ways. The king sent a tutor to him who appealed to him saying, "Repent, my son." The son, however, sent him back to his father [with the message], "How can I have the effrontery to return? I am

---

[86]Asher Feldman, _The Parables and Similes of the Rabbis_ (Cambridge: University Press, 1924).

[87]Ignaz Ziegler, _Die Königsgleichnisse des Midrasch_ (Breslau: Schlesische Verlags-Anstalt, 1903).

[88]See esp. Israel Abrahams, _Studies in Pharisaism and the Gospels_ (Cambridge: University Press, 1917), pp. 90-107; David Flusser, _Die rabbinischen Gleichnisse und der Gleichniserzähler Jesu_, vol. 1 (Frankfurt a. M. and Las Vegas: Peter Lang, 1981), p. 38.

ashamed to come before you." Thereupon his father sent back word, "My son, is a son ever ashamed to return to his father? And is it not to your father that you will be returning?" Similarly, the Holy One, blessed be He, sent Jeremiah to Israel when they sinned, and said to him: "Go, say to My children, 'Return.' " (Midrash Rabbah on Deuteronomy 2:24; cf. Lk 15:11-24)[89]

R. Judah the Prince used to cite this parable: To what is the matter like? To a king who possessed a vineyard which he handed over to a tenant. The king said to his servants, "Go, cut down the grapes of my vineyard, take away my portion and leave behind the portion which belongs to the tenant." They at once went and carried out his order. The tenant began to cry and lament; so the king said to him, "Have I taken anything of yours? I have only taken my own!" He replied to him, "My lord king, so long as your portion was with mine, my portion was guarded from plunder and theft; but now that you have removed your portion, behold my portion is exposed to plunder and theft!" The king is the supreme King of kings, the Holy One, blessed be He; the tenant is the father and mother. So long as the soul is within the human being, he is preserved; but when he dies he is for the maggot and worm. (Midrash Rabbah on Ecclesiastes 5:10, 2; cf. Mk 12:1-9 pars.)[90]

R. Meir illustrated it by a parable. To what is the matter like? To a king who prepared a banquet and invited guests without fixing a time when they should leave. The shrewd among them left at the ninth hour, returned home and went to bed while it was still light; others left at sunset while the shops were still open and the lamps burning, entered their homes and went to bed by the light of the lamps; still others left at two or three hours in the night when some shops were open and some shut, some with their lamps alight and some with their lamps extinguished, entered their homes and went to bed in the dark. Those remaining at the banquet became intoxicated, and wounded and killed each other; as it is stated, "I saw the Lord standing beside the altar; and He said: Smite the capitals, that the posts may

---

[89]Trans. J. Rabbinowitz, in *Midrash Rabbah* vol. 3, sec. 2, 53.

[90]Trans. A. Cohen, in ibid., vol. 4, sec. 3, 148.

shake; and break them in pieces on the head of all of them; and I will slay the residue of them with the sword." (b. Semachoth 8.10; cf. Mt 22:1-10, 25:1-13)[91]

The first two parables seem self-explanatory. The last occurs in the context of a discussion of the Roman massacre of the Jews following their rebellion in the 130s A.D. Perhaps Rabbi Meir was suggesting that Jews who died before this bloodbath died in peace.

5. *The rabbis interpreted their parables in a variety of ways, but almost always with some allegorical element.* These same three examples also nicely illustrate various approaches to interpretation. In the first case, a generalizing conclusion summarizes a main point; in the second, a point-by-point explanation provides greater detail; in the third, a Scripture is cited, but the meaning of several of the parable's elements remains unclear. All three of these approaches are common in the rabbinic literature and in the parables of Jesus.

What is clear in each of these three narratives is that at least some, if not most, of the details stand for a (usually scriptural) counterpart, that the parable is meant to be read at two levels throughout, and that, by any of the definitions previously surveyed, the parables are decidedly allegorical. Some of the referents involved are stereotypic and recur regularly throughout the rabbinic literature—the king for God, the son for Israel, the tutor or servant for one of Israel's leaders or prophets, the banquet and its guests as the coming (often eschatological) judgment and those who will be either blessed or cursed at that time. All of these "equations" have exceptions, however; context always takes priority over convention.[92] In the second passage cited above, for example, Rabbi Judah uses the vineyard, which usually stands for Israel, in an innovative way to illustrate the connection between soul and body.

6. *The purposes of the rabbinic parables involve both disclosure and concealment.* These three samples, finally, also represent the larger body of Tannaitic parables in that they reflect the same purposes already

---

[91]Trans. A. Cohen, *The Minor Tractates of the Talmud,* vol. 1 (London: Soncino, 1965), p. 367. For further parallels to Gospel parables, not limited to Tannaitic times, see Oesterley, *Parables.*

[92]For a full catalog of "standard metaphors" with noteworthy exceptions, see Johnston, "Interpretations," pp. 582-96. On p. 597, Johnston notes that "ad hoc metaphors" (those which appear to have been created especially for the specific parables in which they occur) are even more numerous. On the relationship between rabbinic *mashal* and allegory more generally, cf. David Stern, "Rhetoric and Midrash: The Case of the Mashal," *Prooftexts* 1 (1981):261-91.

identified for Jesus' parables and for other allegories: while clearly intended to illustrate and elucidate, the details are not all transparent without subsequent application or explanation. They thus conceal as well as reveal.[93] More precisely, they lead the reader unwittingly along until he acknowledges the validity of the *vehicle* (picture-part) of the parable and is therefore forced to side with the storyteller concerning the *tenor* (spiritual truth) involved as well.

In addition, the rabbinic parables contain features which in many contexts have metaphorical referents but in other places do not. The best example of this is the role of servants in a given story. About half of the time they stand for identifiable characters in Israel's history (or occasionally for angels) whom God used in a special way. Yet the rest of the time they simply function as narrative devices for accomplishing a particular activity on behalf of their master. Most of the metaphors in the rabbis' parables, however, become fairly self-evident once the significance of the (usually two or three) main characters is determined.

2.2.2.2 Differences from the Parables of Jesus

1. Despite a few exceptions, most of the rabbinic parables reinforced conventional wisdom or scriptural exegesis. David Flusser, in an important German work on the parables of Jesus and the rabbis, goes so far as to play down virtually every distinction between these two collections of teachings. He argues that the more exegetical, conventional parables of most of the later rabbis replaced an earlier "classical" form of rabbinic parable which, like those of Jesus, sought to inculcate a fairly radical "moral" of some kind.[94] Flusser's study has now been popularized in English by one of his students, Brad Young.[95]

But this view misrepresents the nature of the parables of both Jesus and the rabbis. To be sure, there are unconventional messages from a few of the Tannaim. In Mekilta Bachodesh 5:2-10 (a midrash or commentary on Exodus 20:2), for example, a theology of grace rather than merit is apparent, as God's giving the Mosaic covenant to the Israelites only after he delivered them out of Egypt is com-

---

[93]Johnston and McArthur, *Parables.* Cf. David Daube, "Public Pronouncement and Private Explanation in the Gospels," *ExpT* 57 (1945-46):175-77.

[94]Flusser, *Gleichnisse,* pp. 19-27.

[95]Brad H. Young, *Jesus and His Jewish Parables* (New York and Mahwah: Paulist, 1989).

pared to a king who built a city wall, brought in the water supply, and fought the town's battles, before ever demanding its inhabitants' allegiance.[96] But examples like this are few and far between; it is hard to find enough illustrations of Flusser's "classical" type to be convinced that it was ever a common form.[97]

Much more common is the attitude reflected in an anonymous narrative from a Tannaitic midrash on Leviticus:

> It is like a king who hired many laborers. And along with them was one laborer that had worked for him many days. All the laborers went also. He said to this one special laborer: I will have regard for you. The others, who have worked for me only a little, to them I will give small pay. You, however, will receive a large recompense. Even so both the Israelites and the peoples of the world sought their pay from God. And God said to the Israelites: My children, I will have regard for You. The peoples of the world have accomplished very little for me, and I will give them but a small reward. You, however, will receive a large recompense. Therefore it says: "And I will have regard for you." (Sifra on Lev 26:9)[98]

How diametrically opposed to the message of Jesus' parable of the laborers in the vineyard (Mt 20:1-16)! In fact the vast majority of the rabbinic parables staunchly reinforce conventional Jewish values, serving primarily to exegete Scripture. They thus stand in marked contrast to Jesus' often "subversive" counterparts, which almost never refer back to God's written word, but gain their force from the personal authority of Christ as he claims to enunciate God's word for his new covenant.[99]

---

[96]Cf. the impetuous Samuel the Little who dispels the notion that God had brought rain in response to a fast due to the merit of the community by comparing the situation to a servant who asked his master for a favor and received it only so that the latter could be rid of the former! (b. Taanith 25b; cf. Lk 11:5-8, 18:1-8).

[97]Flusser himself can only give a handful of examples (*Gleichnisse*, pp. 23-25), though he suggests that many did not survive the destruction of the temple. Hans Weder's review is perhaps overly condemnatory but at least on target with this key criticism (*TLZ* 109 [1984]:195-98). Cf. Pheme Perkins, *CBQ* 45 (1983):131-33, for a less vitriolic (though scarcely uncritical) assessment.

[98]Trans. Harvey K. McArthur, in Johnston, "Interpretations," p. 256.

[99]Perhaps the most significant aspect of Crossan, *Parables*, is to underline this revolutionary quality of Jesus' teaching, but Crossan goes too far in "The Good Samaritan: Towards a Generic Definition of Parable," *Semeia* 2 (1974):98, by limiting the term to "a story whose artistic surface structure allows its deep structure to invade one's hearing in direct contradiction to the deep structure of one's expectation." This would preclude labeling virtually any of the rabbinic *meshalim* as parables. A substantial improvement is Crossan's more recent simplification (though now bordering on too little specificity): a parable is "a very short metaphorical narrative" (*Cliffs of Fall: Paradox and Polyvalence in the Parables of Jesus* [New York: Seabury, 1980], p. 2).

2. The parables of Jesus further distinguish themselves by their consistent reference to the kingdom of God, personally inaugurated through the ministry of Jesus. Flusser and Young also overly reduce the distance between Jesus and the rabbis by dismissing virtually all eschatological and Christological features in the Gospel parables. It is true that commentators have often overlooked ways in which these elements might be interpreted differently. The parables in which a master leaves his servants to return at some unspecified future time (e.g., Lk 12:35-38, 19:11-27) might just as plausibly have originally referred to the Jewish expectation of the Day of the Lord as to the Christian hope of Christ's return. This in turn might yield better insights into how at least some in Jesus' original audience would have interpreted the so-called parousia parables (and, incidentally, bolster the case for their authenticity).

But unless one rejects massive amounts of previous research, it remains undeniable that Jesus' parables are explicit illustrations and signs of the in-breaking kingdom of God, personally ushered in by his own ministry and message, in a way that applies to none of the rabbinical texts. To this extent Klaus Berger is correct in emphasizing that the uniqueness of Jesus' parables lies neither in their form nor in their content but in "their function in the context of the transmission of Jesus' proclamation."[100] For the most part, Jesus' parables subvert Jewish tradition, whereas the rabbinic stories reinforce it.

3. The degree of explicit interpretation in the rabbinic texts regularly exceeds that of the Gospels. This distinction is more one of degree than of kind. A high percentage (76%) of the Tannaitic parables are given explicit application or interpretation.[101] Parables centered around a king standing for God comprise over half of the total surveyed, whereas in the Gospels they are primarily limited to a few instances in Matthew.[102] Seldom do the evangelists precede their parables with an "illustrand" (a specific statement of the topic or text to be illustrated), while the rabbinic literature regularly includes one. Perhaps

---

[100]Klaus Berger, "Materialen zu Form und Überlieferungsgeschichte Neutestamentlicher Gleichnisse," *NovT* 15 (1973):37. Cf. Johnston and McArthur, *Parables.*

[101]Johnston, "Interpretations," p. 559.

[102]Cf. M. D. Goulder, "Characteristics of the Parables in the Several Gospels," *JTS* 19 (1968):51-69. However, the historical conclusions Goulder draws from these observations do not follow.

most importantly, a larger fraction of the Tannaitic parables contain the type of point-by-point allegory that is seemingly limited in the Gospels to the parables of the sower and of the wheat and tares.

The differences between the parables of Jesus and those of the rabbis thus primarily involve choice of themes and frequency of certain features. They do not suggest any fundamental generic distinction. Rules for interpreting the parables of Jesus may therefore closely approximate principles for interpreting the rabbinic parables, and one of those principles should admit the presence of allegory. To put it more strongly still,

> the study of rabbinic parables renders unusable the distinction between parable and allegory in respect to the parables of the Gospels: if the parables of Jesus are generically the same as those of the rabbis, which seems inescapable from the standpoint of morphology and inner structure, then the classical Jülicherian model must be discarded as inapplicable to the Gospel parables.[103]

2.3 Conclusions

The evidence gleaned from a study of the rabbinic literature only reinforces what the survey of modern literary analyses of allegory elicited. The parables of Jesus are sufficiently similar to other demonstrably allegorical works that many of them too must probably be recognized as allegories. This does not mean that every detail in the parables must stand for something; neither their rabbinic counterparts nor allegories in general manifest this trait. Usually many details provide only local color or human interest to enhance the fictional picture constructed.

Commonly, the primary details which disclose an allegorical level of meaning are the narratives' principal characters, and the meanings ascribed to them must be ones which the stories' original audiences could have been expected to grasp in their historical setting. Finally, a survey of both rabbinic and other literary parallels should lay to rest the notion that a good parable is one that does not need to be interpreted.

As allegories, however artistic or incarnational, even the clearest of parables drives home its point with much more force if its au-

---

103Johnston, "Interpretations," pp. 636-37.

dience's hunches are confirmed by some kind of specific conclusion. Such a conclusion need scarcely tie up all loose ends; the enigmatic character of a parable may well persist. One may endorse with confidence, however, the recent conclusions of Gregoire Rouiller, who finds "the notions opposing parable and allegory dangerous, if not frankly unusable, whether one considers their application to the parables of the rabbis or of the Gospels." Rouiller immediately adds that "this renders equally suspect the research which seeks to name the [sole] 'point' of the parable."[104] Or in the words of John Sider,

> The one-point theory is the most influential and the most pernicious part of Jülicher's legacy to a century of interpretation. What every seminary graduate remembers about the parables is that allegorizing is wrong and that every parable makes one main point. But any informed student of literature knows nowadays that these options are ill-framed—that an extended analogy of Spenser, Shakespeare, or Milton, or a metaphysical conceit of Donne's, is neither an allegory to be interpreted down to the last minute detail nor a comparison limited to a single point of resemblance.[105]

The Gospel parables, with or without the alleged additions and interpretations of later tradition, are allegories, and they probably teach several lessons apiece. But does this mean, as for Drury (see above, p. 45), that they are largely creations of early Christians? Can one affirm that the parables as they stand in the New Testament are both allegorical and authentic? An answer to this question requires an examination of the two primary tools of modern historical-critical analysis of the Gospels—form and redaction criticism—an examination to which the next two chapters turn.

---

[104]Gregoire Rouiller, "Parabole et mise en abysme," in *Mélanges Dominique Barthélemy*, ed. Pierre Casetti, Othmar Keel & Adrian Schenker (Fribourg [Suisse]: Éditions Universitaires; Göttingen: Vandenhoeck & Ruprecht, 1981), p. 329.

[105]John W. Sider, "Nurturing Our Nurse: Literary Scholars and Biblical Exegesis," *Christianity and Literature* 32 (1982):17-18.

3
Form Criticism
& the Parables

DOES THE PARABLE OF THE TEN VIRGINS REALLY EXHORT CHRIStians to stay awake and watch for the Second Coming of Christ as its conclusion suggests (Mt 25:13)? After all, in the story both the five foolish and the five wise girls fell asleep! Or does the parable of the laborers in the vineyard really intend to suggest that "the last shall be first and the first shall be last," as Matthew claims (20:16)? The narrative itself seems to imply clearly enough that all will be equal in the kingdom of heaven.

At first glance, neither of these conclusions seems to fit its story. Many scholars therefore believe that they do not represent the way Jesus originally ended his parables. In another vein, why do pairs of parables like the pounds and talents (Lk 19:12-27; Mt 25:14-30) or the great banquet and wedding feast (Lk 14:16-24; Mt 22:1-14) exhibit the types of similarities and differences which they do? If they are variant accounts of the same originals, then at least one of them in each case has been very poorly preserved.

These issues raise questions about the reliability of the Gospel tradition, inasmuch as the teachings of Jesus circulated primarily by word of mouth until they were first put into writing no earlier than twenty or thirty years after Jesus' death. The question of how to interpret a parable as Jesus originally spoke it cannot be divorced from the question of how much of that parable in its current form Jesus actually spoke. If it has not been accurately preserved, then interpreters will try to reconstruct as best they can what Jesus himself said in order to comment on the meaning of the parable in its original context.

This "quest for the historical Jesus" has occupied a sizable portion of twentieth-century parable research. The discipline which addresses these concerns most directly is form criticism.[1] An understanding of its approach to the parables will require a few comments concerning the overall method, with a critique of its strengths and weaknesses, followed by a more detailed analysis of the ways the parables were modified as they were transmitted in the oral tradition. A survey of some alternate hypotheses concerning this transmission will round out this chapter.

3.1 Classical Form Criticism
3.1.1 The Method
Rudolf Bultmann, Martin Dibelius and K. L. Schmidt comprise the trio of German scholars who pioneered form-critical analysis of the Gospels.[2] Their agenda involved three main tasks.

1. *Each Gospel passage is categorized according to form. Specific forms include parables, miracle stories, proverbs, pronouncement stories,[3] and the like. Identifying the form of a passage enables one to interpret it properly, since each form involves distinct interpretive procedures. Pronouncement stories* build to a climactic and usually controversial saying of Jesus on which all attention is focused. *Miracle stories* present the public plight of someone in need who cries out for help, and they conclude with an acclamation by Jesus' audience, which marvels at how anyone can perform such wonders.

---

[1]The best detailed introduction to this discipline is Edgar V. McKnight, *What Is Form Criticism?* (Philadelphia: Fortress, 1969). More briefly, cf. Keith F. Nickle, *The Synoptic Gospels: An Introduction* (Atlanta: John Knox, 1981; London: SCM, 1982), pp. 11-54.

[2]Rudolf Bultmann, *The History of the Synoptic Tradition* (Oxford: Blackwell; New York: Harper & Row, 1963 [Germ. orig. 1921]); Martin Dibelius, *From Tradition to Gospel* (Cambridge: J. Clarke, 1934; New York: Scribner's, 1965 [Germ. orig. 1919]); K. L. Schmidt, *Der Rahmen der Geschichte Jesu* (Darmstadt: Wissenschaftliche Buchgesellschaft, 1969 [repr. of 1919 ed.]).

[3]This term derives from the first main English form critic, Vincent Taylor, *The Formation of the Gospel Tradition* (London: Macmillan, 1933), p. 30. Bultmann had used the term *apophthegm;* Dibelius, *paradigm.* Neither was as descriptive and as long-lasting.

Parables subdivide into three categories: (a) *similitudes,* short comparisons between two basically unlike objects using present tense verbs (in Jesus' case, usually comparing the kingdom of God to some common activity of everyday life); (b) *parables proper,* complete stories narrated in past tenses, with metaphorical significance; and (c) *example stories,* narratives in past tenses simply depicting behavior to be imitated, with no metaphorical level of meaning. Thus the comparison of the kingdom of God to a mustard seed is a similitude (Mk 4:30-32), the prodigal son is a parable proper (Lk 15:11-32), and the good Samaritan is an example story (Lk 10:29-37).[4] The parables in categories (b) and (c) are fictitious narratives which are not intended to systematize theological doctrine. In most instances, the parables make only one point, derived from the *tertium comparationis* (third [term] of comparison), which links the *vehicle* (the story of the parable) with the *tenor* (the message about the kingdom).

2. *The form critic next seeks to determine, if possible, the* Sitz im Leben *(situation in life) in which each form was likely employed by the early church.* Pronouncement stories are usually thought to have been most commonly used in Christian preaching; miracle stories, in apologetic debate with paganism; and parables, in popular storytelling. If any or all of a given form can also be traced back to Jesus, then one may go on to postulate a *Sitz im Leben Jesu* (situation in the life of Jesus). For parables, form critics usually stress that the original audiences whom Jesus taught contained large numbers of relatively uneducated Galilean village folk, so that he would have had to employ simple, down-to-earth and engaging illustrations in order to communicate effectively.

3. *The most significant facet of form-critical study, however, is the final one: reconstructing the history of the oral transmission of each form.* To use the same three examples yet once more, it is argued that pronouncement stories most likely preserved their climactic sayings quite carefully, but the narratives leading up to them were subject to drastic alteration, much like the highly divergent ways a given joke can be

---

[4]This scheme of classification, most commonly associated with Bultmann, actually stemmed from Adolf Jülicher, *Die Gleichnisreden Jesu,* vol. 1 (Freiburg: Mohr, 1899), pp. 80-118. It has been widely adopted by many who otherwise diverge from the original form critics at several points: e.g., A. M. Hunter, *Interpreting the Parables* (Philadelphia: Westminster; London: SCM, 1960), pp. 9-11; Dan O. Via, Jr., *The Parables: Their Literary and Existential Dimension* (Philadelphia: Fortress, 1967), pp. 11-13; Simon J. Kistemaker, *The Parables of Jesus* (Grand Rapids: Baker, 1980), p. xiv.

told so long as the punch line remains intact. Miracle stories tended to embellish the supernatural aspects of Jesus' wondrous deeds. Parables were subject to the "laws" of oral storytelling or popular folklore. Many of these affected primarily the way the stories were phrased.

Bultmann here relied on the ground-breaking study of ancient European folk tales by Axel Olrik. Based on Olrik's discoveries, Bultmann contended (1) that in parables normally only two characters appear at a time, with each parable containing no more than three main characters or groups of characters, (2) that successive episodes often depict close parallels or sharp contrasts and build to a climax at the end, and (3) that superfluous details are omitted so that the plot is single-stranded and tightly unified.[5]

Other proposed tendencies of the parabolic tradition, however, led form critics more directly to call into question its historicity. Here the work of Joachim Jeremias offers the classic discussion. Jeremias identified ten "laws of transformation" in the oral tradition: (1) translation from Aramaic into Greek, (2) representational changes which transformed certain imagery from what was familiar in rural Palestine to what was appropriate for a more urban Greco-Roman milieu, (3) embellishment of detail, (4) addition of details under the influence of Old Testament or folk-story themes, (5) changes in the audiences to which the parables were addressed, most notably by applying to the disciples what Jesus originally intended for his opponents, (6) changes in emphasis from warning to exhortation, (7) modification of details in light of new situations in which the early church found itself, (8) allegorization, (9) formation of collections of parables which were originally independent or the combination of parts of two parables to form a new one, and (10) changes in setting, primarily through alterations in the parables' introductions and conclusions.[6]

---

[5]Axel Olrik, "Epic Laws of Folk Narrative," in *The Study of Folklore*, ed. Alan Dundes (Englewood Cliffs, N.J. and Hemel Hempstead, Herts.: Prentice-Hall, 1965 [Germ. orig. 1909]), pp. 129-41. Cf. Bultmann, *History*, pp. 166-205; Eta Linnemann, *Parables of Jesus: Introduction and Exposition* (London: SPCK, 1966 [= *Jesus of the Parables: Introduction and Exposition* (New York: Harper and Row, 1967)]), pp. 8-16.

[6]Joachim Jeremias, *The Parables of Jesus* (London: SCM; Philadelphia: Westminster, 1972), pp. 23-114. Cf. A. T. Cadoux, *The Parables of Jesus: Their Art and Use* (London: J. Clarke, 1930; New York: Macmillan, 1931), pp. 60-79; B. T. D. Smith, *The Parables of the Synoptic Gospels* (Cambridge: University Press, 1937), pp. 30-60.

Although most form critics still believe that a substantial core of each parable goes back to the historical Jesus himself, they clearly do not believe one may simply come to the texts as they are currently found in the Gospels and expect to interpret them as Jesus originally intended. The *ipsissima vox Jesu* (the "authentic voice of Jesus") has to be separated from the accretions of later tradition.

3.1.2 Critique

Form criticism has been subjected to intense scrutiny in recent years.[7] Each of the three main items on its agenda has been shown to have serious shortcomings as well as valid insights.

1. Recognizing that different forms often require different principles for their interpretation is the most valid of the three items on the form-critical agenda, but the value of various subclassifications of form has been overestimated. It is doubtful if the subdivision into similitudes, parables proper and example stories is the most significant way of classifying the parables. Inasmuch as Jesus usually taught in Aramaic, a distinction between past and present tenses (and thus between similitude and parable proper) would seem somewhat irrelevant. The Semitic perfect tense, which regularly characterizes Hebrew narrative, can at times refer to past, present and even future action, while even in Greek (or English!) the meaning of a story seems to have little to do with what tense is used to narrate it. To be sure, many of the parables proper involve longer and more detailed narratives than many of the similitudes, but it is not clear that this makes the two groups of texts qualitatively different from each other.[8]

Nor is it certain that the example story is an entirely helpful concept. In the case of the good Samaritan, for example, it can lead interpreters astray, making them think that the parable intends simply to provide a model for humanitarian compassion rather than

---

[7]The three best brief reviews are E. Earle Ellis, "New Directions in Form Criticism," in *Jesus Christus in Historie und Theologie,* ed. George Strecker (Tübingen: Mohr, 1975), pp. 299-315; Stephen H. Travis, "Form Criticism," in *New Testament Interpretation,* ed. I. Howard Marshall (Exeter: Paternoster; Grand Rapids: Eerdmans, 1977), pp. 153-64; and Graham N. Stanton, "Form Criticism Revisited," in *What about the New Testament?* ed. Morna Hooker and Colin Hickling (London: SCM, 1975), pp. 13-27. Much more massive and trenchant, though largely unacceptable in the alternatives to form criticism which he proposes, is Erhardt Güttgemanns, *Candid Questions concerning Gospel Form Criticism* (Pittsburgh: Pickwick, 1979).

[8]Georg Baudler, *Jesus im Spiegel seiner Gleichnisse* (Stuttgart: Calwer; München: Kösel, 1986), pp. 58-79, therefore prefers a more fluid distinction between shorter "procedure parables" *(Vorgangsgleichnissen)* and longer "parables with a plot" *(Handlungsgleichnissen).*

to answer the question posed by the lawyer who first approached Jesus: "Who is my neighbor?" (Lk 10:29).[9] A recent detailed analysis of the example story has shown that it was never really identified on the basis of formal features in the first place and that it refers to a kind of passage which overlaps with the rest of the parables more than most commentators have recognized.[10]

As for distinctive rules of interpreting the parables, the "one main point" principle derives directly from the assumption that the parables are not allegories, a claim which I have argued in chapter two is seriously misleading. In fact, the "laws" of oral storytelling which focus attention on the two or three main characters in each parable suggest that one point is associated with each. The contrasts between bad and good behavior which feature so regularly in Jesus' parables (priest and Levite vs. Samaritan, Pharisee vs. publican, unfaithful vs. faithful stewards, foolish vs. wise virgins) match the dual nature of many of his audiences (opponents and disciples). It is difficult to resist the conclusion that Jesus may have intended his parables to make one point for one group and a very different one for the other, offering both a model for discipleship by means of the good character in the story and a warning of judgment by means of the bad one.[11]

Many commentators, including Jeremias, have admitted this for obvious examples like the parable of the prodigal son, which divides so neatly into two different sections (Lk 15:11-24, 25-32),[12] but the principle would seem valid for shorter narratives as well. And if the third main character, usually a king/master/father figure, is also taken into account, then perhaps a final point about the character of God is present in many instances too. For example, scholars have long debated what the "one main point" of the prodigal son involves: God's unfailing love, ever ready to forgive; the need and possibilities for repentance from sin, however shameful; or the wickedness of

[9]Robert W. Funk, "The Good Samaritan as Metaphor," *Semeia* 2 (1974):74-81; Bastiaan van Elderen, "Another Look at the Parable of the Good Samaritan," in *Saved by Hope,* ed. James I. Cook (Grand Rapids: Eerdmans, 1978), p. 113.

[10]Ernst Baasland, "Zum Beispiel der Beispielerzählungen," *NovT* 28 (1986):193-219.

[11]Cf. esp. Philip B. Payne, "Metaphor as a Model for Interpretation of the Parables of Jesus with Special Reference to the Parable of the Sower" (Ph.D. diss., Cambridge, 1975), p. 267.

[12]Jeremias, *Parables,* pp. 131, 186. The other two-pointed parables which Jeremias admits are Luke 16:19-31; Mt 20:1-16; and 22:1-14 (p. 38).

resentment for the undeserving upon whom God showers his grace. Most likely the solution to this debate is to affirm that Jesus taught all three points, since each stems from an analysis of the behavior of one of the parable's three main characters.[13]

Nevertheless, it remains valid to insist that many of the details of a parable not be pressed into the service of systematic theology. Even if the sleeping farmer in the parable of the seed growing secretly in some sense stands for God (Mk 4:26-29), no one concludes that God therefore sleeps (cf. Ps 121:4)!

A few have complained that the prodigal son is granted forgiveness without any substitutionary sacrifice, but the standard, well-taken reply points out that a parable of salvation is not designed to teach everything about that doctrine there is to know. But it is remarkable how many commentators violate this principle with the story of the rich man and Lazarus, constructing elaborate theories about the nature of the "intermediate state" of those who die before the final resurrection (or, for some theologians, of those who died before the crucifixion of Christ).[14]

Nor can the objection be sustained that this latter narrative relates a real, historical event, based on the fact that Luke does not specifically label it a parable. Here form criticism proves very helpful. Approximately half of the passages in the Gospels commonly identified as parables are not specifically labeled as such, but are recognized on the basis of their common form. In this case, the introductory formula alone (Lk 16:19) accomplishes this task, with ἄνθρωπός τις ("a certain man") functioning much like the English phrase "once upon a time" to indicate the beginning of a fictitious narrative.[15] This is also the identical formula with which Jesus in-

---

[13]So Cadoux, *Parables*, p. 123; Alex Stock, "Das Gleichnis vom verlorenen Sohn," in *Ethische Predigt und Alltagsverhalten*, ed. Franz Kamphaus and Rolf Zerfass (München: Kaiser; Mainz: Grünewald, 1977), pp. 82-86; and esp. Pierre Grelot, "Le père et ses deux fils: Luc XV, 11-32," *RB* 84 (1977):321-48, 538-65. For more detail on how this principle should be applied to other parables, see Craig L. Blomberg, "Preaching the Parables: Preserving Three Main Points," *PRS* 11 (1984):31-41; and cf. below, pp. 171-253.

[14]This appears mostly in popular expositions (e.g., James M. Boice, *The Parables of Jesus* [Chicago: Moody, 1983], pp. 213-15; Robert C. McQuilkin, *Our Lord's Parables* [Grand Rapids: Zondervan, 1980], pp. 189, 194-97) and systematic theologies (e.g., James O. Buswell, *A Systematic Theology of the Christian Religion*, vol. 2 [Grand Rapids: Zondervan, 1963], pp. 305-10; Henry C. Thiessen, *Introductory Lectures in Systematic Theology* [Grand Rapids: Eerdmans, 1949], pp. 488-89).

[15]Recall the probable parallel with the introductory formula for rabbinic parables discussed above, p. 60. A ground-breaking study of this particular form of parable was Heinrich Greeven, " 'Wer unter euch . . . ?' " *Wort und Dienst* 3 (1952):86-101.

troduces the two immediately preceding parables of the prodigal son and the unjust steward.

2. The second item on the form critic's agenda proves more speculative. *Determining the* Sitz im Leben *of a form can suggest relevant ways in which it might be employed today, but most of the suggestions that have been made rest on little evidence and much guesswork.* If the parables were most often retold as part of popular folklore, the probability of distortions creeping in, even unwittingly, would seem great. Such an inference, however, probably underestimates the conservative nature of ancient oral traditions and the highly trained memories that Jesus' contemporaries undoubtedly had.[16] And the classic form-critical notion of the Gospels being fashioned out of traditions that could have been handed down by virtually anyone in the Christian community and which could have undergone modification dozens of times over is almost certainly wrong, as will be discussed in more detail below (see pp. 94-98).

With the *Sitz im Leben Jesu,* one is on firmer ground, but still one must not overestimate the naiveté of Jesus' audiences. Boys were required to attend school until at least age twelve and by that time had mastered large portions of biblical teaching.[17] Men, women and children alike probably knew what Christians now call the Old Testament far better than do most modern followers of Jesus, so that he may well have expected at least some of them to pick up on scriptural allusions or subtle meanings which contemporary interpreters have difficulty detecting. This assumption forms a foundation for the discipline of midrash criticism, which is noted again below (pp. 85-86).

3. *The final objective of the form critics, to trace the "tradition history" of a passage, is the most complex and subjective of the three.* It therefore requires more detailed analysis, especially because form critics themselves often assert that this is the most objective of all their endeavors. If there really are laws of transformation which applied to the parables

---

[16]René Latourelle, *Finding Jesus through the Gospels* (New York: Alba, 1979), pp. 178-79. Cf. the remarkable examples of massive quantities of oral tradition preserved intact cited in R. P. C. Hanson, "The Enterprise of Emancipating Christian Belief from History," in *Vindications,* ed. Anthony Hanson (London: SCM; New York: Morehouse-Barlow, 1966), pp. 58-60.

[17]See esp. Rainer Riesner, *Jesus als Lehrer* (Tübingen: Mohr, 1981), pp. 186-99; idem, "Jüdische Elementarbildung und Evangelienüberlieferung," in *Gospel Perspectives,* vol. 1, ed. R. T. France and David Wenham (Sheffield: JSOT, 1980), pp. 209-23. More generally, cf. S. Safrai and M. Stern, eds., *The Jewish People in the First Century,* vol. 2 (Assen: Van Gorcum, 1976), pp. 946-58.

as they circulated in the early church, then one should be able to determine how the texts were modified. In fact the term *law* is a serious misnomer, for neither Olrik nor any other student of folklore ever claimed to be offering more than useful generalizations.[18]

For minor differences among the Gospel parallels these "tendencies of the tradition" can often prove quite instructive. The account of the parable of the wicked tenants in Luke, for example, abbreviates and streamlines Mark's account of the various servants whom the landlord sent and of the mistreatment they received. Mark refers to one servant beaten, a second wounded on the head, another killed, and finally, many others, some beaten and some killed (Mk 12:3-4). Luke's version is more structured, following the form critics' laws of "threefoldness" and "endstress" (Lk 20:11-12— one beaten, one beaten and treated shamefully, and a third wounded and thrown out). At the end of this sequence only the son is killed.

The most convincing explanation for these differences, which do not alter the lessons taught by the passage, is that they resulted from the tendency of popular storytelling to use groups of three characters or episodes which build to a climax.[19] In other cases, however, the implications of Jeremias's "laws of transformation" are more far-reaching. His nine proposals (excluding the "law" of allegorizing which we examined at length in chapter two) therefore merit closer scrutiny.

1. Translation into Greek. Although Jesus and his disciples could hardly have avoided knowing some Greek, given three centuries of Hellenistic influence in Palestine, they undoubtedly spoke Aramaic most of the time. For this reason very few of the teachings ascribed to Jesus in the Gospels represent his exact words *(ipsissima verba)*. Yet no competent historian would question the reliability of the Gospel tradition on this ground alone. Translations, summaries, paraphrases and the use of indirect instead of direct speech can all faithfully reflect what a speaker says (his *ipsissima vox* or "authentic voice")

---

[18]On this and other general criticisms of Jeremias's work on the parables, see John W. Sider, "Rediscovering the Parables: The Logic of the Jeremias Tradition," *JBL* 102 (1983):61-83. My critique will go into a more detailed assessment of each individual law.

[19]Werner H. Kelber, *The Oral and the Written Gospel* (Philadelphia: Fortress, 1983), p. 59; Hans-Josef Klauck, *Allegorie und Allegorese in synoptischen Gleichnistexten* (Münster: Aschendorff, 1978), p. 292; Tim Schramm, *Der Markus-Stoff bei Lukas* (Cambridge: University Press, 1971), p. 160.

even if they do not reproduce his original words verbatim.[20]

At the same time, subtle nuances of a speaker's meaning can be lost in these processes, so not surprisingly scholars have often sought to reconstruct the Aramaic originals behind Jesus' teachings, including his parables. Matthew Black, for example, has suggested that a play on words originally linked Jesus' reference to the son *(ben)* in the parable of the wicked husbandmen with the accompanying citation from Psalm 118:22 about the stone *('eben)* the builders rejected (Mk 12:6, 10 pars.).[21] Such a link at least partially explains the choice of this Old Testament text, which at first glance seems unrelated to the parable. Both son and stone mirror the Messiah in his rejection by the Jewish leaders. And this choice must have been made at least as early as when Christians were still primarily an Aramaic-speaking community. But given Jesus' use of wordplays elsewhere, there is no good reason not to ascribe this linkage to him.[22]

Showing a Semitic substratum underlying the teaching attributed to Jesus thus enhances the case for its authenticity. But the converse does not follow; texts which are not easily rendered in Aramaic need not be later creations of the church. Since they may well simply have been more freely translated, other criteria are needed before one can justify a claim of inauthenticity. Thus Jeremias's argument is invalid when he concludes that the interpretation of the parable of the sower ascribed to Jesus (Mk 4:13-20) is actually a product of the early church because of its distinctive vocabulary and style.[23]

Philip Payne has convincingly defended the authenticity of this parable's interpretation against numerous objections. To this one

---

[20]The standard evangelical expositions of the doctrine of inerrancy regularly recognize that Scripture need only present a speaker's *ipsissima vox*, not his *ipsissima verba*. See esp. Paul D. Feinberg, "The Meaning of Inerrancy," in *Inerrancy*, ed. Norman Geisler (Grand Rapids: Zondervan, 1979), p. 301.

[21]Matthew Black, "The Christological Use of the Old Testament in the New Testament," *NTS* 18 (1971):11-14. Cf. Ellis, "Form Criticism," pp. 313-14.

[22]One of the most famous is his saying about the camel (Aramaic *gamla)* and the needle's eye *(qalma)*. For this and other examples, see Robert H. Stein, *The Method and Message of Jesus' Teaching* (Philadelphia: Westminster, 1978; Exeter: Paternoster, 1981), pp. 13-14.

[23]Jeremias, *Parables*, pp. 77-79. Because he also views the interpretation as unjustifiable allegorizing his discussion comes under that heading. But his admission that for him only the linguistic features make the argument persuasive means that if this objection is removed then no barrier remains to a full acceptance of the passage as authentic.

he properly replies: "It is natural that the translation of Jesus' teaching into Greek in the church community would use 'church vocabulary' where that vocabulary faithfully expressed Jesus' teaching. *Greek* vocabulary statistics cannot determine the authenticity of Jesus' *Aramaic* sayings."[24]

2. Representational Changes. Parallel versions of a given parable often differ in imagery employed, even though the message remains unaltered. Only Luke's version of the parable of the mustard seed has the plant grow in a "garden" (Lk 13:19) rather than just in the "earth" (presumably of the fields). Jewish tradition forbade the planting of this kind of seed in a garden, whereas Greeks commonly cultivated it there. The imagery has been changed to be more intelligible for a Greco-Roman audience.[25]

Matthew's parable of the two builders apparently envisages a Palestinian *wadi*—a waterless ravine with steep sides which occasionally turned into a raging river after severe rains (Mt 7:24-27). Luke instead portrays a broad river like the Orontes at Syrian Antioch where summer shelters had to be abandoned before the winter rains set in (Lk 6:47-49).[26] He also speaks of building a foundation for the house, an architectural feature much more common outside of Palestine than within. Once again the changes reflect the natural adaptation of the story to a Hellenistic context.

Such transformations may surprise the very conservative reader who often advocates a highly literal translation and interpretation of Scripture, but in fact they fit in very well with the tenets of modern translation theory. Often the form of a message must change precisely in order to *preserve* its meaning in a new culture, whereas a literal word-for-word translation might well prove unintelligible.[27] Modern versions of Scripture which employ "dynamic

---

[24]Philip B. Payne, "The Authenticity of the Parable of the Sower and Its Interpretation," in *Gospel Perspectives*, vol. 1, ed. R. T. France and David Wenham (Sheffield: JSOT, 1980), p. 178. For replies to other objections to its authenticity, cf. idem, "The Seeming Inconsistency of the Interpretation of the Parable of the Sower," NTS 26 (1980):564-68.

[25]Jeremias, *Parables*, p. 27, n. 11. The prohibition among Jews was one of their many laws of purity distinguishing what types of plants could be cultivated together (see m. Kilaim 3:2).

[26]J. Alexander Findlay, *Jesus and His Parables* (London: Epworth, 1950) pp. 95-96; Joseph A. Fitzmyer, *The Good News according to Luke I-IX* (Garden City: Doubleday, 1981), p. 644; Kistemaker, *Parables*, pp. 7-8.

[27]Eugene A. Nida and Charles R. Taber, *The Theory and Practice of Translation* (Leiden: Brill, 1969), p. 173; Charles H. Kraft, *Christianity in Culture* (Maryknoll: Orbis, 1979; Exeter: Paternoster, 1980), pp. 276-90.

equivalence" theory (most notably the United Bible Society's many translations) as well as freer paraphrases (like those of Phillips or Taylor) regularly employ similar representational changes, especially with metaphorical language which can easily be misunderstood.[28]

Popular preachers even of the most conservative stripe often contemporize biblical stories by retelling them as if they were happening in modern settings, so it should scarcely cause surprise that the early church occasionally employed a similar method, especially with parables. As fictional narratives, they do not depict historical events, the details of which cannot be changed, but instead illustrate theological truths which can be communicated by a variety of different metaphors.[29]

3. Embellishments. Ever since Rudolf Bultmann first propounded his "law of increasing distinctness,"[30] scholars have regularly assumed that the oral tradition behind the Gospels consistently added to the original stories, making them longer, more detailed and more spectacular than they originally were. At first the parables seem to corroborate this hypothesis with Luke's pounds being turned into Matthew's talents (sixty times more valuable) or Luke's simple banquet being transformed into Matthew's lavish wedding feast (with armies destroying the guests who refuse to come!).

But Bultmann's "law" depended more on the studies of extrabiblical folk traditions than on a careful comparison of the Synoptics. Assuming, as Bultmann did, that Mark was the first of the Synoptics written, that Matthew and Luke both used Mark as one of their sources, and that Q (the non-Markan material common to Matthew and Luke) is usually more closely approximated by Luke than by Matthew, then (contra Bultmann) a detailed study of Gospel parallels actually demonstrates that later versions are in fact consistently

---

[28]John Beekman and John Callow, *Translating the Word of God* (Grand Rapids: Zondervan, 1974), pp. 124-50, offer an insightful analysis of the nature and translation of metaphor and simile. Cf. also their comments on idiomatic translations (pp. 24-25).

[29]Cf. the advice of Gordon D. Fee and Douglas Stuart, *How to Read the Bible for All Its Worth* (Grand Rapids: Zondervan, 1982; London: Scripture Union, 1983), p. 133, on expounding the parables today; and for a discussion of how this approach in general does not deny but rather supports a doctrine of verbal inspiration, cf. David J. Hesselgrave, "Contextualization and Revelational Epistemology," in *Hermeneutics, Inerrancy, and the Bible*, ed. Earl D. Radmacher and Robert D. Preus (Grand Rapids: Zondervan, 1984), pp. 691-738.

[30]Rudolf Bultmann, "The New Approach to the Synoptic Problem," in *Existence and Faith*, ed. Schubert M. Ogden (New York: Meridian, 1960; London: Hodder & Stoughton, 1961 [Germ. orig. 1926]), pp. 41-42.

shorter and less detailed than earlier ones.[31] Studies of oral tradition among the ancient rabbis as well as more general psychological analyses of the processes of human memory demonstrate the same point: detailed narratives (like parables), when they are not simply preserved intact, are quite frequently abbreviated and stripped of inessential detail as they are passed from one person to another by word-of-mouth.[32]

The apparent exceptions to this pattern in the Synoptics more often than not involve passages which may not be genuine parallels at all. In the case of the parables, a statistical analysis of the amount of verbal and conceptual parallelism between such pairs of passages as the watchful servants and doorkeeper (Lk 12:35-38; Mk 13:33-37), great supper and wedding banquet (Lk 14:16-24; Mt 22:1-14), the pounds and talents (Lk 19:11-27; Mt 25:14-30), and possibly even the lost sheep and wandering sheep (Lk 15:4-7; Mt 18:12-14), along with a comparison of the contexts in which they are found, strongly suggests that these are pairs of separate but similar stories which Jesus told at different times during his ministry.

Even if one considers only those portions of the passages which bear some similarity to portions of their supposed parallels, the amount of *verbal* parallelism in each case is significantly less than for the rest of Jesus' multiply attested parables, and what does exist usually involves memorable details and wording which Jesus likely reused in numerous contexts.[33] Yet without these four examples, the case for embellishment in the parables is exceedingly weak.

The other complicating factor is the apocryphal Gnostic Gospel of Thomas, the closest extrabiblical parallel to the Gospel tradition

---

[31]Most notably, Luke is shorter than Mark in 71 of the 92 passages they have in common. For full details, see Craig L. Blomberg, "The Tradition History of the Parables Peculiar to Luke's Central Section" (Ph.D. diss., Aberdeen, 1982), pp. 25-27. Cf. also Leslie R. Keylock, "Bultmann's Law of Increasing Distinctness," in *Current Issues in Biblical and Patristic Interpretation*, ed. Gerald F. Hawthorne (Grand Rapids: Eerdmans, 1975), pp. 193-210.

[32]V. Taylor, *Formation*, pp. 202-9; W. S. Taylor, "Memory and the Gospel Tradition," *TToday* 15 (1958):470-79; Jan Vansina, *Oral Tradition: A Study in Historical Methodology* (London: Routledge & Kegan Paul; Chicago: Aldine, 1965), p. 26; G. N. Stanton, *Jesus of Nazareth in New Testament Preaching* (Cambridge: University Press, 1974), p. 178; M. D. Hooker, "On Using the Wrong Tool," *Theol* 75 (1972):572.

[33]For a detailed defense of these claims, including charts summarizing the varying degrees of verbal and conceptual parallelism among pairs of passages, see Craig L. Blomberg, "When Is a Parallel Really a Parallel? A Test Case: The Lucan Parables," *WTJ* 46 (1984):78-103. Cf. also the incisive remarks of Roland M. Frye, "Literary Criticism and Gospel Criticism," *TToday* 36 (1979):215-17.

currently known. This collection of 114 sayings ascribed to Jesus, strung together with very little connecting narrative, contains eleven clear parallels to Synoptic parables, eight of which are significantly shorter and less detailed than their canonical counterparts. If Thomas's versions represent a development of the tradition later than the Synoptics, as is most likely (despite repeated claims to the contrary), then one might actually reverse Bultmann's law and speak rather of a tendency toward decreasing distinctness.

Whatever the origin of the rest of the Thomas material, the passages which parallel canonical parables are almost certainly later than and dependent on the Synoptic tradition. I have defended this point at some length elsewhere and have referred to numerous studies which corroborate it, so I simply assume it here.[34] One of the most glaring inadequacies of most of the material originating from either the SBL parables seminar or the Jesus Seminar is the wholesale lack of adequate interaction with these and similar studies and the data on which they are based. Thomas is simply assumed, without sufficient argument, to be independent of the Synoptics.[35] On the other hand, Jeremias's appropriation of the evidence from Thomas's parables is remarkably inconsistent. In one discussion he assumes Thomas is late; in another, early, with no adequate rationale for his vacillation.[36] In sum, it is doubtful if a consistent tendency toward "embellishment" is demonstrably pres-

---

[34]Craig L. Blomberg, "Tradition and Redaction in the Parables of the Gospel of Thomas," in *Gospel Perspectives*, vol. 5, ed. David Wenham (Sheffield: JSOT, 1985), pp. 177-205. Cf. also esp. Wolfgang Schrage, *Das Verhältnis des Thomas-Evangeliums zur synoptischen Tradition und zu den koptischen Evangelien-Übersetzungen* (Berlin: Töpelmann, 1964); B. Dehandschutter, "Les paraboles de l'évangile selon Thomas," *ETL* 47 (1971):199-219; William R. Schoedel, "Parables in the Gospel of Thomas: Oral Tradition or Gnostic Exegesis?" *CTM* 43 (1972):548-60; Andreas Lindemann, "Zur Gleichnisinterpretation im Thomas-Evangelium," *ZNW* 71 (1980):214-43; C. M. Tuckett, "Thomas and the Synoptics," *NovT* 30 (1988):132-57. E. P. Sanders, *The Tendencies of the Synoptic Tradition* (Cambridge: University Press, 1969) had already demonstrated that in other NT apocrypha, church fathers and textual variants, no clear tendency toward increasing or decreasing distinctness prevailed, either toward expansion or abbreviation. But Sanders deliberately did not include Thomas in his survey, since he felt its relationship with the canonical Gospels was uncertain.

[35]B. B. Scott, *Hear Then the Parable* (Minneapolis: Fortress, 1989), pp. 30-35, gives more argument than most (six pages). But neither of Scott's two main points proves what he alleges. Granted the order of Thomas cannot be explained by dependence on the Synoptics, that does not exclude them as sources for individual logia. Second, the claim that Thomas never parallels Synoptic redaction is simply false. Thomas frequently resembles Lukan forms of the parables more so than Matthean or Markan ones. And on almost every current major source-critical hypothesis, Luke is the latest of the three Synoptics. Attempts to argue for more primitive forms in Luke based on parallels with Thomas simply reason in a circle.

[36]Cf., e.g., Jeremias, *Parables*, p. 28, n. 16, with p. 31, or p. 32 with p. 49, et passim.

ent in the Gospel tradition. Where later Gospels add material not in earlier parallels, other explanations for the differences should probably be given priority.

4. *Old Testament and Folk-Tale Influence.* The similarities between parts of the parables and various passages from the Hebrew Scriptures, along with certain popular tales well known in first-century Palestine, make it likely that Jesus used already existing stories and themes in composing some of his parables. Proving these specific influences, however, is more difficult. Many recent studies have probed these possibilities more extensively than Jeremias's brief remarks permitted him to explore. These studies often refer to their analysis as "midrash" criticism (using a Hebrew word for the "interpretation" of the Old Testament).[37]

For example, the parable of the great supper has been read in light of Deuteronomy 20:5-8, with the excuses of the invited guests resembling the exemptions from the draft permitted the ancient Israelites. Was Jesus trying to say that reasons for not fighting Israel's physical enemies were invalid when used to reject God's call to enlist in his "kingdom troops"?[38] The very next chapter in Deuteronomy discusses the inheritance rights of firstborn sons and prescribes capital punishment for rebellious offspring (21:15-21). Both of these themes recur in dramatically altered form with the generosity and forgiveness shown by the father of the prodigal son—was the contrast deliberate?[39]

Most of the earlier ventures into midrash criticism argued that demonstrating links with the Old Testament not only shed new light on the meaning of certain parables but also enhanced the case for their authenticity; an increasingly Hellenistic or Greek-oriented

---

[37]For a full-scale survey of this method as applied to the parables, see Jeffrey R. Sharp, "Comparative Midrash as a Technique for Parable Studies" (Ph.D. diss., Southern Baptist Theological Seminary, 1979). The scholar who has used this method more than any other is J. D. M. Derrett. His studies are scattered across a wide range of journals and collections of essays; two helpful anthologies are his *Law in the New Testament* (London: Darton, Longman, & Todd, 1970) and *Studies in the New Testament*, 4 vols. (Leiden: Brill, 1977-86).

[38]Derrett, *Law*, pp. 126-55. Cf. James A. Sanders, "The Ethic of Election in Luke's Great Banquet Parable," in *Essays in Old Testament Ethics*, ed. James L. Crenshaw and John T. Willis (New York: KTAV, 1974), pp. 245-71. Paul H. Ballard, "Reasons for Refusing the Great Supper," *JTS* 23 (1972): 341-50, agrees that the parable is a midrash on Deuteronomy, but thinks it is referring to chap. 28 instead. For a critique of the attempt to read this parable as a midrash, see Humphrey Palmer, "Just Married, Cannot Come," *NovT* 18 (1976):241-57.

[39]So John Drury, *The Parables in the Gospels* (London: SPCK; New York: Crossroad, 1985), p. 145.

church would have been less likely to create such links.[40] More recently, however, several scholars, most notably Michael Goulder, have argued that large portions of the Gospels are midrashic elaborations of the Old Testament, by which they mean that the texts are creations of the early church or Gospel writers inspired by scriptural themes.[41]

These proposals have especially challenged the authenticity of the numerous parables in Luke's so-called travel narrative (9:51-18:14), but the challenge proves unsuccessful. Most of the alleged parallels are too vague and the proposed patterns too full of exceptions to be convincing.[42] But even if they were, the logic of the *earlier* "midrash critics" is more sound. Although Semitic parallels cannot prove authenticity, they can serve only to strengthen rather than to detract from the case for the tradition's early origin, inasmuch as most of the church very quickly lost sight of its Jewish roots.

Determining the influence of noncanonical stories is even more laden with pitfalls, but in a few instances such influence seems undeniable. To return to the example of the rich man and Lazarus, at the turn of the century Hugo Gressmann identified several versions of a popular folk tale, known in both Egypt and Palestine, which depicted the reversal of fates for a rich man and a beggar in the underworld after their deaths.[43] This is all the more reason for not deriving systematic theology from this imagery! What Jesus contributed, however, was the addition to the story of a largely unparalleled section about the testimony of the Law, the need for repentance and the improbability that a resurrection would convince the person who refused to heed Old Testament prophecy (Lk 16:27-31). Here are the themes which Jesus wanted to emphasize, and his use of a well-known story in the first part of the parable

─────────────

[40]In addition to the writings of Derrett and Sanders, see esp. Birger Gerhardsson, "The Parable of the Sower and Its Interpretation," *NTS* 14 (1967-68):192, who sees both parts as authentic and midrashically elaborating Deut. 6:4.

[41]M. D. Goulder, *Midrash and Lection in Matthew* (London: SPCK, 1974); idem, *The Evangelists' Calendar* (London: SPCK, 1978). Cf. esp. Robert H. Gundry, *Matthew: A Commentary on His Literary and Theological Art* (Grand Rapids: Eerdmans, 1982).

[42]For a thorough treatment of this issue, see Craig L. Blomberg, "Midrash, Chiasmus, and the Outline of Luke's Central Section," in *Gospel Perspectives*, vol. 3, ed. R. T. France and David Wenham (Sheffield: JSOT, 1983), pp. 217-61.

[43]Hugo Gressmann, "Vom reichen Mann und armen Lazarus," *Abhandlungen der königlich preussischen Akademie der Wissenschaften, Philosophisch-historische Klasse* 7 (1918):1-90; cf. Jeremias, *Parables,* p. 183.

made his additions that much more striking and effective.

5. *Change of Audience.* A common dictum of form criticism is that the Gospel stories circulated mostly independent of any geographical, chronological or situational information indicating the context in which the various teachings and actions of Jesus first occurred. This assumption seems at least partly valid, inasmuch as, excluding the infancy and passion narratives, the Synoptics only occasionally supply details about the locations of the various events they narrate, and indications of time and sequence are even sparser.

But such is not the case with information about Jesus' audiences. J. Arthur Baird has estimated that 98% of all the Synoptic sayings contain "audience identifiers." What is more, these identifiers are among the most stable elements in all of the Gospel tradition. Rarely do parallel accounts differ as to the makeup of Jesus' audience, although on many occasions Jesus speaks to a crowd which includes both his supporters and his opponents, and one Gospel may well stress the presence or reaction of one of these groups more than another Gospel does.[44]

Philip Payne has demonstrated this stability in detail for the parables. The only two instances of irreconcilable descriptions of audiences (disciples vs. opponents) appear in a comparison of Matthew's and Luke's accounts of the parables of the lost sheep and of the talents/pounds.[45] Because (as already discussed) these are probably not genuine parallels, even here the contradictions seem only apparent and not real. The argument that the oral tradition regularly addressed parables to the disciples which were originally intended for Jesus' opponents involves singularly specious reasoning.

Jeremias discusses in detail only the parables of the lost sheep and of the laborers in the vineyard. This latter example, however, is never assigned to a different audience elsewhere in the Gospels because it is found only in Matthew, so his reconstruction of a different *Sitz im Leben Jesu* from that which Matthew provides is entirely speculative. Jeremias briefly lists a host of other references in support of his claims, but when one takes the time to look each

---

[44]J. Arthur Baird, *Audience Criticism and the Historical Jesus* (Philadelphia: Westminster, 1969), pp. 49, 73.
[45]Payne, "Metaphor," p. 239.

of these up, not one supports his allegations.[46]

6. *Exhortational Use.* This alleged tendency of the tradition is closely
bound up with the last. It also depends on the "one main point" rule
for parable interpretation. If parables originally made only one point
and if they were ascribed to new audiences during their transmission, then one could argue that their usage changed from warnings
against opposing Jesus to encouragement for commitment and discipleship. But if the frequent use of contrasting characters suggests
that Jesus originally intended in many of his parables both a message for his enemies and one for his disciples, then their exhortational use in the early church simply reflects the focus appropriate
for preaching to believers. A shift in emphasis has occurred rather
than a distortion of their message. Once again Jeremias's discussion
is complicated by his appeal to passages probably not genuinely
parallel and by his assumption that the Gospel of Thomas offers
versions of the parables earlier than the Synoptics.[47]

7. *The Influence of the Church's Situation.* According to form criticism,
by far the most significant change in the situation of the church a
generation following Jesus' ministry was its waning expectation of
Christ's imminent return. This recognition of the "delay of the
parousia" allegedly led to the modification of many of Jesus' teachings, including the parables. The parable of the ten virgins, for
example, was transformed into an allegory warning the church to
stay awake even when it seemed her bridegroom tarried. Luke explicitly declared that the parable of the pounds was designed to
refute the notion that the kingdom was going to appear immediately (Lk 19:11). Even minor changes, like Luke's addition to the parable of the wicked tenants about the master going away "for a long
time" (Lk 20:9), were the product of a recognition that Christ might
not be coming back as soon as his followers had first thought.

A number of factors, however, challenge the whole idea that the
timing of Christ's return fundamentally altered Christian theology
in general and the parables in particular.

First, Jesus' formation of a community of followers and the instructions he gave them for living in and evangelizing society pre-

---

[46]For details, see Blomberg, "When Is a Parallel Really a Parallel?" p. 99.
[47]Jeremias, *Parables,* pp. 42-48.

suppose a significant interval of time before the end of the age would come, during which they could put this teaching into practice.[48]

Second, passages which seem to teach that Jesus believed he would definitely return within the lifetime of his disciples (e.g., Mk 9:1; 13:30; Mt 10:23) are better interpreted in other ways. A. L. Moore has studied these at some length and concludes, "It appears that the parousia in Jesus' outlook was *in some sense* near, but that evidence is lacking that he held to a delimited hope."[49]

Third, religious movements seldom alter authoritative traditions when prophecies seem to pass unfulfilled as much as they alter the interpretations of those traditions.[50]

Fourth, the Jews, among whom all the first Christians were numbered, were particularly used to this problem, since the prophets had been warning them for centuries that the Day of the Lord was at hand. World history had continued for over four hundred years since the last prophet, Malachi, but by the first century Israel's Messianic hopes had not diminished but rather increased. The "delay" was often explained by emphasizing that the divine definition of "soon" is not the same as the human one (Ps 90:4).[51] 2 Peter 3:8-9 shows that Christians adopted a similar approach.

Fifth, the specific examples from the parables that seem to reflect the church's growing awareness that their Lord was not immediately coming back make equally good sense when taken as Jesus' authentic teaching that the kingdom of God was not arriving as quickly as the Jews had hoped or taking the political shape for which

---

[48]I. H. Marshall, *Eschatology and the Parables* (London: Tyndale, 1963), pp. 18-19; G. R. Beasley-Murray, *Jesus and the Future* (London: Macmillan; New York: St. Martin's, 1954), pp. 191-99.

[49]A. L. Moore, *The Parousia in the New Testament* (Leiden: Brill, 1966), p. 190. Cf. pp. 175-89. More briefly, cf. Craig L. Blomberg, *The Historical Reliability of the Gospels* (Leicester and Downers Grove: IVP, 1987), pp. 33-34. Donald Guthrie, *New Testament Theology* (Leicester and Downers Grove: IVP, 1981), pp. 794-95, notes that "there is a curious mixture of urgency and delay in the teaching of Jesus" and "it would seem reasonable to suppose that Jesus distinguished between imminence and immediacy." Cf. also Wilhelm Michaelis, "Kennen die Synoptiker eine Verzögerung der Parusie?" in *Synoptische Studien*, ed. J. Schmid and A. Vögtle (München: Karl Zink, 1953), pp. 107-23.

[50]Without endorsing every statement in either work, cf. David Flusser, "Salvation Present and Future," in *Types of Redemption*, ed. R. J. Zwi Werblowsky and C. Jouco Bleeker (Leiden: Brill, 1970), pp. 46-61; and Robert P. Carroll, *When Prophecy Failed* (London: SCM; New York: Seabury, 1979), esp. pp. 112-17.

[51]Richard Bauckham, "The Delay of the Parousia," *TynB* 31 (1980):3-36. Cf. Stephen S. Smalley, "The Delay of the Parousia," *JBL* 83 (1964):53.

many of the them had longed. Apart from the issue of the "delay of the parousia," the changes which Jeremias identifies as due to the altered situation of the church are minor and do not threaten the tradition's reliability, or else they overlap with considerations already treated under (5) and (6).

8. Collection and Conflation. Since classical form criticism assumed the original independence of almost every Gospel passage, collections of passages of like forms were naturally viewed as the work of later tradition. Mark's Gospel clearly relies on such collections, for example, pronouncement stories in 2:1-3:6 and miracle stories in 4:35-6:6. In most cases, the individual passages in each collection are connected together without any references to time or order to suggest that they originally occurred in the sequence in which Mark now presents them. Sometimes the fact that Matthew or Luke arranges the passages in a quite different order reinforces the assumption that one or more of the evangelists is following a topical rather than a chronological outline.

Whether or not the group of parables in Mark 4:1-34 reflects one of these topical arrangements is less clear. Matthew preserves this collection relatively intact, although he includes additional parables which Mark does not (Mt 13:1-52). Luke abbreviates the collection and inserts the parable of the mustard seed into a different context (Lk 13:18-19; cf. Mk 4:30-32), but that context is his "travel narrative" which is demonstrably topical in structure.[52]

The general summary in Mark 4:33-34 of how Jesus continually spoke to the crowds in parables may support the view that Mark has simply gathered together samples of what Jesus said in several different contexts. At the same time Mark 4:35 ("on that day when evening had come") might imply that Jesus uttered all of the preceding parables on one occasion. So too the collection of "parousia parables" (Mt 24:32—25:46), though widely assumed to be composite in origin, may reflect an original, extended eschatological discourse.[53] Either way, though, their authenticity need not be suspect. The question of the fusion or conflation of parables is more difficult. But here Jeremias's examples again rely entirely on those

---

[52]Blomberg, "Midrash."

[53]David Wenham, *The Rediscovery of Jesus' Eschatological Discourse* (Sheffield: JSOT, 1984).

pairs of parables which are probably not genuine parallels, so this problem seems to dissipate as well.

9. Altered Introductions and Conclusions. Of all the proposed tendencies of the parables' transformation, this final one is potentially the most serious for defenders of the Gospels' reliability. For it is the context surrounding a given parable in which interpretations or applications are often spelled out with varying degrees of specificity. If these interpretations are the product of a later misunderstanding of a parable's true meaning, then the whole history of their exegesis has been largely mistaken, even when commentators did not interpret the parables as detailed allegories! Yet here is precisely where Dodd and Jeremias have left their mark. Even where form criticism has been supplanted by newer methods of studying the Gospels, the assumption that a parable's context usually distorts its original meaning nevertheless remains axiomatic.[54]

Much of the evidence in support of this view stems from inconsistencies between the apparent meaning of a parable and the interpretations attached to it, but in each case plausible resolutions suggest themselves quite naturally. To return to the examples with which this chapter began, the conclusion to the story of the ten virgins ("keep watch") cannot possibly mean that Christians will never again sleep before the coming of the end! Wakefulness is a metaphor for preparedness which in no sense contradicts the imagery of the parable itself.

So also the proverbial saying, "the last shall be first and the first shall be last" (Mt 20:16), would be just as true in a situation where all are rewarded equally as in one where earthly priorities are reversed. The belief that the parables' contexts are not accurate cannot logically depend to any great extent on such easily resolvable tensions, but must rather follow from more general assumptions about the nature of parables. The most important of these are: (a) the introductory or concluding statements usually offer only weak generalizations which can scarcely account for the detail and vitality of the parables themselves; (b) a good parable (like a good joke!) will make its point so clearly on its own that subsequent explanation is

---

[54]Cf., e.g., Via, *Parables;* J. D. Crossan, *In Parables: The Challenge of the Historical Jesus* (New York and London: Harper & Row, 1973); Hans Weder, *Die Gleichnisse Jesu als Metaphern* (Göttingen: Vandenhoeck & Ruprecht, 1978); Scott, *Hear.*

unnecessary and demeaning; and (c) as metaphors, parables are not able to be paraphrased propositionally—the meaning is inherent in the form and is lost when one-sentence summaries are formulated.

Objection (c) is a major emphasis of the movement known as the "new hermeneutic" and will be examined in detail in chapter five. In reply to (a) and (b), several points seem necessary. To begin with, many of the sayings surrounding the parables were likely never intended to summarize their main point(s).

Luke 14:28-33 offers a good example. The two little parables about the warring-king and tower-builder clearly call would-be followers of Jesus to "count the cost" of discipleship. Yet in verse 33 one reads that a disciple must give up everything, a much more drastic sacrifice than either of the parables demands! But this verse may well not be intending to summarize the parables' lesson. Actually, the two parables themselves do not seem to be making the identical point. As Cadoux phrases it, in the first instance Jesus says, "Sit down and reckon whether you can afford to follow me"; in the second, "Sit down and reckon whether you can afford to refuse my demands."[55]

But contra Cadoux, verse 33 does not level both parables to a single, unrelated meaning. Rather it provides the climax for a sequence of three points, each building on the previous one. One may easily build a tower without selling everything. The costs of a war generally require much more sacrifice. Discipleship demands total surrender in allegiance to Jesus as Lord.[56] This type of "chain-link" reasoning was a standard feature of the contexts of rabbinic parables, which makes its use by Jesus entirely natural.[57]

In some cases, the context of a parable provides only a partial summary of the parable's meaning. When a parable is viewed as making two or three main points, derived from each of its main characters, many of the so-called contradictions between the story

---

[55]Cadoux, *Parables*, p. 174.

[56]Cf. William Hendriksen, *Exposition of the Gospel according to Luke* (Grand Rapids: Baker, 1978 [= *The Gospel of Luke* (London: Banner of Truth, 1979)]), p. 736; Philippe Bossuyt and Jean Radermakers, *Jésus: Parole de la Grâce selon saint Luc* (Bruxelles: Institut d'études theologiques, 1981), pp. 335-36.

[57]Robert M. Johnston, "Parabolic Interpretations attributed to Tannaim" (Ph.D. diss., Hartford Seminary Foundation, 1978), pp. 556-81; Derrett, *Law*, pp. 82-92; G. V. Jones, *The Art and Truth of the Parables* (London: SPCK, 1964), pp. 14, 35.

and its framework evaporate. Interpretations like those of Jeremias and Dodd may have simply emphasized one of the main points, whereas the Gospel writers stressed a different point. Thus the dichotomy between the parable of the unjust judge teaching about the patience and generosity of God (Lk 18:2-8) and Luke's introduction on praying without despair (v. 1) is a false one. The former is the point to be derived (by a fortiori logic) from the actions of the judge; the latter, from the persistence of the widow.

In other cases, a parable's context itself may suggest more than one point. The story of the unjust steward concludes with no less than three appendices (Lk 16:8a, b, 9), generally taken as positive proof of its repeated modification by the later tradition.[58] At the same time each of these three interpretations elegantly dovetails with the purpose of one of the parable's main characters or groups of characters: the master's praise reflects God's commendation of his followers, the steward's cleverness (not his injustice!) models a character trait needed for discipleship, and the debtors' future welcome of the steward mirrors the heavenly reception awaiting God's people. All three points make perfect sense as Jesus' original conclusion to the parable.

It is worth noting, finally, that the vast majority of the Synoptic parables have some kind of interpretation or application attached, however brief. If it were a case of only a few parables deviating from a pattern in which they were usually left uninterpreted, one might be more sympathetic to the form critics' hypotheses.[59] Nor does the rabbinic tradition offer any evidence for such a pattern. The rabbis almost always provide for their parables explanations even more detailed than those found in the Synoptics. The objection that a good parable does not need to be interpreted seems to be an arbitrary assertion.

---

[58]Vv. 10-13 complicate the picture even more. For a full survey of the plethora of interpretations and tradition-critical dissections of this parable and its appendages, see Michael Krämer, *Das Rätsel der Parabel vom ungerechten Verwalter* (Zürich: PAS-Verlag, 1972). For a defense of the authenticity of all thirteen verses in their Lukan context, see Markus Barth, "The Dishonest Steward and His Lord: Reflections on Luke 16:1-13," in *From Faith to Faith*, ed. D. Y. Hadidian (Pittsburgh: Pickwick, 1979), pp. 65-73.

[59]Cf. Olof Linton, "Coordinated Sayings and Parables in the Synoptic Gospels: Analysis versus Theories," *NTS* 26 (1980):159: "This widespread occurrence is per se an indication that the pattern [of coordinating sayings and parables] has deep roots in the synoptic tradition. It must go back to the beginning, and most probably was used by Jesus himself."

Even astute audiences often fail to grasp the full import of metaphorical discourse and, according to the Gospels, Jesus' audiences,
including his disciples, were far from astute in this respect! As Walter Magass explains, concluding generalizations provide the necessary "concretization" of the parables, their re-orienting and application to the world of the hearer after he has been transformed into
the imaginary world of the parables. If the conclusions seem pale
or weak by comparison, it may be because this is required to ease
the hearer back to reality.[60] Roland Frye points out examples from
secular literature where authors complete carefully structured
forms by appending aphorisms.[61] And Claus Westermann does the
same for Old Testament analogues.[62]

To sum up, none of the form critics' proposals concerning the
way the tradition modified Jesus' parables requires a rejection either
of the authenticity of the Synoptic accounts as they now stand or
of the appropriateness of the interpretive comments attached. A
comparison of Gospel parallels proves that the wording of many of
the parables was noticeably altered, and form criticism can help one
understand why some of that variation occurred, but increasingly
greater numbers of these differences are being explained in other
ways. Specifically, form criticism has largely given way to redaction-
critical explanations in recent parable research. Nevertheless, form-
critical views are still often presupposed rather than defended, and
redaction criticism can be equally or even more skeptical of the
Gospels' reliability (see chap. four). On the other hand, certain alternatives to classical form criticism actually bolster the case for the
trustworthiness of the Gospels.

3.2 Hypotheses of the "Guarded Tradition"
A number of general considerations support the claim, over against
traditional form criticism, that the oral tradition of Jesus' teachings
and deeds was guarded with considerable care. Robert Stein itemizes six of these: (a) the presence of eyewitnesses who could confirm

---

[60]Walter Magass, "Die magistrale Schlusssignale der Gleichnisse Jesu," *LingBib* 36 (1975):9, 14,
16.
[61]Frye, "Literary Criticism," pp. 210-15.
[62]Claus Westermann, *Vergleiche und Gleichnisse im Alten und Neuen Testament* (Stuttgart: Calwer,
1984), pp. 11-104.

or refute the early Christian claims, (b) the existence of a center of leadership in the Jerusalem church to exercise control over the tradition, (c) the respect for tradition that the rest of the New Testament shows the first Christians exercising (e.g., Rom 6:17; 1 Cor 7:10, 12), (d) the faithfulness of the early church in transmitting awkward or embarrassing sayings of Jesus (e.g., Mk 10:18; 13:32; Mt 10:5), (e) the lack of traditions attributed to Jesus dealing with important controversies that arose in later first-century Christianity but not during Jesus' lifetime (e.g., circumcision or speaking in tongues), and (f) the generally conservative nature of oral tradition in societies that do not emphasize writing to the extent that the modern Western world does.[63] Most of these points were made by critics of form criticism right from its inception, but without offering an alternate model for the circulation of the oral tradition. More recently, however, two such models have been proposed.

3.2.1 Memorizing Jesus' Teachings

In the late 1950s and early 1960s two Uppsala scholars, Harald Riesenfeld and Birger Gerhardsson, argued that Jesus taught his disciples to memorize his teachings and the narratives of his deeds much as the rabbis did in the centuries immediately following the birth of Christianity. These scholars recognized that the church at some stage had felt free to change the wording of the various accounts, because Synoptic parallels are obviously not word-for-word identical, but they felt that these changes were made thoughtfully and carefully and did not represent the inevitable distortions of incautious storytellers.[64]

Reaction to this "Scandinavian school" was largely negative, inasmuch as it relied on analogies from later rabbinic tradition and seemed to ignore the great differences between Jesus and other Jewish teachers of his day.[65] Important support, though, was sup-

---

[63]Robert H. Stein, "The 'Criteria' for Authenticity," in *Gospel Perspectives*, vol. 1, pp. 226-27.

[64]Harald Riesenfeld, "The Gospel Tradition and Its Beginnings," in *The Gospel Tradition* (Philadelphia: Fortress, 1970 [art. orig. 1959]), pp. 1-29 (for his specific treatment of the parables cf. "Parables in the Synoptic and in the Johannine Traditions," pp. 139-69); Birger Gerhardsson, *Memory and Manuscript: Oral Tradition and Written Transmission in Rabbinic Judaism and Early Christianity* (Lund: Gleerup, 1961); idem, *Tradition and Transmission in Early Christianity* (Lund: Gleerup, 1964). For an update of Gerhardsson's views, see idem, *The Origins of the Gospel Traditions* (London: SCM; Philadelphia: Fortress, 1979).

[65]For a good overview of the reaction, see Peter H. Davids, "The Gospels and Jewish Tradition: Twenty Years after Gerhardsson," in *Gospel Perspectives*, vol. 1, pp. 75-99.

plied from a study by Heinz Schürmann, who pointed to the need for the disciples to pass on accurate teaching of and about Jesus even during his lifetime, when they were sent out on their various missions (e.g., Mk 6; Mt 10; Lk 10), and also to the common ancient practice of keeping private, written notes against which public, oral teaching could be checked.[66] More recently, the case for memorization has been enormously strengthened by the erudite dissertation of a young German scholar, Rainer Riesner.[67]

Rather than focusing exclusively on the model of a rabbi and his disciples, which Jesus might not have adopted, Riesner comprehensively surveys the many situations in which education occurred both in ancient Israel and among her neighbors. In every instance, he concluded that memorization was the dominant practice. Furthermore, Jesus' distinctives would have made it more, rather than less, likely that his followers would have passed on his teachings with care.

Viewed as a prophet, Jesus would have had his words preserved at least as carefully as Old Testament prophecy (considered by many scholars to be among the most faithfully preserved of all the Old Testament traditions). Viewed as Messiah, he would have been expected to be a teacher of wisdom, whose aphorisms required safeguarding. Finally, a careful study of the forms of Jesus' teaching reveals that over 90% of them are phrased in ways which make them easy to remember, by means of parallelism, rhythm, catchwords and striking figures of speech.

With reference to the parables, Riesner draws heavily on the work of Kenneth Bailey. He admits the parables are not as strictly poetic as some of Jesus' teachings but notes that they were carefully styled with various types of parallelism, especially inverted or chiastic (A-B-B-A) patterns, which facilitated their accurate transmission.[68] Further, their enigmatic nature suggests that, as in much elementary

---

[66]Heinz Schürmann, "Die vorösterlichen Anfänge der Logientradition," in *Der historische Jesus und der kerygmatische Christus,* ed. H. Ristow and K. Matthiae (Berlin: Evangelische Verlagsanstalt, 1960), pp. 342-70; cf. Latourelle, *Jesus,* pp. 157-68.

[67]Riesner, *Jesus.*

[68]Ibid., pp. 367-71; Kenneth E. Bailey, *Poet and Peasant: A Literary-Cultural Approach to the Parables in Luke* (Grand Rapids: Eerdmans, 1976); idem, *Through Peasant Eyes: More Lucan Parables* (Grand Rapids: Eerdmans, 1980). Cf. esp. Marcel Jousse, *Le style oral rythmique et mnemotechnique* (Paris: Gabriel Beauchesne, 1925), pp. 163-64.

education in the ancient near and middle East, they were learned first and then meditated on afterward. Jesus' call to his disciples in Mark 13:28 to "learn this parable" may point to such a practice.[69]

3.2.2 New Insights into Oral Folklore

A second alternative to form criticism does not deviate from it quite as radically. Agreeing with the original form critics that analogies from popular storytelling are relevant, this approach goes on to emphasize that recent studies of oral folklore have entirely revised the way in which the transmission of tradition is viewed. No one is more responsible for this revolution in folkloristics than the classicist and anthropologist A. B. Lord. Lord's studies, ranging from the epics of Homer to the ballads of illiterate Yugoslavian folk singers to the Synoptic Gospels, suggest that the Gospel narratives were memorized but that "memorization" needs to be defined more loosely than the way in which contemporary Westerners are accustomed to thinking of it.

Oral folksingers past and present might have committed stories of up to 100,000 words to memory. Nevertheless they might vary the wording and sequence of their presentation by up to 40% of the story from one "performance" to the next. In the same manner, the Synoptics could be explained as the result of a process of flexible transmission within fixed limits. Incidental features might vary as the stories were retold, while the core of each episode remained inviolate. In Lord's studies, if the singer or storyteller erred in significant details, his audience would know it and correct him.[70] Similar conclusions have resulted from the studies of African oral tradition by Jan Vansina and by Bruce Chilton of the Jewish targums (at first oral and then later written explanatory paraphrases of the Hebrew Scriptures).[71]

---

[69]Riesner, *Jesus*, p. 443. Gerhardsson has warmly commended Riesner's study, citing it frequently in his "Der Weg der Evangelientradition," in *Das Evangelium und die Evangelien*, ed. Peter Stuhlmacher (Tübingen: Mohr, 1983), pp. 79-102.

[70]See esp. A. B. Lord, *The Singer of Tales* (Cambridge, Mass.: Harvard Univ. Press, 1960); idem, "The Gospels as Oral Traditional Literature," in *The Relationships among the Gospels*, ed. William O. Walker, Jr. (San Antonio: Trinity University Press, 1978), pp. 33-91.

[71]Vansina, *Oral Tradition*; Bruce D. Chilton, "Targumic Transmission and Dominical Tradition," in *Gospel Perspectives*, vol. 1, pp. 21-45; idem, "A Comparative Study of Synoptic Development: The Dispute between Cain and Abel in the Palestinian Targums and the Beelzebul Controversy in the Gospels," *JBL* 101 (1982): 553-62.

Parallels to the Gospels are not as close here as in the memorization hypotheses, and none of the studies of the folklorists inspires as much confidence in assigning the Gospel traditions to the *ipsissima vox Jesu* as do Gerhardsson and Riesner. But some who are reluctant to refer to the *ipsissima vox* are willing to speak of the Gospels preserving the *ipsissima intentio* (actual intention) or *ipsissima structura* (actual structure) of Jesus' teaching.[72] The same essential meaning may be communicated by a variety of different "performances." This leaves the door open for viewing Jesus as using a similar plot in several different settings. Variations on a theme need not automatically be ascribed to later tradition.[73]

3.3 Conclusions

Form criticism offers valuable insights into the interpretation of the parables, but its attempt to limit each passage to one main point fails to convince. It points to ways in which the oral tradition modified Jesus' original teachings but usually exaggerates the extent of the modifications. Most likely Jesus' disciples did memorize much of the Gospel tradition, while feeling free to vary certain details when recounting it orally. But there is enough evidence in support of a relatively conservative oral tradition so that all claims about the inauthenticity of portions of the Synoptics, or of incompatible interpretations at different stages of the tradition, should be based on actual, irreconcilable contradictions in the texts themselves—either within a given passage or between that passage and its parallel in a different Gospel. This is all the more true in the case of the parables, which already have a core of material recognized as authentic by almost all schools of interpretation and where certain

---

[72]Respectively, P.-G. Müller, *Der Traditionsprozess im Neuen Testament* (Freiburg: Herder, 1982), p. 144; and Crossan, *Parables*, p. 117. For a more detailed survey of this understanding of the tradition as both fixed and flexible in light of modern folklore studies, see Kelber, *Gospel*, pp. 1-43. Kelber's section headings are insightful—classical form criticism becomes "evolutionary progression"; Gerhardsson's model is "passive transmission"; and this final trend in scholarship, a "process of social identification and preventive censorship." But Kelber has overestimated the differences between Lord and Gerhardsson. The two models are complementary rather than mutually exclusive. Kelber's mistake lies in a one-sided appropriation of the "autonomous" theory of literacy development (associated e.g., with Walter Ong and Eric Havelock), which overestimates the disjunction between orality and textuality, and in ignoring the "ideological" theories (associated e.g., with Brian Street or S. Scribner and M. Cole), which see individuals and societies valuing or devaluing literacy according to varying social settings.

[73]A point recognized in principle by Scott, *Hear*, p. 42, and then entirely ignored throughout the rest of his work.

arguments for the unreliability of the tradition elsewhere usually do not apply.[74] But this shifts the focus from form criticism to redaction criticism, the next main topic for discussion.

---

[74]E.g., the issue of whether early Christian prophets invented sayings of Jesus. The most forceful advocate of this position, M. Eugene Boring (*Sayings of the Risen Jesus* [Cambridge: University Press, 1982]) only rarely includes parables within the material he believes the prophets created, but see his comments on Mt 22:3 [p. 215] and Lk 12:35-38 [p. 224]). But the thorough studies by David Hill, *New Testament Prophecy* (London: Marshall, Morgan & Scott; Richmond: John Knox, 1979) and David E. Aune, *Prophecy in Early Christianity and the Ancient Mediterranean World* (Grand Rapids: Eerdmans, 1983), neither of which was available to Boring, go a long way toward laying to rest the notion of early Christian prophecy being preserved under the guise of sayings of the earthly Jesus.

4
Redaction Criticism
of the Parables

Ⅰ N WHAT WAYS DO GOSPEL PARALLELS ACTUALLY DIFFER FROM EACH other? Are there irreconcilable contradictions which require commentators to speak of an evangelist having created certain details which have no foundation in the life of the historical Jesus? Or are the differences simply the product of selection, arrangement and rewording in order to highlight particular theological or stylistic emphases? To try to answer these types of questions is to practice redaction criticism, the study of how the Gospels were "redacted" or edited. This is an endeavor in which the church has been engaged ever since the four Gospels were collected into one canon,[1] even if the terminology now used stems from more recent, critical study.[2]

---

[1]For a selection of primary sources, see Helmut Merkel, *Die Widersprüche zwischen den Evangelien: Ihre polemische und apologetische Behandlung in der Alten Kirche bis zu Augustin* (Tübingen: Mohr, 1971); and for a discussion of the data, idem, *Die Pluralität der Evangelien als theologisches und exegetisches Problem in der Alten Kirche* (Frankfurt a. M.: Peter Lang, 1978).

[2]The three studies generally credited with the development of modern redaction criticism are Günther Bornkamm, Gerhard Barth, and Hans-Joachim Held, *Tradition and Interpretation in Matthew* (London: SCM; Philadelphia: Westminster, 1963); Willi Marxsen, *Mark the Evangelist* (Nashville: Abingdon, 1969); Hans Conzelmann, *The Theology of St. Luke* (New York: Harper & Row; London: Faber & Faber, 1960).

Redaction criticism nevertheless remains perhaps the most controversial and certainly the most scrutinized of the various methods for analyzing the Gospels, largely because it means many different things to different people. In the hands of its most radical practitioners, it seems to provide the rationale for assigning all but a handful of the sayings of Jesus to the fertile imaginations of the Gospel writers.[3] Among more conservative scholars, it is a tool for highlighting distinctive emphases of Jesus' teaching without necessarily questioning the historical reliability of the Gospels in recording that teaching.[4] A whole spectrum of intermediate positions complicates matters further.

Perhaps the most objective and neutral definition is that of Richard Soulen: redactional study "seeks to lay bare the theological perspectives of a Biblical writer by analyzing the editorial (redactional) and compositional techniques and interpretations employed by him in shaping and framing the written and/or oral traditions at hand (see Luke 1:1-4)."[5]

A few writers have called for the complete rejection of redaction criticism, believing that attention to the distinctives of the various Gospels will inevitably lead one to denigrate their historical accuracy and to pit the theology of one evangelist against another.[6] Yet there are differences among Gospel parallels which must be explained in some way. The traditional approach has been to write harmonistic "lives of Christ," combining information from all the Gospels into one unified narrative. Yet it was precisely this approach which inadequately accounted for the recurring themes

---

[3]The classic example is the work of Norman Perrin. For his methodological reflections, see his *What Is Redaction Criticism?* (Philadelphia: Fortress, 1969; London: SPCK, 1970). Robert Gundry, *Matthew: A Commentary on His Literary and Theological Art* (Grand Rapids: Eerdmans, 1982), writing as an avowed evangelical, adopts almost an equally skeptical position for Matthew's Gospel, but believes he can still hold a doctrine of inerrancy by combining redaction criticism with midrash criticism.

[4]See esp. the commentaries by William L. Lane, *The Gospel according to Mark* (Grand Rapids: Eerdmans, 1974; London: Marshall, Morgan & Scott, 1975), and I. Howard Marshall, *The Gospel of Luke* (Exeter: Paternoster; Grand Rapids: Eerdmans, 1978).

[5]Richard N. Soulen, *Handbook of Biblical Criticism* (Atlanta: John Knox, 1976; Guildford: Lutterworth, 1977), pp. 142-43.

[6]The intra-evangelical debate on the issue is well-chronicled in David L. Turner, "Evangelicals, Redaction Criticism and the Current Inerrancy Crisis," *GTJ* 4 (1983):263-88; idem, "Evangelicals, Redaction Criticism and Inerrancy: The Debate Continues," *GTJ* 5 (1984):37-45; and Grant R. Osborne, "Round Four: The Redaction Debate Continues," *JETS* 28 (1985): 399-410. One of the most outspoken critics of redaction criticism has been Robert L. Thomas; see his "Hermeneutics of Evangelical Redaction Criticism," *JETS* 29 (1986):447-59.

and patterns in each individual Gospel that led modern criticism to seek an alternative. Nevertheless, there are unwarranted, vitiating assumptions that often accompany redaction criticism, which must be avoided if a study of the Gospels is to be as objective as possible.[7]

This chapter seeks to illustrate both the strengths and weaknesses of redaction criticism when applied to the parables, by giving a sample of the many differences between the various Synoptic parallels along with possible explanations for the variation. The texts chosen for discussion illustrate a broad cross-section of all the major types of differences and the most well-known and perplexing of the apparent contradictions. A successful treatment of the most glaring divergences should inspire confidence that the less significant ones can be handled adequately as well.

One other introductory matter must be dealt with. Since redaction criticism by definition involves an analysis of how the Gospel writers used their sources, some approach to the literary interrelationship of the Synoptics must be presupposed. The greatest bulk of the last two centuries of scholarship has endorsed the "two-source hypothesis," arguing that Matthew and Luke used both Mark and Q[8] in the composition of their Gospels, and this hypothesis is presupposed here.[9]

Recent additions and challenges to this view have not overturned this consensus, but they make it clear that no hypothesis which limits itself to two documents can account for the origin of all the

---

[7]See esp. D. A. Carson, "Redaction Criticism: On the Legitimacy and Illegitimacy of a Literary Tool," in *Scripture and Truth*, ed. D. A. Carson and John D. Woodbridge (Grand Rapids: Zondervan; Leicester: IVP, 1983), pp. 119-42; Stephen S. Smalley, "Redaction Criticism," in *New Testament Interpretation*, ed. I. Howard Marshall (Grand Rapids: Eerdmans; Exeter: Paternoster, 1977), pp. 181-95.

[8]The abbreviation used to denote material common to Matthew and Luke not found in Mark, largely involving the sayings of Jesus, and likely (but still only hypothetically) written down in a document much like the form (but not the contents) of the Coptic Gospel of Thomas. The question of Q is clearly less certain than that of Markan priority. For surveys of research, see Howard C. Bigg, "The Q Debate since 1955," *Themelios* 6, no. 2 (1981):18-28; idem, "The Present State of the Q Hypothesis," *VoxEvang* 18 (1988):63-73.

[9]Two of its most convincing defenses are Donald Guthrie, *New Testament Introduction* (London: Tyndale; Downers Grove: IVP, 1970), pp. 121-87; and Joseph A. Fitzmyer, "The Priority of Mark and the 'Q' Source in Luke," in *Jesus and Man's Hope*, vol. 2, ed. D. Y. Hadidian (Pittsburgh: Pickwick, 1970), pp. 131-70. Most recently, and in slightly more popular form, cf. Robert H. Stein, *The Synoptic Problem: An Introduction* (Grand Rapids: Baker, 1987). The leading competitor, the Griesbach hypothesis, in which Luke depends on Matthew, and Mark abridges both Matthew and Luke, has been thoroughly analyzed by C. M. Tuckett, *The Revival of the Griesbach Hypothesis* (Cambridge: University Press, 1983) and found wanting.

information in the Gospels. The complexity of the evidence points to additional sources as well as overlapping sources.[10] Occasionally Mark and Q seem to have contained the same passages. Mark and Luke, for example, both present versions of the parable of the mustard seed, but they differ noticeably from each other. When one observes that Matthew combines distinctives of both, it makes sense to assume that Mark and Q each preserved independent versions of the parable which Matthew later conflated.[11]

Further, Matthew and Luke almost certainly had access to other sources as well, either oral or written, both for the material unique to each of their Gospels as well as for what is paralleled elsewhere.[12] So we should not naively assume where Matthew or Luke differ from Mark that their additions are not based on tradition; they may simply be following different sources. But redaction criticism has shown that such deviations reflect deliberate choices by the evangelists, often to highlight their particular theological concerns.

4.1 Positive Contributions

The valid insights of redaction-critical study of the parables thus fall into two categories. First, redaction criticism highlights ways in which the distinctives of a particular evangelist's version of a parable fit in with the themes which he emphasizes elsewhere in his Gospel. These distinctives may point to a particular emphasis in Jesus' teaching which that evangelist wants to preserve. Second, redaction criticism looks for connections between a parable and its larger context in the Gospel so that the significance of its location in the author's outline is clarified. This second task has sometimes been distinguished from redaction criticism by the term "composition criticism," but the distinction is not often maintained.

---

[10]Cf. the excellent overview in D. A. Carson, "Matthew," in *The Expositor's Bible Commentary*, ed. Frank E. Gaebelein, vol. 8 (Grand Rapids: Zondervan, 1984), pp. 11-17.

[11]Charles E. Carlston, *The Parables of the Triple Tradition* (Philadelphia: Fortress, 1975), p. 26; Hans Weder, *Die Gleichnisse Jesu als Metaphern* (Göttingen: Vandenhoeck & Ruprecht, 1978), pp. 128-29.

[12]This is based both on ancient testimony, which is not as lightly dismissed as many allege (e.g., the second-century testimony of Papias that something like Matthew in either Hebrew or Aramaic was the first "Gospel" written and Luke's reference in his prologue to "many" predecessors), and on linguistic evidence for distinctive sources behind the unparalleled material in Matthew and Luke. Cf. Johannes H. Friedrich, "Wortstatistik als Methode am Beispiel der Frage einer Sonderquelle im Matthäusevangelium," *ZNW* 76 (1985):29-42; and Joachim Jeremias, *Die Sprache des Lukasevangeliums* (Göttingen: Vandenhoeck & Ruprecht, 1980).

4.1.1 The Illustration of Distinctive Themes

Six examples should suffice to illustrate the typical ways in which the evangelists reshaped the accounts of the parables which they acquired from their sources in order to stress particular theological concerns important elsewhere in their Gospels. The examples involve some of the shorter metaphorical sayings of Jesus, not always called parables, as well as some of the longer, undisputedly parabolic narratives. The comparison of parallels will also include an examination of certain interpretations of the parables attributed to Jesus.

1. *Luke 5:31-32 (cf. Mark 2:17).* In their accounts of the parable (or proverb) of the physician, both Mark and Luke agree on the wording, "it is not the healthy but the sick who have need of a doctor."[13] Both go on to add Jesus' application: "I did not come to call righteous people but sinners." Only Luke, however, concludes with the additional phrase "unto repentance." Both Matthew and Mark agree that an apt summary of Jesus' entire message was the calling of his listeners to repent (Mk 1:15; Mt 4:17), a summary widely recognized as historically accurate,[14] but only Luke repeatedly stresses this theme.

Even a mere glance at a concordance reveals that the words *repent* and *repentance* occur fourteen times in Luke's Gospel and only ten times in the other three Gospels put together. Most likely, Luke has added "unto repentance" to this passage to clarify what type of calling Jesus had in mind. In the immediate context, one could have supposed that Jesus was referring only to the invitation of the outcasts of Jewish society to the meal with Levi, but the wider context of Jesus' ministry makes it clear that his concern for the despised and dispossessed included their spiritual needs as well.[15]

---

[13]Luke clarifies Mark's "strong" by substituting the Greek word "healthy." In Aramaic one word can mean both, so this is probably only a translation variant. See Joachim Jeremias, *The Parables of Jesus* (London: SCM; Philadelphia: Westminster, 1972), p. 125, n. 42; Marshall, *Gospel of Luke,* p. 220.

[14]Leander E. Keck, *A Future for the Historical Jesus* (Nashville: Abingdon, 1971; London: SCM, 1972), p. 32. One important recent challenge to the consensus that Jesus stressed repentance in his teaching comes from E. P. Sanders, *Jesus and Judaism* (London: SCM; Philadelphia: Fortress, 1985), pp. 106-13, but Sanders's arguments have been effectively answered by Norman H. Young, " 'Jesus and the Sinners': Some Queries," *JSNT* 24 (1985):73-75; and Dale C. Allison, Jr., "Jesus and the Covenant: A Response to E. P. Sanders," *JSNT* 29 (1987):68-74.

[15]Cf. Marshall, *Gospel of Luke,* p. 221: "Luke thus brings out an element which was integral to the teaching of Jesus . . . although it is often expressed in other categories." Contra Conzelmann, *Luke,* p. 227, who believes that Luke's addition has changed the meaning of Jesus' statement.

2. Matthew 9:12-13 (cf. Mark 2:17). Matthew also carefully preserves Mark's wording of the "parable" of the physician. But instead of adding "unto repentance" at the end as in Luke, he inserts into verse 13 Jesus' command, quoting Hosea 6:6, "But go and learn what this means: 'I desire mercy and not sacrifice.' "

Again the addition fits in perfectly with Jesus' authentic teaching elsewhere. He consistently treats the Law as still binding in principle but with certain regulations no longer literally applicable inasmuch as they are fulfilled in him (cf., e.g., Mt 5:17, Mk 2:27-28 pars.; 7:18-19; Lk 11:39-42).[16] But the addition also fits in with Matthew's distinctive emphasis on the Law and the relationship between Judaism and Christianity. In fact Matthew includes the very same quotation from Hosea in his account of Jesus' reply to his critics when his disciples were found plucking grain on the Sabbath (Mt 12:7; cf. Mk 2:26-27).

Not surprisingly, many scholars therefore declare this to be an unhistorical addition or at best a saying of Jesus taken out of its original context and reinserted here. But unless they deny that Matthew could have had access to any additional information about Jesus' teaching on this occasion besides what he learned from Mark and Q, this does not follow. The verse begins with the typical rabbinic formula "go and learn," and it is entirely appropriate in its immediate context. The quotation justifies Jesus' lack of concern for Pharisaic purity regulations by appealing to Old Testament precedent—the common prophetic theme condemning participants in religious ritual who neglect the needy in their midst.[17] What redaction critics can legitimately stress is that Matthew, as over against Mark and Luke, highlights a different portion of Jesus' teaching from this occasion: his rejection of external religion in which legalism supplants true love.[18]

3. Luke 8:12 (cf. Mark 4:15). Despite substantially abbreviating and

---

[16]The meaning and authenticity of these and related sayings continue to be disputed. For balanced assessments see Robert Banks, *Jesus and the Law in the Synoptic Tradition* (Cambridge: University Press, 1975). More briefly, cf. Douglas J. Moo, "Jesus and the Authority of the Mosaic Law," *JSNT* 20 (1984):3-49.

[17]Cf. Pierre Bonnard, *L'évangile selon saint Matthieu* (Neûchatel: Delachaux et Niestlé, 1963), pp. 130-31.

[18]Cf. Eduard Schweizer, *The Good News according to Matthew* (Richmond: John Knox, 1975; London: SPCK, 1976), p. 226; Francis W. Beare, *The Gospel according to Matthew* (San Francisco: Harper & Row; Oxford: Blackwell, 1981), pp. 227-28.

stylistically rephrasing Mark's account of the parable of the sower and its interpretation (Lk 8:4-8, 11-15; Mk 4:1-9, 13-20), Luke does not make any changes which significantly alter the meaning of any portion of the passage.[19] But in 8:12 he does introduce one of his favorite themes—salvation—into Jesus' interpretation of the seed which fell alongside the road and was eaten by birds. Luke adds the unparalleled phrase, "in order that they might not believe and be saved."

Of course, the concept of salvation is integral to Jesus' entire ministry and message (cf., e.g., Mt 18:11 par.; Mk 5:34 pars.; 13:13 par.; which all use the verb "to save"). Yet, interestingly, the nouns *savior* and *salvation* occur nowhere in Matthew or Mark but eight times in Luke. One of Luke's most distinctive characteristics is his emphasis on saving the lost, especially among the neglected and ill-treated strata of society. I. Howard Marshall, in fact, persuasively argues that *salvation* is the one word that best captures the essence of Luke's message.[20] Luke's explanatory addition here does not bring him into conflict with Matthew or Mark. Rather, he "is simply bringing out what is already in his sources, namely that physical healing and spiritual salvation are dependent upon faith in Jesus" (cf. esp. Mk 2:5).[21]

4. *Luke 20:13 (cf. Mark 12:6)*. One of the most common ways in which Matthew and Luke edit Mark is by clarifying awkward, ambiguous or potentially embarrassing language. In the parables one of the clearest examples comes with Luke's insertion of "perhaps" before Mark's statement in the parable of the wicked tenants about the landlord's belief that his son will be respected.

As an expression on the lips of the fictitious landlord in the parable, the belief makes perfect sense as a confident though misguided expectation that an emissary who is his own offspring will command a better audience than did the servants who preceded him. But at the allegorical level, it could lead people to imagine that Jesus was teaching that God was caught by surprise when the leaders of

---

[19]For detailed demonstration see I. Howard Marshall, "Tradition and Theology in Luke (Luke 8:5-15)," *TynB* 20 (1969):56-75.

[20]Idem, *Luke: Historian and Theologian* (Exeter: Paternoster, 1970; Grand Rapids: Zondervan, 1971), pp. 93-102.

[21]Idem, *Gospel of Luke*, p. 325.

the Jews rejected his son.[22] Luke's addition of "perhaps," while changing a small portion of the parable's dialog, thereby preserves what he believes is the proper interpretation of its theological message.

5. *Matthew 21:41, 43 (cf. Mark 12:9-12).* Matthew's additions to Mark's account of the parable of the wicked tenants are lengthier. Most notably, he expands the conclusion of the parable to include the prediction that in due course the new tenants will give their master the fruits of the vineyard. Matthew also adds the allegorical application of the parable to the Jewish leaders hostile to Jesus: "Therefore I say to you that the kingdom of God will be taken away from you and given to a people producing the fruit of it." For many commentators these additions bear no resemblance to what Jesus originally said or meant but instead are among the most decisive pointers in the whole Gospel to the fact that the community for which Matthew was writing had "parted company with Judaism."[23] Many find them unduly harsh and anti-Semitic and conclude that Matthew himself created them.

It is quite probable that Matthew did choose to include these verses because of some particular relevance for the people to whom he was writing, but this deduction proves nothing about their historicity. They are not inappropriate as words of the historical Jesus in the context of this parable. They are no harsher than the consistent condemnation of hypocrisy which characterizes Jesus' teaching in numerous portions of the Gospels. And they are scarcely anti-Semitic, since Jesus never condemns all Jews en masse but only those who reject his call to repentance.

Matthew, in fact, is the Gospel which most emphasizes Jesus' ministry to the Jews (cf. the unparalleled statements in 10:5 and 15:24 on his concern to offer the Gospel exclusively to the Jews during his earthly ministry). In retrospect, and in light of the use of the term elsewhere, it is easy to assume that the ἔθνος (a "people" or "nation") which produces the fruits of the kingdom and replaces the corrupt Jewish leaders must be exclusively Gentiles, but the

---

[22]Cf. Carlston, *Parables,* p. 79; Josef Ernst, *Das Evangelium nach Lukas* (Regensburg: Pustet, 1977), p. 537.

[23]Graham Stanton, "Introduction," in *The Interpretation of Matthew,* ed. Graham Stanton (Philadelphia: Fortress; London: SPCK, 1983), p. 5.

context nowhere demands this assumption. The New Testament regularly conceives of the community of God's people who produce "good fruit" as a combination of Jewish and Gentile followers of Jesus.[24] Even the most universalist text in Matthew's Gospel, the Great Commission (Mt 28:18-20), with its call to preach to all the ἔθνη ("nations"), does not exclude the Jews from its purview.[25]

In a detailed analysis, Wolfgang Trilling persuasively argues that although the language of Matthew 21:43 may be the evangelist's, this verse should be seen as simply reiterating and emphasizing Jesus' original conclusion to the parable.[26] Redaction criticism nevertheless correctly calls attention to Mt 21:41, 43 as the most important portions of the parable for Matthew. His distinctive interest in the offer of the Gospel to the Jews as well as the need to evangelize the world must not be minimized, as so often occurs in harmonizations with parallel accounts. In essence, Matthew highlights what Paul would later encapsulate in the formula: "to the Jew first and also to the Greek" (Rom 1:16).[27]

6. Matthew 11:19 (cf. Luke 7:35). Luke usually preserves the wording of Q more literally than Matthew. This at least appears to be true in the case of the parable of the children in the marketplace,[28] although Matthew has not changed his source very much. By far the most striking difference is in the concluding sentence where Matthew has substituted "works" for "children" as the agent of wisdom's justification. The word _work_ occurs six times in Matthew but only twice in Mark and twice in Luke. More significantly, Matthew is the Gospel which most emphasizes Jesus' mighty works, especially with a dramatic emphasis on his miracles. Both Matthew and Luke agree that Jesus interpreted the children's festive play as

---

[24]Richard J. Dillon, "Towards a Tradition-History of the Parables of the True Israel (Matthew 21, 33-22, 14)," *Bib* 47 (1966):12-37, discusses in detail the non-Matthean nature of the language of 21:41b, 43 and of parallels to this theme in 1 Pet 2:9-10; Mt 3:7-12; Mk 4:1-9 pars.; Rom 6:21-22, 7:4-6; Gal 5:22-24; Phil 1:11; Eph 5:8-11; and Col 1:10-14 which suggest that these concepts are deeply rooted in the tradition of the early church.

[25]Despite the views cited above (p. 108; cf. n. 23), Graham Stanton himself admits this much in his "The Gospel of Matthew and Judaism," *BJRL* 66 (1984):275.

[26]Wolfgang Trilling, *Das wahre Israel* (München: Kösel, 1964), pp. 55-65.

[27]Cf. Carson, "Matthew," pp. 22-23, 244-45, 355, 596-99.

[28]Thus, e.g., M. Jack Suggs, *Wisdom, Christology, and Law in Matthew's Gospel* (Cambridge, Mass.: Harvard Univ. Press, 1970), pp. 33-58; Heinz Schürmann, *Das Lukasevangelium*, vol. 1 (Freiburg: Herder, 1969), pp. 423-29.

symbolizing his joyful ministry, their mourning as reflecting John the Baptist's more austere lifestyle, and their immovable playmates as the Jews who rejected both John and Jesus.

But God's wisdom is justified by his emissaries (Luke's "children") and their deeds (Matthew's "works"). Matthew has probably used synecdoche to refer to the key element which demonstrates the righteousness of God's children—their actions. But there is no contradiction here. As Harald Sahlin explains,

> wisdom retains its claim to righteousness as much through "her works," that is through the course of events in the history of salvation, as also through "all her children," that is through the prophets and messengers of God who have conducted the affairs of God.[29]

These six examples, then, illustrate a variety of ways in which the evangelists have reworded Jesus' parables so as to clarify potential ambiguities and underline distinctive emphases. In some instances one evangelist has probably drawn on more than one source in order to add material not included in parallel accounts. In other cases, the Gospel writers have more likely just paraphrased and explained what they believed was the true meaning or significance of Jesus' words. In each example, the alterations have led many scholars to deny that the edited version could fairly reflect Jesus' *ipsissima vox*, but these denials seem to be unwarranted. If one is trying to assess the historical reliability of the Gospels, harmonization remains a legitimate and achievable endeavor.[30] But if one wants to interpret a particular passage in a given Gospel in the way in which that evangelist intended it, then redaction criticism becomes a necessary and profitable tool, when used with care.

4.1.2 The Significance of the Larger Contexts

The second major contribution of redaction criticism involves the examination of the way in which an evangelist has located a particular passage in the overall structure of his narrative. The Gospels

---

[29]Cf. Harald Sahlin, "Traditionskritische Bemerkungen zu zwei Evangelienperikopen," *ST* 33 (1979):84.

[30]See esp. Craig L. Blomberg, "The Legitimacy and Limits of Harmonization," in *Hermeneutics, Authority, and Canon,* ed. D. A. Carson and John D. Woodbridge (Grand Rapids: Zondervan; Leicester: IVP, 1986), pp. 139-74; cf. idem, *The Historical Reliability of the Gospels* (Leicester and Downers Grove: IVP, 1987), pp. 113-89.

are often topical rather than chronological in their outlines, as a glance at any synopsis of Gospel parallels quickly reveals, and parables are regularly included in these topical sections. Of many possible examples, four will be discussed briefly.

1. *Luke 8:4-8, 11-15.* Luke does not have an extensive collection of parables corresponding to Mark 4 or Matthew 13. Instead he juxtaposes the parables of the sower and the lamp (Lk 8:4-18) with the pronouncement story about Jesus' true family (vv. 19-21), which in Mark precedes these two parables rather than following them (Mk 3:31-35). Moreover, Luke has reworded Jesus' climactic pronouncement from Mark's "whoever does the will of God is my brother and sister and mother" to "my mother and brothers are those who hear the word of God and do it." This corresponds to Luke's explicit emphasis in the interpretation of the parable of the sower that "the seed is the word of God" (8:11), which Mark phrases less directly, "the sower sows the word" (Mk 4:14).

In both Gospels the intervening parable of the lamp concludes with the warning to take heed how one hears. Thus not only a comparison of Luke with Mark, but also an analysis of the structure of Luke's Gospel on its own, leads to the conclusion that the main point of Luke 8:4-21 deals with the proper hearing of the Word of God, which leads to right action.[31] This theme is not absent from Mark or Matthew, but it is not as prominent for them as for Luke.

2. *Mark 4:1-34/Matthew 13:1-52.* In Mark's chapter of four main parables (sower, lamp, seed growing secretly and mustard seed), the most striking features are Jesus' discussion of why he speaks so cryptically and his reaction to the disciples' obtuseness, features which Luke conspicuously abbreviates. Jesus claims in some way to be concealing as well as revealing the truth of God's kingdom, leading some commentators to level serious charges of self-contradiction. When Mark says that Jesus spoke in parables as much as the crowds were able to take in (4:33) but then adds immediately that in private he had to explain everything to his disciples (v. 34), Charles Carlston remarks: "It is impossible to believe that Jesus or Mark or any other single individual held both of these conceptions at the same time."[32]

---

[31]Cf. Charles H. Talbert, *Reading Luke* (New York: Crossroad, 1982), pp. 93-94; Joseph A. Fitzmyer, *The Gospel according to Luke I-IX* (Garden City: Doubleday, 1981), pp. 699-700.

[32]Carlston, *Parables*, p. 98.

Chapter two has already suggested a way in which this tension may be lessened (see p. 55): Jesus' audiences were not baffled by the cognitive meaning of the parables but hindered by their unwillingness to accept the claims made on their lives by the parables' descriptions of the kingdom of God.[33] Knowledge in this instance does not become true understanding until it is translated into action. This problem affected the disciples no less than the crowds, but Jesus did not want the Twelve to remain as marginally committed as the rest, hence the private elaboration.

Moreover, the crowds might understand the basic thrust of his teaching, but Jesus wanted his most intimate followers to grasp the full import of specific details, hence the allegorical explanations. And the significance of Mark's unparalleled verse 13 must not be missed. Understanding the parable of the sower is the key to understanding "all the parables."[34]

It will not do, as most recent conservative exegetes have argued, to accept the parable of the sower and perhaps one or two others as allegories, since Jesus explicitly interpreted them in that way, but then to argue that all the other parables are of a different nature. Either virtually every one is allegorical, though undoubtedly to varying degrees, or, if Mark's testimony is rejected and the prevailing opinion adopted, none is allegorical. In the latter event, one would be left with the remarkable situation in which every layer of the Synoptic tradition now recoverable entirely misrepresented the most characteristic component of Jesus' teaching.[35] Surely the

---

[33]Cf. also Madeleine Boucher, *The Mysterious Parable* (Washington: Catholic Biblical Association of America, 1977), pp. 83-84; Jack D. Kingsbury, *The Christology of Mark's Gospel* (Philadelphia: Fortress, 1983), p. 17.

[34]This is an important contribution of Joel Marcus's recent study, *The Mystery of the Kingdom of God* (Atlanta: Scholars, 1986), p. 213, though Marcus is concerned to examine only Mark's understanding at the redactional level. In a similar vein, Mary Ann L. Beavis, "Literary and Sociological Aspects of the Function of Mark 4:11-12" (Ph.D. diss., Cambridge, 1987) shows that Mark 4:11-12 reflects Mark's understanding of the entire Gospel, especially Jesus' teaching, rather than representing an anomalous seam in the tradition history of the text.

[35]Most recent commentators identify the Markan parable collection, along with the engimatic vv. 11-12, as pre-Markan, and many see them as stemming from at least the primitive Palestinian-Christian community, but they have not faced up to the implications of accepting such an early dating for the tradition without also assigning it to the historical Jesus. Cf. Hugh Anderson, *The Gospel of Mark* (London: Oliphants, 1976; Grand Rapids: Eerdmans, 1981), p. 130; Eduard Schweizer, *The Good News according to Mark* (Richmond: John Knox, 1970; London: SPCK, 1971), pp. 92-93; Rudolf Pesch, *Das Markusevangelium*, vol. 1 (Freiburg: Herder, 1976), p. 238; Joachim Gnilka, *Das Evangelium nach Markus*, vol. 1 (Zürich: Benziger; Neukirchen-Vluyn: Neukirchener Verlag, 1978), p. 167.

former alternative is more plausible.

An exegesis of Mark 4, however, is complicated by the fact that Jesus' statements of his purposes for speaking in parables are often linked with another pervasive theme of Mark's Gospel—the so-called "Messianic secret" motif (see above, pp. 33, 39-41). Yet, as noted previously, these issues should probably be kept distinct. Jesus never tells anyone not to spread the word which he preaches by means of parables.

The focus on the disciples' lack of understanding may well stem from the frank testimony of Peter himself, who is traditionally believed to be the source for much of Mark's information. In a religious community which quickly elevated Peter to the highest level of authority, few others would be likely to emphasize so consistently the shortcomings of the group of disciples which he led.[36] At least Matthew and Luke seem to play down this motif.

More important, Mark's emphasis is probably pastorally motivated. If the church to which he wrote, most likely the church in Rome which was beginning to undergo considerable persecution, could see that even the twelve apostles were as fallible as Mark describes them, then they could be encouraged that God could use them too despite their weaknesses and insecurities. In fact, only that which by human standards reflected powerlessness could allow for divine power to work in their midst.[37] The key contribution of redaction criticism here, then, is not a challenge to the credibility of any of Mark 4:1-34 but simply the observation that Mark uniquely edits his sources so as to underline the cryptic side of the parables. His comments may serve today as an important corrective to any exaggerated claims about the parables' clarity.

In his pivotal chapter 13, Matthew groups together no less than eight parables (omitting Mark's secretly growing seed but adding the wheat and tares, the treasure in the field, the pearl of great price, the dragnet, and the scribe) in an intricately structured chi-

---

[36]For this and other arguments reaffirming a Petrine connection with Mark's Gospel, see now esp. Martin Hengel, *Studies in the Gospel of Mark* (London: SCM; Philadelphia: Fortress, 1985).

[37]Dorothy A. Lee-Pollard, "Powerlessness as Power: A Key Emphasis in the Gospel of Mark," *SJT* 40 (1987):173-88. Cf. Ernest Best, *Mark: The Gospel as Story* (Edinburgh: T & T Clark, 1983), pp. 93-99. C. M. Tuckett, "Mark's Concerns in the Parables Chapter," *Bib* 69 (1988):1-26, demonstrates Mark's hand in warning and encouraging his community throughout material which has often been viewed largely as un-Markan or pre-Markan.

astic (inverted parallel) sequence. David Wenham diagrams the chiasmus as follows:

Crowd

A. *Sower*   Parable on those who hear the word of
                                                             the kingdom

B. (Disciples' question and Jesus'
   answer about purpose of parables
   for crowd and about understanding
   parables; + interpretation of sower)

C.*Tares*   Parables of kingdom—good and evil

D. *Mustard seed* ⎫   Parable of kingdom
                  ⎬ Pair
E. *Leaven*   ⎭   Parable of kingdom

Disciples

F. (Conclusion of crowd section +
   interpretation of tares)

E. *Treasure* ⎫   Parable of kingdom
              ⎬ Pair
D. *Pearl*   ⎭   Parable of kingdom

C. *Dragnet* (with interpretation)   Parable of kingdom—good and evil

B. (Jesus' question and disciples'
   answer about disciple's understanding of parables)

A. *Scribe trained*   Parable on those trained for the king-
                                                            dom[38]

The center and climax of this chiasmus (point F.) focuses on the allegorical interpretation of the parable of the wheat and tares. Matthew no less than Mark sees allegory as the key to interpreting the parables.[39] Further, by evenly dividing the chapter into teaching

---

[38]David Wenham, "The Structure of Matthew XIII," *NTS* 25 (1979):517-18.

[39]In fact if Greg Fay ("Introduction to Incomprehension: The Literary Structure of Mark 4:1-34," *CBQ* 51 [1989]: 65-81) is correct, Mark 4:1-34 is also a (seven-member) chiasmus with the interpretation of the sower at the center. But this outline requires vv. 21-25 to represent "parabolic method" rather than "parabolic material," which is unlikely.

to the crowds and teaching to the disciples, he illustrates the same tension as in Mark 4:33-34 without feeling compelled to reject either the revelatory or the esoteric function of Jesus' teaching. Many argue that Matthew substituted "because they see but do not perceive . . ." (Mt 8:13) for "in order that they might see but not perceive . . ." (Mk 4:12) in order to soften the force of Mark's difficult ἵνα (purpose) clause. But in fact he expands the quotation from Isaiah 6 to emphasize the role of the proclamation of God's word in the hardening of the people's hearts.[40] D. A. Carson offers a better explanation for the variation in the wording:

> Matthew has already given Jesus' answer in terms of divine election (v. 11); now he gives the human reason. While this brings him into formal conflict with Mark 4:12, he has already sounded the predestinarian note of Mark 4:12. Here Matthew includes much more material than Mark; and in the ordered structure that results from the inclusion of such new material, verbal parallels are lost in favor of conceptual ones.[41]

Once again redaction criticism may sensitize us to the different ways parallel accounts present similar themes without necessarily challenging the historical reliability or literary integrity of any of them.

Perhaps this appears nowhere as clearly as in Matthew's distinctive conclusion to his parable chapter, with his illustration about the scribe trained for the kingdom of heaven, who "brings out of his treasure new things and old" (13:52). Of the diverse suggestions for the meaning of this text, the best is again Carson's: Matthew teaches that "the scribe who has become a disciple of the kingdom now brings out of himself deep understanding of [Old Testament promises, law and piety] and their transformed perspective affecting all life."[42] The point is unique to Matthew's account but profoundly consistent with Jesus' teaching elsewhere.

---

[40]J. D. Kingsbury's attempt to avoid the force of Matthew 8:14-15 by arguing that it embodies post-Matthean scribal additions is a counsel of despair in light of the lack of extant textual variants to support his view (*The Parables of Jesus in Matthew 13* [London: SPCK; Richmond: John Knox, 1969], pp. 38-39).

[41]Carson, "Matthew," p. 309; cf. pp. 304, 307, where he debunks the notion that Matthew introduces parables in chapter 13 for the first time as a way for Jesus no longer to speak plainly to the Jews since they have decisively rejected his earlier, clearer teaching.

[42]Ibid., p. 333. Cf. Kingsbury, *Parables,* p. 128; Joachim Gnilka, *Das Matthäusevangelium,* vol. 1 (Freiburg: Herder, 1986), p. 511.

3. Luke 9:51-18:14. The entire central section of Luke, though seemingly a "travel narrative," contains fewer references to time and place than any other major section of the four Gospels. It also contains a higher concentration of parables than any other comparable section, approximately twenty of which are found only in this Gospel. Probably the material is arranged topically, with the parables as the key to the various subheadings in Luke's outline. Thus, for example, 11:1-13 combines two parables on prayer (the friend at midnight and the asking son) with Luke's version of the Lord's prayer. Luke 13:10-14:24 describes a series of teachings on "kingdom reversals," climaxing with three parables on the topic (the places at table, the invited guests and the great supper). And 16:1-31 begins and ends with major parables on the use and abuse of riches (the unjust steward and the rich man and Lazarus), with several related sayings linking them together.[43]

This last theme is one of the most prominent in both Luke and Acts, to the extent that Luke is sometimes seen as so emphasizing the physical, this-worldly aspects of salvation, especially in his concern for the poor and for social justice, that he contradicts Matthew's and Mark's more spiritual, otherworldly conceptions of the kingdom. Again the distinction is overly pressed. Luke's is the Gospel most concerned for the poor, but it is more often than not the poor Israelite, the pious Jew humbly awaiting the coming Messiah in the midst of a corrupt nation, who is in view.

Conversely, Luke's critique of the wealthy always hints at their godlessness, never suggesting that riches are evil in and of themselves.[44] They can very easily lead to greed and covetousness, and redactional studies of Luke rightly alert "first world" Christians to grave dangers here.[45] But Luke's redaction gives no countenance to thoroughgoing Marxist brands of liberation theology as the solu-

---

[43]For details of all three of these passages, see Craig L. Blomberg, "Midrash, Chiasmus, and the Outline of Luke's Central Section," in *Gospel Perspectives*, vol. 3, ed. R. T. France and David Wenham (Sheffield: JSOT, 1983), pp. 244-47.

[44]On both these points, see esp. David P. Seccombe, *Possessions and the Poor in Luke-Acts* (Linz: Studien zum Neuen Testament und seiner Umwelt B. 6, 1982). Cf. Thomas E. Schmidt, *Hostility to Wealth in the Synoptic Gospels* (Sheffield: JSOT, 1987), pp. 135-62.

[45]One of the best of these is Walter E. Pilgrim, *Good News to the Poor* (Minneapolis: Augsburg, 1981). For a challenging evangelical appropriation of liberation theology more generally, but with special reference to Luke on pp. 50-59, see Thomas D. Hanks, *God So Loved the Third World* (Maryknoll: Orbis, 1983).

tion to economic inequity, despite frequent claims to the contrary.

4. *Matthew 18:12-14, 23-35; 20:1-16; 21:28-32; 22:1-14; 24:45-25:46*. Most of these parables are unique to Matthew's Gospel; a few come from Q but are located in a different place in Matthew than in Luke. All of them illustrate the teachings of Jesus which immediately precede them. This pattern very much resembles the rabbinic method of illustrating legal principles *(halakah)* with popular stories *(haggadah)*. There is no reason why Jesus himself could not have employed this method; many or all of these contexts may thus be original.[46] At the same time, Matthew, whose style is the most Jewish of the four evangelists, may have made the connections topically.[47] Either way the important contribution of redaction criticism is to note the links between the parables and their contexts and so to highlight Matthew's key emphases.

The parable of the lost sheep (18:12-14) portrays God's concern for all of his people, explaining why one should not cause any of his "little ones" to sin (v. 6) nor "despise them" (v. 10). The parable of the unforgiving servant (18:23-35) warns against neglecting Jesus' teaching on forgiveness (vv. 21-22). The parable of the laborers in the vineyard (20:1-16) concludes with the same "moral" ("the first will be last and the last first") as Jesus' promise to those who have forsaken all to follow him (19:30).

The parable of the two sons (21:28-32) hints at the answer to the Jewish leaders' question about Jesus' behavior (19:23), which he refused to provide directly: the authority for his actions came from the same God who welcomes repentant outcasts and who rejects those who only mouth confessions of loyalty but do not demonstrate true obedience to God's will. The wedding banquet (22:1-14) expands on the previous story of the wicked tenants (21:33-46), further illustrating who comprises "true Israel."[48] Matthew's version of Jesus' eschatological discourse, finally, concludes with more than a full chapter of parables not found in Mark (24:45-25:46). All of these elaborate the implications of the uncertain timing of

---

[46]Cf. esp. David Wenham, *The Rediscovery of Jesus' Eschatological Discourse* (Sheffield: JSOT, 1984), on the parables of Matthew 24—25.

[47]Cf. esp. John Drury, *The Parables in the Gospels* (London: SPCK; New York: Crossroad, 1985), p. 91. Drury's further conclusion that Matthew *composed* the parables does not follow.

[48]See esp. Dillon, "True Israel," pp. 1-42.

Christ's return, with which the previous section of his discourse had concluded (24:36-44).

Redaction critics have thus pointed out important distinctives among the evangelists both in the details they include or omit and in the larger arrangement of their material. Overall, the similarities among the Synoptics in general, and between parallel versions of individual parables, significantly outweigh the differences. Divergent accounts can be harmonized, so that it is not fair to speak of one Gospel contradicting another. At the same time, harmonization can too quickly lose sight of the unique emphases or nuances of meaning which a particular Gospel writer wished to communicate. Here redaction criticism offers a healthy corrective.

4.2 Invalid Allegations

A less balanced use of redaction criticism, however, also plagues many of its practitioners. Besides too frequently exaggerating the differences between parallel accounts of the same passage, the method often suffers from at least seven other problems. The first four deal with invalid presuppositions; the last three, with faulty exegesis.

4.2.1 Misleading Parallels

Just as form criticism derived faulty conclusions about the tendencies of the tradition by comparing similar parables which probably came from different contexts in Jesus' ministry, so redaction criticism has erred in the same way (see above, p. 83). Nothing can be assumed with confidence about the distinctives of the evangelists vis-à-vis their sources from pairs of passages like the wedding banquet and great supper, the talents and pounds, and the lost sheep and the wandering sheep, since they may well not be true parallels. Yet it is precisely from such a comparison that many unwarranted conclusions are often drawn about Matthew's greater propensity for allegorizing or his heightened Christology. Many of the shorter metaphorical sayings in Luke's central section also may be independent of their counterparts in Matthew—for example, the little parables of the animals in the well and sheep in the pit (Lk 14:5; Mt 12:11) and of the armed guard and strong householder (Lk 11:21-22; Mt 12:29).

4.2.2 Dictional Analysis

Some redactional studies begin by going to great lengths to separate the vocabulary and grammar characteristic of each individual evangelist from that common to the Synoptic tradition. Then only the latter is accepted as part of what the Gospel writers inherited; the former is ascribed entirely to their creative invention.[49] This fallacy also resembles one discussed in the previous chapter (pp. 80-81); vocabulary statistics cannot determine authenticity. One may be able to argue that a particular writer has freely rewritten or paraphrased a passage in his own style, but one can deduce nothing about the presence or absence of a source which contained identical information in other wording. Ancient writers often reworked their sources with varying degrees of freedom from one section to another,[50] so very little may legitimately be concluded about historical accuracy from fluctuations in writing style.

4.2.3 The Theology-History Dichotomy

Despite repeated refutation, the notion still persists that if a passage or portion of a passage epitomizes the distinctive theology of a particular evangelist, it must reflect his own composition and cannot rest on a historical foundation in the life of Jesus. This has particularly affected the assessment of a number of the parables peculiar to Luke, especially those which so marvelously encapsulate Luke's theology of grace (e.g., the prodigal son or the Pharisee and tax-collector). No less a careful scholar than E. P. Sanders draws on such studies, albeit tentatively, in his attempt to narrow the distance between Jesus and the Jewish leaders, and to attribute the most "radical" characteristics of the Gospel to the later church.[51] But the logic remains flawed. Christian theology is based on histor-

---

[49]For a drastic example of this approach, see Gundry, *Matthew,* passim. For a very cautious example, cf. Graham N. Stanton, "Matthew as Creative Interpreter of the Sayings of Jesus," in *Das Evangelium und die Evangelien,* ed. Peter Stuhlmacher (Tübingen: Mohr, 1983), pp. 273-87. Both writers include a number of the Matthean parables in their list of redactional creations. A recent example of a study of an individual parable which errs in this respect is E. D. Freed, "The Parable of the Judge and the Widow (Luke 18:1-8)," *NTS* 33 (1987):38-60.

[50]Tessa Rajak, *Josephus: The Historian and His Society* (London: Duckworth, 1983; Philadelphia: Fortress, 1984), p. 233.

[51]Sanders, *Jesus and Judaism,* pp. 179, 281, 320; cf. the literature cited in n. 6, p. 385, and n. 24, p. 386.

ical fact, not on opposition to it.[52] It is virtually certain that much material in each of the Gospels is both theologically significant and historically accurate.[53]

4.2.4 Prophecy after the Event

In his Synoptic sayings, Jesus often prophesies concerning future events. The most well-known examples are his passion predictions and his eschatological discourse. But the parables too contain hints of the future. A few of these seem to describe the destruction of Jerusalem by the Romans in A.D. 70, and they are often seen as redactional touches added by the evangelists *ex eventu* (after the event). By far the most famous example is Matthew 22:7 (in the parable of the wedding feast), in which the slighted king sends his troops to destroy the would-be guests who had murdered his servants and to burn their city.

Nothing like this appears in Luke's great supper parable, the details are obviously allegorical (the overreactions of both invitees and king seem unimaginable in real life), and the parallelism with the fall of Jerusalem remains striking. But if, as already suggested, the wedding feast and great supper are not true parallels, and if Jesus did use allegory, then the first two objections pose no problem. Neither does the third, per se, unless an antisupernatural bias prevents one from believing that Jesus could truly foresee the future.

In this instance, however, there are good reasons for questioning whether either Matthew or Jesus meant to refer to the Roman onslaught in A.D. 70 at all. In the other parables which describe the actions of kings, the monarch always stands for God rather than a human ruler. Yet if this parable were an allegory of the fall of Jerusalem, the king would most naturally stand for the emperor. Similarly, other parables of judgment all refer to the final reckoning at the end of the age, not to any political conquest.

The invited guests, moreover, have to stand for those who refused God's invitation to the kingdom through Jesus, but the Zealots who rebelled against Rome were only a small group of those Jews who had rejected Jesus. Finally, in the parable the city is

---

[52]For more detail, see Stewart C. Goetz and Craig L. Blomberg, "The Burden of Proof," *JSNT* 11 (1981):44-52, and the literature there cited.

[53]See esp. Marshall, *Luke: Historian and Theologian*, pp. 21-52.

burned, but in A.D. 70 only the temple and not all of Jerusalem was destroyed by fire. A redactor inventing "prophecy" after the event would probably have made the parable more closely correspond to historical fact (cf., e.g., 2 Baruch 7:1, 80:3).[54]

For all of these reasons, it is more likely that Matthew 22:7 refers more generally to the end-time destruction of God's enemies, using graphic, warlike language amply paralleled in Old Testament and intertestamental history, as well as in rabbinic parables (cf., e.g., Judg 1:8, 1 Macc 5:28, Test Jud 5:1-5, Sifre Num 131).[55]

4.2.5 Characterizing the Parables in Different Synoptic Sources

In his influential article, "Characteristics of the Parables in the Several Gospels," Michael Goulder argues that the peculiarly Lukan and peculiarly Matthean parables so differ from those of Mark that they are more likely the product of the evangelists than of Jesus.[56] He claims that Mark presents predominantly nature parables in simple, rural settings with no clear-cut contrast between good and bad characters, a high degree of allegorizing, and a call for only a vague or general response. Matthew's parables are about people in grander or more urban settings, with clear-cut contrasts between characters, and slightly less allegorizing, but similarly vague in specifying the desired response. Luke also prefers "people parables" with marked contrasts but locates them in smaller towns, with more down-to-earth characters, much less allegorizing and very specific applications.

Just as with his analysis of the Gospels as midrash (see above, p. 86), however, Goulder reads the evidence through highly selective lenses. Some of his generalizations are marginally true—three of

---

[54]Bo Reicke, "Synoptic Prophecies on the Destruction of Jerusalem," in *Studies in the New Testament and Early Christian Literature*, ed. David E. Aune (Leiden: Brill, 1972), p. 123; J. A. T. Robinson, *Redating the New Testament* (London: SCM; Philadelphia: Westminster, 1976), pp. 19-21.

[55]K. H. Rengstorf, "Die Stadt der Mörder (Matt. 22:7)," in *Judentum, Urchristentum, Kirche*, ed. W. Eltester (Berlin: Töpelmann, 1960), pp. 106-29. Cf. Alexander Sand, *Das Evangelium nach Matthäus* (Regensburg: Pustet, 1986), p. 438, who refers to Lev 26:31; Josh 6:5; 2 Kings 23:27; Is 1:7-9.

[56]Michael Goulder, "Characteristics of the Parables in the Several Gospels," *JTS* 19 (1968):51-69. Cf. its surprising endorsement by Simon J. Kistemaker, *The Parables of Jesus* (Grand Rapids: Baker, 1980), pp. 275-79; and Leland Ryken, *How to Read the Bible as Literature* (Grand Rapids: Zondervan, 1984), p. 148. Although neither of these writers accepts Goulder's conclusions about inauthenticity, it is not clear that his claims about the differences among the Gospels can be detached from these conclusions. And his figures concerning the percentage of allegorical details in the various parables also seem inflated.

Mark's five narrative parables are nature parables (sower, seed growing secretly, and mustard seed), and the latter two of these three admittedly show no clear-cut contrasts, but this hardly gives him the right to jettison from the other Gospels as inauthentic the several dozen "people parables" with sharper contrasts. The latter are the typical kind; the three nature parables in Mark, more the exception (along with Matthew's wheat and tares, dragnet, field, and pearl, and Luke's fig tree).

Some of Goulder's generalizations are simply inaccurate—if Mark's and Matthew's are the more allegorical parables, and they probably are, then their applications are more specific rather than less. And for almost every example of a parable set in village, town or city in the particular Gospel which supposedly emphasizes those locations and their corresponding scales of simplicity or grandeur, an exception can be found elsewhere in that Gospel to counter Goulder's perceived patterns.

Mark's mustard "bush" may not be the larger "tree" that it is in Luke, but it is still called "the greatest of all shrubs" (Mk 4:32; cf. Lk 13:19). Matthew has the largest number of parables featuring a king but also the largest number of nature parables. Similar attempts to pit one group of Synoptic parables against another fail equally badly (see below, pp. 146-48). In fact, when careful studies of style and vocabulary are taken into account, what uniformity exists in the unparalleled parables of Matthew and Luke supports the M-and L-hypotheses (i.e., that Matthew and Luke drew on special sources for their unique material) rather than theories of redactional invention. That is to say, these parables more often than not display fewer of the evangelists' favorite words and forms of speech than do many other sections of their Gospels.[57]

4.2.6 Mistaking Stylistic for Theological Redaction

This mistake is undoubtedly the most common of all so far mentioned. The vast majority of the differences between Gospel parallels, including the parables, are minor variations in wording that are

---

[57]Eduard Schweizer, "Zur Sondertradition der Gleichnisse bei Matthäus," in *Matthäus und seine Gemeinde* (Stuttgart: Katholisches Bibelwerk, 1974), pp. 98-105; Craig L. Blomberg, "The Tradition History of the Parables Peculiar to Luke's Central Section" (Ph.D. diss., Aberdeen, 1982), pp. 300-341.

probably more motivated by matters of style than of substance. One can imaginatively ascribe theological motives to almost any conceivable variation in wording, but equating those ascriptions with the original purposes of the Gospel writers is extremely risky. Of dozens of possible examples, two may be cited.

1. *Matthew 21:39/Luke 20:15; cf. Mark 12:8.* Most commentators assume that Matthew and Luke reversed the sequence of verbs in the description of the fate of the son in Mark's parable of the wicked tenants to correspond to the historical details of Jesus' death. Thus instead of the son being killed first and then cast out of the vineyard, he is first cast out and then killed, just as Jesus was taken outside the walls of Jerusalem and then crucified. The vineyard in the parable, however, is not a metaphor for Jerusalem but for Israel (see below, p. 248), and Jesus was not put to death outside of his native land. Rather it is more likely that these are incidental or coincidental changes.

If a motive must be found, it is more probably stylistic. Especially in Luke's version, a number of features point to his improving the literary quality of Mark's more rugged Greek. He has omitted the superfluous "they took him" and turned a finite verb into a participle (thus literally reading,"having cast him out of the vineyard, they killed [him]"). This places the more important action—the death of the son— squarely in the limelight, and mentioning it last gives it climactic force.[58] It is possible that the same change of order in Matthew without a corresponding grammatical improvement indicates that this alteration occurred already in the oral tradition or that a version of the parable also appeared in Q, but neither of these hypotheses is demonstrable. Certainly it is tenuous to derive with confidence major claims about contradictory meanings from so minor a syntactical change.

2. *Luke 12:42; cf. Matthew 24:45.* The parable of the faithful and unfaithful servants is nearly word-for-word identical in Matthew and Luke. The variations which do occur almost all involve the substitution of one synonym or grammatical form of a word for another. Two of these substitutions, however, have often been invested with greater significance. In the opening sentence of the

---

[58]Cf. esp. Michel Hubaut, *La parabole des vignerons homicides* (Paris: Gabalda, 1976), p. 52.

parable, instead of the common word for "servant" or "slave," Luke uses the more specific term *steward;* instead of the past tense "set him over his household," he utilizes the future "who will set him . . ."

Thus many see Luke as restricting the application of the parable to Christian leaders, perhaps even just the twelve apostles, who in their leadership positions in the early church resembled the chief stewards whom a master would set over lesser servants. Alfons Weiser, for example, observes that if the story had originally spoken of a steward, then his master could not have set him over his household as a reward for faithful service—he would have already had that honor. The reference to the steward must be a redactional alteration, allegorizing the parable in a way which mars its realism.[59]

Nevertheless, if Luke were really trying to emphasize anything by the use of the word *steward,* surely he would have changed his other references to the *slave* as well (vv. 43, 45, 46). The tension felt by Weiser can be resolved by assuming that the steward already had a certain amount of authority over his peers but was invested with even more after his faithful service. And the switch from past to future tense is almost certainly designed to smooth out an awkward tense change, because Matthew, too, goes on to use the future tense for the rest of his narrative (vv. 46, 47, 50, 51).

4.2.7 Misrepresenting the Theology of an Evangelist

At least as frequent as the error of mistaking stylistic changes for theological distinctives is the error of misrepresenting the theological distinctives of a given evangelist. Many times the meaning of one evangelist's version of a passage will seem to contradict a parallel passage only when that version is interpreted so as to fit in with an alleged tendency which in fact may not fairly characterize that evangelist's theological distinctives. Four examples complete this survey of how redaction criticism of the parables has sometimes overstepped its rightful boundaries.

1. Luke 5:39; cf. Mark 2:22. At the end of the little parable of the wineskins, Luke includes an extra statement not found in either

---

[59]Alfons Weiser, *Die Knechtsgleichnisse der synoptischen Evangelien* (München: Kösel, 1971), p. 219.

Mark or Matthew: "and no one drinking old [wine] wants the new, for they say 'the old is good.' " Because Luke is regularly perceived to have a more conservative view of the Old Testament Law than Mark, this addition is often said to conflict with Mark's shorter, more radical parable. Luke, it is alleged, seeks some kind of compromise between Christianity and Judaism which would have been unthinkable for Jesus. In fact, a careful study of both his Gospel and Acts shows that Luke is just as concerned as any of the other evangelists to promote the radical newness of the Gospel.[60] So it is better to interpret this verse not as a toning down of the force of the parable but as an ironic aside reflecting on the way many of the Jewish leaders did actually react to Jesus. In the words of Eduard Schweizer, "more likely Luke is trying to say that unfortunately it is natural for people (including the speakers of vs. 33) to stick with the old than to be open to the new call of Jesus (cf. 18:8b)."[61]

2. *Luke 12:41-42; cf. Matthew 24:45.* In between the parables of the householder and the faithful servant, Luke inserts a question from Peter not found in Matthew's parallel: "Lord, are you telling this parable to us or to all?" Just as many commentators see Luke's switch from "slave" to "steward" in v. 43 (cf. above, p. 124) as indicating a narrower focus on apostles or church leaders generally, so also many find the same significance behind the question of verse 41.

The implied answer to Peter's question is that Jesus is telling this parable primarily for the disciples, because they, with Peter as their head, will be granted authority over Christ's church after his death. Yet it is Matthew, much more than any of the other evangelists, who typically inserts unparalleled material about Peter (his walking on the water, his being given the keys to the kingdom, instructions about forgiving his brother seventy-seven times, etc.), whereas this is not a common practice for Luke.

In fact, nothing in Jesus' parabolic reply suggests that he was not promoting good stewardship for *all* Christians. A better case can be made for Luke's having preserved here an accurate, historical rem-

---

[60]See esp. Craig L. Blomberg, "The Law in Luke-Acts," *JSNT* 22 (1984): 53-80; M. Max B. Turner, "The Sabbath, Sunday, and the Law in Luke/Acts," in *From Sabbath to Lord's Day,* ed. D. A. Carson (Grand Rapids: Zondervan; Exeter: Paternoster, 1982), pp. 99-157.
[61]Eduard Schweizer, *The Good News according to Luke* (Atlanta: John Knox; London: SPCK, 1984), p. 112.

iniscence of what Peter asked on this occasion. And if David Wenham's reconstruction of the eschatological discourse at this point is
correct, then Mark 13:37 ("what I say to you I say to all, watch!")
supplies the most immediate answer to Peter's question.[62] In that
event, Matthew may have omitted this brief interchange precisely
because it did *not* single out Peter or the Twelve in any special way.

3. *Luke 21:31; cf. Mark 13:29.* In the previous examples, redaction
critics often made too much of an evangelist's minor additions to
his sources; in this instance too much has been made of a minor
omission. Unlike Mark and Matthew, Luke's version of the parable
of the budding fig tree deletes the final two Greek words for "at
the very gates," following "when you see these things happening,
know that the kingdom of God is near." As a result Charles Carlston concludes that "the 'kingdom of God' is now de-eschatologized,
in keeping with Luke's general tendency to think of the Kingdom
as the content of Christian preaching rather than that which has
drawn near."[63]

This kind of sweeping inference from a minor change in wording
is unfortunately all too common among many redaction-critical
studies, and its validity in this instance is singularly suspect. If Luke
were playing down the nearness of the kingdom, it is extraordinary
that he should have left even the phrase "the kingdom of God is
near"! If it were not for the common notion that Luke in general
writes under the influence of the delay of the parousia, it is unlikely
that anyone would ever have found theological significance in this
slight alteration of Mark. But, as already indicated (see above, pp.
88-90), the timing of Christ's return was probably not an issue
which caused the early church to modify its presentation of the life
of Christ. It certainly does not place Luke in tension with earlier
stages of New Testament theology.[64] All of them affirm the nearness of Jesus' coming, but all recognize that an interval must precede it. As C. E. B. Cranfield comments in light of a similar debate
about the implications of the parable of the unjust judge,

---

[62]Wenham, *Rediscovery*, pp. 57-62.

[63]Carlston, *Parables*, p. 82.

[64]Contra Conzelmann, *Luke*, pp. 95-136, see esp. E. Earle Ellis, *Eschatology in Luke* (Philadelphia:
Fortress, 1972); Augustin George, *Études sur l'oeuvre de Luc* (Paris: Gabalda, 1978), pp. 321-47;
Emilio Rasco, "Hans Conzelmann y la 'Historia Salutis': A propósito de 'Die Mitte der Zeit' y
'Die Apostelgeschichte,' " *Greg* 46 (1965):286-319.

the Parousia is near . . . not in the sense that it must necessarily occur within a few months or years, but in the sense that it may occur at any moment and in the sense that, since *the* decisive event of history has already taken place in the ministry, death, resurrection and ascension of Christ, all subsequent history is a kind of epilogue, an interval inserted by God's mercy in order to allow men time for repentance, and, as such an epilogue, necessarily in a real sense short, even though it may last a very long time.[65]

Two other verses related to Lukan parables may be similarly explained. In the great supper parable, the master sends his servants out a second time to find new guests (14:23), and in introducing the parable of the pounds Luke explains that Jesus told the parable because some thought the kingdom would appear immediately (19:11). Both of these verses at first seem to point out Luke's reaction to the delay of the parousia.

Robert Maddox, however, stresses that Luke is not trying to discuss the timing of the kingdom's arrival but its nature.[66] It may require extra time for the servants to go out to the highways twice to find guests (in Matthew's wedding banquet parable they only go once), but the main point is about God's concern for society's dispossessed, possibly though not necessarily with an eye on the extension of the kingdom to the Gentiles.[67] The kingdom of God was not appearing immediately at Jesus' triumphal entry because the crucifixion had to come first. Christ's self-consciously Messianic act in riding the donkey (cf. Zech 9:9) was not going to culminate in a revolution against Rome as many would have liked.

4. *Matthew 24:45-25:13.* Just as the strengths of redaction criticism derive not only from its study of how an evangelist altered his sources but also from how he arranged the material within his Gospel, so also some of the errors redaction critics have made stem from a misreading of the larger context of an individual passage. One example from a sequence of parables involves Matthew's jux-

---

[65]C. E. B. Cranfield, "The Parable of the Unjust Judge and the Eschatology of Luke-Acts," *SJT* 16 (1963):300-301.

[66]Robert Maddox, *The Purpose of Luke-Acts* (Edinburgh: T & T Clark, 1982), pp. 49-50.

[67]A reference to the Gentiles could be authentic; Kenneth E. Bailey, *Through Peasant Eyes: More Lucan Parables* (Grand Rapids: Eerdmans, 1980), pp. 101-8, has noted ample Old Testament precedent. But the "highways" and "hedges" are not well-established symbols, and they could simply refer to places for additional Israelites, even more remote from the centers of piety and power.

taposition of the parable of the faithful and unfaithful servants (from Q) with the story of the ten virgins (unique to Matthew). Matthew, like Luke, has often been accused of altering the theology of earlier Christian tradition in light of the diminishing hope for Christ's imminent return. Thus while preserving the former parable about the unknown time of the master's return, he added (or even created) the latter parable about the bridegroom's delay.[68]

But the argument that assumes the Gospel writers were free at will to add to or delete from their sources cuts two ways. It implies not only that their distinctives probably reflect conscious emphases but also that anything which they preserved intact likewise bore their stamp of approval. So Matthew 24:45-51 is no less significant than 25:1-13 for determining Matthew's message.

The parable of the faithful and unfaithful servants is hardly just about the uncertainty of the time of the master's return. Instead it explicitly warns against those who think he will be gone *longer* than he actually will be ("if that wicked servant says to himself, 'my master is delayed' "—v. 48). The parable of the virgins then perfectly balances this warning with a caution not to assume the Lord is returning *earlier* than he is. Matthew emphasizes neither delay nor imminence but rather good stewardship for whatever period of time Christ tarries.[69] The subsequent parables of the talents and of the sheep and the goats which round out Matthew 25 make this crystal clear.

4.3 Conclusions

In many ways this chapter is closely linked with the last. Both form and redaction criticism help to explain many of the differences in wording between parallel accounts of the same passages in different Gospels. Both methods rely on a large dose of subjectivity; it is easy to speculate about why one Gospel differs from another, but the answers proposed can be only educated guesses at best. One may be able to pinpoint a key theme that a given evangelist wanted to highlight which might easily be missed if one simply concentrated

---

[68]E.g., Jean Zumstein, *La condition du croyant dans l'évangile selon Matthieu* (Göttingen: Vandenhoeck & Ruprecht, 1977), p. 280.

[69]Cf., e.g., Victor C. Agbanou, *Le discours eschatologique de Matthieu 24—25: Tradition et rédaction* (Paris: Gabalda, 1983), pp. 204-5.

on those portions of the passage which all the versions share. Since this result emerges more from redaction than from form criticism, it is arguable that redaction criticism is of more value than form.

But neither discipline discloses adequate reason for accepting the consensus that the parables have been so modified by the tradition and/or the Gospel writers that one must speak of contradictory details or theologies. The striking thing about the survey of this present chapter is that even the most clear-cut examples of the evangelists' redaction yield only fairly minor differences. The vast majority of the wording of parallel accounts is remarkably similar from one Gospel to the next.

Of course it could be argued that the data have been skewed by deliberately eliminating questionable pairs of parables (talents/pounds, wedding feast/great supper, etc.), which, if accepted as genuine parallels, would substantially alter these conclusions. In fact, the opposite is more likely true; it is the acceptance of such pairs of passages as parallel which distorts the evidence. If the Gospel writers were as free to alter their sources as they would have had to have been to create a parable like that of the wedding feast out of the great supper, then one would expect similar editorial freedom to be reflected even in passages which have a high enough percentage of verbal similarity to be indisputably parallel.

But this is precisely what never occurs—large stretches of close parallelism with drastic differences interspersed. Instead, *either* the entire passage is radically "altered," making one question whether the "parallel" is genuine or not, *or* the entire passage remains closely aligned to its parallel throughout.[70] This is a more powerful argument for the generally conservative nature of the parables' tradition and redaction than is usually recognized.

A second objection might be that the entire Gospel tradition has not been taken into account; perhaps the editorial methods which the evangelists employed with nonparabolic material make it more likely that the variations in wording among the parables represent actual contradictions after all. Clearly the only adequate response

---

[70]As noted previously, I have elaborated this point at length for the Lukan parables paralleled in either Mark or Matthew in "When Is A Parallel Really A Parallel? A Test Case: The Lucan Parables," *WTJ* 46 (1984):78-103. Matthew is generally even more conservative than Luke with his redaction of Mark, so a fortiori the argument applies to him as well.

to such an objection would be a book even lengthier than this one.[71] Suffice it to say that redaction-critical studies of all three Synoptics, unencumbered by the more radical presuppositions which so easily beset them, have not shown this to be true.

Perhaps the three best of these are the studies of the theologies of Mark by Ralph Martin, of Luke by I. Howard Marshall and of Matthew by R. T. France, all in the "Contemporary Evangelical Perspectives" series.[72] D. A. Carson's recent commentary on Matthew is also fully abreast of redaction-critical studies and shows a sober appreciation and sane appropriation of them.[73] Even more liberal scholars now often make much more modest and valid claims about what redaction criticism can and cannot do than did the method's pioneers. Several excellent, detailed studies[74] as well as briefer overviews demonstrate this.[75]

But one can make the point even more forcefully. Harmonizing the Gospels and analyzing their redactional distinctives are not contradictory but complementary methods.[76] With a full appreciation of all the variations in wording between parallel accounts, not one example has come to light which demands an abandonment of belief in the Gospels' accuracy, provided that accuracy is measured by standards of precision appropriate to the cultures and expectations of the original authors and their audiences.

Biblical theology takes rightful precedence over systematic theology—each Gospel must be heard on its own before a "life of Christ" is written by combining them together—but both tasks are entirely proper and essential.[77] The individual theologies of the various Gos-

---

[71]I have dealt with this question for a full chapter in *Historical Reliability*, pp. 113-52.

[72]Ralph P. Martin, *Mark: Evangelist and Theologian* (Exeter: Paternoster, 1972; Grand Rapids: Zondervan, 1973); Marshall, *Luke: Historian and Theologian*; R. T. France, *Matthew: Evangelist and Teacher* (Exeter: Paternoster; Grand Rapids: Zondervan, 1989).

[73]Carson, "Matthew"; cf. idem, "Jewish Leaders in Matthew's Gospel: A Reappraisal," *JETS* 25 (1982):161-74; idem, "Christological Ambiguities in the Gospel of Matthew," in *Christ the Lord*, ed. Harold H. Rowdon (Downers Grove and Leicester: IVP, 1982), pp. 97-114.

[74]E.g., Graham N. Stanton, "The Origin and Purpose of Matthew's Gospel: Matthean Scholarship from 1945 to 1980," in *Aufstieg und Niedergang der römischen Welt*, II, 25.3, ed. W. Haase (Berlin: de Gruyter, 1985), pp. 1889-1951; Fitzmyer, *Luke I-IX*, pp. 143-258.

[75]Keith F. Nickle, *The Synoptic Gospels: An Introduction* (Atlanta: John Knox, 1981; London: SCM, 1982), pp. 55-81; James L. Mays, *Interpreting the Gospels* (Philadelphia: Fortress, 1981). Cf. also the series of articles in *Themelios* 14.2 (1989) on recent study of the individual Synoptists.

[76]Blomberg, "Harmonization."

[77]See esp. D. A. Carson, "Unity and Diversity in the New Testament: The Possibility of Systematic Theology," in *Scripture and Truth*, pp. 65-95.

pel writers never come into irreconcilable conflict with each other or with the traditions which preceded them so as to prevent a subsequent synthesis of their thought, even if they do have important distinctives which such a synthesis inevitably blurs.

Indirect testimony to these conclusions is provided by many recent studies of the parables, which, while uncritically assuming the unreliability of the Gospels as history and therefore being unable to return to more traditional methods of interpretation, are equally dissatisfied with form and redaction criticism and so have turned to newer literary and hermenuetical tools in the quest for more substantial insights. These form the focus of attention for the final chapter of part one.

5

New Literary &
Hermeneutical Methods

C HAPTERS TWO THROUGH FOUR HAVE DEFENDED TWO MAIN
theses: the Synoptic parables attributed to Jesus are allegories and
they are authentic. They are allegories, not in that every detail in
the parables stands for something else, but in that at least several
of the details in each parable function metaphorically to point to a
second level of meaning in the story. Specifically, the parables illustrate various aspects of the kingdom of God.

Interpreters from Jülicher to the present have been unable to
avoid allegorical interpretations of the parables, however strenuously they deny the validity of the method. This is true even when
they detach the parables from their Gospel contexts. When one
recognizes that there is no good reason to reject the interpretations
of the parables given in the Gospels, the allegorical nature of the
parables is that much more undeniable.

Form and redaction criticism have offered plausible explanations
of why parallel accounts of the same parable differ as they do, but
their attempts to reject the authenticity of any portion of the parables fail to convince. One of the main reasons these critics see the

interpretive summary of a given parable's meaning as inaccurate, be it ascribed to Jesus or added by the evangelists, is its seeming inability to encapsulate adequately *the* central truth of that parable. When one recognizes that in many cases this is not its purpose, this objection dissipates. In many cases these summaries highlight one of two or three main points which the parable makes, perhaps focusing on the significance of one of the two or three main characters in the parable. In other cases they append applications rather than providing interpretations. The exegesis of part two will illustrate these principles in more detail.

For many New Testament scholars not specializing in the field of parable research, Jeremias's book remains the definitive work on the topic. Those who have delved more deeply into the field are quickly overwhelmed by the unabating flood of literature that continues to flow far beyond anything Jeremias ever imagined. In certain circles form and redaction criticism are already passé, and newer models of study drawn more explicitly from secular literary criticism dominate. The purpose of this chapter is not to describe each of these in detail, but instead to focus on the ways in which the newest methods of parable research either challenge or confirm the two main theses put forward here.[1]

5.1 The New Hermeneutic

The "new hermeneutic" is the only method surveyed here that did not originate in literary criticism; it is a development of modern philosophy. Flourishing first in the 1960s and associated in New Testament circles with such names as Ernst Fuchs, Gerhard Ebeling, Hans-Georg Gadamer and Eberhard Jüngel, the new hermeneutic has come to refer to a movement which emphasizes the subjectivity of the process of interpreting the biblical texts, over against the traditional quest for objectivity.[2]

---

[1]For more thorough, though selective, surveys of the recent discussion, see Norman Perrin, *Jesus and the Language of the Kingdom* (Philadelphia: Fortress; London: SCM, 1976), pp. 89-193; Wolfgang Harnisch, "Die Metapher als heuristisches Prinzip: Neuerscheinungen zur Hermeneutik der Gleichnisreden Jesu," *VF* 24 (1979):53-89; Pheme Perkins, *Hearing the Parables of Jesus* (New York: Paulist, 1981).

[2]Two of the best, brief introductions to the method are Anthony C. Thiselton, "The New Hermeneutic," in *New Testament Interpretation*, ed. I. Howard Marshall (Exeter: Paternoster; Grand Rapids: Eerdmans, 1977), pp. 308-33; and William G. Doty, *Contemporary New Testament Interpretation* (Englewood Cliffs, N.J.: Prentice-Hall, 1972), pp. 28-51. For a fuller treatment, cf. Robert W. Funk, *Language, Hermeneutic and Word of God* (New York and London: Harper & Row, 1966).

More technically, it seeks to overcome the traditional distinction between subject (interpreter) and object (text) through a "fusion of the horizons" of text and interpreter. In other words, it focuses on ways in which the "text interprets the reader," challenging his inherited presuppositions (a process often called a "language event"), instead of looking simply at ways in which the reader interprets the text, often finding in it just what he expected before looking.

Most scholars have come to accept this as a valid, if sometimes overstated, principle. A common approach to biblical interpretation now involves the establishment of a "hermeneutical circle" (or, better, a "spiral"), through which the interpreter continually seeks to let the text stand over him, correcting his misconceptions of it, even as he stands over the text, trying to explain and elucidate it for others.[3] One might diagram the procedure as follows:

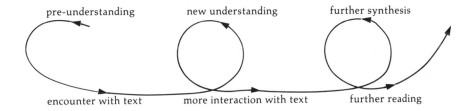

pre-understanding   new understanding   further synthesis

encounter with text   more interaction with text   further reading

Many applications of the new hermeneutic to the Gospels focus on the parables, because Jesus consistently used this form of teaching to challenge conventional beliefs of his day. Speaking in parables also runs contrary to standard conceptions of theological language and the nature of preaching. Jesus did not address his congregations by stating universal truths and then expounding them; he told stories!

More specifically, he spoke more in metaphors than in straightforward propositions. Chapter two (see above, pp. 32, 35) has already discussed traditional meanings of *metaphor* (either a figure of speech in general or a specific type of comparison without a comparative word, as over against a simile). The new hermeneutic and related

---

[3]This method is to be distinguished sharply from that kind of circular reasoning in which the interpeter fallaciously presupposes his conclusion(s). The hermeneutical spiral of the new hermeneutic is put forward precisely as an antidote to this question-begging process.

movements in linguistic philosophy and literary criticism have introduced a third important use of the term *metaphor*, which has proved
widely influential.[4] This use puts metaphor and allegory in direct
opposition to one another and so clearly requires further attention.

5.1.1 The New View of Metaphor

Although others identified with the new hermeneutic have written
more detailed exegetical studies of the parables,[5] perhaps no one is
a more prominent spokesman for the significance of the parables as
metaphor than Paul Ricoeur. Ricoeur itemizes six differences between the traditional and modern understandings of metaphor, and
in each case he endorses the latter. (1) The fundamental unit of
meaning is not the individual word but an entire sentence. (2) A
metaphor is not a deviation from the literal sense of a word but the
creation of tension by juxtaposing words which do not normally go
together ("that man is a wolf" or "a good Samaritan"). (3) Understanding the metaphor does not come from noting the resemblance
between the literal and figurative meaning of the words used, but
from recognizing the shock created by the juxtaposition of typically
incompatible words. (4) Metaphors are thus not substitutes for literal language but semantic innovations. (5) Similarly, they are not
translatable into propositional speech as traditionally conceived. (6)
Therefore metaphors are not mere ornaments of literature but devices conveying new information about reality.[6]

If the "new" view of metaphor is correct, then as metaphors the

---

[4]The literature is enormous. David S. Miall, ed., *Metaphor: Problems and Perspectives* (Brighton:
Harvester; Atlantic Highlands, N.J.: Humanities Press, 1982) is a helpful, recent overview from
the literary perspective; Samuel R. Levin, *The Semantics of Metaphor* (Baltimore and London: Johns
Hopkins, 1977), a thorough linguistic analysis; and Mark Johnson, ed., *Philosophical Perspectives on
Metaphor* (Minneapolis: Univ. of Minnesota Press, 1981), a helpful survey and analysis of the
philosophical alternatives. Cf. also the entire issues of *New Literary History* 6 (1974) fascicle 1, and
Critical Inquiry 5 (1978) fascicle 1. Many of the articles in the latter are also collected in Sheldon
Sacks, ed., *On Metaphor* (Chicago and London: Univ. of Chicago Press, 1978).

[5]The standard works are Ernst Fuchs, *Studies of the Historical Jesus* (London: SCM; Naperville:
Allenson, 1964); Eberhard Jüngel, *Paulus und Jesus* (Tübingen: Mohr, 1962), pp. 87-174; Eta Lin-
nemann, *Parables of Jesus: Introduction and Exposition* (London: SPCK, 1966 [= *Jesus of the Parables:
Introduction and Exposition* (New York: Harper & Row, 1967)]).

[6]Paul Ricoeur, "Biblical Hermeneutics," *Semeia* 4 (1975):27-148, esp. pp. 76-77. Cf. also idem, *The
Rule of Metaphor* (Toronto and London: Univ. of Toronto Press, 1977), esp. pp. 173-215, in which
Ricoeur offers a more nuanced approach, allowing in certain contexts for some irreducible
cognitive element to metaphor. For more detail and subdivision of these "old" and "new" views
of metaphor, cf. J. J. A. Mooij, *A Study of Metaphor* (Amsterdam: North Holland, 1976), pp. 29-
38.

parables cannot also be allegories. Details of the parables cannot stand for anything which could be substituted in their place, like a king for God or servants for his angels. This is the nature of the simile (where one thing is explicitly said to be "like" something else) rather than the metaphor.

Parable and allegory thus remain as antithetical as Jülicher or Jeremias ever alleged they were. But over against Jülicher and Jeremias, one can no longer even talk of summarizing the one main point of a parable.[7] Metaphors simply cannot be expressed in non-metaphorical language; their meanings are inextricable from their form. To rephrase the sentence, "that man is a wolf" as "that man is adventuresome" (or "vicious" or "aggressive" or "competitive") results in a substantial loss not only of force but of content, since no one-word substitution can do justice to all the nuances that might be involved in the original figure of speech.

Borrowing from the language of philosophy, the parables as metaphors are *performative* rather than *propositional*—utterances which do not convey information but perform an action, such as promising, warning, giving a gift or making a demand.[8] Thus Ernst Fuchs describes the parable of the laborers in the vineyard (Mt 20: 1-16) as one in which Jesus is *pledging* that "there will be no disappointment for those who, in face of a cry of 'guilty,' nevertheless found their hope on an act of God's kindness" and *determining* that he will "give up everything else for this faith."[9] The italicized action verbs highlight the difference between this type of exposition and commentary which attempts to state the main points of the parables as universal principles. The new hermeneutic describes what the parables do rather than what they mean.

Bernard Scott employs this procedure as consistently as anyone, emphasizing that he is not expounding the parables' meaning but only talking "about" them in the hopes of facilitating "insight" at a

---

[7]This, e.g., is Norman Perrin's primary critique of Jeremias, whose work he otherwise highly praises. For Perrin, "parables as parables do not have a 'message' " (*Jesus*, p. 106).

[8]This use of *performative* is to be distinguished from the more general performative nature of all language (i.e., all speech accomplishes something). The germinal studies of language's "speech acts" (which include making statements, giving commands, asking questions and expressing desires) are J. L. Austin, *How to Do Things with Words* (Oxford: Univ. Press; Cambridge, Mass.: Harvard Univ. Press, 1962); and John R. Searle, *Speech Acts* (Cambridge: Univ. Press, 1969).

[9]Fuchs, *Jesus*, p. 37, italics mine.

"pre-conceptual" level.[10] And John Donahue entitles the introductory chapter of his recent book, "How Does A Parable Mean?" because he does not believe one can definitively determine *what* the parables mean.[11] From this perspective, Sallie Te Selle admits that "a critic, when asked what a poetic metaphor 'means,' is finally reduced to repeating the line of poetry or even the entire poem, for there is no other way of saying what is being said except in the words that were chosen to say it."[12] If the main points of the parables cannot be expressed even in simple sentences, then they surely cannot be dealt with by detailed allegorical equations.

5.1.2 A Critique of the New View of Metaphor

Much of the new hermeneutic's appropriation of the modern analysis of metaphor proves quite valuable. Ricoeur's first two points may be freely granted, but they need not lead to the type of opposition between allegory and metaphor which he imagines. We may agree that a word in isolation cannot stand for anything other than itself and that it requires the context of a complete, meaningful utterance, namely, the sentence.[13] And in Jesus' parables part of that context *will* regularly involve as shocking a juxtaposition as the acts of mercy attributed to a Samaritan must have originally seemed to Jesus' Jewish audience.

But, although the Samaritan plays an unconventional role, he still functions symbolically[14]—standing for one's most hated

[10]B. B. Scott, *Jesus, Symbol-Maker for the Kingdom* (Philadelphia: Fortress, 1981), pp. 12-18. In his *Hear Then the Parable* (Minneapolis: Fortress, 1989), p. 420, he writes, "Instead of accenting what the parable means, I have chosen to describe how it creates meaning."

[11]John R. Donahue, *The Gospel in Parable* (Philadelphia: Fortress, 1988), pp. 1-27.

[12]Sallie M. Te Selle, *Speaking in Parables: A Study in Metaphor and Theology* (Philadelphia: Fortress; London: SCM, 1975), p. 49.

[13]The discipline of "discourse analysis" is now arguing that paragraphs and other larger units of thought are even more fundamental than the sentence in the structure of language and speech. See, e.g., Robert D. Bergen, "Text as a Guide to Authorial Intention: An Introduction to Discourse Criticism," *JETS* 30 (1987):327-36.

[14]Literary critics themselves disagree on the definition of a symbol. This book adopts the broader sense specified by Gay Clifford, *The Transformations of Allegory* (London and Boston: Routledge and Kegan Paul, 1974), p. 11: "objects or events or persons standing for something other and generally greater than themselves." If one adopts the narrower definition of Philip Wheelwright, *Metaphor and Reality* (Bloomington: Indiana Univ. Press, 1962), p. 92, which adds the restriction that the element which stands for something else is "relatively stable and repeatable," then of course the good Samaritan is not a symbol. But many writers simply refer to Wheelwright's kind of symbol as a "stock symbol." René Wellek and Austin Warren, *Theory of Literature* (New York: Harcourt, Brace & World, 1956; London: Jonathan Cape, 1966), p. 189, prefer to distinguish between "images" which may be invoked once as a metaphor and "symbols" which persistently recur. Here "image" and "symbol" are used more interchangeably for both senses.

enemy.[15] The question of whether the parable of the good Samaritan is a pure parable or an example story complicates matters somewhat and probably makes this a bad illustration from which to generalize, although many have tried.[16] The situation is clearer with a more typical comparison, such as a king symbolizing God, a consistent image both in Jesus' parables and those of the rabbis.

Nevertheless, one does well to apply Ricoeur's principle and stress that only the entire context of the sentences describing a given character's action can confirm what (or whom) he represents in a particular parable. In the case of servant-characters in the parables of both Jesus and the rabbis, this principle becomes obvious. Sometimes they stand for angels, sometimes for the people of God, sometimes for the faithless; and often they are mere props with no independent significance. Only the context can help one determine the meaning in any given passage.

Point (3) is even more crucial. Over against Dodd's and Jeremias's emphasis on the realism of parabolic imagery, Ricoeur stresses their "extravagant" language. Fathers often do not run down the road welcoming home prodigal sons, those who throw banquets very rarely invite the outcasts of society, and landlords whose servants have been killed by their tenants would probably never send an only son to risk a similar fate![17]

But rather than speaking of this extravagance fairly obliquely, as Ricoeur does, in terms of "limit" language which reveals the transcendent impinging on ordinary life (an affirmation of the revelatory quality of Jesus' parables for an age which no longer believes in the supernatural), it is better to see the unusual features in Jesus' parables as more straightforward pointers to their allegorical nature. Many fathers don't welcome prodigals, but God does; when the father is seen as standing for God, the problem disappears. So also for the behavior of the banquet-giver and wealthy landlord.

Points (4) through (6) prove more subtle, masking hidden premises. Each poses a false dichotomy. One can admit that metaphors

---

[15]As practitioners of this method tacitly admit in their own expositions. Cf. esp. Robert W. Funk, "The Good Samaritan as Metaphor," *Semeia* 2 (1974):74-81.

[16]Cf., e.g., the various other views represented in *Semeia* 2 (1974), which is entirely devoted to studies of this parable.

[17]Ricoeur, "Biblical Hermeneutics," p. 115. Cf. the thorough list of such features compiled by Norman A. Huffman, "Atypical Features in the Parables of Jesus," *JBL* 97 (1978):207-20.

cannot be replaced by exactly equivalent substitutes, translated into propositional speech or viewed as mere rhetorical flourishes without sacrificing some of their meaning and certainly much of their power. Undoubtedly modern preaching of the parables would gain much by carefully crafted contemporizations or re-presentations of the parables in modern garb to stir today's audiences more in the manner in which Jesus' originals affected his listeners.[18] But although metaphors are not propositions nor merely artistic figures of speech, they do not exclude either of these. Ricoeur himself seems to admit as much but he does not therefore diminish his disjunction between parable and allegory.[19] At this point the new view of metaphor is fundamentally misleading for at least six main reasons.

1. *Performative language presupposes certain propositional truths.*[20] One cannot give a gift, for example, without implying certain statements ("I have such-and-such an object," "I want you to have it," "I have the authority and ability to transfer ownership rights at no cost to you," etc.). The fact that different interpreters seldom encapsulate the propositional meaning of a given parable with precisely the same formulation shows that something is lost and irrecoverable when metaphors are "translated." But the fact that such encapsulations, even when independently formulated, often greatly resemble each other shows that metaphorical meaning may be closely approximated by more straightforward discourse.[21]

---

[18]Cf. the excellent illustrations in Gordon D. Fee and Douglas Stuart, *How to Read the Bible for All Its Worth* (Grand Rapids: Zondervan, 1982; London: Scripture Union, 1983), p. 133; David Wells, "Prayer: Rebelling Against the Status Quo," *Christianity Today* 23 (1979):1465. On narrative preaching more generally, see the excellent discussion in James E. Massey, *Designing the Sermon* (Nashville: Abingdon, 1980), pp. 35-49.

[19]Ricoeur, "Biblical Hermeneutics," p. 80: "To say that [metaphors] are untranslatable does not mean that they cannot be paraphrased, but the paraphrase is infinite and does not exhaust the innovation in meaning." But very similar observations were made in chapter two about the nature of allegory too (see above, pp. 53-54).

[20]Thiselton, "New Hermeneutic," p. 326. Cf. idem, *The Two Horizons* (Exeter: Paternoster; Grand Rapids: Eerdmans, 1980), p. 443. Thiselton's latter work is without question the most comprehensive and incisive study of the new hermeneutic and related issues, and his criticisms are leveled only after much sympathetic appropriation of the positions he surveys. Kevin J. Vanhoozer, "The Semantics of Biblical Literature: Truth and Scripture's Diverse Literary Forms," in *Hermeneutics, Authority, and Canon*, ed. D. A. Carson and John D. Woodbridge (Grand Rapids: Zondervan; Leicester: IVP, 1986), pp. 53-104, surveys the various definitions of the word *proposition* current in the philosophical literature and argues that the term should be given its "ordinary meaning" as that which a text "propounds" or "is about" (pp. 91-92).

[21]See esp. A. C. Thiselton, "The Parables as Language-Events: Some Comments on Fuchs's Hermeneutics in the Light of Linguistic Philosophy," *SJT* 23 (1970):437-68.

2. *The modern emphasis on the meaning of a metaphor as closely bound up with its literary context undercuts the new hermeneutic's concern for the autonomy of the parables.*[22] If, as I have argued, the interpretive comments in the Gospels surrounding the parables reflect Jesus' original meaning, then those contexts must be taken into account. Yet many of those interpretive comments are highly propositional in nature—"he who exalts himself will be humbled and he who humbles himself will be exalted" (Lk 18:14), "there is rejoicing in the presence of the angels of God over one sinner who repents" (15:10), or "from everyone who has been given much, much will be demanded" (12:48).

For the most part, the new hermeneutic has simply built on the foundation laid by earlier higher-critical study of the parables which rejected these "generalizing" conclusions. But if this foundation is cut out from under it, much of the edifice erected on top will collapse as well. Ricoeur believes that it is fair to translate the parables into other biblical modes of discourse about the kingdom of God, such as proverbs and prophecy.[23] But much of the New Testament's discourse about the kingdom is propositional (e.g., it was offered first to the Jews, then to the Greeks), including at least some of Jesus' undeniably authentic teaching (e.g., it is "at hand," or it has "arrived"). So to be consistent Ricoeur should stress the legitimacy of this type of translation of the parables as well.

3. *The fact that many of the Gospel parables are expressed as similes ("the kingdom of God is like . . .") but with apparently little if any difference in function from those which are pure metaphors (i.e., with no comparative term) renders a hard-and-fast distinction between the two forms seriously suspect.*[24] In the transmission of both the Gospel and rabbinic traditions, the introductory formulas were more often abbreviated or omitted, rather than added to pre-existing stories. So it is likely that the

---

[22]Wayne C. Booth, "Metaphor as Rhetoric: The Problem of Evaluation," *Critical Inquiry* 5 (1978):60, goes so far as to say that metaphor "cannot be judged without reference to a context."

[23]Ricoeur, "Biblical Hermeneutics," p. 101. Cf. David Tracy, "Metaphor and Religion: The Test Case of Christian Texts," *Critical Inquiry* 5 (1978): 101-2: "there is no need to hold that this interpretation of the metaphorical character of the parables of Jesus makes it impossible to employ conceptual, theological language that does maintain hermeneutical fidelity to the originating Christian root metaphor. Indeed, strictly theological discourse of the later New Testament language does maintain that hermeneutical fidelity." If later New Testament writers could legitimately do this, why could Jesus not have interpreted his own parables similarly?

[24]See Jonathan Culler, *The Pursuit of Signs: Semiotics, Literature, Deconstruction* (London: Routledge & Kegan Paul, 1981), pp. 207-8, on the difficulty of rendering a clear distinction between metaphor and simile more generally. Cf. Booth, "Metaphor," p. 55. Contra, e.g., Perrin, *Jesus,* p. 135.

simile rather than the metaphor was actually the most original form for many of the parables. Where comparisons and substitutions are left implicit the parables are no less allegorical but only more economical and forceful in their wording.

4. *The very power of parables to create a "language event," persuasively challenging traditional beliefs, sets these metaphors off as different from more enigmatic ones which are harder to translate into propositional language.* In order to persuade, the parables must communicate content. Mysterious riddles may defy conceptualization, but then they often leave their audience uncertain as to how it should respond. The parables as language events are calls to action—to count the cost of discipleship (Lk 14:28-33), to rejoice over God's abundant grace (Lk 15:3-7) or to be faithful stewards of everything with which God entrusts a person (Mt 25:14-30).

To make these demands the parables must communicate propositionally. Or in Wayne Booth's words, whatever may be true of other types of metaphor, those used in rhetoric as weapons of persuasion are part of a "communication in a context that reveals a predetermined purpose that can be paraphrased, intended to be recognized and reconstructed with stable, local meanings that can be evaluated as contributing to that purpose."[25] Once again the new hermeneutic undermines itself. It can have its language events, but then it must also accept propositional truths in the parables.

5. *Some types of metaphors are more susceptible to substitution than others, most notably those in which the metaphors are largely restricted to the subjects or nouns of a sentence.*[26] This is precisely what occurs in the parables. The activity of the characters in the parables is largely expressed in verbs which apply quite literally to the people for which they stand (asking, sending, repenting, serving, etc.). Only the identities of the people (and thus the nouns or subjects) have been changed. Even Max Black, whose work *Models and Metaphors* is widely heralded as the seminal study for the new view of metaphor, admits that only a "very small number of cases" of what are usually called metaphors fall into the category of irreducible, nonpropositional

---

[25]Booth, "Metaphor," p. 55. Cf. Amos Wilder, *Jesus' Parables and the War of Myths*, ed. James Breech (Philadelphia: Fortress; London: SPCK, 1982), pp. 31-32.

[26]See esp. Mooij, *Metaphor*, pp. 129-31.

examples which interest him.[27]

6. Finally, even the best attempts at consistently applying a nonpropositional approach to interpreting the parables fail. Scott, for example, concludes his analysis of the good Samaritan with these words: "The parable can be summarized as follows: to enter Kingdom one must get in the ditch and be served by one's mortal enemy." This interpretation may be somewhat unconventional, but it is solidly propositional. Scott recognizes this and so immediately adds: "Of course to summarize the parable in this manner is already to risk a loss of meaning. That is, to truly understand one must enter the parable so that its contours can resonate."[28]

Yet merely "risking a loss of meaning" is a far cry from Scott's starting point which seemed to deny categorically any possibility of capturing even partial meaning through such a summary statement. It is not a little ironic that virtually all the devaluation of propositional language and all the acclaim given to metaphor in the new hermeneutic comes in books and articles written almost entirely in nonmetaphorical, propositional language.[29] A theology of the parables true to their metaphorical nature would be a theology in narrative, a series of retellings of the parables in contemporary metaphorical idiom. Undoubtedly, there is a need to write about the method before applying it in practice, but after more than two decades it is somewhat surprising that not one practitioner of the new hermeneutic has written such a narrative.

It is safe to say that for all its contributions to the study of the parables, the new hermeneutic poses no challenge to the propositional nature of the parables such as would call into question their allegorical nature. To repeat, I am not claiming that valid nonmetaphorical paraphrase is either easy or that it exhausts a parable's meaning but rather that it can capture a substantial portion of it.

---

[27]Max Black, *Models and Metaphors* (Ithaca: Cornell, 1962), pp. 45-46.

[28]Scott, *Jesus*, p. 29. Cf. Mary A. Tolbert, *Perspectives on the Parables* (Philadelphia: Fortress, 1979), p. 42, on Te Selle's similar self-contradiction.

[29]If anything, the genre of writing has become more woodenly propositional with the appearance of books and articles subdivided into small sections, without subtitles, clear transitions between each part or standard narrative flow. See esp. many of the contributions to the journal *Semeia*. Cf. also Eberhard Jüngel, "Metaphorische Wahrheit," in *Metapher*, ed. Paul Ricoeur and Eberhard Jüngel (München: Kaiser, 1974), pp. 119-122, who finds the most useful way to summarize his discussion of the nonpropositional nature of metaphor to be an itemization of 25 propositional theses.

As such it is both a legitimate and essential endeavor.[30]

5.2 Structuralism

However different the practitioners of the new hermeneutic first seem from more traditional, historical-critical exegetes, both groups agree that the interpreter's task goes beyond an analysis of the text. Older literary criticism, in secular and biblical circles alike, sought the intention of the author in writing what he did. But representatives of this view are now few and far between.[31] In secular literary criticism, the long-standing preoccupation with authorial intent was largely abandoned in the earlier decades of this century with the rise of the so-called new criticism or formalism.

New criticism focused almost exclusively on the structures and form of a piece of literature and greatly played down the value of seeking information about the life and times of its author as an aid to interpretation. One movement with formalist roots borrowed from developments in the study of linguistics and anthropology and became known as structuralism. This method of interpretation deliberately ignores the historical background of a text but instead seeks to show universally recurring features in fictional narratives of all cultures and ages, which reveal a text's most fundamental meaning irrespective of its author's conscious intentions.[32]

For the most part, New Testament scholars have come to appropriate structuralist methodologies only within the last fifteen years. Because the parables are the most obvious examples of fiction in the

---

[30]Cf. Edmund P. Clowney, "Interpreting the Biblical Models of the Church: A Hermeneutical Deepening of Ecclesiology," in *Biblical Interpretation and the Church*, ed. D. A. Carson (Exeter: Paternoster, 1984; Nashville: Thomas Nelson, 1985), pp. 96-97. The two most detailed studies of metaphor and parable are also the most esoteric. Mogens S. Kjärgaard, *Metaphor and Parable* (Leiden: Brill, 1986) distinguishes present, imperfect and perfect metaphors, arguing that only the last are susceptible to propositional paraphrase, and that the original parables of Jesus do not fall into this category. But he fails to observe that, despite their fresh twists, Jesus' parables are filled with stock symbolism which would have yielded conventional interpretations of certain details and have given them some qualities of the perfect metaphor. Edmund Arens, *Kommunikative Handlungen: die paradigmatische Bedeutung der Gleichnisse Jesu für eine Handlungstheorie* (Düsseldorf: Patmos, 1982) is much more persuasive in his discussion of parables as speech-acts, by which they must be tied to a particular context and presuppose certain propositional truths.

[31]But cf. Helen Gardner, *The Business of Criticism* (Oxford: Clarendon, 1959), p. 75; and Walter C. Kaiser, Jr., *Toward an Exegetical Theology* (Grand Rapids: Baker, 1981), pp. 106-14.

[32]The standard introduction to literary structuralism is Jonathan Culler, *Structuralist Poetics* (Ithaca: Cornell; London: Routledge & Kegan Paul, 1975). To see how this movement affected other disciplines as well, cf. Jean-Marie Benoist, *The Structural Revolution* (London: Weidenfeld & Nicolson; New York: St. Martin's, 1978).

New Testament, it is not surprising that much of that appropriation initially focused on them. Detailed, specialized studies with highly technical language appeared, analyzing the "deep structure" of the parables—the subtle relationships between episodes or stages in a particular plot, the functions, motives and interaction between the main characters and objects in a narrative, and most notably the types of oppositions and their resolutions (if present) that develop as a story unfolds.[33]

The significance attached to such analyses varies. It is helpful to consider structuralism under three distinct headings: (a) an ideology which considers itself to be the only valid method for interpreting literature; (b) a method of studying certain structures underlying a text, usually neglected by but compatible with other more traditional methods; and (c) a method of studying certain surface features of the text and the connections between them, usually overlooked by other approaches.[34]

5.2.1 The Ideology

As a world view, structuralism is inherently bound up with dialectic philosophy, determinism and atheism.[35] It is determinist and atheist in that it claims that language determines thought. Thus it denies the possibility of both transcendent revelation and true personal freedom. Language controls speech and writing rather than vice versa. It is dialectic in that it seeks to identify oppositions in texts and how they are mediated or overcome. Ironically, structuralism as an ideology is more amenable to a propositional interpretation of the parables than the less radical new hermeneutic, inasmuch as structuralists believe that the text has a fixed meaning and that

---

[33]Daniel Patte, *The Gospel according to Matthew: A Structural Commentary on Matthew's Faith* (Philadelphia: Fortress, 1987), helpfully identifies many of the oppositions that occur throughout Matthew, including among characters in the parables.

[34]The best detailed introduction to New Testament structuralism, focusing largely on the parables, is idem, *What Is Structural Exegesis?* (Philadelphia: Fortress, 1976). Cf. also Raymond F. Collins, *Introduction to the New Testament* (Garden City: Doubleday; London: SCM, 1983), pp. 231-71. A very good survey and critique of biblical structuralism more broadly, but with pertinent references to the parables, is David C. Greenwood, *Structuralism and the Biblical Text* (Berlin, Amsterdam and New York: Mouton, 1985).

[35]Robert Detweiler, "After the New Criticism: Contemporary Methods of Literary Interpretation," in *Orientation by Disorientation*, ed. Richard A. Spencer (Pittsburgh: Pickwick, 1980), p. 13; Vern Poythress, "Philosophical Roots of Phenomenological and Structuralist Literary Criticism," *WTJ* 41 (1978):166.

exegesis is a relatively scientific and objective enterprise. Pure structuralist exegesis, however, results in a translation of the Gospel into secular language in which God becomes a mere cipher for anything unusually good in human experience.[36]

5.2.2 The Method

Few of the structuralist studies of the parables actually embrace a full-orbed structuralist ideology, although they may accept some of its deterministic and atheistic presuppositions. Usually structuralism is seen as simply one more method to add to the existing arsenal of approaches. Like the new hermeneutic, it takes for granted the standard tradition-critical dissection of the Gospel texts and then applies its own analysis to the remaining, autonomous core of authentic parable material. At this level important implications for the authenticity as well as the interpretation of the parables emerge.

1. Although initially disavowing historical concerns, several structuralist analyses of the parables have discerned patterns of narrative which they believe characterize the authentic parables of Jesus. Substantial divergences from these patterns then render certain other parables suspect as inauthentic. Gerhard Sellin, for example, argues that most of the parables found only in Luke have three main characters—a king/father/master figure with two subordinates (sons/servants), one of whom is a good example and the other bad. One thinks, thus, of the parables of the prodigal son, the rich man and Lazarus, or the Pharisee and publican (where God himself is implicit as the third figure hearing the prayers of the other two).

In each case the protagonist of the story is the good subordinate, even if Jesus' definition of "good" may overturn conventional expectations. In the other Gospels, however, this triadic structure is less frequent, and when it does appear, the main character seems to be the authority figure, for instance the king who gave the marriage feast for his son (Mt 22:1-10) or the vineyard owner who destroyed his wicked tenants (Mk 12:1-9 pars.). Sellin concludes, therefore, that the peculiarly Lukan parables are largely inauthentic.[37]

---

[36]Of many possible examples, a particularly interesting one is Earl Breech, "Kingdom of God and the Parables of Jesus," *Semeia* 12 (1978): 15-40.

[37]Gerhard Sellin, "Lukas als Gleichniserzähler: die Erzählung vom barmherzigen Samariter (Lk 10, 25-37)," *ZNW* 65 (1974):166-89; 66 (1975): 19-60; idem, "Gleichnisstrukturen," *LingBib* 31 (1974):89-115.

Sellin's structural analysis, however, greatly resembles Goulder's redactional study (see above, pp. 121-22) in that he approaches the evidence very selectively. Several of the distinctively Lukan parables have only one or two main characters—for instance, the rich fool, the barren fig tree, the friend at midnight and the unjust judge— while a distinctively Matthean parable like that of the two sons (Mt 21:28-32) almost exactly reflects the structure and significance of the parable of the prodigal in Luke. In addition, the parable of the lost coin (Lk 15:8-10) has as its protagonist the "authority" figure (the woman) while the unjust steward (Lk 16:1-13) fits into neither of Sellin's main categories. Despite its polemical nature, W. G. Kümmel's response to Sellin seems justified: "this self-defeating stand against 'almost all parable research' leads him fully astray, in spite of all his exerted erudition, and it is incomprehensible to me how such a faulty argument could be accepted as part of a dissertation."[38]

2. *In fact, more careful structuralist analysis enhances the case for the parables' authenticity.* Dan Via evaluates the fourteen major narrative parables in the Gospels under eight headings, which correspond to the standard types of binary oppositions which structuralists typically examine. These include (a) tragic vs. comic plot, (b) sequence of episodes (crisis-response-denouement vs. action-crisis-denouement), (c) subject does or does not receive the object or goal of the narrative, (d) subject desires to retain this object vs. communicating it to someone else, (e) causal vs. chronological connection between events, (f) subject unifies action vs. being only a part of the action, (g) subject ordains his own activity vs. acting on behalf of another, and (h) subject and ordainer are inferior/superior vs. equal.

Via determines that six of Jesus' parables are identical on all eight of these counts—three found only in Matthew, one found only in Luke, one common to Matthew, Mark and Luke, and one common to Matthew and Luke—and that the others vary only minimally from this pattern. Thus, far from pitting the parables in one Gospel source against those in another, structuralist analysis confirms that a cross-section of all the Gospel sources shows Jesus speaking in a consistent way, with the "deep structures" of his parables revealing

---

[38]Werner G. Kümmel, "Jesusforschung seit 1965," *ThRu* 43 (1978):141.

consistent patterns not readily imitated by a later author writing in Jesus' name.[39]

3. *Although Sellin's conclusions concerning the inauthenticity of the parables are unwarranted, his structural analysis does offer a helpful way of classifying the parables.* Focusing on the number and nature of main characters provides a more objective criterion for classification than the vague, thematic headings so commonly used in books on the parables (cf., e.g., Jeremias's chapter titles—"Now Is the Day of Salvation," "God's Mercy for Sinners," "The Great Assurance," "The Imminence of Catastrophe," "It May Be Too Late," "The Challenge of the Hour," etc.—most parables could easily fit under several if not all of these headings).

Helpful, too, are Via's study of the plots of the parables, identifying those which are "comic" (ending with a note of hope), "tragic" (ending with the threat of disaster) or open-ended, and Crossan's threefold categorization of parables of "advent" (disclosing God's surprising grace), "reversal" (rewarding or punishing behavior in unconventional ways) and "action" (enjoining specific ethical activity).[40] Robert Funk has introduced additional categories by combining the type of analysis of characters begun by Sellin with the analysis of plot instituted by Via to distinguish parables with comic or tragic reversals of fates, each in turn subdivided according to whether the protagonist is a master or subordinate figure.[41]

For the purposes of this study, the most significant implication of this structuralist analysis is that each parable looks slightly different depending on which character a given member of its audience identifies with. If it is legitimate to speak of three main points in the parable of the prodigal son, associated with each of its three main characters, then the structuralists' recognition of this triadic pattern in many other passages suggests that a similar approach to interpretation will apply quite widely among Jesus' parables. One point may be emphasized more than others, however, if one character is more dominant in the narrative. Funk himself earlier observed that

---

[39]Dan O. Via, Jr., "Parable and Example Story: A Literary-Structuralist Approach," *Semeia* 1 (1974):105-33.

[40]Idem, *The Parables: Their Literary and Existential Dimension* (Philadelphia: Fortress, 1967); J. D. Crossan, *In Parables: The Challenge of the Historical Jesus* (New York and London: Harper & Row, 1973).

[41]Robert W. Funk, *Parables and Presence* (Philadelphia: Fortress, 1982), esp. pp. 35-54.

Jesus aims the parables of grace in three different directions: (1)
he sometimes directs attention to the poor and the sinners
(. . . Mk. 2:17 . . .), (2) he sometimes invites the righteous and
wealthy to consider themselves (. . . Mt. 12:34 . . .); or, (3) he
may draw attention indirectly to God (. . . Lk. 15:7)[42]
In light of his more recent structuralist studies, it seems logical to
conclude that all three of these aims may play a part in any given
triadic parable, even if one is more noteworthy in one specific context than another. Going beyond Funk, but based on his studies,
this also suggests that the parts of a particular parable most likely
to be invested with allegorical import are the two or three main
characters which regularly appear as images of God, his faithful
followers and the rebellious in need of repentance.

    4. *Much structuralist study of the parables, however, focuses on other issues,*
the most popular of which is actantial *analysis.* This approach identifies six
actants—characters or objects—which are fundamental to every narrative plot. Specifically, a *sender* seeks to communicate an *object* to a
receiver by means of a *subject* who may be aided by a *helper* and hindered by an *opponent*. Not all of the six actants appear in every
narrative, and two or more actantial roles may be filled by the same
character. Identifying the actants supposedly reduces the story to
its most basic level. These are often exhibited in diagrammatic form
as follows:

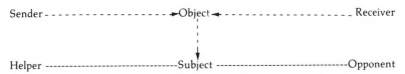

Pheme Perkins has integrated this type of structuralism with other
more traditional forms of exegesis in her semipopular book on interpreting the parables. She diagrams the parable of the rich man
and Lazarus, for example, in the following fashion:[43]

[42]Funk, *Language,* p. 15. Arens, *Handlungen,* pp. 358-59, agrees that most of the parables operate
on three levels at the same time: expressing Jesus' solidarity with the outcasts of Israel, justifying
Jesus' behavior over against his critics, and claiming as his rationale the in-breaking of God's
kingdom. Cf. also Wolfgang Harnisch, *Die Gleichniserzählungen Jesu* (Göttingen: Vandenhoeck &
Ruprecht, 1985) passim.
[43]Perkins, *Parables,* p. 69.

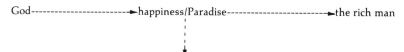

God----------------------►happiness/Paradise----------------------►the rich man

Moses/Prophets - - - - - - - - - the rich man - - - - - - - - his own pleasure/negligence

In other words, God wants to communicate eternal happiness to all, but the rich man, who in this instance is both subject and would-be receiver, cannot obtain this gift because his lifestyle stands in the way. Obedience to Scripture (Moses and the prophets) could have removed this obstacle.

This kind of diagram quickly enables the interpreter to separate the essential elements of a passage from subordinate details. In this case, for example, the diagram reinforces the observation that the parable of the rich man and Lazarus is not about the nature of the afterlife but about the need to exhibit true godliness through stewardship in this life. Nevertheless, one does not need structuralism to come to this realization. Most of the valid insights of actantial analysis simply restate in fairly technical and esoteric terminology what careful interpreters knew anyway, so it is not surprising that the movement has already noticeably waned.[44]

5.2.3 Surface Structures
Structuralism as an ideology plays down the importance of more traditional formalist or new critical concern for the surface features of a text in favor of analyzing its deep structures. So some scholars do not refer to an analysis of surface structures as structuralist at all, preferring some term like *rhetorical criticism* or *stylistics* (although these terms also refer to much broader lines of inquiry). Regardless of the label, recent research has been immeasurably enhanced by a number of studies which concentrate on various literary features of the parables and suggest that they are more tightly woven unities than tradition-critical dissection typically asserts. Most notable in this category are Kenneth Bailey's expositions, which pay careful attention to repetition and parallelism, highlighting those elements intended to have climactic significance. Bailey has been

---

[44]In retrospect, Norman Perrin's insights to this effect, published already in 1976, have proved very prophetic (*Jesus,* p. 205). One recent evangelical attempt to promote actantial analysis of the parables is an exception: Christian R. Davis, "Structural Analysis of Jesus' Narrative Parables: A Conservative Approach," *GTJ* 9 (1988):191-204.

especially sensitive to the presence of chiasmus or inverted parallelism.

To cite just one of many possible examples, Luke's parable of the lost sheep turns out to be a carefully constructed chiasmus in which the concluding sentence ("I tell you that in the same way there is more rejoicing in heaven over one sinner who repents than over ninety-nine righteous who need no repentance"—Lk 15:7), far from being the secondary addition it is usually alleged to be, perfectly balances the opening question ("Which of you having a hundred sheep and losing one of them does not leave the ninety-nine . . . ?"— v. 4). Both verses begin with a direct address to "you," then refer to the "one," and conclude with the "ninety-nine." In between, vv. 5-6 introduce the themes of "losing," "finding" and "rejoicing," and then repeat them in inverse order. This leaves the first part of verse 6 ("he goes home and calls his friends and neighbors together") as the climactic center, a detail not always emphasized in treatments of this narrative.

A. Which one of you
B. one
C. ninety-nine
  1. the lost
    2. find
      3. joy
        4. restoration
      3'. joy
    2'. find
  1'. the lost
A'. I say to you
B'. one
C'. ninety-nine

Such communal celebration over a lost sheep would have been extraordinary among Palestinian shepherds; it is one of those "atypical features" which emphasizes the nonliteral referents of the parables. Although a shepherd may search almost as diligently for a lost sheep as God does for unredeemed humanity, the heavenly celebration over a saved sinner, without a doubt, far surpasses the typical shepherd's relief at finding his strayed animal.[45]

This type of structural analysis clearly enhances both the case for the parable's authenticity and our grasp of its meaning, and it is to be welcomed appreciatively. Similar studies of the parable of the prodigal son and of the rich man and Lazarus have pointed out intricate synonymous parallelism between the respective "halves" of each narrative (Lk 15:11-24, 25-32; 16:19-23, 24-31), thus challenging the view which sees the second "half" in each case as a later addition to Jesus' original, as well as highlighting the details most emphasized in each story.[46] But too few studies of the parables have utilized this kind of careful structural analysis. Clearly, much productive work in this area remains to be done. The valid contributions of formalism or new criticism in secular literary studies offer a well-established model to point the way ahead.[47]

5.3 Poststructuralism

The late 1960s and early 1970s not only provided the new hermeneutic and structuralism with their first widespread appropriation by New Testament scholars, but they also spawned a number of other avant-garde movements in literary criticism. Two of these originated in direct repudiation of certain key principles of structuralism and have therefore been labeled poststructuralist. These are generally referred to as "deconstruction" and "reader-response criticism." Applications in the field of biblical studies have arisen almost entirely in the last decade, so assessment of their potential contribution remains rather tentative.

What is clear is that both reject the structuralists' claim to find objective meaning in the text, while accepting the structuralists' critique of previous approaches to interpretation which tried to reconstruct authorial intention. But if the meaning of a work of literature is not to be found in the thoughts of its original author

---

[45]Kenneth E. Bailey, *Poet and Peasant: A Literary-Cultural Approach to the Parables in Luke* (Grand Rapids: Eerdmans, 1976), pp. 144-56. Cf. passim and idem, *Through Peasant Eyes: More Lucan Parables* (Grand Rapids: Eerdmans, 1980), for additional illustrations.

[46]Tolbert, *Parables*, pp. 98-101; F. Schnider and W. Stenger, "Die offene Tür und die unüberschreitbare Kluft," *NTS* 25 (1979):276.

[47]An excellent, concise introduction to those elements of new criticism most relevant to biblical studies appears in Lynn M. Poland, *Literary Criticism and Biblical Hermeneutics: A Critique of Formalist Approaches* (Chico: Scholars, 1985), pp. 65-105. Scott, *Hear*, regularly includes a section on "surface structure" in his commentary on each of the parables.

or in the language of the text which he wrote, then the only remaining option is that meaning is the creation of the individual reader. Less radical forms of poststructuralism ameliorate this view somewhat by speaking of the interaction between text and reader, but they agree that meaning is largely subjective and varies from one person to the next.

5.3.1 Deconstruction

By far the most unorthodox movement to unsettle the literary horizon in recent generations, deconstruction is a method most closely associated with the French philosopher and interpreter of Nietzsche, Jacques Derrida. Its avowed purpose is one of "generating conflicting meanings from the same text, and playing those meanings against each other" to show how every piece of writing ultimately "deconstructs" or undermines itself.[48] The interpreter or reader is free to associate apparently unrelated texts, interpreting one in light of the other by common vocabulary, themes or structures, however marginal, so long as the resulting interpretation is interesting and provocative. Cleverness rather than validity is the goal, inasmuch as there is no objective standard by which to judge the rightness or wrongness of a particular interpretation. The catchword for this practice in deconstructive terminology is *freeplay.*

John Dominic Crossan, whose prolific writing leaves him unmatched in total output among recent commentators on the parables, has adopted almost every new literary method somewhere in his work, including deconstruction.[49] Some of the deconstructive tendency surfaces in his thesis that parables "subvert world," or in his more technical definition of parables as "paradoxes formed into story by effecting single or double reversals of the audience's most profound expectations."[50] But deconstructionists' delight in turning

---

[48]T. K. Seung, *Structuralism and Hermeneutics* (New York: Columbia, 1982), p. 271, who offers a vigorous but justified critique of the movement. More neutral but relatively clear introductions to a discipline not intended to be readily understandable appear in Jonathan Culler, *On Deconstruction: Theory and Criticism after Structuralism* (Ithaca: Cornell, 1982; London: Routledge & Kegan Paul, 1983); and Christopher Norris, *Deconstruction: Theory and Practice* (London and New York: Methuen, 1982).

[49]For an outline of Crossan's methodological pilgrimage, see Frank B. Brown and Elizabeth S. Malbon, "Parabling as a Via Negativa: A Critical Review of the Work of John Dominic Crossan," *JR* 64 (1984):530-38.

[50]J. D. Crossan, *Raid on the Articulate: Comic Eschatology in Jesus and Borges* (New York and London: Harper & Row, 1976), p. 98.

a text in on itself appears most explicitly in his analysis of the parable of the sower as a parable about how parables are heard, and even more clearly in his discussion of "polyvalent" (multilayered) interpretation.[51]

Ironically, Crossan here discloses his greatest openness to allegory, but he distinguishes between allegory which is "mimetic" (depicting reality) and that which is "ludic" (simply "playing" with the text, because all reality is play!). The latter, a clever but unchecked association of concepts, is practiced because the text has no fixed meaning: "Since you cannot interpret absolutely, you can interpret forever." Thus the parable of the prodigal son can be read as "an allegory of Western consciousness's path from mimetic to ludic realism"—the father standing for reality, the older son representing that type of interpretation which tries to be faithful to reality and the prodigal as the one who abandons such a quest. Thus the inversion of the two sons' roles at the story's conclusion proves that, with respect to reality, "he who finds the meaning loses it, and he who loses it finds it"![52]

There is no question that deconstruction applied to the parables can be clever and entertaining. To the extent that it focuses on the revolutionary and subversive force of Jesus' speech, so often lost to modern audiences immunized against its radical nature by centuries of domesticating interpretation, it performs a valuable service. But as a full-fledged method of interpretation, by its own principles it is self-defeating. Deconstructive criticism inevitably undermines itself.

Because deconstruction does not believe that reality is an objective entity to be taken seriously, we might fairly question whether deconstructive critics should be taken seriously.[53] Not surprisingly, most deconstructionists sooner or later break away from the extremes with which they elsewhere flirt, and stress that the value of their method lies more in its greater emphasis on the role of the

---

[51]Idem, *Cliffs of Fall: Paradox and Polyvalence in the Parables of Jesus* (New York: Seabury, 1980), pp. 25-64, 65-104.

[52]Ibid., pp. 102, 103, 101.

[53]Cf. the incisive assessment of M. H. Abrams, "The Limits of Pluralism II. The Deconstructive Angel," *Critical Inquiry* 3 (1977):425-38. From a very different perspective, but equally critical, cf. Bruce J. Malina, "Reader Response Theory: Discovery or Redundancy?" *Creighton University Faculty Journal* 5 (1986):55-66. Although Malina's title refers only to reader-response criticism, his critique applies to all of poststructuralism and especially to deconstruction.

reader in imparting meaning to texts and in observing usually over-looked, marginal details and hidden tensions in those texts.[54]

Paul de Man apparently backs away even further by seeming to suggest that performative utterances are exempt from deconstruction. A promise, for example, is grounded in a historical context from which it may not be detached.[55] In this event, the parables as performatives should be equally immune to deconstruction. So too Michael LaFargue persuasively argues that a substantial measure of indeterminacy in the meaning of a text does not hinder it from having a "determinative substantive content," which ought to be the primary focus of interpretation.[56] In fact, the popularity of deconstruction overall is already beginning to fade and is not likely to survive even in many poststructuralist circles, which are rapidly turning instead to reader-response criticism.

5.3.2 Reader-Response Criticism

Less unified than the other movements so far described, reader-response criticism has come to refer to a diverse collection of approaches which all focus on the factors that influence interpreters as they read a given text. These approaches agree that at least a part of the text's meaning is created by the reader during the process of interaction with the text, often in conjunction with previous approaches to the work with which the reader is familiar. Thus, like the new hermeneutic, they stress the subjectivity of interpretation. Over against the new hermeneutic they do not attribute this to the transcendent power of words to create "language events" but to the belief that meaning is, at least to a large extent, in the eye of the beholder.[57]

---

[54]See the helpful summary and assessment by Edgar V. McKnight, *The Bible and the Reader* (Philadelphia: Fortress, 1985), pp. 84-94. Cf. also the relatively sympathetic evaluation, from an evangelical perspective, in Clarence Walhout, "Texts and Actions," in Roger Lundin, Anthony C. Thiselton and Clarence Walhout, *The Responsibility of Hermeneutics* (Grand Rapids: Eerdmans; Exeter: Paternoster, 1985), pp. 34-42.

[55]Paul de Man, *Allegories of Reading* (New Haven and London: Yale Univ. Press, 1979), pp. 270-77.

[56]Michael LaFargue, "Are Texts Determinate? Derrida, Barth, and the Role of the Biblical Scholar." *HTR* 81 (1988):341-57.

[57]One of the best introductions is the anthology edited by Jane P. Tompkins, *Reader-Response Criticism* (Baltimore and London: Johns Hopkins, 1980); more briefly, cf. Robert M. Fowler, "Who Is 'The Reader' in Reader Response Criticism?" *Semeia* 31 (1985):5-23. For application to the Gospels, see James L. Resseguie, "Reader-Response Criticism and the Synoptic Gospels," *JAAR* 52 (1984):307-24.

The application of reader-response criticism to the parables in many ways resembles that of deconstruction, most notably in its openness to allegory—not as the most legitimate way to understand their original meaning but as one of an unlimited number of viable interpretations.[58] The ambiguous and enigmatic nature of many of the parables would seem to support this new movement's claim that meaning lies not so much (and, for some, not at all) in what the original author intended nor in what the text actually says, but rather in what the interpreter chooses to make of it. If so, the best that could be said of the type of allegorical approach I will elaborate in part two is that it is one of many possible approaches, but not a very good (i.e., creative) one since it focuses almost exclusively on what the details of the parables most likely meant in their original contexts![59] Obviously the question about the locus of meaning in a work requires more careful attention.

5.3.2.1 The Location of Meaning

1. Clearly an author's intention cannot be the sole key to understanding the meaning of a text. An author may fail to execute his intention and produce a text which says something different from what he wanted it to say. Or he may not realize the full extent of his text's meaning, as when he unwittingly writes something susceptible of a double entendre, where more than one meaning arises from the words he has chosen. Many authors have responded to reviews of their work by admitting the validity of certain interpretations which they had not consciously foreseen. Wimsatt and Beardsley's celebrated article on the "intentional fallacy" challenged long-cherished views by making these and other telling points.[60] As a result, virtually no literary critic today endorses a full-fledged "intentionalism."

---

[58]See esp. Frank Kermode's celebrated *The Genesis of Secrecy* (Cambridge, Mass.: Harvard Univ. Press, 1979) based largely on his interpretation of Mark 4:11-12. Cf. the evenhanded but penetrating critique by David S. Greenwood, "Poststructuralism and Biblical Studies: Frank Kermode's *The Genesis of Secrecy*," in *Gospel Perspectives*, vol. 3, ed. R. T. France and David Wenham (Sheffield: JSOT, 1983), pp. 263-88.

[59]Mikeal C. Parsons, " 'Allegorizing Allegory': Narrative Analysis and Parable Interpretation," *PRS* 15 (1988):147-64, is more positive about allegorical interpretation—at the level of reader-response not of authorial intention.

[60]W. K. Wimsatt and M. C. Beardsley, "The Intentional Fallacy," in *The Verbal Icon*, ed. W. K. Wimsatt (Lexington: Univ. of Kentucky Press, 1954), pp. 2-18.

Perhaps the closest anyone comes to this is E. D. Hirsch. Yet even he can juxtapose three potentially contradictory statements: "*Meaning* is that which is represented by a text; it is what the author meant by his use of a particular sign sequence; it is what the signs represent."[61] The first and third of these clauses assign the locus of meaning to the text. Only the middle one speaks of authorial intent, and even then not apart from the actual written symbols which are produced to convey that intention.

Formalists or new critics have undoubtedly undervalued the role of historical and biographical information about the life and times of the author as an aid to understanding the meaning of his writing, especially when they imagine a text as an autonomous entity divorced from the external circumstances of its composition. But they nevertheless rightly stress that the immediate literary context of any given passage must take priority over background information, acquired from other sources, in interpreting that passage's meaning.

2. One does well to emphasize just as strenuously the impropriety of the notion of many reader-response critics that meaning is the construct of the individual reader. This is to confuse meaning with significance, interpretation with application.[62] To be sure, reader-response criticism has very properly stressed that different readers disagree on the original meaning of texts and that a certain type of pluralism in interpretation is inevitable.[63] Further, every author writes with a certain kind of audience in mind, and valid interpretation needs to try to reconstruct that audience in order best to understand the meaning of the texts designed for it.

Reader-response critics' study of the "implied reader" in a text (or even better the "authorial reader"—the actual reader envisaged by the author rather than simply the one implied by the text) rightly

---

[61]E. D. Hirsch, *Validity in Interpretation* (New Haven and London: Yale Univ. Press, 1967), p. 8. Hirsch's *Aims of Interpretation* (Chicago and London: Univ. of Chicago Press, 1976) makes it clear that meaning is not limited solely to authorial intent (e.g., pp. 79-80). For an insightful analysis of Hirsch's inconsistencies see William E. Cain, "Authority, 'Cognitive Atheism,' and the Aims of Interpretation: The Literary Theory of E. D. Hirsch," *College English* 39 (1977):333-45.

[62]That such a distinction even exists, of course, is repudiated by most reader-response critics, but see P. D. Juhl, *Interpretation* (Princeton and Guildford: Princeton Univ. Press, 1980), pp. 12-14.

[63]See esp. Wayne C. Booth, *Critical Understanding: The Powers and Limits of Pluralism* (Chicago and London: Univ. of Chicago Press, 1979).

focuses on this fact.[64] But when one speaks of an unlimited number of often largely unrelated interpretations as valid, varying widely from one reader to the next, then one falls into the same self-defeating trap as ensnares the deconstructionists. Sooner or later most all reader-response critics back away from a fully reader-centered hermeneutic and insist that every valid interpretation must meet specific criteria of coherence and must fit various details of the text.

Stanley Fish, perhaps the most famous advocate of reader-centered theories, is more consistent in his method than many, but frankly admits that the position he puts forward is one by which no one could live.[65] But many critics do live by the belief that there are numerous models of interpretation that one may adopt, each with its own rules and none with any necessary claim to superiority.[66]

3. Most desirable is a holistic model that interprets the words of a text in the context of the larger semantic structures in which they are embedded and that includes what the text discloses concerning the author's original intentions for the type of audience he envisaged as readers.

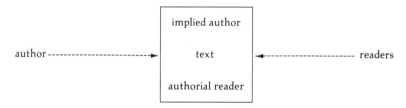

Certain less radical reader-response critics have proposed precisely such models,[67] although they need to be supplemented, on the one hand, with an openness to using any relevant information outside

---

[64]To use the terms of Wolfgang Iser, *The Implied Reader* (Baltimore and London: Johns Hopkins, 1974), and Norman R. Petersen, "The Reader in the Gospel," *Neotestamentica* 18 (1984):38-51, respectively.

[65]Stanley Fish, *Is There a Text in This Class?* (Cambridge, Mass., and London: Harvard Univ. Press, 1980), p. 370. Stephen D. Moore, "Negative Hermeneutics, Insubstantial Texts: Stanley Fish and the Biblical Interpreter," *JAAR* 54 (1986):707-19, is less pessimistic but does make it clear that reader-response criticism does not allow for traditional belief in biblical authority.

[66]Cf. McKnight, *Bible and Reader*, pp. 115-34.

[67]Cf. ibid.; Hubert Frankemölle, "Kommunikatives Handeln in Gleichnissen Jesu," *NTS* 28 (1982):61-90; and from the perspective of a critique of reader-response criticism, Steven Mailloux, *Interpretive Conventions: The Reader in the Study of American Fiction* (Ithaca and London: Cornell, 1982), p. 112.

the text which sheds further light on the intentions of the author and, on the other hand, with a humble recognition of the substantial, often unconscious, interpretive filters through which every reader sifts texts as he responds to them.

P. D. Juhl, who would vigorously disassociate himself from most forms of poststructuralism, has perhaps come as close as any among modern literary critics to articulating such an approach. Juhl also incorporates a robust defense of the view that a text has one determinable, fixed interpretation, even though it may be a complex composite of several related, partial interpretations arrived at only after much hard work.[68]

I do not make as ambitious claims as these for the exegetical chapters of part two. These chapters' comments more closely resemble Juhl's preliminary, partial interpretations, but they seek to improve on many of the current views which compete for supporters.

5.3.2.2 Application to the Parables

Biblical scholarship's appropriation of reader-response criticism is still in its infancy, so many of the possible applications to a collection of passages like the parables remain to be explored. Initial studies have tended to combine this method with others, a strategy which may prove to be the most helpful.

Susan Wittig, for example, advocates a combination of structural analysis (of both surface and deep structures) with reader-response criticism, in order to generate a "first-order system" of fixed meaning for a given narrative, which in turn leads to "second-order systems" of meanings of indeterminate nature.[69] But the systems are linked "iconically," that is, the significance and relationship of the various components of the parable with respect to each other remain constant.

Thus, a typical historical-critical reading of the prodigal son might see the father reflecting God's love, the prodigal representing the tax collectors and sinners with whom Jesus associated, and the older

---

[68]Juhl, *Interpretation*, esp. pp. 199-200.

[69]Susan Wittig, "Meaning and Modes of Signification: Toward a Semiotic of the Parable," in *Semiology and Parables*, ed. Daniel Patte (Pittsburgh: Pickwick, 1976), pp. 319-47; cf. idem, "A Theory of Multiple Meanings," *Semeia* 9 (1977):75-103. Cf. also Tolbert, *Parables*, pp. 68-72.

brother as an image of the Pharisaic objectors to Jesus' mercy. But in the later church, these same three figures might more naturally point to two different types of Christians responding to beneficent pastoral leadership. For modern psychoanalysts, they quite readily resemble the contrasting roles played by the id and superego in response to the mediation of the ego.[70] For Crossan, as already noted, they can even be taken to reflect two types of allegory responding to reality. But there is something analogous in all these interpretations—one figure is a reckless, undisciplined, surprising recipient of grace, who contrasts with a conventional, moralistic, and unsympathetic opponent, while both respond to the same mediating authority.

As Sandra Perpich has convincingly demonstrated, however, once Wittig's theory is more felicitously phrased in terms of Hirsch's distinction between meaning and significance, what Wittig is doing is not demonstrating polyvalent or pluralist interpretation but multiple contexts for application.[71] The original setting provides the context for interpreting a text's meaning. Subsequent readers then translate that meaning into analogous terminology in order to apply the text in a significant way to themselves. The first task is bounded by objective constraints; the latter, in principle, is endless.

Parables like the prodigal son, where the reaction of the older brother to his father's appeals remains unspecified at the end, are so self-evidently and purposefully incomplete that they cry out for the reader's involvement. Will one be willing to love the unlovely or not? The text compels its reader to respond existentially. To the extent that reader-response criticism requires commentators to apply the parables to their own lives rather than being satisfied with an exegesis which stops short of personally involving the interpreter, it provides an invaluable service. But this is not the way it usually advertises itself, and many of its claims mislead readers into thinking that they have the power actually to create meaning for texts.

---

[70]Mary A. Tolbert, "The Prodigal Son: An Essay in Literary Criticism from a Psychoanalytic Perspective," *Semeia* 9 (1977):1-20.

[71]Sandra W. Perpich, *A Hermeneutic Critique of Structuralist Exegesis, with Specific Reference to Lk 10.29-37* (Lanham, Md.: University Press of America, 1984), pp. 184-94.

5.4 Other Methods

Additional trends in literary criticism have occasionally impinged on parable interpretation, such as the psychological analysis of the parable of the prodigal son noted above (p. 160).[72] Sociological and cultural-anthropological studies have illuminated the Gospels at many points, and these affect a reading of the parables especially where Jesus addresses economic topics.[73] But these applications of social science, though often set forward as part of another competing method alongside historical, form, redaction, hermeneutic, structuralist or poststructuralist criticism, seem instead just to be specialized forms of either historical criticism or poststructuralism.

To the extent, for example, that a study of the economics of first-century Palestine illuminates the class conflict between the few wealthy landowners and the majority of poor, landless peasant workers, the realism of the revolt of the wicked tenants against their absentee landlord takes on an added dimension. This is simply another branch of historical criticism, enabling one to realize that what is unusual and therefore most significant in the parable is not the tenants' violence as much as the landlord's patience and apparent foolishness in sending his son to die at their hands.[74]

On the other hand, when certain liberation theologians filter such a passage through an interpretive grid of Marxist economics so that Jesus becomes an explicit opponent of capitalism, then they are anachronistically imposing a modern ideological grid on an an-

---

[72]Cf., e.g., Louis Beirnaert, "The Parable of the Prodigal Son, Luke 15:11-32, Read by an Analyst," in *Exegesis: Problems of Method and Exercises in Reading (Genesis 22 and Luke 15)*, ed. François Bovon and Gregoire Rouiller (Pittsburgh: Pickwick, 1978), pp. 197-210; Dan O. Via, Jr., "The Prodigal Son: A Jungian Reading," *Semeia* 9 (1977):21-43; idem, "The Parable of the Unjust Judge: A Metaphor of the Unrealized Self," in *Semiology*, ed. Patte, pp. 1-32.

[73]For a sympathetic, evangelical survey of a large number of these studies, see Derek Tidball, *An Introduction to the Sociology of the New Testament* (Exeter: Paternoster, 1983 [= *The Social Context of the New Testament* (Grand Rapids: Zondervan, 1984)]). Cf. esp. Bruce J. Malina, *Christian Origins and Cultural Anthropology* (Atlanta: John Knox, 1986). The field may in fact soon dwarf all of the literary and hermeneutical methods surveyed in this chapter. A detailed bibliography appears in Daniel J. Harrington, "Second Testament Exegesis and the Social Sciences: A Bibliography," *BTB* 18 (1988):77-85. For sample applications which most closely impinge on this discussion, cf. Paul H. Hollenbach, "From Parable to Gospel," *Forum* 2, no. 3 (1986):67-75. Scott, *Hear*, regularly utilizes Malina's research to illuminate the background of numerous texts.

[74]See, e.g., Klyne Snodgrass, *The Parable of the Wicked Tenants* (Tübingen: Mohr, 1983), pp. 31-40.

cient text in a way which does violence to that text.[75] Such a reading of the economics of Jesus has to disregard numerous data which do not fit its grid. To that extent, broadly speaking, they mirror post-structuralists' lack of concern for the historical context of a given work.[76]

5.5 Conclusions

In sum, interpreters of the parables today face a bewildering array of methods from which to choose. If anything, scholarship is becoming more and more fragmented and specialized, leaving the nonspecialist baffled as to where to turn. Certainly every method has made important contributions, and a full-orbed exegesis will do its best to adopt an eclectic approach, incorporating the valid insights of each.[77]

The more limited concern of this chapter has been to see if the two theses concerning the authenticity and allegorical nature of the parables are either threatened or reinforced by the newer literary criticisms. Nothing has emerged which convincingly challenges the authenticity of the parables; practitioners of virtually all of the newer methods are relatively uninterested in historical questions. Usually they just presuppose the conclusions of form and redaction criticism, complete with all their strengths and weaknesses. When they occasionally do join in the "quest for the historical Jesus," their most reliable findings, as with the structuralist studies surveyed, actually support the defender of the parables' authenticity.

The case for the allegorical character of the parables can also be strengthened. More significant than the approach which encourages allegorizing, not all that dissimilar from that which plagued ancient and medieval commentators (more for the sake of its imag-

---

[75]E.g., Fernando Belo, *A Materialist Reading of the Gospel of Mark* (Maryknoll: Orbis, 1981), pp. 185-86. For a better assessment of Jesus' attitude to politics and economics, see Richard J. Cassidy, *Jesus, Politics and Society* (Maryknoll: Orbis, 1978); and cf. the important refinements by Charles H. Talbert, "Martyrdom in Luke-Acts and the Lukan Social Ethic," in *Political Issues in Luke-Acts*, ed. Richard J. Cassidy and Philip J. Scharper (Maryknoll: Orbis, 1983), pp. 99-110.

[76]Cf. Edwin Yamauchi, "Sociology, Scripture and the Supernatural," *JETS* 27 (1984):169-92. On the link between deconstruction and Marxism, see David L. Jeffrey, "Caveat Lector : Structuralism, Deconstructionism, and Ideology," *CSR* 17 (1988):436-48.

[77]Cf. the approach advocated toward literary criticism more generally by Wilfred L. Guerin, Earle G. Labor, Lee Morgan and John R. Willingham, *A Handbook of Critical Approaches to Literature* (New York and London: Harper & Row, 1979); and, specifically for the Gospels, by Charles T. Davis, "A Multidimensional Criticism of the Gospels," in *Orientation*, p. 95.

inative nature than for its legitimacy!), is the recognition that the parables need to be examined as specific examples of the general category of fictional narratives. The meaning of a narrative, in turn, is closely tied to the roles and functions of its main characters, as Funk observed (see above, pp. 148-49).[78]

The evidence which has been accumulating throughout part one therefore suggests a very attractive proposal which would enable commentators to affirm more than just one point per parable without moving to the opposite extreme and endorsing an unlimited number of points: *each parable makes one main point per main character— usually two or three in each case—and these main characters are the most likely elements within the parable to stand for something other than themselves, thus giving the parable its allegorical nature.* It may well be frequently possible to combine these main points into a statement of one central truth that the passage teaches. But the shorter and more concise such a statement becomes, the more it risks missing some of the wealth of the parable's detail. At the same time, elements other than the main characters will have metaphorical referents only to the extent that they fit in with the meaning established by the referents of the main characters, and all allegorical interpretation must result in that which would have been intelligible to a first-century Palestinian audience. This last restriction will sharply distinguish the type of allegory defended here from the largely anachronistic allegorizing both of patristic and medieval exegesis and of many forms of post-structuralism. Part two will test these hypotheses via individual discussions of each of Jesus' major parables.

---

[78]So also Robert C. Tannehill, "The Disciples in Mark: The Function of a Narrative Role," *JR* 57 (1977):386-405; Resseguie, "Reader-Response Criticism," p. 321; Roland M. Frye, "The Jesus of the Gospels: Approaches through Narrative Structure," in *From Faith to Faith*, ed. D. Y. Hadidian (Pittsburgh: Pickwick, 1979), p. 79; Kaiser, *Exegetical Theology*, p. 205; Frederick H. Borsch, *Many Things in Parables: Extravagant Stories of New Community* (Philadelphia: Fortress, 1988), p. 2 et passim.

Conclusions to Part One

THE MOST IMPORTANT CONCLUSIONS TO WHICH THIS HALF OF the book has pointed may now be listed ad seriatim. They may be divided into conclusions which deal with the interpretation of the parables and those which deal with their authenticity.

Interpretation

1. Two of the most well-entrenched principles of twentieth-century parable interpretation are: (a) at least for the most part, the parables of Jesus are not allegories, and (b) each parable makes one main point.

2. In light of the nature of the earliest rabbinic parables and in light of the developments of modern secular literary criticism, both of these principles are more misleading than helpful.

3. A better approach distinguishes among various degrees of allegorical interpretation, recognizing that every parable of Jesus contains certain elements which point to a second level of meaning and others which do not.

4. To avoid the errors of past allegorizers, modern interpreters must also assign meanings to the details of parables which Jesus' original audiences could have been expected to discern.

5. While the parables do present largely lifelike portrayals of first-century Palestinian Judaism, key details in them are surprisingly unrealistic and serve to point out an allegorical level of meaning.

6. Recent literary and hermeneutical challenges to the viability of propositionally paraphrasing the parables offer important insights but fail to disprove its legitimacy.

7. The same must be said of those who denigrate the importance or possibility of reconstructing a fixed, original meaning of a text. No interpreter will capture it all, but some will do better than others.

Two additional principles of interpretation suggest themselves as hypotheses to be tested:

8. The main characters of a parable will probably be the most common candidates for allegorical interpretation, and the main points of the parable will most likely be associated with these characters.

9. The triadic structure of most of Jesus' narrative parables suggests that most parables may make three points, though some will probably make only one or two.

Authenticity

1. The Synoptic parables may be accepted as authentic sayings of Jesus, assuming that authenticity is defined in terms of *ipsissima vox Jesu* and not just *ipsissima verba Jesu.*

2. This authenticity extends to all of the words attributed to Jesus in conjunction with the parables, including introductions, conclusions and aphoristic generalizations, contra Jeremias's "laws of transformation."

3. Differences between parallel accounts of the same parable nevertheless prove that both the oral tradition and the evangelists in their editorial activity have modified the exact wording of Jesus' original speech.

4. But these differences serve only to improve style and intelligibility and to highlight distinctive redactional themes; they do not in any way distort what Jesus originally said or meant.

5. Other data which impinge on the historical reliability of the Gospels, such as the practices of ancient oral tradition more generally, reinforce a fairly conservative model of the transmission of Jesus' teaching.

6. The common argument for the authenticity of the parables of Jesus based on their distinctives vis-à-vis the rabbinic parables is probably exaggerated.

7. On the other hand, newer literary analyses, such as structuralism, can demonstrate literary unity in parables often dissected by tradition critics and can point out distinctive deep structures not readily fabricated by imitators.

8. Moreover, Jesus' radical message, regularly subverting his audiences' expectations, sets his parables off from most other forms of teaching in the ancient Jewish and Greco-Roman worlds.

Part II
The Meaning &
Significance
of Individual Parables

6
Simple Three-Point Parables

MANY OF JESUS' PARABLES HAVE THREE MAIN CHARACTERS. Quite frequently, these characters include an authority figure and two contrasting subordinates. The authority figure, usually a king, father or master, typically acts as a judge between the two subordinates, who in turn exhibit contrasting behavior (see diagram below).

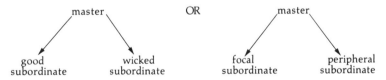

These have been called *monarchic* parables, since in each case the central or unifying character (the character who directly relates to each of the other two) is the master or king figure.[1] Often the particular underling, a servant or son, who would have seemed to a first-century Jewish audience to have acted in a praiseworthy

[1]See esp. Robert W. Funk, *Parables and Presence* (Philadelphia: Fortress, 1982), pp. 29-54; cf. Gerhard Sellin, "Lukas als Gleichniserzähler: die Erzählung vom barmherzigen Samariter (Lk 10, 25-37)," *ZNW* 65 (1974):180-89.

manner, is declared to be less righteous than his apparently wicked counterpart. Jesus stands conventional expectation on its head.[2]

One of the best-loved of all Jesus' parables, the story of the prodigal son, clearly illustrates this structural paradigm. It also highlights the problems facing those who would divorce parable from allegory and restrict a parable's meaning to one main point. This parable will be examined in some detail, therefore, followed by a more cursory look at other parables with this same simple three-point or "triadic" structure. Since chapters three and four have already surveyed the most significant differences between parallel accounts of the same parable, usually only the earliest version of each passage will be discussed here. Exceptions include those parallels which are so similar that no version is demonstrably earlier, and those which may not be parallel at all.

6.1 The Prodigal Son (Lk 15:11-32)

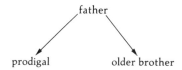

The parable of the prodigal son poses special problems for the theory that parables can make only one main point. Its traditional title suggests that the main purpose of the narrative is to encourage all sinners to repent, regardless of the extent to which they may have degraded themselves.[3] This is the feature of the story which first strikes many readers, challenging their natural inclination to judge the prodigal severely. Yet many scholars would point to the second, climactic portion of the story and find the primary emphasis on the rebuke to the hardhearted older brother.[4] Then the main point

---

[2]Cf. esp. J. D. Crossan, *In Parables: The Challenge of the Historical Jesus* (New York and London: Harper & Row, 1973), pp. 53-78, who speaks of "parables of reversal."

[3]E.g., Michael Wilcock, *The Saviour of the World: The Message of Luke's Gospel* (Leicester and Downers Grove: IVP, 1979), pp. 149-57, and William F. Arndt, *The Gospel according to St. Luke* (St. Louis: Concordia, 1956), p. 350, who say next to nothing in their expositions about vv. 25-32.

[4]Thus Frederick W. Danker, *Jesus and the New Age: A Commentary on St. Luke's Gospel* (Philadelphia: Fortress, 1988), p. 275, relabels it "the parable of the reluctant brother"; and Charles H. Talbert, *Reading Luke* (New York: Crossroad, 1982), p. 147, "the response of elder brothers."

becomes one about the need to rejoice in the salvation of others.

Some commentators solve this dilemma by affirming both points and conceding that this is a rare example of a "two-pointed" parable.[5] They observe that the story subdivides neatly into two episodes—verses 11-24 focusing on the younger brother, and verses 25-32 on the older one—whereas most of Jesus' parables are shorter and less clearly divisible. By far the most common approach suggests yet a different main point by concentrating on the role of the father of the two sons as the character who unites both "halves" of the narrative. Then the theme of the story is revealed in the father's extraordinary love and patience with both his sons.[6]

It is hard to deny the presence of any of these three themes in the parable, and it is not easy to combine them all into one simple proposition. A few commentators have rejected the authenticity of verses 25-32 precisely because it does seem to tack on an extra section to an otherwise self-contained story about the return of the wayward son.[7] But Mary Tolbert has shown that there is close structural parallelism between both halves, suggesting that they were a unity from the start. Each section divides into four units alternating between narrated discourse (ND) and direct discourse (DD):

A.	[ND] the younger son's journey away	(vv. 12b-16)
B.	[DD] his decision to return	(vv. 17-19)
C.	[ND] his father's reception	(v. 20)
D.	[DD] his confession and his father's response	(vv. 21-24a)
A'.	[ND] the older son's return home	(vv. 24b-26)
B'.	[DD] the servant's explanation	(v. 27)
C'.	[ND] his father's reception	(v. 28)
D'.	[DD] his accusation and his father's response	(vv. 29-32)

---

[5]Classically, Joachim Jeremias, *The Parables of Jesus* (London: SCM; Philadelphia: Westminster, 1972), p. 131.

[6]See esp. Helmut Thielicke, *The Waiting Father* (London: J. Clarke; New York: Harper & Bros., 1959), pp. 17-40. Cf. Eduard Schweizer, *The Good News according to Luke* (Atlanta: John Knox; London: SPCK, 1984), pp. 247-48; I. Howard Marshall, *The Gospel of Luke* (Exeter: Paternoster; Grand Rapids: Eerdmans, 1978), p. 604.

[7]Esp. Jack T. Sanders, "Tradition and Redaction in Luke xv. 11-32," *NTS* 15 (1968-69):433-38. Sanders also argues that vv. 25-32 are more distinctively Lucan in language, but this claim has been decisively refuted by Joachim Jeremias, "Tradition und Redaktion in Lukas 15," *ZNW* 62 (1971):172-89; and Charles E. Carlston, "Reminiscence and Redaction in Luke 15:11-32," *JBL* 94 (1975):368-90.

Verbal parallels further highlight this symmetry—references to the field in A and A', to the father and his servants in B and B', to coming in and out in C and C', and most importantly to killing the fatted calf and making merry in D and D'. The key refrain of "was dead and is alive" and "was lost and is found" then concludes both major sections.[8] Even the opening verses of the parable by themselves require the episode about the prodigal to have a sequel. Otherwise there would be no need to include the phrases *"two sons,"* "the *younger* of *them,"* "give me the *share,"* and "he *divided* between *them."*

In fact, the parable may just as easily subdivide into three rather than two episodes, one for each of the three main characters: verses 11-20a—the younger son's departure and return; verses 20b-24—the father's welcome; verses 25-32—the older son's reaction.[9] The most compelling resolution of the problem of the parable's meaning therefore seems to be to affirm that it teaches three main points, one per character, and, in this case, one per episode. *(1) Even as the prodigal always had the option of repenting and returning home, so also all sinners, however wicked, may confess their sins and turn to God in contrition. (2) Even as the father went to elaborate lengths to offer reconciliation to the prodigal, so also God offers all people, however undeserving, lavish forgiveness of sins if they are willing to accept it. (3) Even as the older brother should not have begrudged his brother's reinstatement but rather rejoiced in it, so those who claim to be God's people should be glad and not mad that he extends his grace even to the most undeserving.*

Different members of Jesus' audience would have identified themselves most closely with different characters in the parable, so that one of these points might have come across more strongly to them than the others. Those who hear the parable today may also tend to identify with just one of the individuals in the story, so that it is helpful to listen to the parable three times, trying to understand the action from the perspective of a different character each time.[10] But any attempt to exclude a particular perspective loses sight of

---

[8]Mary A. Tolbert, *Perspectives on the Parables* (Philadelphia: Fortress, 1979), pp. 98-100.

[9]A. T. Cadoux, *The Parables of Jesus: Their Art and Use* (London: J. Clarke, 1930; New York: Macmillan, 1931), p. 123; Alex Stock, "Das Gleichnis vom verlorenen Sohn," in *Ethische Predigt und Alltagsverhalten,* ed. Franz Kamphaus and Rolf Zerfass (München: Kaiser; Mainz: Grünewald, 1977), pp. 82-86.

[10]Pierre Grelot, "Le pére et ses deux fils: Luc, XV, 11-32," *RB* 84 (1977): 321-48, 538-65.

a key teaching of Jesus.

The three main points of the parable also illustrate the impossibility of avoiding an allegorical interpretation. Each character clearly stands for someone other than himself. Virtually every commentator notices the close correlation between the prodigal and the "tax collectors and sinners" (v. 1), with whom Jesus was criticized for associating, and between the older brother and the "Pharisees and scribes" who leveled that criticism (v. 2), even though many think that these two verses reflect Luke's later interpretation.

Some find the portrait of the older brother as either too stark or too muted to be a true representation of the Jewish leaders,[11] but these criticisms overlook the great diversity of viewpoints and behavior found within ancient Pharisaism. On the one hand, Jesus is not tarring all Pharisees with the same brush, merely those who have criticized him at this particular time.[12] On the other hand, the father's approach to the older brother is gentle enough to suggest that, at least on this occasion, Jesus is not challenging the sincerity of the Pharisees' questions or the genuineness of their loyalty to God.[13]

Since the prodigal speaks of having sinned against "heaven" (i.e., God) as well as his father (vv. 18, 21), the direct equation of the father with God at first glance seems dubious. Nevertheless, as noted previously (p. 42), even Jeremias admits that the father is at least "an image of God."[14] A. M. Hunter's conclusion seems sound when he declares, "beyond doubt, in the mind of Jesus the father stood for God, the elder brother for the Scribes and Pharisees, and the prodigal for publicans and sinners."[15] But, contra Hunter, this

---

[11]E.g., Luise Schottroff, "Das Gleichnis vom verlorenen Sohn," *ZTK* 68 (1971):27-52; and José Alonso Díaz, "Paralelos entre la narración del libro de Jonás y la parábola del hijo pródigo," *Bib* 40 (1959):637-39, respectively. Schottroff nevertheless recognizes the unity of the parable and so therefore ascribes it all to Luke!

[12]See esp. Charles H. Giblin, "Structural and Theological Considerations on Luke 15," *CBQ* 24 (1962):29.

[13]François Bovon, "The Parable of the Prodigal Son, Luke 15:11-32, First Reading," in *Exegesis: Problems of Method and Exercises in Reading (Genesis 22 and Luke 15)*, ed. François Bovon and Gregoire Rouiller (Pittsburgh: Pickwick, 1978), p. 61, speaks of the father's "indefectible affection toward the elder son: the vocative τέκνον, even as the σύ, grammatically superfluous, are two indications of this paternal love." Cf. further, below, pp. 182-83.

[14]Jeremias, *Parables*, p. 128. Cf. Robert H. Stein, *An Introduction to the Parables of Jesus* (Philadelphia: Westminster, 1981; Exeter: Paternoster, 1982), p. 118.

[15]A. M. Hunter, *Interpreting the Parables* (London: SCM; Philadelphia: Westminster, 1960), p. 61.

symbolism is precisely what makes the parable an allegory, as chapter two has demonstrated. The "life-likeness" of the narrative in no way undermines this literary classification.

The parable, however, is not quite as lifelike as many have alleged. Would a first-century Jewish son have dared to ask his father for his share of the inheritance while the father was still alive and in good health? Would the father have capitulated so readily? Although a few scholars have argued that both practices were not at all unusual,[16] it seems likely that at the very least such behavior would have appeared as "deplorable."[17] Kenneth Bailey goes so far as to interpret the son's request as equivalent to a wish that his father were dead, and the father's response as an almost inconceivable expression of patience and love.[18]

The issue is complicated by a lack of detailed evidence for the legal situation presupposed by the narrative. It is more generally agreed that the father's later welcome for the returning prodigal was certainly atypical. However inwardly glad he may have been to see his son again, no older, self-respecting Middle Eastern male head of an estate would have disgraced himself by the undignified action of running to greet his son (v. 20). Nor would he have interrupted the son's speech before a full display of repentance (cf. v. 21 with vv. 18-19) or instantly commanded such a luxurious outpouring of affection for him (vv. 22-23).[19] All of these details strongly suggest that Jesus wanted to present his audience with more than a simple, realistic picture of family life. Rather he used an extraordinary story to illustrate God's amazing patience and love for his ungrateful children.

A history of the interpretation of this parable shows that commentators from earliest days recognized that the father and his two sons each stood for individuals or groups of people other than

---

[16]E.g., Eta Linnemann, *Parables of Jesus: Introduction and Exposition* (London: SPCK, 1966 [= *Jesus of the Parables: Introduction and Exposition* (New York: Harper & Row, 1967)]), p. 75; Karl Bornhäuser, *Studien zum Sondergut des Lukas* (Gütersloh: C. Bertelsmann, 1934), pp. 105-7.

[17]J. D. M. Derrett, *Law in the New Testament* (London: Darton, Longman & Todd, 1970), p. 106. Wolfgang Pöhlmann, "Die Abschichtung des verlorenen Sohnes (Lk 15, 12f.) und die erzählte Welt der Parabel," *ZNW* 70 (1979):198-201, believes the practice was acceptable but frowned upon.

[18]Kenneth E. Bailey, *Poet and Peasant: A Literary-Cultural Approach to the Parables in Luke* (Grand Rapids: Eerdmans, 1976), p. 161.

[19]See esp. ibid., pp. 181-87.

themselves. The only debate centered on how that symbolism was to be defined. Yves Tissot identifies four main approaches that proliferated in the first centuries of the church's existence. All agreed that the father stood for God (or Jesus), but they differed as to the identities of the two sons: (1) A "gnosticizing" approach equated the older son with the angels and the younger son with humanity. (2) An "ethical" view saw in these two figures the righteous and sinners of the world in general. (3) An "ethnic" interpretation linked them with Israel and the heathen. (4) A "penitential" option, finally, saw the Christian rigorist contrasted with the less legalistic believer.[20]

Of these four, modern scholars have opted more for (3) than for (1), (2) or (4).[21] (1) and (4) are clearly anachronistic for a *Sitz im Leben Jesu*, while (2) does not anchor the parable in as specific a life-setting as (3). But none of these four does justice to Luke 15:1-2, where both outcasts and righteous are groups of Israelites. On the other hand, each of the four is intelligible as an attempt to *apply* the parable in a different religious context. Here the previously discussed distinction between meaning and significance is helpful (see above, pp. 159-60).

Only the people in view behind the characters of the parable when it was originally spoken may be said to reflect its meaning, but to the extent that analogous groups or individuals appear in other life-settings, the parable may be applied more widely. John Purdy offers an insightful contemporary illustration of this process in his application of selected parables to the modern world of daily work, and he effectively balances the significance of each of the main characters in this particular passage:

> *The workplace, which knows all too well the wasteful tendencies of the younger son and the harshness of the elder, needs also the extravagant love of the father.* Such mercy can season the workplace and make it more humane. It can bring peace to the inner warfare of the individual worker. It can bring peace between the overachievers and those who fall

---

[20]Yves Tissot, "Patristic Allegories of the Lukan Parable of the Two Sons," in *Exegesis,* ed. Bovon and Rouiller, p. 366.

[21]E.g., Daniel Patte, "Structural Analysis of the Parable of the Prodigal Son: Toward a Method," in *Semiology,* ed. Daniel Patte (Pittsburgh: Pickwick, 1976), p. 141; Bernard B. Scott, "The Prodigal Son: A Structuralist Interpretation," *Semeia* 9 (1977):65.

far short of perfection. We do not have to choose between the two sons. We may choose to be like the father.[22]

In no sense does this exposition describe the original meaning of the parable, but it aptly encapsulates its significance in one particular, later context.

Admitting that the parable is allegorical to the extent that each of the "secular" characters stands for his "spiritual" counterpart does not require one to allegorize additional details. All the remaining elements of the narrative are props, used only to illustrate the nature and fortunes of the primary actors. The servants function only to carry out their masters' bidding; they are simply the means by which the family members act. Praying to "heaven" is not an independent detail which disqualifies the father from functioning as a symbol for God but is just part of the story line in which God and the father *are* separate.

The particular nature of the prodigal's sin and his first attempts to remedy it when famine comes add poignancy to his plight and indicate the depths of his degradation but should not be taken to stand for specific types of misfortune or squalor. The robe, ring, shoes, and fatted calf which await his return all highlight the extent of his restoration but once again should not be given independent significance. All these details fit in with known customs and experiences of Jesus' day and merely add to the force of the main points which derive from the main characters.[23] They could easily have been abbreviated, expanded or replaced without altering the three key lessons of the parable. Here is where the ancient allegorizers so often went astray.[24]

A final point stemming from Purdy's exposition is appropriate. Unlike several of the parables discussed below, which contrast good and bad subordinates of a master, this narrative presents neither

---

[22]John C. Purdy, *Parables at Work* (Philadelphia: Westminster, 1985), p. 72.

[23]Cf. the parable attributed to R. Hanina b. Gamaliel in b. Kidd. 61b, which begins with the strikingly parallel phrase, "[It is like] a man who divided his estate among his sons" but then goes on to deal with issues of payment and possession to make a point about the rights of Gad and Reuben to have a portion of the land of Canaan.

[24]One possible explanation of the details of the prodigal's departure and return involves formal, Jewish procedures to cut off and reinstate the son as a member of the household. See Karl H. Rengstorf, *Die Re-Investitur des verlorenen Sohnes in der Gleichniserzählung Jesu: Luk. 15, 11-32* (Köln: Westdeutscher Verlag, 1967). But the details of the parable do not fit these procedures closely enough for them to be pressed too far.

son as a model uniformly to be followed or avoided. God delights in the repentance of prodigals, but he would prefer that they not have to sink so low before coming to their senses. God cherishes the faithfulness of those who obey his will but does not want them to despise the rebellious who have repented. The parable is strikingly open-ended. Did the older brother come in the house and join the festivities? Jesus does not say, and it misreads the parable to attempt to answer the question. The important fact is that the invitation remains for all who hear or read and are willing to respond and rejoice.

6.2 The Lost Sheep and Lost Coin (Lk 15:4-10; cf. Mt 18:12-14)

How widely do the methods used to understand the parable of the prodigal son apply? One need look no further than the immediately preceding context to discover two additional passages whose themes and structure closely resemble those of the parable of the prodigal. There are of course differences. The parables of the lost sheep and lost coin involve animals and inanimate objects as main "characters." They each use groups of characters (the ninety-nine and the nine) as collective units to fill the role of one of the subordinates. The lost sheep and lost coin are also much shorter and less detailed, and each is introduced with a rhetorical question beginning with τίς ἐξ ὑμῶν "what man (or woman) of you . . . [would not do such-and-such]?"

This question, with analogies in the rabbinic parables (see above, pp. 60-61), regularly anticipates a negative answer and utilizes a logic which is a fortiori. In other words, the question introduces a situation which requires so clear-cut a response that the audience would be forced to acknowledge, "of course, no one would not do that"—that is, "everyone would do it." And the logic progresses from the lesser to the greater; if sinful humans usually conduct certain affairs in a particularly reasonable or ethical way, how much more must God behave in comparable fashion.

Nevertheless, the same triadic structure may be perceived as in the parable of the prodigal: an authority figure (shepherd, woman) with contrasting subordinates (one hundred sheep, divided into ninety-nine which are safe and one which is lost; and ten coins, nine safe and one lost). The emphasis seems to rest mostly on the response of the human figure—the joy of discovering what was lost. Still, it is likely that some would have also identified with the sheep or the coins and seen in them symbolic significance.

The metaphors of sheep and shepherd symbolizing Israel and her leaders (including God) were well known from Old Testament and intertestamental times (most notably from the allegory of Ezek 34:1-31). Interestingly, although the biblical shepherd was a cherished image of care for God's people, first-century shepherds were generally despised by the average Jew, due to their reputation for lawlessness and dishonesty (cf. b. Sanhedrin 25b).[25] Jesus thus places his audience in a bind; the Pharisees naturally would have tried to identify with the authority figure in each case but would have balked when that figure turned out to be a shepherd or a woman!

In the case of the parable of the lost coin, an additional observation points out the importance of the subordinate "characters" (the coins). J. D. M. Derrett has shown that *zuzim,* the Hebrew word for the coins described here, can also mean "those that have moved away, departed." Derrett suspects that Jesus employed a deliberate play on words, so that the coins are "excellent representatives of people who have somehow rolled away . . . and yet are still within the house, only waiting to be swept up by some sweeping operation (which is exactly what Jesus was about)."[26]

Further hints emerge that the figures in the parables are meant to point beyond the level of a simple, realistic story of first-century Palestine. If this were a purely historical narrative, one would expect to hear that the shepherd safeguarded the ninety-nine left behind in the wilderness, and one would not expect him to rejoice quite so extravagantly or to carry the sheep on his shoulders when no reason was given for why it should not walk. All of these fea-

---

[25]Talbert, *Luke,* p. 33.

[26]J. D. M. Derrett, "Fresh Light on the Lost Sheep and the Lost Coin," *NTS* 26 (1979):51.

tures can be sidestepped and are not wholly unnatural, but their cumulative effect suggests an unusual emphasis on the joy of the recovery.[27]

A controlled allegorical interpretation therefore seems proper: the shepherd and woman stand for God, the lost sheep and coins for the tax collectors and sinners, and the remaining sheep and coins for the scribes and Pharisees. Both parables suggest three main points, not unlike those derived from the prodigal son. *(1) Just as the shepherd and woman go out of their way to search diligently for their lost possessions, so God takes the initiative to go to great lengths to seek and to save lost sinners. (2) Just as the discovery of the lost sheep and coin elicit great joy, so the salvation of lost men and women is a cause for celebration. (3) Just as the existence of the ninety-nine sheep and nine coins afford no excuse for not searching for what is lost, those who profess to be God's people can never be satisfied that their numbers are sufficiently great so as to stop trying to save more.*

This triadic interpretation is more concisely summed up by the concluding refrains of verses 7 and 10, which contrast (a) the joy in heaven over (b) one sinner who repents with that for (c) those who need no repentance. Since these refrains clearly establish the allegorical referents of the three main characters, they are widely assumed to be secondary additions to the parables.[28]

But Bailey has shown the integral part the conclusions have in the structures of the overall passages. As noted above (p. 151), the lost sheep is a brief three-stanza poem in which verse 7 (stanza 3) balances the first part of verse 4 (stanza 1). Some find unbearable tension between the shepherd (or woman) searching and finding the entirely passive sheep (or coin) in verses 4-6 (and 8-9) and a sinner's more active repentance (vv. 7, 10), yet this is precisely the kind of tension between divine sovereignty and human response which characterizes much of Scripture.[29]

Other details in these two parables—the wilderness and the shep-

---

[27]For the historical realism, see E. F. F. Bishop, "The Parable of the Lost or Wandering Sheep," *ATR* 44 (1962):44-57; for the cumulative effect of the unusual, Denis Buzy, "La brebis perdue," *RB* 39 (1930):50-51.

[28]E.g., C. H. Dodd, *The Parables of the Kingdom* (London: Nisbet, 1935; New York: Scribner's, 1936), p. 119; Joseph A. Fitzmyer, *The Gospel according to Luke X-XXIV* (Garden City: Doubleday, 1985), p. 1073.

[29]See esp. D. A. Carson, *Divine Sovereignty and Human Responsibility* (London: Marshall, Morgan & Scott; Atlanta: John Knox, 1981), passim. Contra C. W. F. Smith, *The Jesus of the Parables* (Philadelphia: United Church Press, 1975), pp. 72-73.

herd's home, or the lamp with which the woman searches her house—add nothing more to the meaning of the narratives but simply act as the logical "stage props" for the action of the central characters. Verse 10 may suggest a lone exception. Although the reference to the "angels of God" may simply be an indirect way of speaking about God himself, it might imply that the woman's friends and neighbors (v. 9) stand for the angels. Then presumably the shepherd's friends would play a similar role in the preceding parable (v. 6). This would introduce a fourth allegorical detail into the parable but not at the expense of the triadic structure, since it would simply reinforce the point associated with the shepherd and woman, namely, rejoicing in heaven. The friends therefore correspond to what Honig terms an "allegorical waver"—a detail which may or may not be designed to contribute to the overall second level of meaning of the story (see above, p. 56).

One controversial exegetical conclusion has been assumed in the foregoing analysis. The phrase "persons who need no repentance" (v. 7) has been taken at face value. But if Jesus had the Pharisees and scribes in mind as those who were not rejoicing at the salvation of sinners, how could he refer to them so positively? Many assume that Jesus' reference to those who do not need to repent reflects irony or sarcasm; by the "righteous" he really meant the "self-righteous."[30]

Yet this interpretation flies in the face of the consistently positive meaning of δίκαιος ("righteous") elsewhere in the Gospels (cf., e.g., Mt 5:45, 10:41; Mk 6:20)[31] and renders the conclusion that God rejoices more over the convert than over the hypocrite so self-evident as to be trite. There is certainly nothing in the depiction of the ninety-nine sheep or nine coins to suggest they were in any way blemished or counterfeit.

In Luke's Gospel, moreover, the "righteous" consistently refers to those who are already right with God, the pious in Israel expectantly awaiting their salvation (cf., e.g., Lk 1:6, 2:25, 23:50). The word

---

[30]E.g., Peter R. Jones, *The Teaching of the Parables* (Nashville: Broadman, 1982), p. 172; Bailey, *Poet and Peasant*, p. 155.

[31]Cf. esp. David Hill, *Greek Words and Hebrew Meanings* (Cambridge: Univ. Press, 1967), pp. 130-31; and R. T. France, *Matthew* (Leicester: IVP; Grand Rapids: Eerdmans, 1985), p. 168. Of course, irony works best where it is unanticipated, so this argument is not as conclusive as the next.

does not refer to people who are sinless but to those who place their hope in God. So Jesus here more likely had a wider group of Jews in view than just those whom he elsewhere denounces as hypocrites. And he addressed the particular issue of Luke 15:1-2, not by directly challenging his critics' claim to be part of the people of God, but by seeking to woo them more gently back to a right attitude toward their fellow Jews.[32] This fits well with the understandable but misguided complaints of the prodigal's older brother in verses 25-32, where the father's reaction is remarkably restrained and solicitous.[33] Direct rebukes would occur elsewhere and more consistently as Jesus' ministry neared its end.

Matthew's parable of the wandering sheep (Mt 18:12-14) may or may not be a variant of the same story from the same occasion in Christ's ministry (see above, pp. 83, 118). Either way, the triadic structure and three main points derivable from it are virtually identical to those of Luke's account, even if the emphasis shifts from the point associated with the lost sheep (the joy of salvation) to that associated with God (concern that none should perish). When we see that many parables make three points rather than just one, this change of emphasis may be readily accepted without allegations of one of the evangelists having altered the meaning of the story.

The two groups of people contrasted also seem to have changed, from repentant vs. unrepentant Israelites to trusted followers of Jesus vs. those in danger of abandoning their commitment. This illustrates the way in which a parable could be reapplied to new situations analogous to its original context. But both pairs of people correspond to the types of individuals Jesus regularly encountered, so it is inappropriate to reject either version of the parable as a later development of the other.[34] Matthew himself may have had yet a third situation in mind with his reference to "not despising these little ones" (v. 10), since μικροί ("little ones") for him elsewhere

---

[32]Cf. E. Earle Ellis, *The Gospel of Luke* (London: Oliphants, 1974; Grand Rapids: Eerdmans, 1981), pp. 196-97; Léonard Ramaroson, "Le coeur du Troisiéme Évangile: Lc 15," *Bib* 60 (1979):357.

[33]Cf. B. T. D. Smith, *The Parables of the Synoptic Gospels* (Cambridge: Univ. Press, 1937), p. 194; J. Alexander Findlay, *Jesus and His Parables* (London: Epworth, 1950), p. 76.

[34]See, e.g., W. O. E. Oesterley, *The Gospel Parables in the Light of Their Jewish Background* (London: SPCK; New York: Macmillan, 1936), p. 177; Marshall, *Luke*, p. 600. Even Joachim Jeremias, "Tradition und Redaktion in Lukas 15," *ZNW* 62 (1971):172-89, after careful linguistic analysis, concludes that Luke's version is *literarily* independent of Matthew. There may be no reason for it not to be seen as *historically* independent as well.

seems to refer to the community he was addressing (cf. Mt 10:42, 18:6). Perhaps Matthew envisioned a contrast between faithful and apostate members of his church. So long as meaning and significance are not confused, this type of application is perfectly legitimate and clearly relevant for contemporary Christians as well.

6.3 The Two Debtors (Lk 7:41-43)

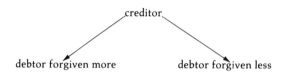

Tucked away in the longer narrative about Jesus' dinner with Simon the Pharisee (Lk 7:36-50), this little parable concisely sums up much of the meaning of the parables of Luke 15. The two debtors are not complete opposites, since both are forgiven, but the focus lies on the contrasting responses of the two. Like Nathan's parable of the ewe lamb designed to make David indict himself (2 Sam 12:1-7), Jesus' question and his host's answer make it clear that Simon himself corresponds to the debtor who was forgiven less, and that the unwelcome woman who had anointed Jesus corresponds to the debtor who was forgiven more. Jesus' further remarks (vv. 44-47) spell out these identifications and obviously treat the parable as an allegory of God's love for sinners of all kinds. Not surprisingly, then, many critics have viewed this Lukan context for the parable as secondary.[35]

B. T. D. Smith advances further reasons for this traditio-critical dissection: (1) Only Luke represents Jesus as accepting the hospitality of Pharisees, whereas in the other Gospels they are quite hostile to him. (2) The parallel in Mark 14:3-9 does not contain the parable. (3) Both the host's treatment of Jesus and Jesus' complaint about it seem too harsh to be realistic. (4) The conclusion assumes the woman's love led to her forgiveness, while the parable talks about the love which follows from forgiveness.[36]

---

[35]E.g., Joseph A. Fitzmyer, *The Gospel according to Luke I-IX* (Garden City: Doubleday, 1981), p. 687; Heinz Schürmann, *Das Lukasevangelium*, vol. 1 (Freiburg: Herder, 1969), p. 436.
[36]B. T. D. Smith, *Parables*, pp. 213-16.

In response, the following observations are appropriate. Objection (1) is not really a problem between Luke and the other Gospels; this passage also differs from many of Luke's harsher portraits of the Pharisees (see esp. 11:37-54). Simon may have invited Jesus because it was viewed as meritorious to treat a guest preacher to a meal, or because he wanted to trap him in his conversation, as the Pharisees frequently tried to do elsewhere.[37] Objections (3) and (1) somewhat cancel each other out; the one claims the actions are too harsh, the other that they are too mild. Both value judgments go beyond what historical criticism can fairly establish. Objection (2) appeals to a parallel which is dubious; this is probably an entirely separate incident in Christ's ministry.[38]

Objection (4) is clearly the most substantial charge, but it involves a tension not only between the parable and its context but between vv. 47-48 ("her sins are forgiven . . . for she loved much") and v. 50 ("your faith has saved you"). To alleviate this tension, one must assume that the passage presupposes that the woman had already come to believe at some prior time and that Jesus now is simply making that fact public and assuring the woman of the forgiveness which faith brings. It is better, therefore, to interpret v. 47a as implying, "*One can see* that her many sins are forgiven, because she loved much."[39] Granted this interpretation, there are no legitimate objections to the authenticity of the parable in its present context.

Not only do the three characters of the parable in some sense correspond to the three key individuals at dinner in Simon's house, but more specific lessons may easily be derived from each. *(1) Like the man owing fifty denarii, those who take their spiritual condition for granted and are not aware of having been forgiven of numerous gross wickednesses should not despise those who have been redeemed from a more pathetic state. (2) Like the*

---

[37]Jeremias, *Parables*, p. 126; and Norval Geldenhuys, *Commentary on the Gospel of Luke* (London: Marshall, Morgan & Scott, 1950; Grand Rapids: Eerdmans, 1951), p. 235, respectively.

[38]This conclusion is vigorously disputed. But see the list of exegetes from a wide variety of perspectives who support it in Robert Holst, "The One Anointing of Jesus: Another Application of the Form-Critical Method," *JBL* 95 (1976):435, nn. 1-2. Holst himself believes that one incident has been elaborated in different ways but believes Luke's was the earliest.

[39]Cf. Jeremias, *Parables*, p. 127. The view that the woman's display of affection for Jesus led to her forgiveness has often been maintained by Roman Catholic theologians because of its obvious affinities with their traditional dogma of good works meriting grace. But the Catholic scholar, José de Urrutia, "La parábola de los dos deudores Lc 7, 39-50," *Estudios eclesiásticos* 38 (1963):472-73, offers a long list of Roman Catholic scholars, both ancient and modern, who agree with the interpretation offered here.

debtor owing five hundred denarii, those who recognize they have much for which to be thankful will naturally respond in generous expressions of love for Jesus. (3) Like the creditor, God forgives both categories of sinners and allows them to begin again with a clean slate.

These three points are virtually spelled out, in turn, by verses 44-46 (contrasting the behavior of Simon and the woman) and verses 47-50 (the declaration of forgiveness). The second point undoubtedly forms the heart of Jesus' message on this occasion, but it may not be entirely divorced from the other two.

Of course if one removes the parable from its context, these points would not be as clear, but it is doubtful if the details of the parable would suggest any radically different interpretation.[40] The unusual generosity of the creditor in cancelling both debts, the larger of which equalled a year and a half's wage for a common laborer, points to an allegorical understanding of the imagery from within the parable itself. The common Synoptic usage of the words *debtors, owe,* and *forgive* to refer both to financial and to spiritual obligations (as esp. in the Lord's Prayer—Mt 6:11-12) reinforces the suggestion that two levels of meaning are present. To try to summarize the parable with one bland phrase, such as "salvation is only for sinners,"[41] misses crucial nuances that the narrative articulates.

6.4 The Two Sons (Mt 21:28-32)

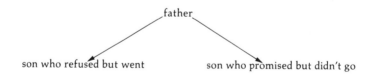

The parable of the two sons offers yet another passage remarkably parallel to the story in Luke 15 of the prodigal and his family. It too describes a father with contrary offspring—one who says he will go to work in the family vineyard but does not do so, and one who says

---

[40]Conservative scholars are by no means the only ones who agree that this parable is in its original context. Cf., e.g., Ulrich Wilckens, "Vergebung für die Sünderin (Lk 7, 36-50)," in *Orientierung an Jesus,* ed. Paul Hoffmann (Freiburg: Herder, 1973), p. 400; Hans Drexler, "Die grosse Sünderin Lucas 7, 36-50," ZNW 59 (1968):165.

[41]As in Peter Fiedler, *Jesus und die Sünder* (Frankfurt: Peter Lang; Bern: Herbert Lang, 1976), p. 248. Cf. Walter Schmithals, *Das Evangelium nach Lukas* (Zürich: Theologischer Verlag, 1980), p. 99.

he will not go but then changes his mind. The Greek manuscripts differ as to the order of these two episodes but the overall meaning of the parable is unaffected.[42] As in Luke 15, the parable is applied to the Jewish leaders and to "sinners."

This time the specific groups in view are the chief priests and elders (v. 23) and the tax collectors and prostitutes (v. 32). Again only a relative comparison appears; the latter group enters the kingdom of God *before* the former. In verse 31 the words "enter before" (προάγουσιν) might also be translated "enter instead of," but even then the parable is open-ended and the invitation implicit for the chief priests and elders to turn and enter as well. The tone is harsher and more urgent than in the parables previously discussed, but, in the context of the final week of Christ's earthly life, this is entirely natural.

Despite frequent denials, the application and context fit the parable perfectly. Any assessment of this story as a secondary insertion into Matthew's narrative must be made on other grounds.[43] To be sure, Mark's narrative omits it, but his use of the plural "parables" in a context where he gives only one (Mk 12:1) could suggest that he knew Jesus spoke others on the same occasion. Luke's partial parallel to verse 32 (Lk 7:29-30) is not similar enough to require Matthew's verse to be a later development of it.[44] The reference to John the Baptist's preaching rather than to Jesus' ministry is not surprising, for Jesus had just asked the Jewish leaders their opinion of John (vv. 25-27).

Verse 32 does not suggest an allegorical equation of the father in the parable with John so much as it focuses on John as one who, like Jesus, came in "the way of righteousness"—i.e., as a true spokesman for God. Instead of directly defending his own ministry as fulfilling God's will, as in the parables of Luke 7 and 15, Jesus brilliantly deflects attention away from himself toward one whose

---

[42]One less well-attested variant has the son who said he would go (but did not) gain approval as the more obedient one! For a valiant attempt to defend the authenticity and intelligibility of this variant, see J. Ramsey Michaels, "The Parable of the Regretful Son," *HTR* 61 (1968):15-26, but it is doubtful if his argument can overcome the paucity of external evidence for the reading (limited to codex Bezae and various Old Latin and Syriac versions).

[43]Sjef van Tilborg, *The Jewish Leaders in Matthew* (Leiden: Brill, 1972), pp. 47-52; Eduard Schweizer, *The Gospel according to Matthew* (Richmond: John Knox, 1975; London: SPCK, 1976), pp. 411-12.

[44]Julius Schniewind, *Das Evangelium nach Matthäus* (Göttingen: Vandenhoeck & Ruprecht, 1936), p. 217.

message was thoroughly consistent with his. Just as the Jewish leaders had been trapped by Jesus' reference to John in reply to their question concerning Jesus' authority (vv. 23-27), once again they could give no retort (v. 32).

We need not look outside the parable itself, however, to find hints of intended allegorical referents. The odds of two sons both deciding at the same time to do exactly the opposite of what they promised their father are rather small. The picture is conceivable but not typical. Francis W. Beare admits that the two sons represent two kinds of people, but he misses the point when he argues that the son who fails to obey could not stand for the Jewish leaders. Granted, they "would be astonished to have it suggested that they were not working in the vineyard of God as they had promised,"[45] but that is precisely Jesus' point. Through a shocking parable of reversal he upends conventional Jewish wisdom concerning God's will. Because they rejected John's call to repentance, the leaders were not truly right with God, however scrupulously they continued to follow other laws and rituals.

The parable may once again be summarized under three main headings. *(1) Like the father sending his sons to work, God commands all people to carry out his will. (2) Like the son who ultimately disobeyed, some promise but do not perform rightly and so are rejected by God. (3) Like the son who ultimately obeyed, some rebel but later submit and so are accepted.*

It is not enough, with Jülicher, to claim that the parable can be encapsulated in the one concept of the need to avoid a discrepancy between doing and saying.[46] This could be taken to mean that the one who promises nothing will have nothing required of him! An anonymous rabbinic parable offers a striking parallel to the structure and contents of the story of the two sons:

> The matter may be compared to someone sitting at a crossroads. Before him were two paths. One of them began in clear ground but ended in thorns. The other began in thorns but ended in clear ground. . . .
>
> So did Moses say to Israel, "You see how the wicked flourish in this world, for two or three days succeeding. But in the end

---

[45]Francis W. Beare, *The Gospel according to Matthew* (San Francisco: Harper & Row; Oxford: Blackwell, 1981), p. 424. For the previous point, see p. 423.

[46]Adolf Jülicher, *Die Gleichnisreden Jesu*, vol. 2 (Tübingen: Mohr, 1899), pp. 365-85.

they will have occasion for regret." So it is said, "For there shall be no reward for the evil man" (Prov. 24:20). . . . "You see the righteous, who are distressed in this world? For two or three days they are distressed, but in the end they will have occasion for rejoicing." And so it is said, "That he may prove you, to do you good at the end" (Dt. 8:16). (Sifre Deut. 53)[47]

The kind of detail which this parable exhibits can scarcely be squeezed into one solitary proposition but divides neatly into a tripartite outline—the conditions into which God places an individual and the contrasting reactions and fates of the righteous and the wicked.

Because the vineyard was a stock symbol for Israel in Old Testament and intertestamental Judaism, and because it is used that way in the adjacent parable of the wicked tenants (Mt 21:33-46), it is tempting to give it a similar meaning in the parable of the two sons.[48] Jesus would then be referring specifically to two types of *Jewish* responses to God's call to serve him. But, as with the neighbors of the shepherd and woman of Luke 15:4-10, this does not add another *independent* allegorical element to the narrative so much as spell out in a *Sitz im Leben Jesu* the logical inference of the nationality of the two sons and the jurisdiction of their work. The significance of the vineyard will change as the parable is reapplied in different situations. One nineteenth-century expositor phrased it this way:

The father is God; the vineyard is the church. The sons are two classes of men to whom the command to labor in the church comes from God: the first is the type of openly abandoned and regardless sinners, who on receiving the command of God defiantly refuse obedience, but afterward, on sober second thought, repent and become earnest in working the work of God; the second is the representative of the hypocrites who in smooth and polite phrase make promises which they never intend to keep, and who, never changing their mind, take no further thought either of God or of his service.[49]

---

[47]Trans. Jacob Neusner, *Sifre to Deuteronomy*, vol. 1 (Atlanta: Scholars, 1987), pp. 175-76.

[48]Cf. Hans Weder, *Die Gleichnisse Jesu als Metaphern* (Göttingen: Vandenhoeck & Ruprecht, 1978), p. 236.

[49]William M. Taylor, *The Parables of Our Saviour Expounded and Illustrated* (London: Hodder & Stoughton; New York: George H. Doran, 1886), pp. 122-23.

As an interpretation of the parable's original meaning, most of this would be anachronistic; as an elucidation of its contemporary significance it is highly apropos.

Apart from this one obvious symbol of the vineyard, however, it is doubtful if the details should be pressed any further. James M. Boice feels differently and derives three additional lessons from the opening command alone. Besides being commanded to do God's work, the sons have to recognize that they must leave home and "go" elsewhere, do the work with a sense of urgency ("today"), and view it as a "duty."[50] Milking such commonplace details for these kind of principles ignores most of the valid insights of modern parable scholarship and overinterprets to an extent which is not justifiable even by Boice's homiletical designs. One might just as easily conclude that Jesus was teaching his followers not to leave home (the vineyard was most likely adjacent to the farmhouse) and that most of the time the sons were not required to work (otherwise why give a special command for this day?)! Better to stick with the three main points and view these details merely as the necessary preface to the plot of the narrative.

6.5 Faithful and Unfaithful Servants (Lk 12:42-48; Mt 24:45-51)

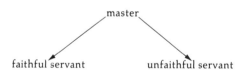

The parables of the prodigal son and of the two sons contrast disobedient and obedient offspring. Several other parables of Jesus contrast faithful and unfaithful servants. In addition to this passage from Q, Luke 12:35-38 and Mark 13:33-37 describe, respectively, the watchful servant and the alert doorkeeper. The relationship among these three passages is disputed.[51] There is some ground for

---

[50]James M. Boice, *The Parables of Jesus* (Chicago: Moody, 1983), pp. 135-38.

[51]Luke 12:35-38 and Mark 13:33-37 are frequently seen as variant forms of the same original. See esp. David Wenham, *The Rediscovery of Jesus' Eschatological Discourse* (Sheffield: JSOT, 1984), pp. 15-49. For the view that these are two separate parables, see Craig L. Blomberg, "When Is a Parallel Really a Parallel? A Test Case: The Lucan Parables," *WTJ* 46 (1984), esp. pp. 83-85, which also lists a variety of other interrelationships which have been postulated.

believing that the latter two have begun to be "de-parabolized" by the early tradition.

In their current form, each begins as a simple command to be alert but then shifts to the use of simile ("it is like a man going away . . ."/ "like men waiting for their master to return"). Since later Christian writings often reworded Jesus' parables as commands it is possible that these parables too once exhibited a "purer" form.[52] Their main points, however, are quite similar to those of the Q parable (Lk 12:42-48; Mt 24:45-51), which is worded almost identically in both Matthew and Luke and is seemingly quite close to its original form. So attention here will focus exclusively on this doubly-attested servant parable.

As with the other triadic, monarchic parables, an authority figure judges between two types of behavior of his subordinates. Here Jesus uses the imagery of master and servant. A variation in pattern occurs since the same individual is used to depict both good and bad behavior ("it will be good for that servant . . . but if that servant is wicked"—Mt 24:46, 48; Lk 12:43, 45). Still, the outcome in each instance is the same. The tone of judgment is harsher here than elsewhere, probably because the original setting of the parable was most likely Jesus' eschatological discourse.[53] Then Jesus was alone with his disciples and able to speak frankly. Furthermore, his life was virtually over, his fate sealed and the seemingly unflinching opposition of the authorities most clear.

The most obvious feature which suggests that the narrative is more than a realistic description of a typical event is the fate of the wicked servant—being cut in pieces. Even if one accepts the possible translation of this verb as "cut off," as in the Old Testament banning of a member from the community,[54] this sentence seems unnaturally harsh for a first-century Palestinian setting. The rewards and punishments must refer to Judgment Day at the end of the age. Matthew makes the allegorical interpretation more explicit with his unique addition, "there will be weeping and gnashing of teeth" (Mt

---

[52]Richard Bauckham, "Synoptic Parousia Parables and the Apocalypse," *NTS* 23 (1977):165-69. Cf. also idem, "The Two Fig Tree Parables in the Apocalypse of Peter," *JBL* 104 (1985):269-87.

[53]See esp. Wenham, *Rediscovery*, pp. 62-66.

[54]See esp. Otto Betz, "The Dichotomized Servant and the End of Judas Iscariot," *RevQ* 5 (1964):46-47; Paul Ellingworth, "Luke 12.46—Is There an Anti-climax Here?" *BT* 31 (1980):242-43.

24:51), language elsewhere used exclusively of punishment in hell (e.g., Mt 25:30; Lk 13:28 par.).

On the other hand, one ought not to deduce specific referents for the type of work the servant is given (distributing food), the type of reward offered the faithful steward (control over the master's possessions) or the particular nature of the evil servant's wickedness (assault and drunkenness). These are dictated simply by the standard responsibilities, rewards and vices of servants in first-century Jewish households. In retrospect, the motif of the master's absence seems obviously to point to the delay of the parousia.

The problem in the parable, though, is not that the master was gone away too long but that he came back too soon and caught the servant unprepared. As noted above (p. 89), the Jews themselves grappled with the problem of the apparent delay of the Day of the Lord, and it is this type of delay that Jesus' original audience would have readily recalled if they placed any emphasis on the interval prior to the master's return. For Christians who believe that the parousia and the Day of the Lord coincide, however, a further *application* of the text to the return of Christ appears legitimate.[55]

Luke 12:47-48 elaborates the destiny of the wicked servant by contrasting the severe punishment meted out to one who knew his master's will but failed to do it with the lighter beating appropriate for one who disobeyed out of ignorance. These verses are unparalleled in Matthew but not necessarily secondary.[56] Even verses 42-46 by themselves focus more attention on the behavior to be avoided than on that to be emulated; in literary terms the parable is "tragic," culminating in the death of one who could have avoided it.

The concept of different punishments for different sins is well-anchored in the Old Testament and intertestamental literature.[57] These verses rank among the clearest in all the Bible in support of degrees of punishment in hell. Still, it does not seem possible to do justice to the entire passage if only this aspect is given attention.

---

[55]As Paul apparently does with his allusions to these parables in the Thessalonian correspondence. See David Wenham, "Paul and the Synoptic Apocalypse," in *Gospel Perspectives*, vol. 2, ed. R. T. France and David Wenham (Sheffield: JSOT, 1981), pp. 345-75.

[56]Wenham, *Rediscovery*, pp. 67-76. Cf. T. W. Manson, *The Sayings of Jesus* (London: SCM, 1949; Grand Rapids: Eerdmans, 1979), pp. 118-19.

[57]For references, see Marshall, *Luke*, p. 544. Cf. also the parable attributed to R. Simeon b. Halafta in Deuteronomy Rabbah 7:4.

One point per main character again yields the full sense of the parable: *(1) God rewards and punishes people at the final judgment on the basis of their stewardship of the tasks assigned to them. (2) Faithful stewardship requires perseverance and consistency, for the end could come at any time. (3) Those who postpone their responsibilities and do evil in the meantime may sadly discover that it is too late for them to make amends for their errors.* These three points closely correspond to the three main episodes of the parable (Mt 24:45 par., 46-47 par., and 48-51 par.).

The differences between Matthew's and Luke's intended applications of the parable were discussed in chapter four (pp. 123-24). There it was noted that many have viewed Luke's version as re-applying an original warning for Israel to the context of early church leadership, but that the evidence for this position is meager. Nevertheless such an application would be perfectly consistent with the original meaning of the parable in both Matthew and Luke. While the good and bad servant originally no doubt stood for faithful and faithless Jews, with faith being defined in terms of allegiance to Jesus, there is no reason not to reapply the imagery in an evangelistic context to Christian disciples as over against all those who reject the Gospel, or in an ecclesiastical setting to genuine vs. spurious Christians within the membership of a local church.

In the context of Matthew's and Luke's narratives, however, the thrust of the parable is not just the responsibility given the follower of Jesus but also the need for the Jews who heard Jesus to respond positively to him.[58] The disciples model faithful following, but they are not castigated en masse as potentially wicked servants.

6.6 The Ten Virgins (Mt 25:1-13)

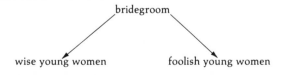

bridegroom

wise young women   foolish young women

---

[58]Cf. Walter L. Liefeld, "Luke," in *The Expositor's Bible Commentary*, ed. Frank E. Gaebelein, vol. 8 (Grand Rapids: Zondervan, 1984), p. 967. Hunter, *Parables*, p. 79, and Dodd, *Parables*, p. 160, correctly identify this as the original meaning in the parable's *Sitz im Leben Jesu* but deny that Matthew and Luke have preserved this meaning.

If the problem facing the wicked servant in the previous parable was the surprisingly quick return of his master, then the opposite problem faces the five foolish bridesmaids in the very next passage in Matthew's Gospel. Here the theme of delay definitely enters in. But the delay of the bridegroom was a standard feature of Jewish weddings, so this detail need not reflect any late stage of the tradition. In fact, most of the parable is extremely realistic by the standards of Jesus' day. Much damage has been done by commentators, especially older ones, who have read too much symbolism out of the details of the text. Thus some have argued that the five women in each category could stand for the five senses, used either for good or for evil; the sleep of the ten, for death; and the sellers of oil, for the poor who bestowed merit on those who gave them alms.[59] Modern commentators can scarcely protest this improbable allegorizing too loudly.

Nevertheless, not every detail is typical of ancient Hebrew wedding festivities. The most implausible is the reaction of the bridegroom in refusing to open the door for the foolish bridesmaids and in claiming not even to know them.[60] But at an allegorical level these features make good sense, when the story is seen as warning about the irreversible judgment which awaits those who have masqueraded as true people of God.

Armand Puig i Tárrech, in the only full-scale monograph on this parable in modern scholarship, believes he has recovered an originally non-allegorical parable by structural analysis. He judges verses 5, 7a and 11-13 to break the passage's three-part symmetry (vv. 1-4; 6, 7b-9; and 10) and so assumes them to be secondary. But even then he is left with the feature of the shut door in the latter half of verse 10. Thus, without any other warrant, he excises this clause as well, further diminishing an already disproportionately small third section of the parable.[61]

It is easier to believe that the parable was an allegory from its

---

[59]These and other examples are cited in Thomas Aquinas, *Commentary on the Four Gospels*, vol. 1, pt. 3 (Oxford: John Henry Parker; London: J. G. F. & J. Rivington, 1842 [Latin orig. in 13th cent.]), pp. 843-51.

[60]France, *Matthew*, p. 352; Beare, *Matthew*, pp. 484-85. A. W. Argyle, "Wedding Customs at the Time of Jesus," *ExpT* 86 (1975):214-15, argues that all of the dubious features of the parable are realistic after all, but he does not discuss these specific ones.

[61]Armand Puig i Tárrech, *La parabole des dix vierges* (Rome: BIP, 1983).

inception. The lack of preparation by the foolish virgins, at the core of any reconstructed original form, is in itself highly unrealistic, because delays before wedding processions were common.[62] At the same time, the allegorical elements are limited to the three main characters: the bridegroom as a natural symbol for God, stemming from the Old Testament concept of God as the husband of his people (e.g., Is 54:4-6; Ezek 16:7-34; Hos 2:19),[63] and the wise and foolish virgins as those who, spiritually, are either prepared or unprepared for Judgment Day.

This limited allegorical interpretation actually supports the parable's authenticity. If the story were a creation of the early church, one would have expected the character corresponding to the faithful believer to be the bride, since Christians quickly adopted the Pauline metaphor of the church as the bride of Christ as a favorite form of self-reference.[64]

The main points of the parable may thus approximate to the following: *(1) Like the bridegroom, God may delay his coming longer than people expect. (2) Like the wise bridesmaids, his followers must be prepared for such a delay—discipleship may be more arduous than the novice suspects. (3) Like the foolish bridesmaids, those who do not prepare adequately may discover a point beyond which there is no return—when the end comes it will be too late to undo the damage of neglect.*

The climax of the parable suggests an emphasis on (3) but not to the exclusion of (1) and (2). Given these three points, verse 13 ("keep watch, because you do not know the day or the hour") cannot be faulted for misrepresenting the meaning of the parable. It is simply a concluding command which epitomizes the necessary response true disciples must make in light of all three points of the passage. Nor does its injunction to "watchfulness" contradict the fact that all ten girls slept. Γρηγορέω ("to keep watch") does not necessarily mean to "stay awake" but merely to "be prepared."[65]

As with the parables of the lost coin and two sons, there is one

---

[62]Findlay, *Jesus*, pp. 111-12.

[63]D. A. Carson, "Matthew," in *Expositor's Bible Commentary*, vol. 8, p. 511. Cf. Weder, *Gleichnisse*, p. 244.

[64]A few, mostly late, textual witnesses make passing reference to such a bride in v. 1, probably added out of this very motivation.

[65]David Hill, *The Gospel of Matthew* (London: Oliphants, 1972; Grand Rapids: Eerdmans, 1981), p. 327. Contra, e.g., Hunter, *Parables*, p. 86.

additional detail which commentators seem unable to ignore. The three points enumerated above could have been made just as effectively completely apart from verses 8-9, in which the bridesmaids who have run out of oil ask the others to share with them and are rebuffed. This suggests that the oil stands for something specific, especially as it was a frequent symbol in earlier Hebrew literature for joy or for the anointing of a priest or king.

As a result, scholars have suggested a wide variety of identities for the oil. Good works, saving faith or grace, and the Holy Spirit are three of the most prominent.[66] But each of these runs aground on the command of the wise women to their companions to go and purchase more oil as if that were a viable alternative. No one can buy good works, faith and grace, or the Holy Spirit. Probably the incident with the oil simply supports the main theme of preparedness and is to be interpreted in the broadest possible sense as anything which an individual must do to be ready to meet the Lord.[67] Then the sellers have no independent significance in the parable's interpretation. The inability of the wise virgins to share their supply at least suggests the theme of individual accountability—spiritual preparedness is not transferrable from one person to the next. But this is an allegorical waver; one may not affirm its import with as much confidence.[68]

As noted in chapter two (pp. 63-64), a partial rabbinic parallel contrasts wise and foolish guests invited to a banquet which would end at an unspecified time. The wise guests went home while their lamps were still lit. The foolish stayed late, got drunk and began to kill each other (b. Semachoth 8:10). Rabbi Meir concludes by quoting Amos 9:1 ("Strike the tops of the pillars so that the thresholds

[66]E.g., respectively, Karl P. Donfried, "The Allegory of the Ten Virgins (Matt. 25:1-13) as a Summary of Matthean Theology," *JBL* 93 (1974):423; R. V. G. Tasker, *The Gospel according to St. Matthew* (London: Tyndale; Grand Rapids: Eerdmans, 1961), p. 234; and John F. Walvoord, "Christ's Olivet Discourse on the End of the Age: The Parable of the Ten Virgins," *BSac* 129 (1972):102.

[67]A. H. M'Neile, *The Gospel according to St. Matthew* (London: Macmillan, 1915), p. 362. Cf. Carson, "Matthew," pp. 513-14.

[68]See esp. Robert H. Mounce, *Matthew* (San Francisco: Harper & Row, 1985), p. 240. J. Dwight Pentecost's attempt to limit the parable to Israel during the tribulation (*The Parables of Jesus* [Grand Rapids: Zondervan, 1982], p. 152) depends on a doubtful interpretation of Matthew 24—25 and is hard to reconcile with the theme of delay around which the parable centers. As with the parable of the faithful and unfaithful servants, the lessons of the ten virgins may be applied widely to Israel and the church so long as meaning and significance are distinguished, although it is always possible that Jesus had more than one application originally in mind.

shake. Bring them down on the heads of all the people; those who are left I will kill with the sword"). Interestingly, this is one of the few early rabbinic parables which does not append a clear explanation, so the meaning of the passage remains uncertain. Apparently, as in Jesus' parable, the emphasis lies on the impending destruction of the foolish individuals, while the lit and unlit lamps have no independent significance.

6.7 The Wheat and the Tares (Mt 13:24-30, 36-43)

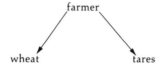

At first glance, the parable of the wheat and tares seems entirely different from those discussed above. The imagery is agricultural; the main "characters" include not just people but wheat and weeds. Several subordinate characters appear in more prominent roles than usual—servants, reapers and an enemy. Of course, the most striking difference is Jesus' *detailed* allegorical interpretation. No less than seven elements of the parable are directly equated with "spiritual" counterparts. If the brief conclusions of other parables with only limited allegorical interpretations are generally regarded as inauthentic, then it is scarcely surprising that virtually all but the most conservative commentators vigorously deny that Jesus could have intended this parable to teach anything remotely resembling the specifics of Matthew 13:36-43.[69]

A closer look, however, reveals some important structural similarities with the other triadic, monarchic parables. There is a central authority figure—the man who sows the seeds and oversees their harvest. There are contrasting subordinates—the wheat and the weeds. Nor is the symbolism of the interpretation ascribed to Jesus at all inappropriate. The use of seeds and plant growth to refer

---

[69]A few go so far as to dismiss the authenticity of the parable as well, often viewing it as a Matthean creation, modifying and elaborating Mark's little parable of the seed growing secretly. Cf., e.g., Robert H. Gundry, *Matthew: A Commentary on His Literary and Theological Art* (Grand Rapids: Eerdmans, 1982), pp. 261-62; Beare, *Matthew*, p. 303. But structurally these two parables are quite different (cf. below, pp. 263-66).

to righteous behavior had ample Old Testament precedent (cf., e.g., Hos 10:12; Jer 4:3-4; Is 55:10).[70] The harvest was a standard metaphor for judgment. Unusual details suggest that the parable is meant to point to a second level of meaning. The enemy's coming stealthily to sow the tares and the farmer's refusal to make any attempt at weeding can both be explained by ancient horticultural practices but nevertheless remain atypical.[71]

Even if the parable were left uninterpreted, it would seem fair to summarize its meaning under three headings, related to each of the main "characters." *(1) God permits the righteous and the wicked to coexist in the world, sometimes superficially indistinguishable from one another, until the end of the age. (2) The wicked will eventually be separated out, judged and destroyed. (3) The righteous will be gathered together, rewarded and brought into God's presence.*[72]

Each of the main "characters" of the story takes a turn holding the upper hand as the parable unfolds over three periods of time. At the beginning, the enemy and the weeds which he sowed seem to have triumphed (vv. 24-28a). In the middle, the wheat has survived, growing despite the presence of the weeds (vv. 28b-30a). In the end, the farmer still harvests his crop, destroying the weeds and salvaging the wheat (v. 30b).

Similarly, Jesus could see the world in his day as in bondage to sin and Satan, offer his message and ministry as the first stage in the solution to the problem, and promise a future day when God's people would win a total victory over their enemies. Dividing the message of the parable into "thirds" ends the needless debate over whether the emphasis of the parable lies in the period of the simultaneous growth of the wheat and weeds or in the final harvest, and it refutes the notion that the interpretation of the passage ascribed to Jesus must be inauthentic because its emphasis does not match that of the parable.[73] Beginning, middle and end—the obstacles to God's kingdom, the inauguration of that kingdom and its final con-

---

[70]John Drury, *The Parables in the Gospels* (London: SPCK; New York: Crossroad, 1985), p. 52.

[71]Jeremias, *Parables,* pp. 224-25.

[72]Thus Hill, *Matthew,* p. 235, declares: "The point of the interpretation, then, is exactly that of the parable itself: only God himself may distinguish the good from the evil: it is God's business alone to decide who belongs to the Kingdom." Note the three key referents—God, good and evil.

[73]As held by Pheme Perkins, *Hearing the Parables of Jesus* (New York: Paulist, 1981), p. 84; Jeremias, *Parables,* p. 81.

summation all are in view. A climactic stress may fall on the last of these but not to the exclusion of the other two.

Jesus' interpretation in verses 36-43 may then be viewed not as arbitrary allegorizing but as spelling out the natural referents of additional details in the parable, fitting in with the symbolism of the farmer, wheat and weeds. Not all the details identified in verses 37-39 are equally important nor is the list exhaustive, for verses 40-43 refer only to some of the same details while introducing others.

Specifically, Jesus does not again speak of the devil, although he goes on to imply equations between the burning of the weeds and the fiery furnace and between the barn and the "kingdom of the Father." Curiously, the field which verse 38 clearly associates with the world is subsequently matched with the kingdom (v. 41). Michel de Goedt picks up on these and other distinctions between verses 36-39 and verses 40-43 to argue that the latter probably reflect Christ's original interpretation, while the former were added at a secondary stage of the tradition.[74] But an equally viable approach simply recognizes that Jesus has appended two similarly sketchy but suggestive ways of understanding the elements of the parable.

Once the referents of the three main characters are identified, the other equations all fall into place naturally. God's enemy is obviously the devil. God's Word is preached throughout the world. The harvesters are the angels, who regularly figure in Jewish descriptions of the final judgment as God's helpers. The kingdom in verse 41, in keeping with Jesus' consistent use of the expression elsewhere in the Gospels, must refer to God's universal, sovereign reign rather than being equated with the church. Thus, the "contradiction" with verse 38 disappears.

The remarkable number of interpreters, who despite these verses make the field stand for the church,[75] shift too hastily from meaning to significance, or from a *Sitz im Leben Jesu* to a life-setting in early Christianity. Yet both Jesus' parable and his interpretation are comprehensible as authentic teachings if this shift is not made at the

---

[74]Michel de Goedt, "L'explication de la parabole de l'ivraie (Matt. xiii, 36-43): création matthéene, ou aboutissement d'une histoire littéraire?" *RB* 66 (1959):32-54.

[75]The classic representative of this view is St. Augustine (Sermons on New Testament Lessons 23). Cf. also Richard C. Trench, *Notes on the Parables of Our Lord* (London: Macmillan, 1870; New York: Appleton, 1873), p. 91; William Hendriksen, *Exposition of the Gospel according to Matthew* (Grand Rapids: Baker, 1973 [= *The Gospel of Matthew* (London: Banner of Truth, 1976)]), p. 573.

outset.[76] The one detail which is left uninterpreted throughout all of verses 36-43 is the servants. They are a different group than the reapers and, as in many of Jesus' other parables where the servants are not among the three primary characters, they are simply props to do the bidding of the master and to allow the storyteller to reveal the master's thoughts through dialog form.[77]

A final debate surrounding the interpretation of this parable involves its intended audience. A common view of the original setting of this story imagines Jesus denouncing the exclusiveness of the various Jewish sects, in keeping with the decidedly nonseparatist nature of his teaching and practice.[78] This scenario may reflect a valid application of the parable, but its original meaning is perfectly intelligible in the setting which Matthew has given it. No particular Pharisaic opposition appears here, the parable is spoken to the crowds who generally approved of Christ, and the interpretation is given only to the disciples.

More likely, the foremost danger in Jesus' mind was the attitude of his supporters, who were already growing discontent with the opposition they faced. Like the disciples who wanted to call down fire from heaven on the unreceptive Samaritans (Lk 9:54), they would have preferred to invoke God's wrath more directly on their opponents. In reply, Jesus enjoins patience and alerts them to expect continued hostility from those who would reject his message.[79] At a later date, the church could legitimately apply the same lessons within her own ranks, when false teachers or nominal adherents hindered the work of the truly redeemed. To conclude that a "mixed church" was inevitable, however, and to use this parable as a justification for doing nothing to attempt to purify the church (as with St. Augustine) goes well beyond anything demanded by the imagery of the narrative. Jesus elsewhere certainly charged his would-be disciples with single-minded service and devotion to him (e.g., Lk 14:25-33; Mt 8:18-22 par.).

---

[76]Cf. France, *Matthew*, p. 225; more tentatively, G. R. Beasley-Murray, *Jesus and the Kingdom of God* (Exeter: Paternoster; Grand Rapids: Eerdmans, 1986), p. 135.

[77]Cf. Stein, *Parables*, pp. 144-45.

[78]E.g., Schweizer, *Matthew*, p. 304; Hunter, *Parables*, p. 46.

[79]Stein, *Parables*, p. 144; Findlay, *Jesus*, p. 26.

6.8 The Dragnet (Mt 13:47-50)

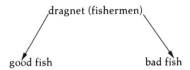

The parable of the dragnet closely resembles the parable of the wheat and tares. Instead of good and bad seed, Jesus describes good and bad fish. Instead of describing the period in which they were mixed together in the sea, he focuses solely on their catch and separation. But otherwise the message and structure are remarkably the same, though the story of the net contains less detail. The closing verses of each passage underline these parallels with the identical refrain "they will throw them into the fiery furnace; there will be the weeping and gnashing of teeth" (vv. 42, 50). The determiner, or unifying figure, could be seen either as the net or the unnamed "they" who do the sorting of the fish. Since the latter seem to correspond to the angels as God's helpers, the former seems preferable. The net becomes a symbol for God's ingathering of all people at the end of the age.

Episodically the parable falls into three clearly delineated parts, corresponding to the three main characters and lessons of the passage. *(1) Verses 47-48a describe the action of the dragnet, which stands for God who will come to judge his people on the last day. (2) Verse 48b describes the fate of the good fish, which stand for those God declares righteous, who are gathered together for further service and safekeeping. (3) Verse 48c describes the fate of the rotten fish, which stand for the unredeemed, who are discarded as worthless.* The conclusion in verses 49-50 develops only this last point, so emphasis must be placed on it. As with the parables of the wheat and tares and of the ten virgins this passage acts out a tragic plot.

Several other details in the text merit attention. First, the fact that the bad fish are merely thrown away while wicked people are thrown into a fiery furnace proves that not every detail on the literal level of meaning perfectly matches its allegorical counterpart. But rather than providing grounds for viewing the conclusion as inauthentic, this observation strengthens the case for seeing the passage as an authentic unity.[80] Later stages of the tradition would probably have tried to remove such inconsistencies. Second, the surfacing of "every kind" of fish in one part of the lake is the most obviously unusual feature of the text, especially since the word for "kind" (γένος) is more commonly used for a "race" or "tribe" of people. An allegorical meaning for these details is thereby confirmed; the different kinds of fish stand for different nationalities of human beings.[81]

Third, a common deduction from the reference to all kinds of fish is that Jesus' disciples must preach to all people regardless of ethnic background.[82] Jesus' earlier command to his followers to become "fishers of men" (Mk 1:17 pars.) gives this interpretation an aura of plausibility, but it overlooks the fact that all the action of the parable occurs at the time of the final sorting.[83] No interval is described between the catch and the separation. The point must rather be that which the story of the judgment of the sheep and the goats elaborates (Mt 25:31-46)—no race or category of person will escape the final judgment. All will be sorted into one of two groups, those God accepts and those he rejects.[84] Finally, while one must guard against too quickly "Christianizing" the interpretation of the parable (so that the good fish are only Christians rather than God's people of all ages), one must avoid the opposite extreme of restricting exposition to Jewish categories. One dispensationalist commentator observes:

> Every previous form of the theocracy had ended in judgment: the expulsion from the Garden of Eden, the catastrophe of the Flood, the scattering from Babel, and the Exile. The question arose then of how this new form of the theocracy would end. The answer

---

[80]Cf. Simon J. Kistemaker, *The Parables of Jesus* (Grand Rapids: Baker, 1980), pp. 60-61. Contra, e.g., Hill, *Matthew*, p. 238; Beare, *Matthew*, p. 315.

[81]Cf. Jack D. Kingsbury, *The Parables of Jesus in Matthew 13* (London: SPCK; Richmond: John Knox, 1969), p. 120. Joachim Gnilka, *Das Matthäusevangelium* (Freiburg: Herder, 1986), p. 509, points out that the fish-catch would have garnered ritually unclean as well as clean fish. Perhaps Jesus also had in mind the overcoming of the Jew-Gentile barriers.

[82]E.g., J. D. M. Derrett, "ΉΣΑΝ ΓΑΡ ΑΛΙΕΙΣ (Mk i.16): Jesus's Fishermen and the Parable of the Net," *NovT* 22 (1980):125-31; Kistemaker, *Parables*, p. 61.

[83]Dodd, *Parables*, pp. 187-89, recognizes that the "fishers of men" interpretation only works if vv. 49-50 are disregarded. Beare, *Matthew*, p. 316, correctly adds that v. 48 must similarly be excised.

[84]Carson, "Matthew," pp. 330-31. Cf. Pierre Bonnard, L'Évangile selon saint Matthieu (Neûchatel: Delachaux & Niestlé, 1963), p. 208.

was given by Christ in the parable of the net.[85]
However valid an analysis of Old Testament history this may be,
there is not the slightest hint in Matthew's context that such a
question triggered this parable or that the problem even entered
Christ's mind. The parable does not address the question of how
the church age will end but of how all humanity will be judged.

6.9 The Rich Man and Lazarus (Lk 16:19-31)

The rich man and Lazarus is the first of the parables so far surveyed
which does not introduce its authority figure at the outset. Here the
story begins apparently just with a contrast between two men who
are worlds apart from each other in all but geography. After describing each in turn (vv. 19, 20-21), Jesus relates their deaths in
reverse order, highlighting the reversal of their status in the life to
come. The beggar finds himself in Abraham's bosom; the rich man,
in Hades (vv. 22a, 22b-23)—two traditional Jewish names for the
places of the righteous and wicked dead.

In verse 24 the story shifts from narrative discourse to direct
discourse, and Abraham appears as a third, unifying figure who
explains the judgments meted out to the other two men. The rich
man and Abraham carry on a dialog until the end of the parable.
A turning point in the dialog appears in verse 26, when, after learn-
ing about the unbridgeable chasm separating the two speakers, the
rich man stops pleading for himself and turns his thoughts to his
brothers who are still on earth.

This "seam" has understandably caused many to dissect the passage via tradition criticism. A popular approach finds verses 16-26
traditional and verses 27-31 redactional.[86] An ancient Egyptian folk-

---

[85]Pentecost, *Parables*, p. 62.

[86]E.g., Rudolf Bultmann, *History of the Synoptic Tradition* (Oxford: Blackwell; New York: Harper
& Row, 1963), pp. 196-97; Crossan, *Parables*, pp. 66-67; Bernard B. Scott, *Hear Then the Parable*
(Minneapolis: Fortress, 1989), pp. 142-46.

tale, modified and popularized in Jewish circles, strikingly resembles the parable but lacks its emphasis on repentance through obedience to Moses and the prophets. The more well-known Jewish form of this folk-tale narrates the story of the rich tax collector Bar Ma'jan, who died and was given a well-attended, ostentatious funeral. About the same time, a poor scholar died and was buried without pomp or attention. Yet the scholar found himself in Paradise, by flowing streams, while Bar Ma'jan found himself near the bank of a stream unable to reach the water.[87]

Some suggest, therefore, that Luke has simply embellished a popular story of this kind. More plausible is the suggestion that the second "half" of the parable is Jesus' own distinctive addition to a tale which circulated in different forms. Nevertheless, structurally, the break after verse 23 (when the dialog begins) seems more pronounced than the shift in focus between verses 26-27. Tying verses 24 and 27 together, the verbal repetition of an address ("father"), of an imprecation ("have mercy on me," "I beg you") and of a request for Abraham to send Lazarus supports this assessment.[88] So it is perhaps doubtful whether any two-stage development of the parable should be posited.[89] More important still, the theme of "too late" winds through all portions of the passage, weaving it into a tightly-knit unity. The rich man pays attention to Lazarus too late, he sees the unbridgeable chasm too late, he worries about his brothers too late, and he heeds the law and the prophets too late.[90]

The parable remains unique in several respects. It is the only one which does not limit its action to events in this world but carries over into the next. It is the only one in which characters have names.[91] Its characters do not seem to symbolize "spiritual counter-

---

[87]For a detailed summary of the Egyptian original, see Kendrick Grobel, " '. . . Whose Name was Neves,' " NTS 10 (1963-64):373-82. The basic contours of the Jewish form appear in Jeremias, Parables, pp. 178-79, 183.

[88]F. Schnider and W. Stenger, "Die offene Tür und die unüberschreitbare Kluft," NTS 25 (1979):281-82. Cf. Eugene S. Wehrli, "Luke 16:19-31," Int 31 (1977):279-80.

[89]Ronald F. Hock, "Lazarus and Micyllus: Greco-Roman Backgrounds to Luke 16:19-31," JBL 106 (1987):447-63, thinks that this unity makes it less likely that the Bar Ma'jan tale lies in the background. Instead Hock interprets this parable in light of somewhat parallel stories in the writings of Lucian of Samosata, in which the virtuous poor are rewarded in the afterlife and the hedonistic rich are condemned.

[90]Otto Glombitza, "Der reiche Mann und der arme Lazarus," NovT 12 (1970):166-80.

[91]In later traditions, the rich man also received a name—usually Dives—but this simply stemmed from the Latin word for "rich man." For the textual history of this name see Henry J. Cadbury, "A Proper Name for Dives," JBL 81 (1962):399-402.

parts" but simply represent other people in identical situations—
certain rich men, certain poor men, and those who dwell in the
presence of God. Thus the parable has been called an example story
rather than a parable proper (see above, p. 73). It is possible to go
so far as to question whether the story is a fictitious narrative at
all and to suggest that perhaps Jesus was intending to recount the
actual fate of two people known to him and his audience.[92]

This last possibility can be dismissed almost at once. The passage
begins with the same formula as so many of Jesus' parables: "a
certain man was . . ." The indefinite pronoun in Greek has parallels
in the Hebrew introductions to rabbinic parables and weighs against
the suggestion that real individuals were in view. The structure of
the story perfectly mirrors the triadic, monarchic pattern which has
appeared throughout this chapter.[93]

That the parable stems from example more than metaphor is
valid but only up to a point. Abraham, as the father of the Jewish
nation and like the other authority figures surveyed, speaks on
behalf of God. And it is not poor and rich men per se whom Lazarus
and his heartless neighbor depict, but those who demonstrate by
their attitudes to material possessions a proper or improper relationship with God. After all, Abraham too was rich. Verse 30,
moreover, makes it clear that the indictment against the rich man's
brothers addressed their lack of repentance, which amounts to an
admission of the fundamental problem with the rich man himself.
Every Jew knew the Old Testament laws commanding the compassionate use of riches, so the man had no excuse for his wanton
neglect of one whom he regularly saw and could have helped very
easily.[94]

Lazarus, too, is probably meant to be seen as one who had faith
in God. His very name means "God helps" (from the Hebrew "Elie-

---

[92]A viewpoint seldom expressed in contemporary literature on the parables but which still
surfaces surprisingly often in other kinds of studies. See, e.g., Millard Erickson, *Christian Theology*,
vol. 2 (Grand Rapids: Baker, 1984), p. 527. David Gooding, *According to Luke* (Leicester: IVP; Grand
Rapids: Eerdmans, 1987), p. 227, argues that the passage is not a parable since it is not based
on "actual things and activities in this world." But such a limitation seems arbitrary and unwarranted.

[93]Cf. Jones, *Parables*, pp. 143-44; Robert C. McQuilkin, *Our Lord's Parables* (Grand Rapids: Zondervan, 1980), p. 187.

[94]See esp. David P. Seccombe, *Possessions and the Poor in Luke-Acts* (Linz: Studien zum Neuen
Testament und seiner Umwelt, 1982), pp. 176-77.

zer"), which probably explains its inclusion.[95] But rather than focusing on anything he had done to express his piety—his state of helplessness virtually forbade tangible signs except for his uncomplaining acceptance of his plight—Jesus may be hinting at God's sovereignty in salvation by identifying him simply as one whom the Lord had aided.

One may thus suggest that the main lessons of the parable follow these lines: *(1) Like Lazarus, those whom God helps will be borne after their death into God's presence. (2) Like the rich man, the unrepentant will experience irreversible punishment. (3) Through Abraham, Moses, and the prophets, God reveals himself and his will so that none who neglect it can legitimately protest their subsequent fate.*[96]

In keeping with the amount of attention paid to each character, Jesus was probably emphasizing (2) and (3) more than (1), but all three points nevertheless seem present.[97] The parable overturns conventional Jewish wisdom which saw the rich as blessed by God and the poor as punished for their wickedness. The restrictions against unlimited allegorizing and the fact that the source for much of the imagery of the parable probably was popular folklore should warn against viewing the details of this narrative as a realistic description of the afterlife. Attempts to limit those details to teaching about the "intermediate state" of the believer (after death and before the final resurrection) or to the situation of Old Testament saints (before Jesus' crucifixion and resurrection) do not alter this fact.

Nevertheless even the most sober of commentators continues to squeeze more out of this parable than is defensible, probably because there are so few passages in Scripture which clearly teach

---

[95]Jeremias, *Parables*, p. 185; Gerhard Schneider, *Das Evangelium nach Lukas*, vol. 2 (Gütersloh: Gerd Mohn; Würzburg: Echter Verlag, 1977), p. 341. Other suggestions have been made concerning Lazarus's name—it creates a parallel with Abraham's servant Eliezer in Genesis 15 (e.g., C. H. Cave, "Lazarus and the Lukan Deuteronomy," *NTS* 15 [1968-69]:323-25) or it is somehow linked to the Lazarus whom Jesus raised (e.g., R. Dunkerley, "Lazarus," *NTS* 5 [1958-59]:321-27)—but these approaches are less convincing.

[96]Cf. Thorwald Lorenzen, "A Biblical Meditation on Luke 16:19-31," *ExpT* 87 (1975):39-43. Contrast Jeremias's bland, reductionistic one main point: "in the face of this challenge of the hour, evasion is impossible" (*Parables*, p. 182).

[97]An approach which affirms two points in the parable, based on the dialog between the rich man and Abraham, but which relegates Lazarus to the periphery, is found in Hans Kvalbein, "Jesus and the Poor: Two Texts and a Tentative Conclusion," *Themelios* 12 (1987):80-87. Yet Kvalbein accepts the significance of Lazarus's name suggested here, so it is not clear why he should object to a third point.

about the details of life after death. Thus Murray Harris, for example, can at first agree that "the parable of the rich man and Lazarus was told to illustrate the danger of wealth and the necessity of repentance, not to satisfy our natural curiosity about man's anthropological condition after death," and yet immediately seem to ignore this salutary warning by adding, "it is not illegitimate to deduce from the setting of the story the basic characteristics of the *post mortem* state of believers and unbelievers." Among these he includes consciousness of surroundings, memory of one's past, capacity to reason, and acuteness of perception.[98]

If these are true aspects of the afterlife, they will be derived from other passages of Scripture, not from this one. Otherwise one might just as well conclude that it will be possible to talk to those "on the other side," that Abraham will be God's spokesman in meting out final judgment, and that some from "heaven" will apparently want to be able to travel to "hell" ("those who want to go from here to you"—v. 26)![99]

A final thought concerns the parable's concluding reference to the futility of a mission by one who would come back from the dead and try to convert those who neglected the Old Testament revelation. It is probably impossible for a Christian to read this verse (v. 31) without thinking of the resurrection of Christ. If such a reference were originally intended, it would scarcely make the prophecy *ex eventu*, unless one arbitrarily rules out the possibility of Jesus' foreseeing his death and resurrection.

But it is unlikely that many in his audience would have picked up such an allusion before the fact and likely that none was intended. The verb used in Luke's retelling of the story in Greek is not the word commonly used for Jesus' "raising up" from the dead (ἐγείρω) but one which more generally means to stand or get up (ἀνίστημι), and some manuscripts offer an even less theological term meaning "to come out of" (ἐξέρχομαι).

In the parable the request for a messenger applies to Lazarus, not

---

[98]Murray J. Harris, "The New Testament View of Life after Death," *Themelios* 11 (1986):47-48.

[99]At the opposite end of the spectrum, Donald Guthrie, *New Testament Theology* (Leicester and Downers Grove: IVP, 1981), p. 820, remarks: "the only certain fact about the afterlife which emerges from the parable is the reality of its existence." But surely one must add at least that there are both irreversibly good and unalterably evil possibilities for this life.

to a Messiah-figure, and in the Egyptian "parallel" the god Si-Osiris also returns from the world of the dead. It is quite possible that this was simply a conventional feature and an integral part of the folktale.[100] C. J. A. Hickling adds that it could also easily have referred to the resuscitations Jesus had already performed during his ministry, which nevertheless left the Jewish leaders unconvinced.[101]

Still, as an application, if not as the interpretation, the picture fits the resurrection of Christ and the disbelieving response of many of the Jews so perfectly that it seems appropriate to reapply it in light of later events, as an example of the later significance of the original meaning. One is tempted to generalize the third point of the parable even further and agree with Cadoux that the passage illustrates how often "conscience is not convinced nor the spiritual world vindicated by signs."[102] The parable's climax then makes this principle the dominant of the three.

6.10 The Children in the Marketplace (Mt 11:16-19; Lk 7:31-35)

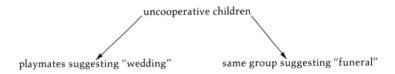

uncooperative children

playmates suggesting "wedding"   same group suggesting "funeral"

The final parable to be considered in this chapter seems to present only two groups of people throughout—two clusters of children at play. The picture is not entirely clear and has been interpreted as depicting two groups proposing alternate games, "wedding" and "funeral," or one group proposing the two different games to their recalcitrant companions who refuse to join in either.

The parable itself can be read both ways, but the verses appended (Mt 11:18-19; Lk 7:33-35) require the latter approach. This interpretation clearly allegorizes the parable in light of Jesus' festive ministry contrasted with John the Baptist's more somber preaching. The one group of children then actually fills both contrasting roles

---

[100]C. W. F. Smith, *Parables*, p. 166.

[101]C. J. A. Hickling, "A Tract on Jesus and the Pharisees? A Conjecture on the Redaction of Luke 15 and 16," *HeyJ* 16 (1975):257.

[102]Cadoux, *Parables*, p. 128.

and the other group, standing for the unresponsive Jews, acts as the judge between them. Whereas in some of the previous parables the determining figures eventually accepted both options presented (e.g., the two debtors), here they reject both.

For those who bracket as later additions the explanations of the parables ascribed to Jesus, this allegorization can be laid to one side. Yet there is nothing in the parable which requires any different approach.[103] Luke's use of "calling to one another" rather than "calling the others" fits equally well with both interpretations. Here at least, then, many commentators are willing to accept that something like the evangelists' conclusion does reflect Jesus' original meaning.[104]

Debate, however, reappears over the details of the children's proposal and the responses elicited. Does the group of children proposing the two games represent, alternately, Jesus and John, so that it is the Jewish leaders who neither danced nor mourned?[105] Or did the Jews try to temper John's stern message with greater levity and Jesus' "permissiveness" with stricter legalism only to find both men uncooperative?[106]

In favor of the latter reading is the *order* of Jesus' conclusion; his comments about John and the Son of man would then parallel the sequence of the two lines of the children's complaint as well as the chronological sequence of the two men's ministries. In favor of the former is the *wording* of Jesus' conclusion; it is the Jews' response to John and Jesus, not John's and Jesus' response to the Jews, that is bemoaned. In light of the parables' propensity for chiastic structures (see above, pp. 150-51), the point about the conclusion's wording carries more weight than the one about its order.

Before enumerating the parables' main points, one further complication must be examined. Both Matthew's and Luke's accounts append a brief, cryptic saying about the justification of wisdom.

---

[103]Inasmuch as the introductory formula compares the kingdom to the entire scenario depicted rather than to just one character or group of characters, Wendy J. Cotter's objections to previous interpretations of the parable are unfounded ("The Parable of the Children in the Market-Place, Q (Lk) 7:31-35," *NovT* 29 [1987]:293-95).

[104]E.g., Jeremias, *Parables*, pp. 161-62; Dodd, *Parables*, p. 114; Schweizer, *Matthew*, p. 259.

[105]So, e.g., Dieter Zeller, "Die Bildlogik der Gleichnisses Mt 11:16f./Lk 7:31f." *ZNW* 68 (1977):252-57; Fitzmyer, *Luke I-IX*, pp. 678-79.

[106]So, e.g., Olof Linton, "The Parable of the Children's Game," *NTS* 22 (1976):159-79; Marshall, *Luke*, pp. 300-301.

Whether Jesus originally attributed this justification to wisdom's deeds or to her children (see above, p. 109), the issue seems to be that the correctness of John's and Jesus' behavior, like that of the more lively group of children, will eventually be proved. A few have taken this ironically, though, as an aside commenting on the futility or "pseudo-wisdom" of the group which balked at both activities.[107] But the terms "wisdom" and "justified" are never used in this sense elsewhere in the Gospels, and because a straightforward reading of them makes perfect sense, it should be preferred.

The parable thus yields the following lessons: *(1) The joyful message of forgiveness should be freely celebrated and not dampened by legalistic restrictions (Mt 11:17a, 19a). (2) The solemn message of repentance should not be ignored but taken with full seriousness (vv. 17b, 18). (3) The truth of both of these principles will be demonstrated by those who implement them (v. 19b).*

The phrasing of this last point incorporates both the readings "deeds" and "children" and permits the emissaries of God's wisdom to be both John and Jesus as well as all those who follow them. It does not seem necessary to try to restrict these referents any more narrowly. The uniqueness of points (1) and (2) lies in the fact that here God's representatives are the subordinates and his opponents have the upper hand in choosing to reject both. Other parables have clearly indicated the reversal of this relationship at the end of the age, but for now the power of the gospel is cloaked with powerlessness. Full vindication awaits a future date.

6.11 Conclusions

If one compiles the three main points associated with each of Jesus' simple, triadic parables, a consistent set of themes emerges. From the various authority figures one learns that God seeks those who are lost, welcomes sinners, forgives all who repent, commands men to do his will, rewards and punishes them in light of their obedience and stewardship, and establishes a day of final judgment, the timing of which is uncertain. But on that day truth will be completely vindicated and evil irreversibly obliterated.

From the "good" subordinates come the lessons that men must

---

[107]B. S. Easton, *The Gospel according to St. Luke* (Edinburgh: T. & T. Clark; New York: Scribner's, 1926), p. 104.

turn to God irrespective of their pasts, repent and show love for all as the fruit which stems from faith, avoid legalism, heed the testimony of Scripture, and persevere with a consistent expectation of the end of the age, at which time they will be rewarded with God's abiding presence. From the "bad" subordinates stem stern warnings against despising the grace God extends to others, complacency in one's spiritual life (even when one appears superficially similar to the truly pious), failure to keep one's promises to God, lack of adequate preparation for the "long haul" of discipleship, and lovelessness or miserliness, especially with respect to the world's needy. For those who act in this fashion, a day may come after which it is too late to repent and eternal judgment will follow.

These themes closely resemble the lessons most modern interpreters have drawn from the parables. Viewing the parables as allegories does not result in a radically different assessment of their meaning, since the allegorical elements are limited in number and interpreted in light of the historical background of Jesus' day. Of course modern scholarship often agrees on the meaning of the parables as they stand in the canonical Gospels but denies that Jesus originally said or meant the same things. This approach has failed to convince for each of the passages examined.

Much of the time scholarly skepticism stems from pitting against one another different interpretations of a parable, when in fact those interpretations each complement one another. Jesus probably intended to affirm these complementary views simultaneously. In many cases the differing interpretations result from focusing on different main characters. Once many of the parables are seen as teaching three distinct lessons from the actions of their three principal characters, no need remains for choosing one of the lessons at the expense of the others. In some instances it may be possible to find one simple sentence which fairly encapsulates the entire sense of the text. In several cases, one or two of the points are more dominant than others. But it often seems easier and fairer to allow the three points to stand on their own, lest the richness of meaning of any individual passage be unduly restricted.

7
Complex Three-Point Parables

SEVERAL OF THE PARABLES OF JESUS HAVE MORE THAN THREE main characters or groups of characters but ultimately display the same triangular structure as the parables discussed in the previous chapter. Often one particular role, usually the good or bad subordinate, may be illustrated with multiple examples, as with the priest and Levite in the parable of the good Samaritan. Two of the parables, the unforgiving servant and the unjust steward, have a simpler triadic structure but are not "monarchic"—the unifying character is not an authority figure, and there is no contrast between equally matched subordinates. One parable, that of the wicked tenants, is perhaps the most complex of all and defies simple categorization. It seems to follow a triadic model which has been complicated by its incorporation into a Hebrew form known as "proem midrash." As a result, it may actually make four points.

7.1 The Talents (Mt 25:14-30; cf. Lk 19:12-27)

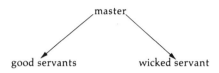

This servant parable contrasts not two subordinate figures but three: men entrusted by their master with five, two and one talents, respectively. The story appears to have four main characters. But the first two servants actually function in identical fashion as positive models. The structure remains triadic but the position of the good subordinate is subdivided into two examples. The exact amounts of money which the servants are given are not relevant, nor are the amounts they make through their investment. The point is that they both invested and received a return. The decreasing quantities simply serve to build to a climax. Surely the one given the least should have the easiest time of all in being a good steward of his trust. The ὡσαύτως ("likewise") in Matthew 25:17, the parallelism of structure in the description of the first two servants' investments in verses 16-17, and the identical phrasing in verses 20-22 in the final reckoning scene with the master all indicate that these two characters have one role to play between them.

The "three characters" are thus the master, the two good servants taken together and the wicked servant. The final reckoning scene, as in the other servant parables, refers to the final judgment that all people will undergo as they give account to God for what they have done with their lives. The extra detail with which the actions and fate of the wicked servant are narrated, along with the harsh conclusion to the parable in verses 28-30, make this a tragic plot—the lesson to be derived from the evil servant is the dominant one.

Nevertheless three points may again be discerned, one per main character. *(1) Like the master, God entrusts all people with a portion of his resources, expecting them to act as good stewards of it. (2) Like the two good servants, God's people will be commended and rewarded when they have faithfully discharged that commission. (3) Like the wicked servant, those who fail to use the gifts God has given them for his service will be punished by separation from God and all things good.*

This final point seems appropriate both for those who are overtly hostile to God and his revelation as well as for those who profess commitment to him but whose lives show no evidence of the reality of their profession. The Matthean context, in which Jesus speaks the parable to his disciples as part of his eschatological discourse, is completely appropriate as the original occasion of its utterance,[1] even if it might just as naturally have fit into a controversy with his opponents. The view that the parable is about "spiritual atrophy"—abilities not used and cultivated in this life will be lost or will deteriorate—seems less likely in light of the consistent use of reckoning scenes in parables to refer to *final* judgment.[2]

The common-sense attitude on which this story seems to rely (wise stewardship involves investment) was probably much less self-evident in ancient Palestine. An oft-cited rabbinic maxim commends the burial of money as one of the safest ways of protecting it (b. Baba Metzia 42a). If the master in the story did have a reputation for being severe, the servant who did not risk losing what he was given may easily have been viewed as taking prudent action. A rabbinic parable further illustrates this point with imagery that affords some striking parallels to the talents:

> To what may the matter be compared? To a reliable person who was in a town, with whom everyone deposited their bailments for safe-keeping. When one of them would come to retrieve his property, [the reliable man] would produce and hand over the object, since he knew precisely where it was. And if [the owner] had occasion to send for a bailment with his son or slave or agent, he would have to turn things topsy-turvy, for he did not know where things were. (Sifre Deut. 357:11)[3]

Jesus' condemnation of the man who hid his master's money may thus have caused strong shockwaves. On the other hand, the Jewish law which commended the burial of money spoke only of safeguarding the trust of a friend or client, not of the appropriate way of dealing with finances intended for investment (cf. Lk 19:13). So

---

[1]Contra most—e.g., Joachim Jeremias, *The Parables of Jesus* (London: SCM; Philadelphia: Westminster, 1972), pp. 58-63; C. H. Dodd, *The Parables of the Kingdom* (London: Nisbet, 1935; New York: Scribner's, 1936), pp. 151-52.

[2]Robert H. Mounce, *Matthew* (San Francisco: Harper & Row, 1985), p. 242, combines both of these points, but it is not clear that the latter necessarily entails the former.

[3]Trans. Jacob Neusner, *Sifre to Deuteronomy*, vol. 2 (Atlanta: Scholars, 1987), p. 458.

perhaps the man's behavior should be seen as rather foolish. Thus neither the action of the servant nor the response of the master is implausible, but each is somewhat unusual.[4]

This suggests an allegorical level of meaning, especially as the concluding refrain breaks the bounds of the parable's imagery by describing a place of eternal punishment where darkness and weeping and gnashing of teeth prevail (Mt 25:30). The master stands for God, and the servants for various kinds of people. Of course, the picture of God as both a generous rewarder and a stern judge is not one that sits well with many modern commentators, but it is a thoroughly biblical portrait.

Other details in the parable must not be pressed. The master's departure need not refer to the postponement of Jesus' return, though it would have been natural to reapply it that way at a later date (cf. above, p. 67). The money distributed among the servants must not be equated with any specific type of gift or ability. God may entrust a person with a wide range of resources and abilities. The ratio of the amounts given to the various servants, like the 100% returns which each of the first two servants gained, has no exact proportional equivalent in spiritual realities, although the differentiation may suggest that "grace never condones irresponsibility; even those given less are obligated to use and develop what they have."[5]

Commentators tend to agree that most of the parable hangs together as a fairly coherent whole,[6] but verses 28-29 seem inauthentic to many. Verse 28 goes beyond saying that faithful stewardship will be rewarded and unfaithfulness punished, by describing the reward for the faithful servant as coming at the lazy one's expense: "take the talent from him, and give it to him who has the ten talents." Verse 29 creates a further problem by speaking not of how the servants used what they had been given, but merely of the raw

---

[4]See esp. Pheme Perkins, *Hearing the Parables of Jesus* (New York: Paulist, 1981), p. 148. Many commentators pick up on one or the other of these but seldom on both.

[5]D. A. Carson, "Matthew," in *The Expositor's Bible Commentary*, vol. 8, ed. Frank E. Gaebelein (Grand Rapids: Zondervan, 1984), p. 517.

[6]Perhaps the most important exception is Lane C. McGaughy, "The Fear of Yahweh and the Mission of Judaism: A Post-exilic Maxim and Its Early Christian Expansion in the Parable of the Talents," *JBL* 94 (1975):235-45, who sees the parable as a creation on the basis of the pre-Christian saying found in v. 26 (cf. the very rough parallels concerning the fear and severity of Yahweh in Job 4:14, 10:16, 23:13-17; Ps 119:120).

totals which they possessed: "to everyone who has more will be given . . . but from him who has not, even what he has will be taken away." Yet both of these verses can make sense as part of the original parable, and they should be given an opportunity to do so before being jettisoned.

Verse 29 fits best in the context of the narrative as referring to "everyone who has" or "has not" *earned* something during his period of stewardship, otherwise the wicked servant would not qualify as one who "had not"—he did still have the one talent given him.[7] That the good servants' rewards came from what was taken from the wicked doesn't necessarily mean anything more than that all possessions are God's and he is free to distribute and redistribute them as he chooses. In the parable, it is possible that the story could not have been told any other way, if we assume that the householder entrusted his servants with almost all his goods (v. 14) and had nothing else substantial on which to draw for his giving of rewards. Francis Beare rightly recognizes that verse 28 is perfectly in keeping with the basic story while also paving the way for the teaching of the next verse, so his rejection of verse 29 as inauthentic is unnecessary.[8]

While most agree that Matthew's parable of the talents fairly closely reflects what Jesus originally spoke, commentators tend to treat Luke's very similar parable of the pounds quite differently. It is similar enough to be seen as a variant of the same narrative but different enough so that most think that some drastic modification or editing must have occurred. The most common explanation is that Luke, or the tradition he inherited, has conflated two parables— the parable of the talents and a parable about a "throne claimant" who is opposed by his citizens and who ends up destroying them (vv. 12, 14, 15a, 27, and the references to cities in vv. 17 and 19).[9]

---

[7]See esp. Leon Morris, *The Gospel according to St. Luke* (London: IVP; Grand Rapids: Eerdmans, 1974), p. 276, commenting on the similar verses (Lk 19:24-26) in Luke's parable of the pounds. Cf. A. H. M'Neile, *The Gospel according to St. Matthew* (London: Macmillan, 1915), p. 367; John F. Walvoord, "Christ's Olivet Discourse on the End of the Age: The Parable of the Talents," *BSac* 129 (1972):210.

[8]Francis W. Beare, *The Gospel according to Matthew* (San Francisco: Harper & Row; Oxford: Blackwell, 1981), pp. 490-91. His rejection of this verse is based on misinterpreting it as teaching the law of "spiritual atrophy" (as described above).

[9]See esp. Max Zerwick, "Die Parabel vom Thronanwärter," *Bib* 40 (1959): 654-74; Francis D. Weinert, "The Parable of the Throne Claimant (Luke 19:12, 14-15a, 27) Reconsidered," *CBQ* 39 (1977):505-14; Wilhelm Resenhöfft, "Jesu Gleichnis von den Talenten, ergänzt durch die Lukas-Fassung," *NTS* 26 (1980):318-31.

This second parable closely parallels the details of the trip of Archelaus, son of Herod the Great, to Rome in 4 B.C. to receive imperial ratification of his hereditary claim to rule Judea, along with the Jewish embassy which opposed him and Archelaus's subsequent revenge on the Judeans (cf. Josephus *Ant.* 17:299-323, *Bell.* 2:80-100). If these details are removed, the remaining text varies only a little from Matthew's talents parable—smaller sums of money are involved, ten rather than three servants appear at the outset, and the wicked servant hides his pound in a napkin. At the same time, neither of the reconstructed parables is entirely coherent on its own. Each must have had additional details which were lost in the conflation.[10] A coherent interpretation of the text as it stands, if one can be discerned, should be preferred.

Four main problems lead most to abandon the search for such an interpretation. (1) It is improbable that a future king would give his servants such small sums of money. One "pound" (mina) was only 100 days wages for a common laborer. (2) It is even more unlikely that he would have them trade with such small sums. (3) Only three of the ten servants give an account of themselves; the other seven appear extraneous. (4) Verse 25 has the first servant's companions complaining merely that he already had ten pounds rather than objecting to the ten cities which had been given him as a reward (v. 17).[11]

Objections (1) and (2) are fairly subjective and not too weighty. In 3 Maccabees 1:4 (describing the intertestamental warfare between the Seleucids and Ptolemies) Arsinoë offered the troops of her brother Antiochus III two minas each if they defeated the Egyptians. Luke's "minas" may be more modest than Matthew's "talents," but the smaller quantity also renders the wrath of the nobleman more intelligible when the wicked servant fails to take the risk of investment even with a relatively paltry sum. Moreover, burial in a napkin had no legal precedent, pointing out even more clearly the untrustworthiness of the servant.

Objection (4) may be countered by the supposition that Jesus

---

[10]See esp. Paul Joüon, "La parabole des mines (Luc, 19,12-27) et la parabole des talents (Matthieu, 25,14-30)," *RSR* 29 (1939):493.

[11]For these four objections, see Jan Lambrecht, *Once More Astonished: The Parables of Jesus* (New York: Crossroad, 1981), p. 174.

wanted to teach the principle that "the smallest gift may be put to good use" (cf. Lk 16:10),[12] or it may be assumed that an extra city came with the extra pound corresponding to the previous parallelism between numbers of cities and pounds. In addition, the fact that several important textual authorities omit verse 25 altogether makes it doubtful whether much should be derived from this verse or that it holds the key to the original form or meaning of the parable.[13]

By far the most troublesome objection is (3). It is strange that the third servant should be called ὁ ἕτερος ("*the* other"; contra RSV, NIV) as if the other seven no longer existed (Lk 19:20). The suggestion that this expression should be taken to refer to the other "class" of servant (i.e., wicked)[14] is not a natural interpretation of the language. A better alternative is to take the expression to mean "the next" (cf. Lk 4:43; Mt 10:23).[15]

The reason the other seven servants do not appear is that the triadic structure is complete with the appearance of three (cf. Lk 20:31 pars.). The reason the ten are there in the first place is that Luke's context presupposes a larger, more diverse audience (the crowds rather than just the disciples as in Matthew). What is more, both an inner core of disciples (symbolized by the servants) and a larger group (symbolized by the citizens) are probably in view.[16] An outline of the episodes of the Lukan parable confirms its unity as it stands. Structurally, it breaks down into three sections as follows:

A. The Missions (vv. 12-14)

   1. The nobleman's journey (v. 12)

---

[12]Morris, *Luke*, p. 276.

[13]I. Howard Marshall, *The Gospel of Luke* (Exeter: Paternoster; Grand Rapids: Eerdmans, 1978), p. 708, suggests that the verse was a pre-Lucan addition to Jesus' original parable; J. M. Creed, *The Gospel according to St. Luke* (London: Macmillan, 1930), p. 235, that it was a post-Lucan addition. The major textual witnesses for the verse include ℵ, A, B, and the majority text; against, D, W and various Old Latin, Syriac and Coptic versions.

[14]E.g., Alfred Plummer, *A Critical and Exegetical Commentary on the Gospel according to St. Luke* (Edinburgh: T. & T. Clark, 1896), p. 441; Norval Geldenhuys, *Commentary on the Gospel of Luke* (London: Marshall, Morgan & Scott, 1950; Grand Rapids: Eerdmans, 1951), p. 478.

[15]Cf. John P. Lange, *The Gospel according to Matthew* (Edinburgh: T. & T. Clark, 1871), p. 192, n. 1, on Mt 10:23.

[16]Joüon, "La parabole des mines," p. 494. Josef Schmid, *Das Evangelium nach Lukas* (Regensburg: Pustet, 1960), pp. 288-89, notes that good style requires that only three of the ten be mentioned in detail. More than that would clutter the narrative.

2. The servants' responsibility (v. 13)
3. The citizens' opposition (v. 14)
B. The Reckonings (vv. 15-23)
1. The nobleman's return (v. 15)
2. Servant A (vv. 16-17)
3. Servant B (vv. 18-19)
4. Servant C (vv. 20-23)
C. The Destinies (vv. 24-27)
1. The fate of the servants (vv. 24-26)
2. The fate of the citizens (v. 27)

The only verse which prevents the parable from falling perfectly into three sections of three divisions each is verse 15; had it come between verses 23 and 24, then sections A and C would balance each other exactly. But of course the nobleman must return before he can call his servants into account, so the literary symmetry had to be broken for the sake of narrative coherence.

The Lukan parable can thus stand on its own as a separate story Jesus told, similar to the parable of the talents, on a different occasion.[17] Luke 19:11 makes this occasion explicit. Jesus is countering the view that his entry into Jerusalem meant that the kingdom would appear immediately. The parable does not presuppose any given length of delay but does require some kind of interval in which the nobleman's servants can go about their trading. The message of the parable fits perfectly with Luke's setting[18] and threatens judgment on those in Jesus' audience who wanted to oppose him. The two contrasting groups of subordinates are thus first of all the servants and the citizens—those on the master's side vs. those against him. Only secondarily are the servants then subdivided into good and bad.

---

[17]Cf. Simon J. Kistemaker, *The Parables of Jesus* (Grand Rapids: Baker, 1980), pp. 264-72; William Hendriksen, *Exposition of the Gospel according to Luke* (Grand Rapids: Baker, 1978 [=*The Gospel of Luke* (London: Banner of Truth, 1979)]), p. 858; Henry C. Thiessen, "The Parable of the Nobleman and the Earthly Kingdom," *BSac* 91 (1934):180-90; J. G. Simpson, "The Parable of the Pounds," *ExpT* 37 (1925-26):299-303; W. O. E. Oesterley, *The Gospel Parables in the Light of Their Jewish Background* (London: SPCK; New York: Macmillan, 1936), p. 144; Theodor Zahn, *Das Evangelium des Lucas* (Leipzig: A. Deichert, 1913), pp. 624-28.

[18]M. Didier, "La parabole des talents et des mines," in *De Jésus aux Évangiles*, ed. I. de la Potterie (Gembloux: Duculot, 1967), p. 259. Luke T. Johnson, "The Lukan Kingship Parable (Lk. 19:11-27)," *NovT* 24 (1982): 139-59, agrees, but goes too far in arguing that the parable was told to reinforce the views expressed in v. 11 rather than to refute them!

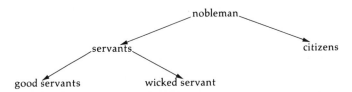

The two main points corresponding to these larger groups of characters therefore involve *(1) the punishment awaiting those in Israel who explicitly reject God's kingship* as well as *(2) the need for his apparently obedient servants to exercise good stewardship lest they too find themselves cut off from his blessing.* The point corresponding to the master remains much the same as in Matthew, though perhaps with a more direct link to Jesus' ministry: *(3) God has acted in Jesus to gain the lordship over all, but his complete dominion still awaits future conquest.*[19]

7.2 The Laborers in the Vineyard (Mt 20:1-16)

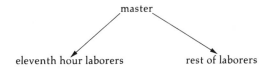

Like the parables of the pounds and talents, the story of the laborers in the vineyard depicts a master with numerous subordinates, this time distinguished by the time of day they were hired. Five groups span the first, third, sixth, ninth and eleventh hours, corresponding to 6 A.M. through 5 P.M. The successively shorter descriptions of the first four groups (vv. 2-5), followed by the more detailed account of the dialog with the workers hired at the eleventh hour (vv. 6-9), suggest, however, that there are really only two groups being compared—all of those hired earlier in the day vs. those hired just for the last hour.

The question then becomes whether an absolute or a relative contrast between these two groups is intended. In favor of the former is the concluding refrain, "the last shall be first and the first

---

[19]For very similar sets of three points, see Charles H. Talbert, *Reading Luke* (New York: Crossroad, 1982), pp. 177-78; Geldenhuys, *Luke*, p. 474.

last" (v. 16). The immediately preceding passage concludes with the identical refrain and reinforces this suggestion. Matthew 19:23-30 promises rewards for those who abandon all to follow Jesus while threatening exclusion from the kingdom for all who trust in their riches to gain entrance.

In favor of the latter is the imagery of the parable itself, in which all the workers receive equal payment despite the unequal duration of their work, as well as the fact that the audience of the parable includes only the disciples (symbolized by the laborers). The servants hired earliest do not seem to symbolize Jesus' opponents, since they do receive a reward. They simply fail to get the bonus for which they were hoping after having seen the master's surprising generosity toward the latecomers.

The interpretation which admits a reversal of status seems also to stem from a natural human sense of fair play which makes every effort to preserve some form of hierarchy among God's people, even if it inverts the type of justice which the world would endorse.[20] But it is hard to reconcile any kind of doctrine of varying rewards in God's kingdom with the notion of grace as something wholly undeserved. Surely J. B. Bauer is correct to stress that the parable teaches not the reversal of order but the abandonment of every form of ordering. All is based on mercy.[21]

Earlier Jesus taught that there are degrees of punishment in hell (Lk 12:47-48); now he makes plain that there are no degrees of reward in heaven. The perfection of the life to come, by definition, does not allow for them. This contrast between heaven and hell fits perfectly with the consistent biblical distinction between salvation by grace and damnation by works. Yet, curiously, a persistent strain of Christian theology continues to affirm that the varying judgments Christians receive ("according to their works"—e.g., Rom 2:6; 2 Cor 5:10) will somehow persist throughout eternity.[22] No

---

[20]J. D. M. Derrett, "Workers in the Vineyard: A Parable of Jesus," *JJS* 25 (1974):64-91, goes so far as to defend the inherent fairness of the hiring and wage-paying policies of the householder in the parable, but succeeds only by reading in all kinds of details not present in the text.

[21]J. B. Bauer, "Gnadenlohn oder Tageslohn (Mt 20, 8-16)," *Bib* 42 (1961): 224-28. Cf. Perkins, *Parables*, pp. 144-45.

[22]E.g., Louis Berkhof, *Systematic Theology* (Grand Rapids: Eerdmans, 1939; London: Banner of Truth, 1971), p. 733, speaks of "degrees of bliss"; while Bruce Milne, *Know the Truth* (Leicester and Downers Grove: IVP, 1982), p. 273, promises "additional degrees of responsibility"!

New Testament texts require this conclusion, and it would seem that grace falls by the wayside in the process.

To be sure, Matthew 19:30 and 20:16 suggest some kind of reversal. For this reason commentators who are persuaded of the "egalitarian" interpretation of the parable often assume that the conclusion and the context are secondary additions.[23] But the refrain about the last being first and the first last could just as easily apply to a situation of equality. If all have identical rewards, then all numerical positions are interchangeable. The refrain is phrased as it is because of the reversal of sequence in payment (v. 8), which in turn is demanded if the laborers hired first are to see and react to the amount the last group receives.[24] No further significance need be read into the reversal. Once again a coherent interpretation of the text as it stands should be given a hearing before the passage is dissected into authentic and inauthentic bits.

The contrast between workers is thus a relative one, much like the contrast between the prodigal and his older brother.[25] Just as their father loved and wooed both of them with equal tenderness, so the landowner pays his laborers the same amount. No one gets less than he was promised; many get much more than they deserve. Diedrick Nelson's complaint, that this type of compassion which "takes from the poor to give to the poorer is not a helpful image for the compassion of an infinitely bountiful God,"[26] fails to take account of the fact that in the parable no one loses anything. B. B. Scott's objection that the Pharisees would not have seen themselves "in the characterization of those first hired" is beside the point. Jesus regularly equated his opponents with suprising role models. Scott's later observation that "almost all readers would identify

---

[23]E.g., Eduard Schweizer, *The Good News according to Matthew* (Atlanta: John Knox, 1975; London: SPCK, 1976), p. 395.

[24]Cf. Robert H. Stein, *An Introduction to the Parables of Jesus* (Philadelphia: Westminster, 1981; Exeter: Paternoster, 1982), p. 126: "The beautiful staging must be observed. Although the order of hiring is, of course, from the earliest to the latest, the payment of the wages is in reverse order. As a result we have a heightening of expectation on the part of the earliest workers."

[25]See esp. G. de Ru, "The Conception of Reward in the Teaching of Jesus," *NovT* 8 (1966):211-13.

[26]Diedrick A. Nelson, "Matthew 20:1-16," *Int* 29 (1975):290. Cf. J. D. Crossan, *In Parables: The Challenge of the Historical Jesus* (New York and London: Harper & Row, 1973), p. 113, who echoes the identical complaint of the workers in v. 13, and misses entirely the expectation-subverting message of the passage, quite ironically, since Crossan elsewhere emphasizes as much as anyone this feature of Jesus' parables.

with the complaint of the first hired" is all that needs to be established and undercuts his earlier objection.[27]

At the level of original meaning, therefore, all of the workers stand for God's true people. Some appear more deserving than others, but all are rewarded equally. The various hours at which the different men began to work merely illustrate the diverse nature of the citizens of the kingdom. At the level of significance, many applications follow. God's people come to repentance at different times in their lives, at different stages throughout history, with varying levels of commitment and faithfulness, and so on.[28]

Nothing in the parable requires the meaning to be limited to the popular interpretation which takes the last group of workers to stand for the Gentiles and the rest to be Jews. And the use of the vineyard metaphor—a stock symbol for Israel—makes it more likely that all the laborers were originally conceived of as Jewish (as were Jesus' disciples).[29] The latecomers would then correspond to the "tax collectors and sinners" who were only recently repenting of their former misdeeds.

The three main points which the three groups of characters suggest may now be enumerated. All deal with the status of individuals before God at the final judgment.[30] *(1) From the earlier groups of workers, one learns that none of God's people will be treated unfairly (cf. v. 4—"whatever is right I will give you"); that is, no one will be shortchanged. (2) From the last group of workers comes the principle that many seemingly less deserving people will be treated generously, due to the sovereign, free choice of God. (3) From the unifying role of the master stems the precious truth that all true disciples are equal in God's eyes.*

The second of these points is certainly the most striking, but all three seem to be present. The master's concluding remarks, in fact, highlight each of these three points in succession (vv. 13-14a, vv.

---

[27]Bernard B. Scott, *Hear Then the Parable* (Minneapolis: Fortress, 1989), p. 293 and n. 8.

[28]For these and other applications, see Robert C. McQuilkin, *Our Lord's Parables* (Grand Rapids: Zondervan, 1980), pp. 104-5. Mounce, *Matthew*, p. 191, finds the distinction between two types of work: "one that is based on a desire for reward and the other upon confidence that God will take care of those who leave everything to him."

[29]Contra Robert H. Gundry, *Matthew: A Commentary on His Literary and Theological Art* (Grand Rapids: Eerdmans, 1982), p. 399; James M. Boice, *The Parables of Jesus* (Chicago: Moody, 1983), p. 60.

[30]On the use of evening or twelfth-hour imagery for the last day, see Hans Weder, *Die Gleichnisse Jesu als Metaphern* (Göttingen: Vandenhoeck & Ruprecht, 1978), p. 223.

14b-15 and v. 16). Commentators who restrict the meaning of a parable to only one main point invariably try to excise one or more of these verses as later appendices. If a parable can make three points, then the entire passage fits together as a tightly knit unity.[31]

The unusual behavior which reinforces the allegorical interpretation of the parable emerges here in the remarkable actions of the master. There are conceivable settings, especially during harvest time, in which a Jewish farmer might have needed this many extra laborers, though his repeated inability to calculate how many were needed in one twelve-hour period is extraordinary. Alternately, one might imagine him deliberately overstaffing his work force in order to provide for the unemployed, but this would have been just as unusual.

The method of payment alone justifies Beare's entitling the passage as "the parable of the eccentric employer."[32] But beyond the obvious details which enable an identification of the main characters, one need not pursue the allegory further. The third, sixth and ninth hours are the natural divisions of the day in the ancient world, and the eleventh hour is chosen obviously because it is the last one before quitting time. The rationale for the last group of workers' idleness—no one had hired them—explains their presence in the marketplace and has no necessary counterpart at the story's spiritual level (lest one infer that God had not given certain people the opportunity to serve him).

The steward who calls in the laborers merely executes his master's will. The view which interprets him as the Messiah runs aground on the fact that where a veiled reference to Jesus is intended in the parables it is usually in the master or father figure, not in one of the incidental characters (see below, pp. 313-23). The parable presents a fresh and striking metaphor of God's grace rather than a detailed account of salvation history.

---

[31]R. T. France, *The Gospel according to Matthew* (Leicester: IVP; Grand Rapids: Eerdmans, 1985), p. 289, succinctly captures all three of these points: "[God's] generosity transcends human ideas of fairness. No-one receives less than they deserve, but some receive far more."

[32]Beare, *Matthew*, p. 401. Interestingly, Beare, pp. 403-4, recognizes that Jeremias's interpretation of the parable (the first workers are like the Pharisees; the last, like the outcasts which Jesus welcomes—*Parables*, pp. 33-38) is "sheer allegorizing"! On the tension between plausibility and atypicality, cf. further Eta Linnemann, *Parables of Jesus: Introduction and Exposition* (London: SPCK, 1966 [= *Jesus of the Parables: Introduction and Exposition* (New York: Harper & Row, 1967)]), pp. 82-83.

7.3 The Sower (Mk 4:3-9, 13-20 pars.)

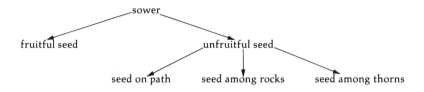

Like the parable of the wheat and tares, the parable of the sower comes with a ready-made allegorical interpretation which is almost unanimously rejected as a secondary creation of the church. Even the limited type of allegory for which this study has been arguing seems clearly transcended. Still, when one looks more closely, the interpretation of the sower does not appear as unique as it first seems. The parable itself describes in detail four kinds of soil. This detail is superfluous if each portion of the ground on which the seed falls does not stand for something fairly specific. As with the other triadic parables a contrast emerges.

The three unfruitful soils are pitted against the fruitful one, and the sower is the unifying figure or third main "character." No variation in length or emphasis distinguishes the description of the final, good soil from its three predecessors, but its distinctive produce clearly sets it apart. Farmers sow seed only in order for it to bear fruit; without this result the plants are good for nothing.[33] The shift from the singulars ὃ μέν ("the one, on the one hand") and καὶ ἄλλο ("and another") to the plural καὶ ἄλλα ("and others") may also point to the contrast between the first three soils and the last.[34] Only the fourth, good soil yields fruit in abundance.

The imagery of God as sower and the people of the world as various kinds of soil was standard in Jewish circles.[35] The imagery

---

[33]In a detailed form-critical study of this parable, Gerhard Lohfink, "Das Gleichnis vom Sämann (Mk 4, 3-9)," *BZ* 30 (1986):36-69, clearly shows that climactic emphasis rests on the good soil.

[34]Thus Weder, *Gleichnisse*, pp. 108-9 speaks of the last soil as the "Grossteil" (great part); and Crossan, *Parables*, p. 41, thinks of three portions of good soil balancing the three bad, though this is probably too specific.

[35]For references see Hans-Josef Klauck, *Allegorie und Allegorese in synoptischen Gleichnistexten* (Münster: Aschendorff, 1978), pp. 92-96. John Drury, *The Parables in the Gospels* (London: SPCK; New York: Crossroad, 1985), pp. 26-27, highlights the especially close parallel in 2 Esdras 4:26-32; while Craig A. Evans, "On the Isaianic Background of the Sower Parable," *CBQ* 47 (1985):464-68, thinks the passage is a midrash on Isaiah 55:10-11. A later rabbinic parable with striking affinities occurs in Aboth Rab. Nathan 8:2.

of bearing fruit, falling on stony ground, having no root or being choked by thorns was so obviously applicable to people as well as to plants that the interpretation ascribed to Jesus in verses 13-20 is entirely natural.[36] Even the birds as Satan fit in with their role as harbingers of evil in Old Testament and intertestamental literature (cf., e.g., 1 Kings 16:4; Jub 11:5-24; Apoc Abr 13).

At the same time, the call to careful listening which frames the parable (vv. 3, 9) suggests that not every detail was entirely self-evident.[37] It is best to see the narrative, then, as one which demanded some kind of interpretation of the primary "characters," but which permitted the rest of the details to fall into place quite naturally. Jesus may not have had to explain as much as he did, but because he viewed this parable as paradigmatic and the disciples' obtuseness as unwarranted (v. 13), he chose to spell things out in full at least on this occasion.

At the same time certain details in the parable have no counterpart in Jesus' interpretation and vice versa. The immediate growth of the seed with no root (v. 6) corresponds to the joyful response of one with only superficial commitment (v. 16), but this does not imply that shallow discipleship is defined as joyful reception of the word! The withering of the scorched plant is not said to occur immediately, as is the falling away of the disciple in tribulation (v. 17). And the thirty-, sixty-, and hundred-fold harvest seems merely to point to the abundance of fruit without any more specific reference (as the variations in number and sequence in the parallel passages in Matthew and Luke tend to confirm). Even the unifying figure, the sower, is not directly explained by Jesus' interpretation. Perhaps this suggests that whereas its primary reference is to God, derivative applications to Jesus or his disciples as sowers of the word (cf. Lk 8:11) are entirely appropriate.

Unusual aspects in the parable confirm its allegorical intentions.

---

[36]As is admitted even by some who reject its authenticity. Cf. Linnemann, *Parables*, pp. 118-19. Rudolf Pesch, *Das Markusevangelium*, vol. 1 (Freiburg: Herder, 1977), p. 233, gives Old Testament and intertestamental parallels, and is willing to admit the allegorical potential of Jesus' original parable even though he rejects the authenticity of the interpretation as it now exists in Mark.

[37]Vincent Taylor, *The Gospel according to St. Mark* (London: Macmillan, 1952), p. 252; William L. Lane, *The Gospel according to Mark* (Grand Rapids: Eerdmans, 1974; London: Marshall, Morgan & Scott, 1975), p. 153. Madeleine Boucher, *The Mysterious Parable* (Washington: Catholic Biblical Association of America, 1977), pp. 48-49, stresses that this is due to the susceptibility of several of the parable's details to multiple interpretations.

As consistently elsewhere, nothing shatters entirely the bounds of possibility in the real world, but the limits are certainly stretched. A somewhat fruitless debate has raged over whether sowing preceded plowing in Palestine, which would make the sower's "wastage" of so much seed on bad ground more intelligible.[38] Philip Payne shows that both sequences were probably employed and that some inadvertent waste would occur in either case, so the imagery would have been intelligible to a Palestinian audience. But the purpose of the parable is not to provide a realistic depiction of Palestinian agricultural practices but to teach a lesson about spiritual fruitbearing.[39] The same is true for the amazing harvest—the quantities are not inconceivable, but they point to the overflowing, abundant blessings of God.[40]

The three main points of the parable thus fall into place. *(1) Like the sower, God spreads his word widely among all kinds of people. (2) Like the three kinds of unfruitful soil, many will respond to his word with less than saving faith, be it (a) complete lack of positive response due to the enticement of evil, (b) temporary superficiality masquerading as true commitment, or (c) genuine interest and conviction about the truth that simply falls short due to the rigorous demands of discipleship. (3) Like the fruitful soil, the only legitimate response to God's word is the obedience and perseverance which demonstrate true regeneration.*[41]

As so often elsewhere, this type of threefold summary avoids the false dichotomies which pit one part of the parable's meaning against another. It seems scarcely coincidental that the two main alternatives for the parable's meaning, for those who would restrict it to one main point, are the *present* growth of the kingdom in spite

---

[38]The leading antagonists are Joachim Jeremias, "Palästinakundliches zum Gleichnis vom Saemann," *NTS* 13 (1966):48-53 (pro); and K. D. White, "The Parable of the Sower," *JTS* 15 (1964):300-307 (con).

[39]Philip B. Payne, "The Order of Sowing and Ploughing in the Parable of the Sower," *NTS* 25 (1978): 123-29 (a study overlooked by Drury, *Parables*, pp. 55-58, in his caustic and unjustified criticism of Jeremias). Cf. France, *Matthew*, p. 218.

[40]Philip B. Payne, "The Authenticity of the Parable of the Sower and Its Interpretation," in *Gospel Perspectives*, vol. 1, ed. R. T. France and David Wenham (Sheffield: JSOT, 1980), pp. 181-86. Cf. Eduard Schweizer, *The Good News according to Mark* (Richmond: John Knox, 1970; London: SPCK, 1971), p. 91. Scott, *Hear*, p. 357, underestimates the goodness of this harvest and therefore misinterprets the parable as implying that in the kingdom the harvest is "ordinary and everyday" (p. 362).

[41]The virtual interchangeability of seed and soil in the imagery and interpretation of the parable is stressed by Philip B. Payne, "The Seeming Inconsistency of the Interpretation of the Parable of the Sower," *NTS* 26 (1980):564-68. The presumed underlying Aramaic as well as the use of the Greek participle σπειρόμενοι ("being sown") suggest that soil "sown with seed" is in view in each case; the variation is not a sign of redactional tampering.

of opposition and its *future* triumph in glory.[42] The former comes from focusing on the unfruitful plants; the latter from concentrating on the fruitful ones. And Peter Jones suggests that the parable is really an "archetype of election" highlighting God's sovereign freedom to "move" toward all persons.[43] This comes from focusing on the third character, the sower. Simon Kistemaker affirms all three of these points but still tries to encapsulate them into "one particular truth":

> the Word of God is proclaimed and causes a division among those who hear; God's people receive the Word, understand it, and obediently fulfill it; others fail to listen because of a hardened heart, a basic superficiality, or a vested interest in riches and possessions.[44]

Surely the correct approach is to affirm all three points (and the three subpoints under the point about unfruitful soils)[45] but to admit them as distinct principles, as the grammar of Kistemaker's complex-compound sentence clearly requires.

7.4 The Good Samaritan (Lk 10:25-37)

Samaritan ◄─────────────man in ditch────────────► priest/Levite

The frequently anachronistic and overly detailed allegorical interpretations of the parable of the good Samaritan have been noted above (p. 31). In light of the fairly detailed allegorical interpretation of the parable of the sower, we might well ask why such an approach is inappropriate here. Several replies merit mention. To begin with, the structure of the good Samaritan is quite different from that of the sower. Instead of evenly balanced vignettes about

---

[42]Cf. David Hill, *The Gospel of Matthew* (London: Oliphants, 1972; Grand Rapids: Eerdmans, 1981), p. 225; Lane, *Mark*, pp. 154-55.

[43]Peter R. Jones, *The Teaching of the Parables* (Nashville: Broadman, 1982), p. 72; cf. Amos N. Wilder, "The Parable of the Sower: Naiveté and Method in Interpretation," *Semeia* 2 (1974):134-51.

[44]Kistemaker, *Parables*, p. 29. C. S. Mann, *Mark* (Garden City: Doubleday, 1986), p. 261, itemizes the three main interpretations of the parable as emphasizing, respectively, the fullness of the harvest, the responsibilities of the hearers of the word, and a picture of the experiences of Jesus.

[45]The attempt of Birger Gerhardsson, "The Parable of the Sower and Its Interpretation," *NTS* 14 (1968):176-77, to correlate each of the soils with a portion of the "Shema" (Deut 6:4-5) draws upon the vaguest of similarities and fails to convince.

four kinds of seed, one reads very briefly of the plight of the wounded man (v. 30) and of the lack of help afforded by priest and Levite (vv. 31-32) but at great length of the compassion of the Samaritan (vv. 33-35).

All of the detail surrounding the care given to the wounded man is entirely realistic and serves only to underline the extent of the Samaritan's love. Similar Old Testament passages about mercy (e.g., Hos 6:1-10) or considerate Samaritans (e.g., 2 Chron 28:5-15) may have inspired some of the imagery.[46] More importantly, the approach which equates each detail of the Samaritan's help with some spiritual counterpart in the process of salvation misses entirely the fact that the parable is told not in order to answer the question of how to inherit eternal life (v. 25) but to answer the question of who one's neighbor is (v. 29).

This is all the more clear because verses 29-37 are linked with 25-28. A similar dialog with a scribe during Jesus' last days of teaching in the temple (Mk 12:28-34 and Mt 22:34-40) coupled with Luke's omission of this passage from his passion narrative, suggest to many that this linkage is not original. But apart from the quotation of the Old Testament love command, all of the central details of the two dialogs differ, and Luke simply may have omitted the later conversation to avoid needless repetition.

It is better to take verses 25-28 as originally belonging with the parable which follows.[47] Verses 25-37 are in fact a carefully wrought unity. The two "halves" (vv. 25-28 and 29-37) parallel each other very closely. Each begins with a question by the lawyer, continues with an answer from Jesus in the form of a counterquestion for the lawyer, proceeds with the lawyer's reply, and concludes with an imperative from Jesus.[48] This structure also weighs against the view that part or all of verses 36-37 are secondary additions, as does

---

[46]See, respectively, Kenneth E. Bailey, *Through Peasant Eyes: More Lucan Parables* (Grand Rapids: Eerdmans, 1980), pp. 49-50; and F. Scott Spencer, "2 Chronicles 28:5-15 and the Parable of the Good Samaritan," *WTJ* 46 (1984):317-49.

[47]So even Jeremias, *Parables*, p. 202. Cf. Josef Ernst, *Das Evangelium nach Lukas* (Regensburg: Pustet, 1977), pp. 345-46; E. Earle Ellis, *The Gospel of Luke* (London: Oliphants, 1974; Grand Rapids: Eerdmans, 1981), p. 159.

[48]See esp. Gerhard Sellin, "Lukas als Gleichniserzähler: die Erzählung vom barmherzigen Samariter (Lk 10, 25-37)," *ZNW* 66 (1975):20, although on faulty methodological grounds Sellin ascribes the entire, unified passage to Luke's redactional invention. For a similar approach, cf. J. D. Crossan, "The Good Samaritan: Towards a Generic Definition of Parable," *Semeia* 2 (1974):82-112.

the fact that verse 37 ("go and do likewise") harks back to the lawyer's original question about how to inherit eternal life (v. 25) and to Jesus' first command to "do this and live" (v. 28).[49] Actually, vv. 25-37 as a whole nicely conform to the Hebraic style of "proem midrash" known as *yelammedenu rabbenu* ("let our master teach us"), which follows the pattern:

(a) introductory question on a text of Scripture (vv. 25-27; cf. Deut. 6:5; Lev. 19:18)

(b) second Scripture (v. 28, cf. Lev. 18:5)

(c) exposition, often by parables, linked with catchwords (vv. 29-36, with πλησίον ["neighbor"]—vv. 27, 29, 36 and ποιεῖν ["do"]—vv. 28, 37a, 37b)

(d) final text or remarks alluding to initial texts (v. 37, with allusion to second text).[50]

The passage thus requires no traditio-critical dissection.

The two main objections to the authenticity of verses 36-37 need not overthrow this verdict. The complaint that Jesus does not answer the lawyer's question, "who is my neighbor?" (v. 29), since he redirects attention to the converse, "who proved neighbor to the man?" (v. 36), can be countered by the observation that Jesus is trying to teach the reciprocal nature of neighborliness or that he feels that the lawyer has simply asked the wrong question.[51]

Even more plausible is the view that sees the parable itself as the answer to the man's question—even one who is as much an enemy as the Samaritan is a neighbor.[52] Verse 36 then forms the transition to the additional point which verse 37 introduces, regarding emulation of the Samaritan. This analysis also offsets the force of the second objection—that verse 37 turns the parable into an example story, that is, that it substitutes the command to model the Samar-

---

[49]See esp. Bastiaan van Elderen, "Another Look at the Parable of the Good Samaritan," in *Saved by Hope*, ed. James I. Cook (Grand Rapids: Eerdmans, 1978), p. 113; cf. Kenneth E. Bailey, *Poet and Peasant: A Literary-Cultural Approach to the Parables in Luke* (Grand Rapids: Eerdmans, 1976), pp. 72-74.

[50]Cf. E. Earle Ellis, "How the New Testament Uses the Old," in *New Testament Interpretation*, ed. I. Howard Marshall (Exeter: Paternoster; Grand Rapids: Eerdmans, 1977), pp. 205-6; Derrett, *Law*, pp. 224-27.

[51]Thus, respectively, Norman H. Young, " 'Once Again, Now, "Who Is My Neighbour?" ': A Comment," *EQ* 49 (1977):178-79; and Léonard Ramoroson, "Comme 'Le Bon Samaritan', ne chercher qu' á aimer (Lc 10, 29-37)," *Bib* 56 (1975):534.

[52]See esp. Robert W. Funk, "The Good Samaritan as Metaphor," *Semeia* 2 (1974):74-81. Cf. Jones, *Parables*, p. 228.

itan's neighborliness for a reply to the lawyer's question about who his neighbor was.

Once we do not restrict a parable to making only one main point, we can see that the parable addresses both of these issues.[53] The passage remains a parable but, as with the parable of the rich man and Lazarus, one which seems to build more on a straightforward example than on a metaphor. Each of the main characters represents the larger group or class of similar people to which they belong. Nevertheless, the example of physical help does not rule out corresponding truths at a spiritual level.[54] Nor need the mention of specific places (Jerusalem and Jericho) lead to the view that Jesus was describing a real event. Specifying the road helps the audience to identify with the acute danger of the Judean wilderness and with the plight of the man left for dead. The direction of travel also highlights the guilt of the clerics. Whatever ritual purity they might have wanted to protect en route to Jerusalem, priestly service there (presuming they thought the man dead and thus unclean) afforded them no excuse for their neglect when they were heading in the other direction.

The structure and message of the passage again fall into three parts, with the Levite and priest sharing one role as the negative model and the Samaritan providing the shocking counterexample. The dramatic reversal of conventional expectations as to who should have been the hero must not be overlooked in a modern world where "Samaritan" is now synonymous with "humanitarian"![55] The third, determining figure is the man in the ditch. Clearly

---

[53]Cf. J. Ramsey Michaels, *Servant and Son: Jesus in Parable and Gospel* (Atlanta: John Knox, 1981), p. 225: "The concluding word of advice, 'Go and do likewise' (v. 37), is not intended as a summary of the story's teaching, but as a further implication of it, resuming the discussion of the love command in verses 25-28."

[54]Contra, e.g., Dan O. Via, Jr., "Parable and Example Story: A Literary-Structuralist Approach," *Semeia* 1 (1974):105-33; Rudolf Bultmann, *The History of the Synoptic Tradition* (Oxford: Blackwell; New York: Harper & Row, 1963), p. 178; Linnemann, *Parables*, p. 56.

[55]D. Gewalt, "Der 'Barmherzige Samariter': Zu Lukas 10, 25-37," *EvTh* 38 (1978):403-17, convincingly demonstrates that the expected sequence of characters, once the priest and Levite had failed to come to the injured man's rescue, would have culminated in an ordinary Israelite providing the necessary service. (An anticlerical segment of the population would have been convinced that an ordinary Jew would have exercised this kind of compassion even if the clergy did not.) The suggestion of Morton S. Enslin, "Luke and the Samaritans," *HTR* 36 (1943):277-97, that the original sequence must have involved priest, Levite and Israelite on the grounds that no Samaritan would act this way toward a Jew, effectively illustrates the trouble Jesus' original audience would have had with the parable but misses entirely the fact that it was just such unusual behavior which gave the parable its meaning.

the parable, though triadic, is not monarchic (hence the diagram at the beginning of this section, in which the central, unifying character is not elevated above the other two characters). The man left for dead is hardly in a position to function as an authority, but he certainly can judge which of the passers-by proved neighbor to him.

The three lessons follow naturally: *(1) From the example of the priest and Levite comes the principle that religious status or legalistic casuistry does not excuse lovelessness. (2) From the Samaritan, one learns that one must show compassion to those in need regardless of the religious or ethnic barriers that divide people. (3) From the man in the ditch emerges the lesson that even one's enemy is one's neighbor.* The third point is perhaps the most crucial. Grace comes in surprising ways and from sources people seldom suspect. Significantly, these three points closely correspond to the three main lessons which the history of interpretation of the parable reveals,[56] even if most of the time commentators have tried to defend one at the expense of the others, rather than admitting all three.

7.5 The Great Supper (Lk 14:15-24; cf. Mt 22:1-14)

With the parable of the great supper, the familiar monarchic pattern returns. What makes the triadic structure complex rather than simple is that both positive and negative subordinates are subdivided, into two and three groups respectively. The meaning of the main characters is nevertheless predictable. The banquet giver stands for God; the invited guests who refuse to come, for those who reject the call to his kingdom; and the second group of guests who do come, for those who accept the call. The imagery of a meal as a symbol for the end-time celebration of God's people was standard

---

[56]Thus G. Bexell, "Den barmhärtige samariern och den teologiska etiken," *SvenskTeolKvart* 59 (1983):64-74, categorizes these approaches as the critical, ethical, and christological dimensions. For a fuller history of interpretation see Werner Monselewski, *Der barmherzige Samariter: Eine auslegungsgeschichtliche Untersuchung zu Lukas 10, 25-37* (Tübingen: Mohr, 1967).

in Jewish thought. The servants are incidental figures, natural props to execute the master's will, though derivatively they could be taken to mirror any who preach God's Word.

Other details prove more ambiguous. The most unusual is the wholesale refusal of the first group of invitees to come. The specific excuses which the three guests give illustrate how "all alike" refused (v. 18). They need not stand for any particular type of reason for rejecting the kingdom; others might just as easily have been listed. What all three share is an extraordinary lameness. They are meant to strike the hearer as ridiculous and to point out the absurdity of any excuse for rejecting God's call into his kingdom.[57] At the level of the story the rejections are just barely conceivable.

The folk-tale which resembles the parable of the rich man and Lazarus (see above, p. 86) contains a similar episode, and as Humphrey Palmer notes, "any guest might decline to come, and usually some will, so it must happen every now and then that everybody does."[58] But the implausibility of all of these extremely unlikely events coinciding suggests an allegorical level.[59] It is just possible that the excuses for participating in a Jewish holy war are in view (Deut 20:5-9), in which case the point would be one of contrast— legitimate excuses against serving in the Israelite army no longer apply to the call to enlist in God's "kingdom troops" (cf. above, p. 85).[60]

Almost as remarkable as the behavior of the first group of guests is the master's response in inviting the poor and handicapped of his community. The two categories of replacements for those originally invited are often taken to stand for Jewish outcasts and Gentiles, but there is nothing in the parable's imagery to suggest that any non-Israelites are in view. The servants simply move further afield within Israel in their quest for guests—from the streets of the city to the highways of the countryside. Verse 23 need not be seen as

---

[57]See esp. Bailey, *Through Peasant Eyes*, pp. 95-99. Contra Robert F. Capon, *The Parables of Grace* (Grand Rapids: Eerdmans, 1988), p. 131.

[58]Humphrey Palmer, "Just Married, Cannot Come," *NovT* 18 (1976):251. On the Bar Ma'jan parallel, see esp. E. Galbiati, "Gli invitati al convito (Luca 14, 16-24)," *BeO* 7 (1965):129-35.

[59]Cf. Ferdinand Hahn, "Das Gleichnis von der Einladung zum Festmahl," in *Verborum Veritas*, ed. Otto Böcher and Klaus Haacker (Wuppertal: Theologischer Verlag, 1970), pp. 68, 71.

[60]Cf. J. D. M. Derrett, *Law in the New Testament* (London: Darton, Longman & Todd, 1970), pp. 126-55; Paul H. Ballard, "Reasons for Refusing the Great Supper," *JTS* 23 (1972):341-50.

an anachronistic reference to the Gentile mission[61] and thus as inauthentic, as it commonly is. Yet even if the Gentiles were in view, there is ample Old Testament precedent to make the concept of the extension of the kingdom to all races entirely natural on Jesus' lips.[62]

The parable is perfectly appropriate in its Lukan setting as Jesus' response to the man who pronounced a blessing on all who eat bread in God's kingdom (v. 15). That man, probably a Pharisee (cf. v. 1), no doubt shared the exclusivist attitude of his fellow sectarians, limiting entrance into God's kingdom to pious Jews. Jesus challenges this narrow-mindedness just as he did earlier during the banquet (vv. 1-14).[63]

Several other features of the narrative deserve brief comment. First, it seems strange that those who refuse to come on their own should also be formally excluded, but ancient banqueting practices often included the host's sending a small portion of food to those unable to come, much like the modern British custom of doing the same with pieces of wedding cake.[64] It is also possible that verse 24 is Jesus' comment to the crowd (note the second-person plural "you") and is only meant to refer to the allegorical level of meaning. Second, there is no particular mention of any significant interval between the callings of the two groups of replacements, so one need not assume a reference to the delay of the parousia or even a long period of Jewish rejection of the Gospel.[65]

Third, the double invitation at the outset merely reflects middle-

---

[61]Rightly, C. W. F. Smith, *The Jesus of the Parables* (Philadelphia: United Church Press, 1975), p. 123; Robert W. Funk, *Language, Hermeneutic, and Word of God* (New York: Harper & Row, 1966), pp. 183-86; Walter Schmithals, *Das Evangelium nach Lukas* (Zurich: Theologischer Verlag, 1980), p. 160.

[62]See esp. Bailey, *Through Peasant Eyes*, pp. 101-8. Cf. Heinrich Kahlefeld, *Parables and Instructions in the Gospels* (New York: Herder & Herder, 1966), p. 88.

[63]See esp. T. W. Manson, *The Sayings of Jesus* (London: SCM, 1949; Grand Rapids: Eerdmans, 1979), pp. 129-30. Even those who find this passage an artificial composite of disparate sayings often acknowledge that each part fits naturally into the larger context. See esp. X. de Meeus, "Composition de Lc., xiv, et genre symposiaque," *ETL* 37 (1961):847-70; Josef Ernst, "Gastmahl-gespräche: Lk 14, 9-24," in *Die Kirche des Anfangs*, ed. Rudolf Schnackenburg, Josef Ernst and Joachim Wanke (Leipzig: St. Benno, 1977), pp. 57-78. For an exclusively literary analysis of vv. 1-24 as a Lucan unity, cf. Timothy Noël, "The Parable of the Wedding Guest: A Narrative-Critical Interpretation," *PRS* 16 (1989):17-27.

[64]See esp. Derrett, *Law*, p. 141.

[65]Rightly, Stein, *Parables*, p. 89. Contra, respectively, Jeremias, *Parables*, pp. 64-65; and Ernst Haenchen, "Das Gleichnis vom grossen Mahl," in *Die Bibel und wir* (Tübingen: Mohr, 1968), pp. 135-55.

Eastern custom; no further meaning should be derived from it. Fourth, the command for the servants to "compel" people to come in reflects the insistence demanded by Oriental courtesy. The fact that such insistence did not force the original invitees to come against their will should prevent it from being misapplied to forced conversions.

The parable focuses, in turn, on the three main activities of the various participants—the invitations of the master (vv. 16-17), the rejection of those first invited (vv. 18-21a), and the subsequent call for replacements (vv. 21b-23). The final verse (v. 24) returns to the action of the master, revealing a second side of his personality.

Three lessons of the parable may therefore be formulated, although the first will have two parts to it. *(1) From the graciousness and severity of the master we learn that God generously and consistently invites all kinds of people into his kingdom but that a day will come when the invitation is rescinded and it is too late to respond. (2) From the excuses of the first group of guests stems the principle that all excuses for rejecting God's invitation are exceedingly lame. (3) From the helplessness of the second group of guests follows the teaching that God's generosity is not thwarted by the rejection of the "establishment," because he extends his invitation even to the dispossessed of this world.* Robert Stein summarizes the parable's meaning under the identical three heads, but he misleadingly thinks they can be collapsed into one point to avoid the problem of allegory:

> It is impossible in reading this parable not to interpret the guests and their replacements as representing the attitudes of the Pharisees/scribes/religious leaders and the outcasts of Israel. . . . The parable was not allegorical, because it posits only one main point of comparison. The point is that the kingdom of God has come and that those who would have been expected to receive it (the religious elite) did not do so, whereas the ones least likely to receive it (the publicans, poor, harlots, etc.) have.[66]

As with Kistemaker's explanation of the parable of the sower, the "one" main point is actually described in a sentence containing three discrete clauses, one per main "character." As in all the parables surveyed so far, the three points are obviously interrelated but difficult to summarize in a simple sentence. And, as Stein makes

---

[66]Stein, *Parables*, p. 89.

clear, it is also authentic, and there is no good reason to try to deny either fact. The characters do stand for people other than themselves. The parable is therefore an allegory.

Matthew's parable of the wedding banquet is usually taken as a secondary, more extensively allegorized reworking of Luke's banquet parable, much as Luke's parable of the pounds was alleged to have expanded Matthew's talents. Once again, though, the structure of the alleged parallel is markedly different. The excuses of the guests who refuse to come are not nearly so neatly delineated. Only one group of replacements is mentioned and no emphasis is placed on them. The destruction of the original guests' city in response to their murderous treatment of the master's (this time a king's) servants gives the narrative an altogether harsher tone and tragic nature. Finally, an episode about the hostile reception of a guest who appeared without a wedding garment brings the parable to an unrelentingly gloomy climax.

Thus despite Hunter's claim that "no reputable scholar nowadays denies" that these two passages are different versions of the same parable,[67] a good case can be made for viewing the two as different teachings of Jesus, using similar imagery, on two different occasions in his ministry.[68] Granted that all kinds of excisions can leave Matthew's text closely resembling Luke's, even-handed exegesis should attempt to interpret the passage as a consistent whole before dissecting it.

The four main objections to seeing Matthew 22:1-14 as a coherent unity are the following: (1) The guests' action and king's response seem extraordinarily violent for the context of invitations to a wedding feast. (2) The destruction and burning of the city read like a "prophecy after the event" of the destruction of Jerusalem by the Romans in A.D. 70. (3) Rejecting a man who appears without a wedding garment makes no sense if he has just been pulled off the street as a last-minute replacement; he could hardly be expected to be dressed for the occasion. (4) Verse 14 is much too general to

---

[67] A. M. Hunter, *Interpreting the Parables* (London: SCM; Philadelphia: Westminster, 1960), pp. 55-56.

[68] Among many who could be cited, cf. Smith, *Parables*, p. 120; Funk, *Language*, p. 163; Palmer, "Just Married," p. 255; Geldenhuys, *Luke*, p. 395, n. 4; Morris, *Luke*, p. 233; Mounce, *Matthew*, p. 210; France, *Matthew*, p. 311.

be the point of the detailed narrative which precedes it.

These objections may be countered in several ways. In response to (1), the details are more realistic than they first appear. The setting of this parable as the marriage feast for the king's son makes refusal to attend tantamount to high treason. The intended guests' violence was a known method of signaling their insurrection and refusal to show allegiance to their sovereign.[69] The question of (2) has already been discussed (above, pp. 120-21), with the supposed allusion to the destruction of Jerusalem being found not close enough to be convincing.

Objection (3) has been dealt with variously. Some believe the custom of a king providing guests with festal clothing, attested from other periods in antiquity, would have applied here too, so that the man who appeared without it was deliberately flouting the king's offer of dress.[70] Klaus Haacker believes this custom could have been inferred from a well-known Palestinian folk-tale about three poor maidens who were invited to appear at the palace and who asked for appropriate garments to be provided because they had none.[71] On the other hand, unlike the Lukan parable, the passage in Matthew says nothing about the second group of guests being poor or having no time to prepare by dressing properly. So perhaps one should assume that the man in verses 11-13 had the ability to arrive with proper attire.[72]

The allegorical level of meaning here of course reads smoothly. One may not stand before God unprepared for judgment and expect to presume upon his grace. A Mishnaic simile attributed to Rabbi Jacob affords an instructive parallel: "This world is like unto a vestibule before the world to come; prepare thyself in the vestibule, so that thou mayest enter the banqueting-hall" (Aboth 4:16).[73]

Concerning (4), verse 14 is best seen not as an attempt to give

---

[69]Derrett, Law, p. 139.

[70]E.g., William Hendriksen, Exposition of the Gospel according to Matthew (Grand Rapids: Baker, 1973 [= The Gospel of Matthew (London: Banner of Truth, 1976)]), pp. 797-98; Kistemaker, Parables, p. 104.

[71]Klaus Haacker, "Das hochzeitliche Kleid von Mt. 22, 11-13 und ein palästinisches Märchen," Zeitschrift des Deutschen Palästina-Vereins 87 (1971):95-97.

[72]G. R. Beasley-Murray, Jesus and the Kingdom of God (Grand Rapids: Eerdmans; Exeter: Paternoster, 1986), p. 121.

[73]Trans. J. Israelstam, in The Babylonian Talmud, ed. I. Epstein, vol. 26 (London: Soncino, 1935), p. 53.

an exhaustive summary of the parable's meaning but rather a valid generalization based on the parable's primary structural distinctive. In successive scenes the number of those who participate in the wedding feast is increasingly narrowed, first by the rejection of the many, then by the rejection of the individual.

Given that Matthew 22:1-14 can stand on its own as a united whole, its triadic structure does not contrast the wicked guests who refuse to come with the good ones who replace them as much as it compares the mass rejection of the first group with the particular rejection of the man who came without the right clothes.

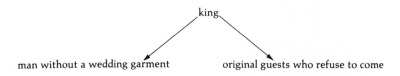

man without a wedding garment   original guests who refuse to come

The three main points which derive from this structure follow: *(1) God invites many people of different kinds into his kingdom; (2) overt rejection of God's invitation leads to eventual retribution; and (3) failure to prepare adequately even when apparently accepted by God proves no less culpable or liable to eternal punishment.*[74] A *Sitz im Leben Jesu* where the first group of guests stands for the Jews who are hostile to Jesus and the second group symbolizes the would-be disciples who fail to "count the cost"[75] is perfectly intelligible and consistent with the setting Matthew gives of Jesus' teaching in the temple during the last week of his life. A striking parallel appears in the Talmud attributed to the first-century rabbi Johanan ben Zakkai:

> This may be compared to a king who summoned his servants to a banquet without appointing a time. The wise ones adorned themselves and sat at the door of the palace, ["for,"] said they, "is anything lacking in a royal palace?" The fools went about their work, saying, "can there be a banquet without prepara-

---

[74]Victor Hasler, "Die königliche Hochzeit, Matth. 22:1-14," *TZ* 18 (1962):25-35, develops a similar set of three points as the main concerns of Matthew's redaction; nothing now prohibits seeing these as Jesus' teaching as well. Alexander Sand, *Das Evangelium nach Matthäus* (Regensburg: Pustet, 1986), pp. 439-40, develops three points from vv. 2-8 (on the invitation and rejection of the Jews), vv. 9-10 (on the formation of the Gentile Christian community) and vv. 11-13 (on the urgency of Christians continuing to obey God).

[75]Interestingly, teaching on this very topic is appended to Luke's great supper parable, in Luke 14:25-33, even though it is not present in the parable itself.

tions?" Suddenly the king desired [the presence] of his servants:
the wise entered adorned, while the fools entered soiled. The
king rejoiced at the wise but was angry with the fools. "Those
who adorned themselves for the banquet," ordered he, "let them
sit, eat and drink. But those who did not adorn themselves for
the banquet, let them stand and watch." (b. Shabbath 153a)[76]

7.6 The Unforgiving Servant (Mt 18:23-35)

Like the parable of the wedding feast, the parable of the unforgiving
servant does not present two equal but opposite servants of a master but successive reckoning scenes with two different subordinates. Unlike all the previous parables surveyed, however, this parable does not describe that reckoning as taking place between
master and servant in both instances. In the second scene it occurs
between servant and fellow servant. The unforgiving servant,
therefore, rather than the master figure, becomes the unifier or
determiner who appears in all of the episodes of the parable (hence
the hierarchical diagram above). The episodes number three—
verses 24-27 (master and first servant), verses 28-31 (first servant
and fellow servant), and verses 32-34 (first servant and master)—
and they are framed by introductory and concluding verses (vv. 23,
35). The unforgiving servant contrasts with his fellow debtor with
respect to the amount forgiven and with the master with respect
to his attitude toward forgiving others.

This parable has for the most part been viewed as authentic; the
context, less so. The link with verses 21-22 (Peter's question on
forgiveness) has been deemed secondary both on the grounds that
by it Matthew intends, unsuccessfully, to answer Peter's query

---

[76]Trans. H. Freedman, in *The Babylonian Talmud*, vol. 4 (1938), pp. 781-82.

more adequately than does Jesus' brief reply concerning seventy-sevenfold forgiveness, and on the grounds that the question has already been answered adequately so that the parable is something of an afterthought.[77] These objections cancel each other out. Probably the "therefore" of verse 23 is a relatively loose connective, and nothing can be determined by it about the parable's original location.

The parable may call to mind the ungrateful attitude of those who overtly rejected Jesus' message, but it is scarcely inappropriate in a context on discipleship.[78] Jesus' ministry is littered with would-be followers who fall by the way, just as the forgiven servant subsequently demonstrated no understanding of the implications of the forgiveness shown him. Verse 35 has also regularly been assigned a later origin in the parable's tradition history, on the grounds that it clearly makes the allegorical equations of king = God, servant = any person, and fellow servants = his or her fellow human beings. But it is hard to see how the parable could be interpreted at all without these basic equations.

Christian Dietzfelbinger's attempt, under the banner of a vague description of humanity's presence within the world, only succeeds in transforming the parable into a platform for modern existentialism,[79] far removed from first-century Judaism. Even though he thinks it is Matthean, Thomas Deidun freely admits that verse 35 fits the parable perfectly, bringing out its point about the change of heart demanded by the love of God made manifest in Jesus.[80]

The extravagance of the servant's debt and the master's cancellation of it place this narrative on the very borders of realism and point to an allegorical meaning. Modern attempts to contemporize the sum have ranged from a few million to several trillion dollars. Pheme Perkins seems to assess the amount best. It would have

---

[77]E.g., respectively, Crossan, *Parables*, p. 106; and Linnemann, *Parables*, pp. 105-6.

[78]So, e.g., Ernst Fuchs, "The Parable of the Unmerciful Servant (Mt 18:23-35)," *TU* 73 (1959):493: to Israel Jesus says "God is harder than you are;" to the church, "God is more indulgent than you are."

[79]Christian Dietzfelbinger, "Das Gleichnis von der erlassenen Schuld," *EvTh* 32 (1972):437-51. Bernard B. Scott, "The King's Accounting: Matthew 18:23-34," *JBL* 104 (1985):429-42, offers a more successful exposition but is forced at the end, despite his protests to the contrary, to admit in through the back door a basic allegorical identification along these lines.

[80]Thomas Deidun, "The Parable of the Unmerciful Servant (Mt. 18:23-35)," *BTB* 6 (1976):219, 221.

reminded a Jewish audience of the fabled riches of Egyptian and Persian kings, neither inconceivable nor within the bounds of their experience.[81]

Subordinate details in the parable add only to the vividness and congruence of the story. The additional servants in verse 23 simply set the stage for their reappearance in verse 31 as means of reporting the first servant's actions to the king. The jailers (or, more literally, "tormentors") in verse 34 could just as easily have been replaced by a jail (or place of torment).[82]

The 6000:1 ratio of the two debts (10,000 talents [= 600,000 denarii] to 100 denarii) has no specific significance except in its enormity. How absurd for one forgiven so much to refuse to forgive so little! The question of whether or not either servant could have repaid his debt is probably unanswerable.

Verse 34 must not be pressed to teach some kind of doctrine of purgatory. The parallelism between the pleas of verses 26 and 29 and the irony in the threat of verse 30 being returned on the servant's own head (v. 34) highlight the contrast between the king's forgiveness and the servant's incorrigibility and stress the fairness of the ultimate verdict. It is not clear that the apparent retraction of forgiveness for the first servant has an exact analog on the spiritual level. The point may be that no true disciple could ever act as this servant did; one who does shows he has not truly received forgiveness. Alternately, one could argue that God's forgiveness is for all, but only those who appropriate it by a life of forgiving others show that they have genuinely accepted the pardon.

The three episodes previously outlined do not focus on just one character apiece, but a different individual does appear dominant in each. One lesson also emerges from each subdivision. *(1) The first section magnificently illustrates the boundless grace of God in forgiving sins, as*

---

[81]Perkins, *Parables*, p. 124. Derrett, *Law*, pp. 32-47 thinks of the king simply postponing the debt until the following year and thus finds the parable on the border of realism. Hill, *Matthew*, p. 278, points out that 10,000 often stood for the highest quantity imaginable for a certain item. Martinus C. De Boer, "Ten Thousand Talents? Matthew's Interpretation and Redaction of the Parable of the Unforgiving Servant," *CBQ* 50 (1988):214-32, recognizes that this extravagance leads to an allegorical interpretation and therefore rejects it as secondary.

[82]This partially offsets the objection of Beare, *Matthew*, p. 383, to the idea of God keeping a "corps of torturers" (cf. Dan O. Via, Jr., *The Parables: Their Literary and Existential Dimension* [Philadelphia: Fortress, 1967], p. 139, who attributes v. 35 to Matthew's "legalistic tendency"). Still, the idea of punishment should not be altogether jettisoned. Unpleasant as it is, it is a thoroughly biblical concept.

the king forgave his servant. (2) In the middle section, the second servant underlines the absurdity of grace spurned; one who has been forgiven so much and yet so mistreats his fellow debtor does not deserve to live. (3) The final section depicts the frightful fate awaiting the unforgiving, as the wicked servant discovered to his ruin.

Again, debates about which of these principles was the original point of the parable[83] are futile once it is seen that all were intended from the outset.[84] Jeremias, in fact, makes three very similar points in his exposition without acknowledging that they are distinct lessons.[85] Rabbi Jose the Priest utilized similar imagery to resolve an apparent scriptural contradiction (between Deut 10:17 and Num 6:26):

> A man lent his neighbour a *maneh* and fixed a time for payment in the presence of the king, while the other swore to pay him by the life of the king. When the time arrived he did not pay him, and he went to excuse himself to the king. The king, however, said to him: The wrong done to me I excuse you, but go and obtain forgiveness from your neighbour. So here: one text speaks of offences committed by a man against God, the other of offences committed by a man against his fellow man. (b. Rosh HaShanah 17b-18a)[86]

Some of the details of the passage differ from those of Jesus' parable, but the same basic allegorical equations appear.

7.7 The Unjust Steward (Lk 16:1-13)

master

steward

debtors

---

[83]As, e.g., in Linnemann, *Parables*, p. 107; Weder, *Gleichnisse*, pp. 211-12.

[84]Cf. esp. Boice, *Parables*, p. 186, who enumerates the three main lessons of the parables as: there is a coming judgment, there is forgiveness, and the only sure proof of having received forgiveness is a changed heart and transformed life. More briefly, cf. Schweizer, *Matthew*, pp. 378-79.

[85]Jeremias, *Parables*, p. 213: (1) "God has extended to you in the gospel, through the offer of forgiveness, a merciful gift beyond conceiving," but (2) "God will revoke the forgiveness of sin if you do not wholeheartedly share the forgiveness you have experienced." Then (3) "God will . . . see that his sentence is executed rigorously."

[86]Trans. Maurice Simon, in *The Babylonian Talmud*, vol. 9, p. 70.

The parable of the unjust steward structurally resembles the parable of the unmerciful servant quite closely. An initial reckoning scene between master and servant (v. 2) gives way to the servant's subsequent interaction with his master's debtors (vv. 3-7) and is followed by a final reckoning between master and servant (v. 8). The servant, not the master, is the unifying figure of the three scenes. Introductory and closing verses bracket the three episodes (vv. 1, 9), although in this case additional sayings of Jesus are appended (vv. 10-13). As in the previous parable, the context is one of instruction for disciples, rather than controversy with opponents. Inasmuch as the teaching is about good stewardship, this is perfectly appropriate.[87] In fact, only as teaching for those already committed does verse 9 form an apt conclusion. Jesus is not saying to the uncommitted that they should use money to earn their salvation, but he is telling those who already are his followers that they must demonstrate the fruits befitting repentance even (or perhaps especially) in the area of worldly wealth.

The parable is somewhat unique in its comic, almost picaresque, portrayal of a master commending an unscrupulous person, and for this reason verse 8 has troubled many commentators.[88] An important line of interpretation argues that what the servant did in reducing the debtors' accounts was perfectly legal; he was merely removing the surcharge or commission he would have received for himself.[89] Thus his master was not out any money rightfully his, the servant himself absorbed the loss, amends for previous wastage were partially made, and the man gained new friends who would care for him after his firing.

All of this is quite plausible and attractive but depends on reading into the parable historical circumstances which are not spelled out

---

[87]At the same time, the crowds and opponents need not have been entirely absent, if this parable was told immediately following those in Luke 15 (cf. Lk 15:1). After all, the Pharisees reappear immediately in 16:14. On the links between Luke 16:1-13 and 15:11-32 in particular, see Michael R. Austin, "The Hypocritical Son," EQ 57 (1985):307-15.

[88]But see now Tim Schramm and Kathrin Löwenstein, Unmoralische Helden: Anstössige Gleichnisse Jesu (Göttingen: Vandenhoeck & Ruprecht, 1986), who show how frequently Jesus uses "picaresque" characters in his parables.

[89]See esp. Paul Gächter, "The Parable of the Dishonest Steward after Oriental Conceptions," CBQ 12 (1950):121-31; Derrett, Law, pp. 48-77; Joseph A. Fitzmyer, "The Story of the Dishonest Manager (Lk. 16:1-13)," TS 25 (1964):23-42. Bailey, Poet and Peasant, pp. 86-110, argues that the servant's action was not moral but enhanced the master's reputation in the community by portraying him as generously absorbing the losses incurred.

and which may or may not have been self-evident to Jesus' original audience. It is just as conceivable that the servant was as unscrupulous in his last actions as in his first, but as the master's primary overseer he had the legal power to enforce what actions he took. The master would then have praised him for his cleverness and prudent self-interest, not any the more consoled for it, but honestly being forced to admit the success of the ploy.[90] The last part of verse 8 might follow just a little more naturally on this reading. The underhanded ethics of the "sons of this world" seem to be implied by the phrase "dealing with their own generation," and the contrast with the lack of shrewdness of the "sons of light" becomes that much starker.[91]

Either way, commentators are generally agreed that the parable itself is authentic, but that the sayings appended to it are not, or at least that they have been relocated secondarily. C. H. Dodd's assessment has often been echoed that in verses 8a, 8b and 9 "we can almost see here notes for three separate sermons on the parable as text."[92] On the other hand, these three lessons correspond remarkably well to the three episodes and three main characters of the story. Perhaps together they form the proper and original interpretation. From verse 8a one learns of the praise of the master; from verse 8b, the shrewdness of the servant; and from verse 9, the grace of the debtors.

Taken in the sequence of the parable and using the familiar allegorical referents for master, servant and debtors, these lessons might be rephrased as: *(1) All of God's people will be called to give a reckoning of the nature of their service to him. (2) Preparation for that reckoning should involve a prudent use of all our resources, especially in the area of finances. (3) Such prudence, demonstrating a life of true discipleship, will be rewarded with*

---

[90]See esp. J.-P. Molina, "Luc 16/1 a 13: L'Injuste *Mamon,*" *ETR* 53 (1978):372. Cf. Stein, *Parables,* p. 110. Scott, *Hear,* pp. 256-60 makes a strong case for this interpretation and then goes one step further, concluding that "the parable breaks the bond between power and justice" and instead "equates justice and vulnerability." The kingdom is therefore "for masters and stewards who do not get even" (p. 266).

[91]M. G. Steinhauser, "Noah in His Generation: An Allusion in Luke 16, 8b, εἰς τὴν γενεὰν τὴν ἑαυτῶν," *ZNW* 79 (1988): 152-57, similarly speaks of "relative righteousness" which would not be considered exemplary in "another generation"—i.e., when compared with superior standards.

[92]Dodd, *Parables,* p. 30. For exhaustive detail of the various traditio-critical dissections of the parable, as well as the history of its interpretation more generally, see Michael Krämer, *Das Rätsel der Parabel vom ungerechten Verwalter* (Zürich: PAS-Verlag, 1972). Most recently, cf. B. B. Scott, "A Master's Praise: Luke 16, 1-8a," *Bib* 64 (1983):173-88.

eternal life and joy.[93]

The problems with seeing all three of these points integrally connected with the passage may be dispensed with fairly easily. Some have seen verse 8 as Luke's words, with "the master" referring to Jesus; a switch to the first person again in verse 9 would then be awkward and a possible sign of later editing. But, as already noted, it is quite plausible that the master in the story could have commended the servant, in which case the change of person in verse 9 more likely implies that Jesus' comments on the parable begin here.

The objectionable clause "make friends for yourselves by means of unrighteous mammon" has received important clarification from discoveries at Qumran which reinforced the view that "unrighteous mammon" was simply a stock idiom for all money, much as one might today use the expression "filthy lucre."[94] It is not a command to use ill-gotten gain for one's own interest. This explanation also does away with the need to interpret verse 9 in some ironic or sarcastic fashion, or as a rhetorical question.[95]

A history of commentary on the parable reveals that it has received two main interpretations. Some take it to teach shrewdness in the use of our money; others, prudence in the time of crisis.[96] It seems unnecessary to choose between these. Each by itself seems somewhat truncated and together they yield good sense. Jesus exhorts his disciples to prepare for the Day of Judgment by wisely using everything God has given them, especially their money. If it is true that we cannot serve both God and mammon (v. 13), in the sense of making an ultimate commitment to both at the same time, then what more

---

[93]Smith, *Parables*, p. 146, notes that all three of the applications of vv. 8-9 are connected with the parable but that none seems to capture its entire message. Perhaps they were meant to be taken together!

[94]See esp. Hans Kosmala, "The Parable of the Unjust Steward in the Light of Qumran," *ASTI* 3 (1964):114-15. For a review of the various interpretations of this detail, see G. M. Camps and B. M. Ubach, "Un sentido bíblico de ἄδικος, ἀδικία y la interpretación de Lc 16, 1-13," *EstBib* 25 (1966):75-82.

[95]Supporting irony, see Donald R. Fletcher, "The Riddle of the Unjust Steward: Is Irony the Key?" *JBL* 82 (1963):15-30; for sarcasm, Geoffrey Paul, "The Unjust Steward and the Interpretation of Luke 16:9," *Theol* 61 (1958):192; and as a question, R. Merkelbach, "Über das Gleichnis vom ungerechten Haushalter (Lucas 16, 1-13)," *VC* 33 (1979):180-81. At a more popular level, Douglas Beyer, *Parables for Christian Living* (Valley Forge: Judson, 1985), p. 76, makes the mistaken claim that the only viable interpretation of the passage is that Jesus was joking!

[96]These two lines of interpretation are concisely summarized in Herbert Preisker, "Lukas 16, 1-7," *TLZ* 74 (1949):85-92. Cf. A. Descamps, "La composition littéraire de Luc xvi 9-13," *NovT* 1 (1956):48.

telling test of true discipleship than in the use of our finances.[97]

Verse 13 seems very apropos here, and the previous verses re-state the same lesson in three parallel ways. One who is faithful in little will be faithful also in much (v. 10). This proverb is then translated in verses 11 and 12 by replacing "little" with "unright-eous mammon" (i.e., earthly riches) and "another's" (that which is loaned from God) and by replacing "much" with "true [i.e., heav-enly] riches" and "one's own" (that which will last into eternity).[98] Although there are few who are willing to countenance the sugges-tion, it is quite natural to take all of verses 1-13 as an original unity in this context. When the parable is seen to be making three points instead of one, and when Jesus is permitted to append further com-mentary, objections to this endeavor should evaporate.[99]

7.8 The Wicked Tenants (Mk 12:1-12 pars.)

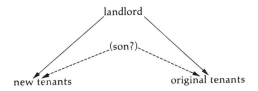

In many ways, the parable of the wicked husbandmen resembles the parable of the wedding feast. In Matthew the two appear back-to-back (Mt 21:33-46, 22:1-14). Each describes an authority figure who replaces a group of rebellious subordinates with more cooperative

---

[97]Smith, *Parables*, p. 149, refers to this verse as the "most inclusive and germane" of all the parable's applications. How Francis E. Williams, "Is Almsgiving the Point of the 'Unjust Stew-ard'?" *JBL* 83 (1964):297, can claim that v. 13 fits neither vv. 1-9 nor 10-12, "since nothing in these twelve verses has suggested the case of a man trying to serve two masters at once," defies all comprehension!

[98]The minor differences which Bailey, *Poet and Peasant*, pp. 110-18, points to in his attempt to identify vv. 9-13 as a self-contained poem separate from the parable may have value for struc-tural analysis, but they do not prove that the two parts were not originally uttered in connection with one another.

[99]Thus esp. Jean Pirot, *Jesus et la richesse: Parabole de l'intendant astucieux (Luc XVI, 1-15)* (Marseille: Imprimerie Marseillaise, 1944), pp. 17-31, who sees vv. 1-8a as teaching about the behavior of the sons of darkness and vv. 9-13 as teaching about the behavior of the sons of light, with v. 8b as the bridge between the two halves of the "diptych"; and Markus Barth, "The Dishonest Steward and His Lord: Reflections on Luke 16:1-13," in *From Faith to Faith*, ed. D. Y. Hadidian (Pittsburgh: Pickwick, 1979), p. 65, who sees 1-8a illustrating the teaching "be as shrewd as serpents" and vv. 10-13, "be as innocent as doves" (with vv. 8b-9 providing the hinge).

ones. Each emphasizes the hostile treatment which the master's servants and son receive. But while the son appears only incidentally in the wedding-feast parable as the banquet's guest of honor, here he occupies a more central position as the focus of attention for three verses (vv. 6-8). It seems hard to deny that here, for the first time, a parable has four primary characters or groups of characters. Nevertheless, it can be argued that the son and servants are still less significant than the master and his two groups of tenants, being simply dramatic vehicles by which the first tenants express their opposition to the landlord. The diagram above indicates the uncertain relationships by means of dotted lines.

At least three clearly allegorical referents thus exist. The vineyard owner stands for God, the first tenants for Israel's leaders,[100] and the second group for those who replace the original, corrupt lot. That verse 1 almost directly quotes the opening lines of Isaiah's vineyard parable (Is 5:1-7) makes these equations certain. The additional detail in the description of the vineyard makes plain this reference and need not serve as more than an illustration of the great care and concern lavished by God on his people.[101]

The new tenants have often been taken to refer to the Gentiles, but, as in the great supper parable, nothing suggests that the story's setting has been transported outside of the nation of Israel (though nothing precludes such an *application* at a later date).[102] Quite possibly some of the Jewish leaders who heard the parable at first might have wondered if the original tenants stood for the Romans who were occupying their land.[103] By the end they clearly recog-

---

[100]Some argue that Jesus deliberately transferred the traditional meaning of the vineyard as Israel to the tenants (so that they stand for the nation as a whole); then their replacements would be either the Gentiles or the church. See, e.g., Josef Blank, "Die Sendung des Sohnes," in *Neues Testament und Kirche*, ed. Joachim Gnilka (Freiburg: Herder, 1974), p. 14; Darrell Bock, *Proclamation from Prophecy and Pattern* (Sheffield: JSOT, 1987), p. 126. But the text is perfectly intelligible without this shift, and Jesus offered no hints in his narrative to suggest to his audience that they needed to abandon their traditional association of the vineyard with Israel.

[101]For a different view, which sees a detailed midrashic interpretation in each of the details, see Craig A. Evans, "On the Vineyard Parables of Isaiah 5 and Mark 12," *BZ* 28 (1984):82-86.

[102]For a similarly balanced assessment, see Akira Ogawa, "Paraboles de l'Israël véritable? Reconsidération critique de Mt. xxi 28-xxii 14," *NovT* 21 (1979):149. Brad H. Young, *Jesus and His Jewish Parables* (New York and Mahwah: Paulist, 1989), pp. 282-305, shows how the entire parable could be interpreted as an intramural Jewish dispute. Young entitles this chapter "Prophetic Tension and the Temple."

[103]Klyne Snodgrass, *The Parable of the Wicked Tenants* (Tübingen: Mohr, 1983), pp. 77-78. The view that Jesus was telling the parable against the Zealots (Jane E. and Raymond R. Newell, "The Parable of the Wicked Tenants," *NovT* 14 [1972]:226-37) is much less likely.

nized that Jesus was telling this story against them, and so they became enraged (Mk 12:12 pars.). The period of the landlord's absence could not, in the first instance, have referred to the time between Christ's first and second comings but would have denoted the era in which the current Jewish leadership and their ancestors had been assigned the stewardship of God's chosen people.[104]

From this central, triadic structure emerge at least the following three points: *(1) God is patient and longsuffering in waiting for his people to bear the fruit which he requires of them, even when they are repeatedly and overtly hostile in their rebellion against him. (2) A day will come when God's patience is exhausted and those who have rejected him will be destroyed. (3) God's purposes will not thereby be thwarted, for he will raise up new leaders who will produce the fruit the original ones failed to provide.*[105]

But what of the servants and the son? Do they disclose a fourth lesson? Christians reading with 20/20 hindsight can scarcely fail to see in the son's rejection and murder the crucifixion of Christ, especially since Jesus concludes with the "cornerstone" quotation from Psalm 118:22, a favorite early Christian Messianic prooftext (cf. Acts 4:11, 1 Pet 2:7). The other servants, then, might well represent the prophets or other messengers from God. The fact that it is hard to imagine any landlord consistently subjecting his servants to such mistreatment and then naively thinking that his son would be exempt, or that the tenants might imagine that such a murderous scheme would succeed, suggests that an allegorical meaning may be intended here too.

Klyne Snodgrass, however, has examined in detail all of the charges of lack of realism in the parable and found them wanting. Information from other historical sources, especially the papyri, has shown that possession was more than nine-tenths of the law of ownership in ancient disputes of this nature. Such hostilities were not uncommon in first-century conflicts between absentee landlords (especially Roman ones) and their tenants. And the tenants could have interpreted the sending of the son as a sign that the

---

104Cf. Marshall, *Luke*, p. 729; Walter Grundmann, *Das Evangelium nach Lukas* (Berlin: Evangelische Verlagsanstalt, 1966), p. 372, n. 1.

105Attempts to collapse the meaning of the parable into one main point again fail to avoid tortuously complex constructions of that "one" point. Cf., e.g., Pesch, *Markusevangelium*, vol. 2 (1978), p. 221; Martin Hengel, "Das Gleichnis von den Weingärtnern Mc. 12, 1-12 im Lichte der Zenonpapyri und der rabbinischen Gleichnisse," *ZNW* 59 (1968):38.

master had died, thus provoking them to try to kill the one whom they would have believed was the sole remaining heir.[106]

These details therefore remain entirely realistic and yet suggestive of additional meaning. An anonymous parable in Sifre Deut. 312 compares God's provision of the land for the patriarchs to a king who leases a field to renters who rob their owner so that he finally retakes possession of the field and gives it to his son. The renters are then compared to Abraham and Isaac who were indirectly responsible for the evil of their sons Ishmael and Esau. With a selective memory, the parable concludes, "When Jacob came along, no chaff came forth from him. All the sons that were born to him were proper people, as it is said, 'And Jacob was a perfect man, dwelling in tents' (Gen. 25:27)."[107]

There is no reason Jesus could not have intended similarly detailed symbolism behind the images of servants and son, including a veiled self-reference. The imminence of a fatal clash with the authorities was by this stage in his ministry a real danger which many might have anticipated. At the same time, there is no reason to assume that most of his original audience would have picked up on such hints. They are subtle allusions, to be recalled and invested with greater significance by the disciples after Christ's death, and thus neither obviously secondary, allegorizing additions nor straightforward indications of Jesus' self-understanding.[108]

As with the parable of the good Samaritan, a proem midrash form may be discerned here, which in part explains why the structure does not fall into any of the neater categories already outlined. E. Earle Ellis provides the outline for Matthew's form, but a similar

---

[106]Snodgrass, *Tenants*, pp. 31-40. For a convenient presentation of the most relevant texts, see Perkins, *Parables*, pp. 186-89; and for full detail, Hengel, "Weingärtnern," pp. 1-39.

[107]Trans. Neusner, *Sifre to Deuteronomy*, vol. 2, p. 332. Cf. the similar imagery used in a much different fashion in Eccl. Rab. 5:10.2—where the need for tenants in a field is compared to the need for the soul to be united to a body!

[108]Cf. esp. Klauck, *Allegorie*, pp. 308-9; Larry W. Hurtado, *Mark* (San Francisco: Harper & Row, 1983; Basingstoke: Pickering & Inglis, 1984), p. 179; Taylor, *Mark*, p. 472. For Matthew, of course, an allegorical meaning may well have been clearer, because of his post-resurrection perspective. Thus Jack D. Kingsbury, "The Parable of the Wicked Husbandmen and the Secret of Jesus' Divine Sonship in Matthew: Some Literary-Critical Observations," *JBL* 105 (1986):643-55, may still be correct that the parable plays a central role in Matthew's Christology. J. C. O'Neill, "The Source of the Parables of the Bridegroom and the Wicked Husbandmen," *JTS* 39 (1988):485-89, agrees that the Son is the Messiah but assigns the origin of this equation to John the Baptist, not Jesus. O'Neill recognizes that Jesus is "chary" of claiming Messiahship elsewhere, but does not realize that the claim here is equally veiled.

outline would fit Mark's account equally well.

Matt. 21:33   initial text: Isa. 5:1f.
vv. 34-41   exposition by means of a parable, linked to the
            initial and final texts by a catchword λίθος
            ("stone"—42, 44, cf. 35; Is. 5:2, *saqal*); cf. οἰκοδομεῖν
            ("build"—33, 42)
vv. 42-44   concluding texts: Ps. 118:22f.; Dan. 2:34f., 44f.[109]

This suggests that the entire passage holds together as a coherent unit of thought, and that there is no reason not to ascribe this unity to Jesus' original teaching. The three points deriving from the vineyard owner and the two groups of tenants are fairly certain; the meaning of the additional detail about the son is more dubious. But the type of veiled self-reference postulated here fits precisely with the nature of Christ's teaching about himself elsewhere in the parables (and in the Synoptics more generally), as the final chapter of this book will demonstrate (pp. 316-23). Ellis, moreover, follows Matthew Black in seeing a deliberate play on words (in the presumed, original Aramaic) between the "son" *(ben)* and the "stone" *('eben)*, in which case both images probably refer to the Messiah Jesus.[110] *Yet even if a fourth point concerning the nature of Christ's rejection derives from the figure of the son, it remains in its context subordinated to the other three.*

7.9 Conclusions

The lessons of the complex triadic parables do not differ in kind from those of the simple triadic form, but they do not always line up as neatly with master and subordinate figures. It is perhaps better to speak of a unifying figure and two additional individuals with whom he interacts. Nevertheless three clusters of themes may be distinguished along the lines of those summarized at the end of chapter six.

One cluster concerns the nature of God. He preeminently

---

[109]Ellis, "How the New Testament Uses the Old," p. 205.
[110]Idem, "New Directions in Form Criticism," in *Jesus Christus in Historie und Theologie*, ed. George Strecker (Tübingen: Mohr, 1975), pp. 313-14; Matthew Black, "The Christological Use of the Old Testament in the New Testament," *NTS* 18 (1971-72):13.

exhibits grace to the undeserving, giving generously far beyond what one expects. He considers all people as equal and emphasizes that even human enemies should be considered neighbors. He waits patiently, repeatedly summoning people into his kingdom, even when they rebel against him. He entrusts all individuals with resources and abilities and expects them to be good stewards of what they have been given.

A second cluster of themes surrounds the model of the faithful disciple. This person bears the fruit of good works which flow from faith, including the outpouring of compassion on the needy, love for the dispossessed and outcast, forgiveness for debtors who are unable to repay (in both the material and spiritual realms), and a shrewd but godly use of one's resources, especially in the financial arena.

A final collection of teachings warns against faithlessness. A day of reckoning will come at which time there is no longer a chance to repent. None will be treated unfairly, but eternal punishment for those who have not proved true disciples will follow inexorably. The condemned will include those who have displayed a temporary, superficial response which produced no lasting fruit, those who have replaced true love for the unlovely with a legalistic purity which avoids helping the genuinely needy, and those who refuse to forgive their fellow human beings despite the massive debts which God has forgiven them. All excuses for rejecting God's kingdom will be unmasked and shown to be ridiculous.

The proposals put forward at the end of part one continue to be confirmed by the exegetical studies of the various parables. Not coincidentally, quite often the history of interpretation of a given parable discloses that three complementary themes have vied for acceptance as the main point of the story. In no instance has any reason emerged for jettisoning any of these themes, except for the arbitrary assertion that parables make only one point. Although one point may sometimes stand out more prominently than another, all the parables discussed in these last two chapters seem to teach three lessons apiece, corresponding to their three main characters. Of course these lessons are always interrelated and can often be combined into one detailed sentence. But most attempts to state "the point" of these parables are reductionistic and fail to account for the three-pronged nature of the texts. So far all of the longest, narrative parables of Jesus have displayed this pattern. Nevertheless, not all of Jesus' parables are as lengthy or complex as these, and many do not appear to be structured triadically. Chapter eight therefore turns to an examination of parables which seem to make only one or two main points.

8
Two-Point &
One-Point Parables

NOT ALL PARABLES HAVE THREE MAIN CHARACTERS OR MAKE three main points, common though that pattern may be. Many shorter narratives and similes have only two key actors or objects, and a few have only one. This does not mean that they are not allegorical but rather that the allegories are less elaborate and the number of referents fewer. Some parables border on being triadic but ultimately prove dyadic, or two-pointed. Others share features of both dyadic and monadic, or one-pointed, forms. Many short metaphors also make just one point but are not included here. The boundary between full-fledged parable and simple metaphor is fluid; two different books on the parables seldom agree exactly as to what should be classified as parabolic. This chapter will survey all the remaining passages in the Gospels usually termed parables and will consider them in order of decreasing complexity.

8.1 Two-Point Parables
8.1.1 The Pharisee and the Tax Collector (Lk 18:9-14)

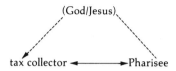

This parable forms a fitting transition from an examination of triadic parables to a study of dyadic ones. It contains the identical type of contrast between good and bad characters, with a surprising role-reversal, found in passages already considered. The parables of the rich man and Lazarus and the good Samaritan offer the closest parallels. The only difference is that here there is no third, unifying figure to judge between the other two. In a sense, Jesus himself fills the role of the judge, pronouncing in the closing verse of the passage God's evaluation of the two men's prayers. But Jesus makes no third point in addition to the obvious two about the one man being justified and the other one not. Indeed, the whole structure of the parable argues for seeing it as two-pointed, with the sharp alternation from Pharisee to tax collector highlighting the contrast between them. The structure may be outlined as A-B-A-B-B-A-A-B, with A standing for the action of the Pharisee and B for that of the tax collector.

1. (A) Pharisee (v. 10a)
2. (B) tax collector (v. 10b)
3. (A) Pharisee (vv. 11-12)
4. (B) tax collector (v. 13)
5. (B) tax collector (v. 14a)
6. (A) Pharisee (v. 14b)
7. (A) Pharisee (v. 14c)
8. (B) tax collector (v. 14d)

The brief inversion of the two elements in the fifth and sixth positions of this outline underlines the climactic reversal of the main characters' status and highlights the shock Jesus' verdict would have created in its first setting. Modern stereotypes concerning the Pharisees must not blind readers to the uniform expectation of Jesus' original audience that the Pharisee would be the hero of the story instead of the tax collector.[1]

On the other hand, one must not go so far as to allege that the portrait of the Pharisee here is a caricature which could not have fit any real-life Jew in a *Sitz im Leben Jesu*, thus requiring one to see part or all of the parable as inauthentic and stemming from a later anti-Jewish polemic.[2] There were both arrogant and humble Pharisees in ancient Judaism, as the Talmud itself later admitted (b. Sot. 22b). The standard prayer in which the pious Jewish man thanks God that he is not a slave, a Gentile or a woman (cf. b. Men. 43b) comes very close to expressing the attitude with which Jesus takes issue here (and cf. Paul in Gal 3:28).[3] In fact, little in the actions or prayers of either man proves extraordinary, except perhaps the tax man's beating on his chest, a dramatic gesture usually reserved for women and used by men only in times of extreme emotion.[4] The parable is perhaps the closest to a pure example story one finds, with each man standing for all others like him—either self-righteous or penitent.

Verse 14b, the only portion of the parable usually labeled inauthentic, captures these conclusions, and so it must not be jettisoned. That this generalizing conclusion appears elsewhere (Mt 18:4,

---

[1]See esp. Anthony C. Thiselton, *The Two Horizons* (Exeter: Paternoster; Grand Rapids: Eerdmans, 1980), pp. 12-15. Cf. Joachim Jeremias, *The Parables of Jesus* (London: SCM; Philadelphia: Westminster, 1972), p. 144.

[2]As esp. in Luise Schottroff, "Die Erzählung vom Pharisäer und Zöllner als Beispiel für die theologische Kunst des Überredens," in *Neues Testament und christliche Existenz*, ed. Hans-Dieter Betz and Luise Schottroff (Tübingen: Mohr, 1973), pp. 439-61. It is Schottroff's view of the parable which is a caricature as she reads in details which simply aren't there—claiming that the Pharisee exalts himself above every other person, denying that anyone else is as righteous as he. Cf. Franz Schnider, "Ausschliessen und ausgeschlossen werden: Beobachtungen zur Struktur des Gleichnisses vom Pharisäer und Zöllner Lk 18, 10-14a," *BZ* 24 (1980):49, who notes that the Pharisee is condemned not for his gratefulness that he has not led a notoriously sinful life, nor for his acknowledgment of his own good works, but only for the comparison which esteems himself as more valuable in God's eyes than the tax collector.

[3]See esp. Helmut Merklein, " 'Dieser ging als gerechter nach Hause . . .' " *Bibel und Kirche* 32 (1977):36. Cf. also b. Berakoth 28b: "I give thanks to thee, O Lord my God, that Thou hast set my portion with those who sit in the Beth ha-Midrash and Thou hast not set my portion with those who sit in [street] corners, for I rise early and they rise early, but I rise early for words of Torah and they rise early for frivolous talk; I labour and they labour, but I labour and receive a reward, and they labour and do not receive a reward; I run and they run, but I run to the life of the future world and they run to the pit of destruction" (trans. Maurice Simon, in *The Babylonian Talmud*, ed. I. Epstein, vol. 1 [London: Soncino, 1948], p. 172). Bernard B. Scott, *Hear Then the Parable* (Minneapolis: Fortress, 1989), p. 97, goes so far as to claim that nothing in the Pharisee's prayer deserved censure. Rather Jesus changed the rules of the game altogether so that one could no longer "predict who will be an insider or outsider."

[4]Kenneth E. Bailey, *Through Peasant Eyes: More Lucan Parables* (Grand Rapids: Eerdmans, 1980), p. 153.

23:12; Lk 14:11) is no counterargument; the maxim is appropriate in numerous contexts. Verse 14a suggests such a radical verdict that some kind of explanation is required to substantiate it. The summary of the two men's behavior as self-exaltation and self-humiliation is apt. Nor should anything be made of the absence of explicit reference to atonement as the necessary ground for justification. These are still pre-crucifixion days, and the natural time for these two men to be praying publicly in the temple would after all be at an hour of sacrifice.[5] In fact, the tax collector's cry, "Be merciful to me" (ἱλάσθητί μοι) might well be translated, "Let me be atoned." The reference to justification actually makes the parable's conclusion one of the most "Pauline" pieces of all of Jesus' teaching.[6]

The parable thus makes two main points which can scarcely be better summarized than by Jesus' own refrain. *(1) He who exalts himself will be humbled, and (2) he who humbles himself will be exalted.* Applications are numerous but the one that is the most crucial involves God's exaltation or humiliation of individuals at the final judgment. Whichever one of these two attitudes has reflected our relationship with God in this life, the opposite will characterize our status in the next. The beatitudes and woes in Luke's Sermon on the Plain (Lk 6:20-26) provide perhaps the best biblical commentary on this parable.[7]

8.1.2 The Two Builders (Mt 7:24-27; Lk 6:47-49)

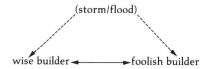

Like the parable of the Pharisee and the publican, the story of the two builders depicts a dramatic contrast between wise and foolish

---

[5]Ibid., p. 145.

[6]F. F. Bruce, "Justification by Faith in the Non-Pauline Writings of the New Testament," *EQ* 24 (1952):66-69.

[7]Thorwald Lorenzen, "The Radicality of Grace: 'The Pharisee and the Tax Collector' (Luke 18:9-14) as a Parable of Jesus," *Faith and Mission* 3, no.2 (1986):73, summarizes the two-pronged message of the parables as follows: "The parable reminds us that even the most religious person can miss the purpose and goal of life. The text therefore invites us to discover God as a living Father and 'that tax collector,' whoever he may be, as a brother."

actions—construction which survives severe testing and that which collapses. Here the imagery is more conventional; the verdict, what one would expect. The fact that people literally do build houses without adequate foundations, however, remains a poignant testimony to the foolishness of human behavior in the material realm and makes the parable an apt illustration of a similar lack of preparation in the spiritual realm.

In the last parable, Jesus' own verdict decided between the two characters; here, the storm, a typical metaphor for judgment or crisis, decides the fate of each. At the level of application one may undoubtedly appeal to this narrative to encourage preparation for numerous types of crises, but in his original preaching Jesus almost certainly had in mind the climactic end of the age. At the same time, the fact that the specific reward granted the wise builder is simply the preservation of his building may point to the fact that the foundations of spiritual structures which will endure in the world to come are laid in the present age.[8]

The parallelism in language, especially in Matthew's version, highlights the similarities and differences between the two builders. Each builds a house, perhaps with no visible, outward differences between them. Each experiences the identical storm or flood, but one building stands while the other falls. The idea of a house on a rock vs. one on sand (Matthew), or of one with a foundation vs. one without (Luke), naturally suggests wise and foolish behavior. But without the specific comparison with those who hear Jesus' words and do not obey them vs. those who hear and do obey, a multitude of interpretations might suggest themselves.

Thus an explanation of the imagery, here by the explicit use of simile, is necessary if the meaning of the parable is to be clear.[9]

---

[8]D. A. Carson, "Matthew," in *The Expositor's Bible Commentary*, vol. 8, ed. Frank E. Gaebelein (Grand Rapids: Zondervan, 1984), p. 194, cites Is 28:16-17, Ezek 13:10-13 and Prov 12:7 as relevant background. Eduard Schweizer, *The Good News according to Matthew* (Richmond: John Knox, 1975; London: SPCK, 1976), p. 191, thinks the flood is reminiscent of the deluge in Noah's day. R. T. France, *The Gospel according to Matthew* (Leicester: IVP; Grand Rapids: Eerdmans, 1985), p. 149, sees the storm as symbolizing both pressures in this world and the ultimate test of God's judgment.

[9]In Aboth 3:17, Rabbi Eleazar b. Azariah recounts a parable which contrasts a tree with good roots and one with poor roots in time of heavy winds, comparing the two kinds of trees to people with sufficient or insufficient good works. Elisha b. Abuyah illustrates the same contrast in Aboth Rab. Nathan 24:1-3 with imagery even more closely parallel—comparing one who builds first with (larger) "stones" and then with (smaller) "bricks" to one who foolishly inverts that sequence.

Interestingly, very few objections have ever been raised to the authenticity of this parable or its interpretation. Details, to be sure, were altered in transmission to preserve the intelligibility of the story in a Hellenistic world (see above, p. 81), inasmuch as the identical lessons can be expressed through diverse imagery. But the unity of the whole is freely admitted.

Ulrich Luz's major critical commentary on Matthew states plainly: "The double parable is a unity and not further divisible. The contents of the picture speak in favor of Matthew's version being the more original. It can stem from Jesus."[10] G. B. Caird is equally forthright and concise about the two main points which then follow from the contrasting pictures of the two builders: "The man who hears and does is safe against every crisis, while the man who only hears is inviting disaster."[11]

One might rephrase Caird's conclusion to focus more explicitly on the ultimate crisis that all persons must face and therefore state the parable's lessons like this: (1) *The person who responds to the gospel with obedience will survive God's final judgment intact.* (2) *The person who refuses to follow Christ in discipleship, on the other hand, will be destroyed on that last day.* Coming at the end of the Sermon on the Mount/Plain, which has graphically depicted Jesus' understanding of discipleship, the parable leaves its hearers with no good reason for refusing Christ's appeal.

8.1.3 The Unprofitable Servant (Lk 17:7-10)

master

servant

A second type of dyadic parable involves a master figure and a subordinate, but with no contrasting foil for that subordinate. A good example is the parable of the unprofitable servant. As in passages previously discussed which began with the rhetorical ques-

---

[10]Ulrich Luz, *Das Evangelium nach Matthäus*, vol. 1 (Neukirchen-Vluyn: Neukirchener; Zürich: Benziger, 1985), p. 412.

[11]G. B. Caird, *The Gospel of St. Luke* (Harmondsworth and Baltimore: Penguin, 1963), p. 107.

tion, "which of you . . . ?" Jesus expects a unanimous chorus to agree that no one would act in the manner here described. No self-respecting master would consider inviting his servant to eat before he did. The conclusion in verse 10, however, shifts attention away from the master and encourages the members of Jesus' audience to place themselves in the position of the servant.

Now the conclusion to which they had tacitly agreed turns on them and requires them to acknowledge their unworthiness before God. They willingly accepted that a servant must put his master before himself, even if he doesn't always feel like it. Now they are forced to admit that this is how they must behave before God, even if they don't feel like it! The logic is also a fortiori—if it applies on the level of human masters and servants, how much more so between man and God.

The shift in perspective from verses 7-9 to verse 10 leads many to a conclusion which has by now become routine—the final verse of the parable was added later and is not original. Once the possibility of multiple lessons in the parables is admitted, then one should demand that at least two points be accepted as inherent in the meaning of the original form of this narrative—one from the nature of the master and one from the behavior of the servant. The parable itself focuses on the former; the conclusion on the latter.

Even without looking for two points, Jacques Dupont has demonstrated the unity of all four verses. He notes the verbal and conceptual parallels between verses 7-9 and 10 (τίς ἐξ ὑμῶν/οὕτως καὶ ὑμεῖς ["which of you/so also you"]; δοῦλος/δοῦλοι ["servant/servants"]; ὅτι ἐποίησεν τὰ διαταχθέντα/ὅταν ποιήσητε . . . τὰ διαταχθέντα ["because he did what was commanded"/Whenever you do what is commanded"]), the necessity of verse 9 as the transition between verses 7-8 and 10, and the role of the double question in verses 7-8 in which the first part is subordinate to the second.

Thus each verse requires the next one, and all views which would attempt to remove one or more of these verses from the original form of the parable are unnecessary and misguided.[12] The shift of

---

[12]Jacques Dupont, "Le maître et son serviteur (Luc 17, 7-10)," *ETL* 60 (1984):233-51. Contra, e.g., Alfons Weiser, *Die Knechtsgleichnisse der synoptischen Evangelien* (München: Kösel, 1971), pp. 107-14, who excises v. 8; J. D. Crossan, "The Servant Parables of Jesus," *Semeia* 1 (1974): 30, who deletes vv. 8-9; and Paul S. Minear, "A Note on Luke 17: 7-10," *JBL* 93 (1974):87, who wants to remove v. 10.

attention from the master to the servant is paralleled in Matthew 7:9-11. In both instances the logic of the parables virtually demands such a shift. If the master stands for God, and the servant for any one of his people, then it is only natural to focus first on the character of God and then on the resultant behavior which his people must display.

The point to be derived from the master's actions is clear enough. God is sovereign. The corollaries which follow from this can be phrased in various ways. God is not the equal of any human being, he requires service, and he does not reward on the basis of merit. The point to be derived from the servant's recognition of his master's sovereignty depends on the translation of ἀχρεῖος.

The traditional renderings—"unprofitable" or "worthless"—are misleading. God's people are of great worth in his sight. "Unworthy" is an improvement and suggests the idea of one who is undeserving or unable to accrue merit.[13] It is even possible that a more strictly etymological translation does most justice to the term, in which case it would mean "without need." Luke 17:10 would then mean that the servant is one to whom nothing is owed or to whom no favor is due.[14] Whatever the precise nuance, it is clear that Jesus is highlighting the need for disciples to renounce any claim they might try to make on God's grace. The parable does not deny that God will reward his people—that point is made elsewhere (e.g., Lk 12:35-38)—but it stresses that an individual's relationship with God is "not a matter of earning or deserving, still less of bargaining, but all of grace."[15]

The context in which Luke places this parable is a series of teachings for his disciples about faith. Like most of the parables addressed to the disciples in the Gospels, many think this one was originally meant for his opponents. Here the most important alleged incongruity is the unlikelihood of many (or any) of Jesus'

---

[13]E.g., Adolf Jülicher, *Die Gleichnisreden Jesu*, vol. 2 (Freiburg: Mohr, 1899), pp. 19-23; John M. Creed, *The Gospel according to St. Luke* (London: Macmillan, 1930), p. 216.

[14]Bailey, *Through Peasant Eyes*, pp. 122-24; J. J. Kilgallen, "What Kind of Servants Are We? (Luke 17, 10)" *Bib* 63 (1982):549-51.

[15]A. Marcus Ward, "Uncomfortable Words IV: Unprofitable Servants," *ExpT* 81 (1970):201. Cf. Georg Eichholz, "Meditation über das Gleichnis von Luk. 17, 7-10," in *Kirche, Konfession, Ökumene*, ed. Karl Halaski and Walter Herrenbruck (Neukirchen-Vluyn: Neukirchener Verlag, 1978), pp. 25-33.

disciples being sufficiently well-to-do to own slaves. But this allegation probably overestimates the poverty of Jesus' followers and underestimates the number of households of only modest income who were able to have *one* slave (and the parable gives no indication of more than one).[16] The family of Zebedee and his sons had at least two servants (Mk 1:20). More importantly, the disciples need not even have had slaves to appreciate the force of the illustration. They would have been well enough acquainted with the practice, even if only second-hand, to appreciate its relevance.[17]

On the other hand, if the context be accepted as authentic, we need not go to the opposite extreme and assume that the teaching was applied only to the twelve disciples, or, in Luke's day, to church leaders. The precious truths of God's sovereignty and grace apply to all Christians. They may perhaps best be summarized as follows: *(1) God retains the right to command his followers to live however he chooses. (2) God's people should never presume that their obedience to his commands has earned them his favor.*

8.1.4 The Seed Growing Secretly (Mk 4:26-29)

The structure of the parable of the seed growing secretly resembles the story of the unprofitable servant. But instead of a master and his slave, Jesus describes a farmer and his seed. One of the two main "characters" is therefore a plant rather than a person. On the heels of the parable of the sower, the most natural interpretation would link the man who sows the seed first of all with God, and then, derivatively, with Jesus and all who preach God's word. The growing seed then represents the fruit of that proclamation—the growth of God's kingdom inaugurated on earth, manifesting itself in the

---

16Bailey, *Through Peasant Eyes*, pp. 114-15; E. Earle Ellis, *The Gospel of Luke* (London: Oliphants, 1974; Grand Rapids: Eerdmans, 1981), p. 208.

17Wilhelm Michaelis, *Die Gleichnisse Jesu* (Hamburg: Furche Verlag, 1956), p. 183. Contra A. R. C. Leaney, *The Gospel according to St. Luke* (London: A & C Black, 1958), p. 228.

creation of disciples. As in the parable of the wheat and tares, the harvest most naturally stands for the final judgment. The reference to putting in the sickle when the grain is ripe harks back to Joel 3:13, which there refers to the coming of the great Day of the Lord. But this allusion is not an extraneous addition which turns the parable into an allegory. It is rather the fitting climax of a narrative which was already allegorical.[18]

The rest of the imagery in the story, however, must not be pressed. If the sower is first of all God, then it is patently false to say that God sleeps and rises or is ignorant of the nature of the growth of his kingdom. These details apply only to the earthly farmer, but, to the extent that the parable may also be applied to human preachers, they reflect ambiguities experienced by all Christians. So too, disciples do not mature automatically or in as orderly a fashion as the progression of events in the parable suggests.[19]

The one main point of comparison in verses 27-28 teaches merely that as the grain does ripen despite all of the forces working against it, so also God's kingdom will grow into all he intends for it, despite the uncertainties of human existence which might cast doubt over its staying power. Yet at the same time, as Schweizer points out, the surprising omission of any reference to ploughing, harrowing or cultivating may point to the message that God's people must wait with a "carefree attitude" for God to act, "without any spiritual maneuvering or misguided efforts."[20] At the very least, Jesus is teaching that human beings cannot control or predict the growth of the kingdom.

Although the center of the parable focuses on the guaranteed but unpredictable growth of the seed, the opening and closing verses highlight the action of the sower. Not surprisingly, two main interpretations have competed with each other for center stage in the history of exegesis. Though traditionally commentators have clas-

---

[18]Contra, e.g., Rudolf Pesch, *Das Markusevangelium*, vol. 1 (Freiburg: Herder, 1977), p. 255.

[19]Contra Claude M. Pavur, "The Grain Is Ripe: Parabolic Meaning in Mark 4:26-29," *BTB* 17 (1987):22, who allegorizes the details of the plant's growth to correspond to specific stages of discipleship.

[20]Eduard Schweizer, *The Good News according to Mark* (Richmond: John Knox, 1970; London: SPCK, 1971), p. 103. In a nice turn of phrase, Scott, *Hear*, p. 371, concludes, "The apocalyptic judge is only a possibility in the future; the God of aftergrowth is here in the sabbatical of his grace."

sified this passage as a parable of growth, the legacy of Jeremias has stressed that the main point should be taken as the promise of future harvest.[21]

When we see that each of these points lines up with one of the parable's main "characters," it is apparent that there is no need to choose between the two emphases. Several commentators seem to recognize this but fail to admit that their encapsulation of the parable's one main point actually combines two independent thoughts. Cranfield, for example, claims to be adopting a Jeremias-like approach, but nevertheless manages to insert into his conclusion the point which Jeremias disputes: "As seedtime is followed in due time by harvest, so will the present hiddenness and ambiguousness of the kingdom of God be succeeded by its glorious manifestation."[22] But the hiddenness and ambiguousness do not correspond to seedtime but to the later growth of the plant!

Others are more forthcoming. Lane, for example, declares: "Emphasis falls not merely upon the harvest which is assured, but upon the seed and its growth as well."[23] Once this is accepted, then all reasons for subdividing the parable into traditional and redactional portions disappear. The passage is a carefully constructed unity with the beginning and ending focusing on the sower, and the center underlining the role of the seed.[24] The parable's message fits in well with a setting in Jesus' ministry. Not long after his ministry was underway, his disciples came to see that his mission was turn-

---

[21]These two options are concisely summarized by Josef Ernst, *Das Evangelium nach Markus* (Regensburg: Pustet, 1981), p. 141; and Werner G. Kümmel, "Noch einmal: Das Gleichnis von der selbstwachsenden Saat," in *Orientierung an Jesus*, ed. Paul Hoffmann, Norbert Brox and Wilhelm Pesch (Freiburg: Herder, 1973), p. 226. Jeremias, *Parables*, p. 152, thinks that the point merely is that the end is implicit in the beginning.

[22]C. E. B. Cranfield, *The Gospel according to St. Mark* (Cambridge: University Press, 1977), p. 168. Cf. Rainer Stuhlmann, "Beobachtungen und Überlegungen zu Markus iv. 26-29," *NTS* 19 (1973):157, who finds the "one" point in the "certainty and inexplicability" of the process leading from planting to harvest.

[23]William L. Lane, *The Gospel according to Mark* (Grand Rapids: Eerdmans, 1974; London: Marshall, Morgan & Scott, 1975), p. 170. Cf. Pheme Perkins, *Hearing the Parables of Jesus* (New York: Paulist, 1981), p. 83.

[24]See esp. Jacques Dupont, "Encore la parabole de la Semence qui pousse toute seule (Mc 4, 26-29)," in *Jesus und Paulus*, ed. E. Earle Ellis & Erich Grässer (Göttingen: Vandenhoeck & Ruprecht, 1975), pp. 96-108 (esp. p. 107); and H. Baltenweiler, "Das Gleichnis von der selbstwachsenden Saat (Markus 4, 26-29) und die theologische Konzeption des Markusevangelisten," in *Oikonomia: Heilsgeschichte als Thema der Theologie*, ed. F. Christ (Hamburg-Bergstedt: Herbert Reich, 1967), pp. 69-75. Contra, e.g., J. D. Crossan, *In Parables: The Challenge of the Historical Jesus* (New York and London: Harper & Row, 1973), pp. 84-85, who deletes v. 28; or Hans Weder, *Die Gleichnisse Jesu als Metaphern* (Göttingen: Vandenhoeck & Ruprecht, 1978), p. 117, who deletes v. 29b as well.

ing in unanticipated directions, so that some decided to leave him
(Jn 6:66). Jesus teaches that the kingdom will eventually come in
triumph but first he must follow the way of the cross. Meanwhile,
he reassures believers that *(1) the kingdom will continue to grow inexorably, though sometimes almost invisibly, and that (2) at the end of the age the
kingdom will have grown into all its fullness, after which Judgment Day will
immediately follow.*

8.1.5 The Rich Fool (Lk 12:16-21)

As with the previous two parables, the story of the rich fool describes an authority figure and his subordinate. In this lone instance, however, that authority appears as God himself rather than
as a character who represents God. Unlike the previous two parables, the ending is tragic rather than comic. Like the Pharisee and
the publican, the passage is as close as one comes to finding a pure
example story. But as in the story of the rich man and Lazarus, the
rich fool does not simply stand for people who are materially rich,
but for those who take no thought for God. Understandably, in
light of Jesus' teaching elsewhere on the spiritually damaging power
of riches, it is natural that he should choose to depict such a person
by describing him as wealthy.

The authenticity of the parable itself is seldom challenged. It is
often alleged, however, that only verse 21 introduces the theme of
one who is not rich toward God, and that the original passage had
a much more radical point to make about the evils of literal, material
riches. There are numerous hints that this is not so. Not only is the
story silent about the man's relationship with God, but it also shows
him taking no thought for anybody but himself. The repeated use
of the personal pronoun "I" in contexts of self-interest is perhaps
the most striking feature of the passage.[25]

---

[25]Cf. Simon J. Kistemaker, *The Parables of Jesus* (Grand Rapids: Baker, 1980), p. 182.

The fact that God addresses the man as a "fool" (not the word which in the Sermon on the Mount Jesus forbids us to use with reference to our fellow human beings—Mt 5:22) suggests that he is also a sinner. Foolishness often has overtones of immorality in the Old Testament and intertestamental literature and is not just an epithet for stupidity. Important background texts include Job 31:24-28; Psalm 14:1; Psalm 49; Ecclesiastes 2:1-11; and Sirach 11:19-20. A. T. Cadoux captures the force of the imagery: "It is the *reductio ad absurdum* of selfishness by showing it at work systematically and unencumbered."[26]

Verses 13-15 are also often suspect as being added later to provide a context for the parable; yet they are entirely appropriate, and there is no reason they should be labeled secondary. The warning against covetousness provides the perfect backdrop for the parable and reinforces the idea that it is not the man's wealth which is condemned but the accumulation of wealth solely for his own enjoyment.[27] Without this framework the parable is left entirely "in the air."[28]

The two main points deriving from the actions of the fool and of God follow naturally. *(1) A purely selfish accumulation of possessions is incompatible with true discipleship. (2) This incompatibility stems from the transience of earthly riches and the coming reckoning which all will face before God.* We need not limit this reckoning either to death or to the final judgment; it applies equally to both.[29]

The two stages of the parable focus in sequence on these two points and the two characters who give rise to them: verses 16-19 describe the actions of the fool, and verse 20 provides God's response. Verses 15 and 21, as the two verses which bracket the parable, suggest two applications nicely corresponding to the two points of the narrative—a warning against covetousness and the

---

[26]A. T. Cadoux, *The Parables of Jesus: Their Art and Use* (London: J. Clarke, 1930; New York: Macmillan, 1931), p. 205. Cf. Michaelis, *Gleichnisse,* p. 223. Scott, *Hear,* p. 135, sees the quantity harvested as miraculous and intended by God for the use of the whole community. Thus the parable poignantly illustrates "how to mismanage a miracle."

[27]See esp. J. D. M. Derrett, "The Rich Fool: A Parable of Jesus concerning Inheritance," in *Studies in the New Testament,* vol. 2 (Leiden: Brill, 1978), p. 116.

[28]Josef Ernst, *Das Evangelium nach Lukas* (Regensburg: Pustet, 1977), p. 396. Cf. Karl H. Rengstorf, *Das Evangelium nach Lukas* (Göttingen: Vandenhoeck & Ruprecht, 1937), p. 159.

[29]Ellis, *Luke,* p. 178. Contra John Drury, *The Parables in the Gospels* (London: SPCK; New York: Crossroad, 1985), pp. 112-13, who sees only death in view; or Jeremias, *Parables,* p. 165, who sees only the eschatological crisis in view.

need to take God into account in one's plans. The rest of the details of the man's building program have no specific referents. Different imagery could just as easily have been used to make the same point.

Jesus chose this particular illustration because he was addressing a largely rural, agricultural people. As Joseph Fitzmyer makes plain: "In the story the 'rich man' is a farmer; but he stands for humans seduced by 'every form of greed' (12:15), whether peasant or statesman, craftsman or lawyer, nurse or doctor, secretary or professor."[30] From a human point of view, then, everything in the parable is natural; from God's point of view, such self-centeredness is absurd! John Purdy offers challenging contemporary applications of the parable to the modern quest for materialist success and happy retirement years. He concludes:

> If we hold that true wisdom is to be rich toward God, then work will have a limited place in our lives. *We shall work hard enough to provide the necessities; we shall leave the future in God's hands.* We will not make work a means of securing our lives against all possible calamities.[31]

8.1.6 The Barren Fig Tree (Lk 13:6-9)

master

fig tree/vinedresser

Just as the unprofitable servant and the seed growing secretly illustrated the comic dyadic pattern of a master and his subordinate, once where the subordinate was human and once where it was a plant, so also the tragic dyadic pattern may take the form of a master and human subordinate (the rich fool) or may employ agricultural imagery in lieu of a human subordinate (the barren fig tree). As noted in the parable of the wicked tenants, the vineyard was a stock metaphor for Israel, so it is natural to take the fig tree here as representing at least some of the Jews. Their fruitlessness

---

[30]Cf. Joseph A. Fitzmyer, *The Gospel according to Luke X-XXIV* (Garden City: Doubleday, 1985), p. 972.

[31]John C. Purdy, *Parables at Work* (Philadelphia: Westminster, 1985), pp. 48-49.

is self-explanatory. In light of Jesus' special condemnation of the corrupt leadership of the Jewish nation elsewhere, the fig tree would naturally symbolize the religious leaders of Israel, though the principle of judgment on those who do not repent obviously applies universally (Lk 13:3, 5).[32]

There are then two characters representing two points of view. The one is the owner of the vineyard; the other is the vinedresser speaking on behalf of the mute tree. The two points are clear: *(1) The threat of imminent judgment hangs over Israel's leaders* (the tree may be cut down), but *(2) God continues for a short while to offer mercy in the hope that they will at last respond properly to him* (the tree will be nurtured for one more year).[33]

The three-to-one-year ratio may highlight the farmer's patience with the tree in the past and his unwillingness to tolerate fruitlessness much longer, but beyond that the numbers seem to signify little. It is probably coincidental that the Torah enjoined that fruit trees be allowed three years to grow before being harvested, otherwise there would be little point to the farmer's protests in the very first year that he could legitimately come to look for fruit.

Derrett thinks the three years were the three following this initial period and that the threat of the axe corresponds to a similar threat in a *halakah* (legal interpretation) for Deuteronomy 20:19.[34] This is possible but not demonstrable. The digging and spreading of manure may be an example of "insult humor," especially if the crowds realized Jesus had the Jewish leaders specially in view,[35] but these details may just reflect natural horticultural practice. Attempts to see Jesus in the figure of the vinedresser risk placing him at odds with God the Father and raise the specter of the ancient Marcionite heresy, which pitted a loving Christ against a vengeful God.

Unlike the parable of the rich fool, but like some of the parables previously discussed (e.g., the prodigal son and two debtors), this narrative concludes in open-ended fashion. The threat of judgment

---

[32]Bailey, *Through Peasant Eyes*, p. 82.

[33]Cf. A. M. Hunter, *Interpreting the Parables* (London: SCM; Philadelphia: Westminster, 1960), p. 82: "The clear implication of the parable is that Israel's time for repentance is short; yet there remains a last chance—a reminder that God is merciful as well as just."

[34]J. D. M. Derrett, "Figtrees in the New Testament," in *Studies in the New Testament*, vol. 2, p. 159.

[35]Bailey, *Through Peasant Eyes*, p. 84.

seems more powerful than the offer of mercy, especially in light of the preceding illustrations of the slaughtered Galileans and the inhabitants of Siloam killed by a falling tower (Lk 13:1-5). But even as Jesus journeys under the shadow of the cross, he suggests that it may not yet be too late for his opponents.

A similar Jewish folk-tale (in the story of Ahikar) altogether lacks any element corresponding to this potential reprieve.[36] As with the rich man and Lazarus, Jesus may have adapted a well-known story to suit his own message, in which case his emphasis on a "second chance" stands out all the more. For Luke, however, looking back on the ultimate response of the Jewish authorities to Jesus would make it seem that for them judgment triumphed over mercy. But disputes about the one main point are futile; both mercy and judgment need to be stressed.

Almost no one contests the authenticity of verses 6-9. John Drury is a rare exception, as he views the parable as a tertiary development of the cursing of the fig tree (Mk 11:12-14, 20-25 par.; the second stage is the metaphor of the budding fig tree—Mk 13:28-31).[37] This hypothesis stands on its head a more common view which assumes that if any of these passages is to be seen as a later development of one of the others, it would be the story of Jesus cursing the fig tree, because of its unique character as the only one of Jesus' miracles which is destructive. In fact, none of the passages needs to be taken as inauthentic; all are coherent in their individual contexts.[38] Drury does recognize that the parable of the barren fig tree is an allegory, but it is no less authentic for being so.

One can go further and note that verses 6-9 are integrally linked with verses 1-5.[39] Like the three parables of the lost sheep, coin and sons in Luke 15, Luke 13:1-9 combines a pair of very short, parallel

---

[36]See Peter R. Jones, *The Teaching of the Parables* (Nashville: Broadman, 1982), p. 120.

[37]Drury, *Parables*, p. 119.

[38]On the present parable, see esp. Jean G. Kahn, "La parabole du figuier stérile et les arbres récalcitrants de la Genése," *NovT* 13 (1971):38-45; on the budding fig tree, David Wenham, *The Rediscovery of Jesus' Eschatological Discourse* (Sheffield: JSOT, 1984), pp. 326-32; on the cursing of the fig tree, see Craig L. Blomberg, "The Miracles as Parables," in *Gospel Perspectives*, vol. 6, ed. David Wenham and Craig L. Blomberg (Sheffield: JSOT, 1986), pp. 330-33, and literature there cited.

[39]Josef Blinzler, "Die Niedermetzelung von Galiläern durch Pilatus," *NovT* 2 (1958):24-49. Günther Schwarz, "Lukas xiii. 1-5: Eine Emendation," *NovT* 11 (1969):121-26, rightly recognizes the tight link between vv. 2b-3 and 4-5, but unnecessarily jettisons vv. 1-2a on linguistic and stylistic grounds.

rhetorical questions with a longer narrative parable which illustrates in more detail the theme of those questions. In each case the two short passages conclude with a refrain about repentance, which proves to be the theme that the third passage takes up.[40] The announcement of judgment becomes a call to turn to God. It is up to each individual in Jesus' audience to determine his or her own response.

8.1.7 The Unjust Judge (Lk 18:1-8)

judge

widow

The parable of the unjust judge provides a further example of a two-pointed parable, in which the two points derive from two characters, one in a position of authority (the judge) and one in a position of powerlessness (the widow). Luke uncharacteristically derives a lesson from the parable right at the outset (v. 1; though compare also 19:11), which apparently describes the point of the narrative—always to pray and not to lose heart.

In the context of Luke 17:20-18:8, the primary prayer in view is probably that which seeks the completion of the kingdom's coming. But Luke's way of phrasing things suggests that verse 1 may not state the meaning of the parable so much as a goal or application of the story. Literally this verse reads, "he was speaking . . . *to the end that* one should always pray . . ." (Ἔλεγεν . . . πρὸς τὸ δεῖν πάντοτε προσεύχεσθαι . . .). The parable itself focuses most of its attention on the judge; only verse 3 is narrated from the point of view of the widow.

Alternately, Luke 18:1 might be seen as the point to be derived from the actions of the widow, and one might expect a second, more prominent lesson to follow from the behavior of the judge. The concluding comments ascribed to Jesus in verses 6-8a support this bipolar outlook.

[40]William R. Farmer, "Notes on a Literary and Form-Critical Analysis of Some of the Synoptic Material Peculiar to Luke," *NTS* 8 (1961-62):305.

Verses 6-8a explicitly begin with the exhortation to "hear what the unjust judge says," while verse 8b returns to the perspective of the widow, querying whether the Son of man will find faith like hers when he returns. The Greek reads literally, "will he find *the* faith on earth?" The definite article suggests that Christ is referring to the specific kind of faith just illustrated. Verse 8b is thus integrally linked with verses 2-8a.[41] I. Howard Marshall compares this parable to that of the prodigal son. Each narrative shifts at the end to focus on the less central character, disclosing a "sting" in its "tail."[42]

Jesus' description of an unscrupulous authority figure does not prevent one from seeing the judge as in some sense standing for God. The logic is a fortiori (from the lesser to the greater); the only aspect of the judge's behavior which makes him resemble God is his rewarding the woman's persistent pleas. God is not being likened to one who normally cares little for justice or who is afraid of getting worn out.[43] That the parable can refer to the judge's relationship with God (or lack thereof) is no more an obstacle to seeing him as a symbol for God than was the dual reference to God and father an obstacle to seeing the father of the prodigal son in a similar light.

The a fortiori logic also suggests that while the judge delayed, God will not delay, although the notorious difficulty of translating verse 7b makes this point less certain.[44] If it does imply a delay, it is at least balanced by the promise of God's quick or swift vindication (v. 8a), and it certainly need not be taken as presupposing the situation of the later church after the so-called delay of the parousia. The Jews themselves had been agonizing for centuries over God's failure to vindicate them against their oppressors.

---

[41]Cf. Gerhard Schneider, *Parusiegleichnisse im Lukas-Evangelium* (Stuttgart: Katholisches Bibelwerk, 1975), p. 78.

[42]I. Howard Marshall, *The Gospel of Luke* (Exeter: Paternoster; Grand Rapids: Eerdmans, 1978), p. 670.

[43]The verb ὑπωπιάζω in v. 5 can mean "to give a black eye," but is probably to be interpreted more metaphorically. Derrett, *Studies*, vol. 1 (1977), p. 44, takes it to mean slander or disgrace; Bailey, *Through Peasant Eyes*, p.136, believes that the phrase is equivalent to "lest she give me a headache."

[44]If v. 7b is translated as an independent rhetorical question, "and will he delay long over them?" as in RSV, NASB, this point is clear. Several studies, however, have suggested that it is a dependent clause in an adversative or concessive relationship to what precedes (the καί perhaps reflecting an underlying Aramaic stative clause)—thus, e.g., "although he delays long over them." See, with varying nuances, Herman Ljungvik, "Zur Erklärung einer Lukas-Stelle (Luk. xviii. 7)," *NTS* 10 (1963-64):292; Harald Riesenfeld, "Zu μακροθυμεῖν (Lk 18, 7)," in *Neutestamentliche Aufsätze*, ed. Josef Blinzler (Regensburg: Pustet, 1963), pp. 216-17; Albert Wifstrand, "Lukas xviii. 7," *NTS* 11 (1964-65):73-74.

Verses 2-5, which form the parable proper, have generally been held to be authentic, but any or all of verses 6-8a, and especially verse 8b, are often attributed to later tradition or redaction. Verse 1 is almost universally said to have missed the point of the parable. When one allows for two main points, the last of these concerns quickly dissipates. The parable teaches both that *(1) God will hear and answer the cries of his people against injustice by again sending the Son of man to earth, although they cannot be sure of the timing, and that, therefore, (2) we must persist in faithful petition for the consummation of the kingdom.*[45]

Often attempts to deny that one of these points is present wind up affirming it anyway.[46] In verse 8b, in addition to the shift of perspective from judge to widow and the use of the article in the expression "the faith," already noted above, the main complaint is that it awkwardly inserts a reference to the Son of man where the passage had been teaching about *God's* vindication of his elect. But, as Gerhard Delling points out, it is precisely by the return of the Son of man that God vindicates his elect, so there is no discrepancy here either.[47]

Objections to verses 6-8a are phrased in numerous ways, but most have to do, not with any inherent traditio-historical tension in this passage, but with the characteristic tension which is found throughout Scripture between God's sovereignty and human responsibility. This tension raises questions about why one should pray at all if God's will is always accomplished, about whether prayers are necessarily more effective the more often one repeats them, or about how to interpret seemingly unanswered prayer.

The parable agrees with passages like James 4:2 and Matthew 7:7-11 that highlight God's conditional will—there are good things which God desires his people to have but which he has determined to give them only if they earnestly seek him in prayer. To be sure, some prayers request that which God has unconditionally willed or

---

[45]Cf. Norval Geldenhuys, *Commentary on the Gospel of Luke* (London: Marshall, Morgan & Scott, 1950; Grand Rapids: Eerdmans, 1951), pp. 446-48; Ceslaus Spicq, "La parabole de la veuve obstinée et du juge inerte, aux décisions impromptues," *RB* 68 (1961):78.

[46]E.g., Weder, *Gleichnisse*, p. 270, states that the emphasis in the parable is not on human perseverance but on divine freedom. But on p. 273, more cogently, he combines these emphases: "the certainty of the fulfillment of the request is at the same time the stipulation of the possibility of perseverance in prayer."

[47]Gerhard Delling, "Das Gleichnis vom gottlosen Richter," *ZNW* 53 (1962): 22. Cf. M.-J. Lagrange, *Évangile selon Saint Luc* (Paris: Gabalda, 1921), p. 468.

rejected; in these instances prayer does not affect what actually happens. But this parable does not concentrate on God's unalterable agenda but on situations in which prayer makes a difference. God will fully establish his kingdom, regardless of individual apathy, but his people can speed its arrival through holy living (2 Pet 3:11-12).

Attempts to assign Luke 18:6-8 to later redaction because it allegorizes the parable's characters fly in the face of the now overwhelmingly cumulative evidence for Jesus' consistent use of allegory in the parables.[48] On the other hand, attempts to preserve the authenticity of these verses by denying that the correspondences they suggest are truly allegorical misunderstand the nature of allegory and, while well-intentioned, are misguided.[49]

Linnemann remarkably rejects the authenticity of all eight verses. Because she believes they form an indissoluble unity and because she finds certain parts of the text objectionable, she must get rid of it all.[50] But this approach can be stood on its head. If the passage is a unity and if the parable itself (vv. 2-5) has seemed to almost all commentators to be characteristic of Jesus' very unorthodox use of imagery on behalf of one of his favorite themes, God's vindication of the dispossessed, then perhaps one should consider more favorably the possibility that verses 6-8 are authentic as well.

8.1.8 The Friend at Midnight (Lk 11:5-8)

man sleeping

friend needing bread

---

[48]Contra, e.g., Fitzmyer, *Luke X-XXIV*, p. 1176, who somewhat uniquely retains v. 6 as authentic while rejecting vv. 7-8.

[49]Thus, e.g., Delling, "Richter," p. 24, who points out the correspondences between elements in vv. 2-5 and 7-8 (e.g., χήρα/ἐκλεκτοί ["widow/elect"]; ἐκδικεῖν ἀπό/ἐκδίκησιν ["avenge/vengeance"]) and argues for the unity of the passage, but refuses to recognize the presence of allegory.

[50]Eta Linnemann, *Parables of Jesus: Introduction and Exposition* (London: SPCK, 1966 [= *Jesus of the Parables: Introduction and Exposition* (New York: Harper & Row, 1967)]), pp. 121, 187-88 (n. 14). Linnemann's other major complaint is against the idea of Jesus gathering a community of "elect" around him. This has been decisively answered by David R. Catchpole, "The Son of Man's Search for Faith (Lk xviii. 8b)," *NovT* 19 (1977):102-4. Interestingly, a number of years after writing her book, Linnemann underwent a charismatic conversion and repudiated much of what she previously wrote.

This little parable is a twin to the parable of the unjust judge. The two parables have identical structure and seem at first glance to make basically the same two points, although the context here is one of general prayer for daily needs, whereas in Luke 18:1-8 the context involved righting injustice and final judgment. Here Luke makes the a fortiori logic explicit by his juxtaposition of 11:9-13 (see esp. v. 13—"if you being evil know how to give good gifts to your children, *how much more* will your Father in heaven give the Holy Spirit to those who ask him").

But, even on their own, verses 5-8 imply an argument of the form "from the lesser to the greater." The rhetorical formula τίς ἐξ ὑμῶν ("which one of you . . . ?") regularly introduces this kind of reasoning. Thus many potential points of comparison are not to be pressed, and some actually contrast human and divine behavior rather than comparing them. Although the sleeping man plays the part of the God-figure, Jesus is not trying to teach that God goes to bed, shuts the door, can't easily get up or doesn't want to be bothered. The point of comparison is simply that, like the sleeping friend, God will give to those who ask him whatever they genuinely need.

The reluctant attitude of the friend contrasts with the eagerness of God to give good gifts to his children. The rhetorical question should be taken as extending to the end of verse 7 and as expecting a clearly negative answer—"no, of course, no one would turn down a friend in these circumstances even despite initial incovenience." One final detail, which is often wrongly allegorized, is the number three. Three hand-sized loaves were simply the standard fare for an evening meal.

The lesson to be learned from the man who asks for bread for his visitor is not as easily determined and depends on the meaning and subject of the word usually translated "importunacy" (ἀναίδεια). Traditionally this has been taken to refer to the persistence on the part of the one asking for help, in which case the point to be derived would deal with perseverance in prayer, very closely parallel to Luke 18:1. Grammatically, though, the antecedent of "his importunacy" is ambiguous; it could refer to the man who had been asleep as easily as to the man calling for help.

Bailey therefore suggests the translation "shamelessness" and attributes this quality to the man in bed. Thus the point is that he rouses himself to help his friend in order to avoid being blamed by his community for not supplying the requested aid.[51] But this involves a subtle semantic shift from the concept of "shamelessness," which would more naturally apply to the man asking for bread despite the discourtesy of doing so in the middle of the night, to the idea of "without blame or disgrace," which would apply more naturally to the other man.

Derrett therefore takes the term as meaning "shamelessness" but applies it to the one asking for aid. He notes that what would seem to modern Westerners as impertinence was the conventional way of stressing the legitimacy and urgency of a request in the ancient Middle East. The man must ask boldly and without shame.[52] That ἀναίδεια rarely means "persistence" in pre-Christian Greek literature goes a long way to refuting the traditional translation, whichever of these alternatives one adopts, and the fact that the other Lukan uses of διὰ τό + εἶναι + an accusative subject ("because . . . [someone] is . . . [something]") usually equate the subject of the infinitive εἶναι with the subject of the sentence (Lk 2:4, 19:11, Acts 18:13; diff. 27:3) tends to support Derrett's interpretation over Bailey's.[53]

In that event, the lesson from the man at the door is that *(1) one should practice bold, unabashed forthrightness in prayer, which does not hesitate to request the good gifts which God has promised to his people if they ask for them.* The lesson from the response of the man who arises and helps his friend is then that *(2) God will provide for the needs of his people even more generously and willingly.* One must not consider God as a remote or distant monarch who does not wish to be bothered with his subjects' concerns. He is interested in even the most trivial and insignificant needs of his people.

Admitting these two distinct points in the parable takes care of

[51]Kenneth E. Bailey, *Poet and Peasant: A Literary-Cultural Approach to the Parables in Luke* (Grand Rapids: Eerdmans, 1976), pp. 119-33. Cf. Alan F. Johnson, "Assurance for Man: The Fallacy of Translating *Anaideia* by 'Persistence' in Luke 11:5-8," *JETS* 22 (1979):123-31; Evertt W. Huffard, "The Parable of the Friend at Midnight: God's Honor or Man's Persistence," *RestQ* 21 (1978):154-60.

[52]J. D. M. Derrett, "The Friend at Midnight: Asian Ideas in the Gospel of St. Luke," in *Donum Gentilicum*, ed. Ernst Bammel, C. K. Barrett and W. D. Davies (Oxford: Clarendon, 1978), p. 83. Cf. A. D. Martin, "The Parable concerning Hospitality," *ExpT* 37 (1925-26):412; Klaus Haacker, "Mut zum Bitten: Eine Auslegung von Lukas 11, 5-8," *TheolBeitr* 17 (1986): 1-6.

[53]Cf. already Jülicher, *Gleichnisreden*, vol. 2, p. 273.

the problem many have seen with the fact that the parable starts from the perspective of the asker and ends with the perspective of the giver. Recognizing two points also dispenses with the typical debates over which of the two lessons is actually the point of the passage.[54]

One of few to separate the passage tradition-critically is Wilhelm Ott, who believes that verses 5-7 were assimilated to the pattern of the parable of the unjust judge by the addition of verse 8.[55] Bailey believes that verses 5-8 and 9-13 were originally separate.[56] David Catchpole offers evidence that verses 9-13 originally stood together in Q with the parable itself, but he agrees with Ott that the parable could not have originally concluded with verse 8 as it now stands.[57] But none of these scholars admit that the parable could be intending to teach something from the actions both of the man asking for help and from the sleeper who is roused. If they did, the need for these reconstructions would be greatly diminished.

8.1.9 The Householder and the Thief (Mt 24:43-44, Lk 12:39-40)

householder ◄————————► thief

The last parable to be discussed in this section still presents two main characters or objects and seems to teach two separate points, but it is so short that it is easy to treat it as monadic in form. It does not fit into any of the patterns previously diagrammed. No inter-action occurs between the two individuals. Thus it forms an appropriate transition to the second main section of this chapter. The little parable of the householder and the thief depicts two human characters, one trying to guard himself against the other.

This parable is, in fact, so short that one is surprised to find scholars still trying to dissect it into authentic and inauthentic

---

[54]So also Ernst, *Lukas*, p. 366. Marshall, *Luke*, p. 462, affirms that the two points belong together as one whole but he later tries to limit the meaning to one central point relating to the man in bed—i.e., on the character of God (p. 465).

[55]Wilhelm Ott, *Gebet und Heil* (München: Kösel, 1965), pp. 25-29, 71-72.

[56]Bailey, *Poet and Peasant*, pp. 134-41.

[57]David R. Catchpole, "Q and 'The Friend at Midnight' (Luke xi. 5-8/9)," *JTS* 34 (1983):418.

bits.[58] Nevertheless, the conclusion is often taken as secondary, because it is said to allegorize the parable: the householder stands for the person who is not a well-prepared disciple of Jesus, and the thief represents the Son of man.[59] This analysis of the allegory is correct; the verdict about inauthenticity does not follow.

The metaphor of the Son of man as thief, like those which compare God to an unjust judge or a disciple to an unjust steward, is so radical as virtually to guarantee its authenticity.[60] The point of comparison is not that Christ is a robber, but that like a burglar he comes at an unexpected time. No delay in the parousia need be presupposed for this message to carry force.[61] The injunction to watchfulness in Matthew's introductory verse (24:42) does not contradict the parable's imagery, because the verb "to watch" (γρηγορέω) implies preparation rather than constant, literal wakefulness. The concluding interpretation concisely summarizes the two main points corresponding to the two characters: *(1) People must constantly be ready for the possible return of Christ, since (2) he might come at any time and catch some off guard.*[62]

8.2 One-Point Parables

It is virtually impossible to tell a story, however brief, without introducing at least two main characters or a subject and an object. Without *inter*action it is very difficult to have *any* action. Conceivably, then, none of Jesus' parables is meant to make only one solitary point. Nevertheless, at least six of the passages usually included in a study of the parables seem to be so brief and to concentrate so intensively on the protagonist of the plot that they may be grouped into a distinct category of parables. These appear to offer only one central truth. Interestingly, the six appear as three pairs of closely matched illustrations.

---

[58]Cf. the detailed study by Adolf Smitmans, "Das Gleichnis vom Dieb," in *Das Wort Gottes in der Zeit*, ed. Helmut Feld and Josef Nolte (Düsseldorf: Patmos, 1973), pp. 43-68.

[59]E.g., Jeremias, *Parables*, pp. 87-88; Schneider, *Parusiegleichnisse*, p. 22.

[60]See esp. Tim Schramm and Kathrin Löwenstein, *Unmoralische Helden: Anstössige Gleichnisse Jesu* (Göttingen: Vandenhoeck & Ruprecht, 1986), pp. 52-53.

[61]Rightly, Fitzmyer, *Luke X-XXIV*, p. 986. Contra Hans Conzelmann, *The Theology of St. Luke* (New York: Harper & Row; London: Faber & Faber, 1960), p. 108.

[62]Cf. Heinrich Kahlefeld, *Parables and Instructions in the Gospels* (New York: Herder & Herder, 1966), p. 105, who takes v. 44b to be an independent reason for the word of warning, and v. 44a to be the original conclusion to the parable.

8.2.1 The Hidden Treasure and Pearl of Great Price (Mt 13:44-46)

These two very brief similes so closely resemble each other in both structure and meaning that they must be considered together. Despite the variation in introductory formulas ("the kingdom is like a treasure/ like a man . . .), it is clear that Jesus is comparing the kingdom of God to the treasure and to the pearl. The man who discovers the treasure, like the merchant who purchases the pearl, stands for anyone who becomes a "child of the kingdom," that is, a disciple of Jesus. In this sense, there are two foci to each parable,[63] but it seems natural to formulate the parables' message in one short sentence: *The kingdom of God is so valuable that it is worth sacrificing anything to gain it.*[64] One could plausibly argue that this sentence in fact contains two points, so that perhaps it should be considered dyadic. Yet it is not clear that the two clauses of the sentence are discrete. The central theme in each remains that of the value of the kingdom. Just as the first two parables in this chapter demonstrated the fluidity of the boundary between triadic and dyadic parables, so these two texts indicate a similar overlap between dyadic and monadic forms.

The refrain which the two passages repeat in identical language highlights the need to sell all for the sake of the treasure or pearl. But we do not purchase the kingdom; quite the contrary, God rules entirely by grace. Some would resolve this apparent contradiction by making the treasure finder and pearl merchant symbols for Christ, who purchased his people with his death, but this approach interprets the metaphor too woodenly.[65]

An early rabbinic parable likens the pilgrimage of the Israelites from Egypt to Canaan to a merchant who in a far-off land discovers a treasure which he purchases (Mekilta Beshallach 2:142ff.). Yet no Jew would have dared to think of Israel as buying the Promised Land from God. Nevertheless, Jesus' teaching elsewhere is clear; for

---

[63]So esp. Jacques Dupont, "Les paraboles du trésor et de la perle," *NTS* 14 (1968) 408-18. Cf. Jack D. Kingsbury, *The Parables of Jesus in Matthew 13* (London: SPCK; Richmond: John Knox, 1969), pp. 115-16; Robert H. Stein, *An Introduction to the Parables of Jesus* (Philadelphia: Westminster, 1981; Exeter: Paternoster, 1982), p. 103.

[64]Cf. C. H. Dodd, *The Parables of the Kingdom* (London: Nisbet, 1935; New York: Scribner's, 1936), p. 112; Linnemann, *Parables*, p. 99, who both emphasize the sacrifice more than the value.

[65]As, e.g., in Jeffrey A. Gibbs, "Parables of Atonement and Assurance: Matthew 13:44-46," *CTQ* 51 (1987):19-43. So also J. Dwight Pentecost, *The Parables of Jesus* (Grand Rapids: Zondervan, 1982), pp. 60-61, who then takes the treasure to stand for Israel and the pearl for the Gentiles!

many individuals financial sacrifice is required before other commitments can give way to the priorities of God (e.g., Lk 19:1-10), and for some this may require selling all (e.g., Lk 18:18-30). For those who do not literally sell anything in becoming disciples, the potential must always be present. They must be willing to risk all, if the priorities of the kingdom threaten the security of their earthly existence.[66]

Crossan's deconstructionist interpretation in which abandoning all includes abandoning the parable and then "abandoning abandonment" discloses the self-defeating results of his method rather than a legitimate interpretation of the passage.[67] At the opposite extreme, the type of new hermeneutic reflected in Fuchs's attempt to make the passage say exactly the opposite of what it does, namely, that would-be disciples should do nothing and leave all the activity to God, proves equally arbitrary.[68]

Details not to be overly stressed include the joy of the discovery of the treasure. Although finding God's kingdom is a joy, this point is not repeated in the parable of the pearl and can scarely be said to summarize the sole main point of the two passages.[69] Even more peripheral are the ethics of the man who hid the treasure he had found in order to purchase the field from its unsuspecting owner. Commentators have taken diametrically opposite stances on the legality and morality of this subterfuge, but enough devious characters have appeared in the parables so far surveyed that interpreters need not be deflected from the main point which lies elsewhere.[70]

Much could be made of the treasure's hiddenness in light of the

---

[66]Perkins, *Parables*, p. 28. Cf. Otto Glombitza, "Der Perlenkaufmann," *NTS* 7 (1960-61):153-61.

[67]J. D. Crossan, *Finding Is the First Act* (Missoula: Scholars; Philadelphia: Fortress, 1979). Carson's critique is quite correct—"ascription of such existentialist results to Jesus or to Matthew is so anachronistic as to make a historian wince" ("Matthew," p. 329). Crossan of course would simply dismiss this criticism as irrelevant since he is self-consciously not employing traditional historical methods.

[68]Ernst Fuchs, *Studies of the Historical Jesus* (London: SCM; Naperville: Allenson, 1964), pp. 127-30. Rightly criticized by Dan O. Via, Jr., *The Parables: Their Literary and Existential Dimension* (Philadelphia: Fortress, 1967), p. 20.

[69]Contra Jeremias, *Parables*, pp. 200-201; and in part, France, *Matthew*, p. 229.

[70]Contra most, and defending the propriety of the action, see J. D. M. Derrett, *Law in the New Testament* (London: Darton, Longman & Todd, 1970), pp. 1-16. Recognizing that the focus of attention lies elsewhere, see David Hill, *The Gospel of Matthew* (London: Oliphants, 1972; Grand Rapids: Eerdmans, 1981), p. 238. John W. Sider, "Interpreting the Hid Treasure," *CSR* 13 (1984):371, believes that the rehiding is significant but only in that it reinforces the commitment required to attain the treasure.

imperceptible growth of the kingdom in the parable of the seed growing secretly. But because the story line requires the man to bury the treasure again in order for his scheme to succeed, it seems dubious to derive any allegorical meaning from it. The main variation between the two passages may be more significant. The two who discover their windfalls include one who is deliberately looking for "good buys" (the pearl merchant) as well as one who stumbles across his treasure (the first man). Jesus may therefore be calling both the individual who is diligently searching for spiritual riches as well as the person who is entirely apathetic toward God to give up whatever stands between them and the kingdom.

8.2.2 The Tower Builder and the Warring King (Lk 14:28-33)

Luke 14:28-32 presents a pair of short τίς ἐξ ὑμῶν ("which one of you . . . ?") parables with closely parallel structure. The basic meaning of the two seems similar and self-evident: do not get involved in something which you are unable to complete. The examples, however, vary in degree of seriousness. The man who is unable to finish building a tower risks only ridicule from his community and the possible loss of financial investment. The man who fails to realize that he is outnumbered in battle risks losing his kingdom, his soldiers and his life. This difference suggests that the passage is arranged in a climactic sequence and explains why Jesus' conclusion seems still more severe: "Whoever of you does not renounce all that he has cannot be my disciple" (v. 33).

This conclusion goes beyond the point of either parable, but it should not therefore be classified as secondary; it brings to a climax the series of three declarations (vv. 28-30, 31-32, 33). The a fortiori nature of τίς ἐξ ὑμῶν parables supports this interpretation. If people must carefully calculate their chances of success in major human endeavors, how much more so must they take seriously the results of spiritual commitments.

Verse 33, however, has posed problems for commentators for other reasons too. Most notably, it seems to be establishing a more radical definition of discipleship than that which Jesus employs elsewhere. Some therefore think that these parables at first applied only to a select core of Jesus' disciples, or that they were addressed only to those who had already committed themselves to him to warn them against half-hearted loyalty.[71] But "to renounce all" does not necessarily mean literally to abandon all. As noted above, Jesus sometimes does make that demand of an individual, but many times he does not. Rather the idea is one of giving up anything which would stand in the way of full-fledged service for Christ. The actual implementation of this principle will vary from person to person and situation to situation, but it probably should involve most modern Westerners in much more serious soul-searching concerning the use of their possessions than they might otherwise suspect.[72]

Problems with the two parables themselves often revolve around the seeming impossibility of counting the cost of Christian discipleship. Most people who come to faith have little idea of what the future will hold or what sacrifices their commitment will involve. Perhaps this reflects more on the shallow nature of many conversions than on any inherent problems in Jesus' parables. Even in the *Sitz im Leben Jesu* in which Luke places this parable, Jesus, as he travels under the shadow of the cross, has given the crowds enough exposure to the nature of his ministry for him to expect them to realize that he is taking the role of a suffering Messiah before his triumphal return. If men and women want to identify with him, they too must be prepared to sacrifice whatever is required to remain faithful to the way of the cross.

In passing, it might be good to note that this passage seems to presuppose some interval of time in which its demands can be implemented. Commitment proves itself only over the long haul. This "delay" before Christ's return balances the often overemphasized theme of imminence in other teachings of Jesus.[73]

A novel approach to the interpretation of these two little parables tries to offset the apparent harshness of their application by assuming that the tower builder and warring king both stand for Jesus (or God) rather than for would-be disciples. God in Christ is thus the one who determined to sacrifice all, by means of the crucifixion. J. D. M. Derrett has set out the case for this interpretation in great

---

[71]Thus, respectively, J. Alexander Findlay, *Jesus and His Parables* (London: Epworth, 1950), p. 99; Ellis, *Luke*, p. 195.

[72]So, e.g., Eduard Schweizer, *The Good News according to Luke* (Atlanta: John Knox; London: SPCK, 1984), p. 242; Jacques Dupont, "Renoncer à tous ses biens," *NRT* 6 (1971):561-82.

[73]A point rarely noted but picked up by Edward A. Armstrong, *The Gospel Parables* (London: Hodder & Stoughton; New York: Sheed & Ward, 1967), pp. 101-2.

detail, noting, for example, that (a) other τίς ἐξ ὑμῶν parables usually teach something about the nature of God from the actions of the main character (recall the sleeping friend in Lk 11:5-8, or the shepherd and woman in Lk 15:3-10); (b) a king regularly stands for God in Jesus' parables; and (c) Jesus elsewhere enjoins his followers to faith rather than to calculation.[74]

On the other hand, contra (a), Luke 12:25 introduces a similar rhetorical question in which the focus is on human actions rather than God's behavior ("which of you by being anxious can add a cubit to his span of life?").

As for (b), verse 31 actually speaks of two kings. Both cannot stand for God, so it is more natural to take the one who is assessing his inferior position to stand for a human individual rather than God. If one of the kings stands for God, it should be the second, more powerful one. But in light of the fact that the parables deal with the challenge of the kingdom rather than the nature of the king, the imagery should probably be taken more generally. Jesus does not elsewhere scare his audiences into the kingdom by asking them to consider if they can withstand God's powerful onslaught, nor would there be any reason to ask them to calculate whether or not they could successfully resist. Destruction would be inevitable.

Derrett's final point (c) sets up a false dichotomy. Jesus teaches both faith and calculation elsewhere, as those passages make clear which warn about not having anywhere to sleep and not putting one's hand to the plow and turning back (Lk 9:57-62 par.). The syntax of verses 31-32, moreover, requires the man who considers whether or not he should sue for peace to be the same figure which Derrett says stands for God, yet it is inconceivable that God should consider surrendering to his enemy (which is what the phrase "asks for terms of peace" seems most likely to mean).[75]

The parables are best taken, then, of human activity, and their one main point may be phrased as follows: *Would-be disciples must consider the commitment required to follow Christ.* The verbal repetition of

---

[74]J. D. M. Derrett, "Nisi Dominus Aedificaverit Domum: Towers and Wars (Lk XIV 28-32)," *NovT* 19 (1977):249-58. More briefly, cf. J. Louw, "The Parables of the Tower-Builder and the King Going to War," *ExpT* 48 (1936-37):478; P. G. Jarvis, "The Tower-builder and the King Going to War," *ExpT* 77 (1966):196-98.

[75]H. St. J. Thackeray, "A Study in the Parable of the Two Kings," *JTS* 14 (1912-13):392-93. Cf. Marshall, *Luke,* p. 594.

the refrain, "does he not first sit down and count the cost/take counsel?" confirms this central focus. Caird's conclusions combine meaning and significance and merit extended citation:

> The twin parables of the tower-builder and the king were not meant to deter any serious candidates for discipleship, but only to warn them that becoming a disciple was the most important enterprise a man could undertake and deserved at least as much consideration as he would give to business or politics. Nobody can be swept into the kingdom on a flood-tide of emotion; he must walk in with clear-eyed deliberation.[76]

8.2.3 The Mustard Seed and Leaven (Lk 13:18-21 pars.)

At least in their Q form, the twin parables of the mustard seed and leaven each introduce one human character, the man who sows the seed and the woman who leavens the bread. Mark, who only records the mustard-seed parable, does not mention a sower but simply uses the passive expression, "it is sown." This makes explicit what is already implicit in Q, that the man and the woman have no significant role to play in the two short similes. The parables are entirely about the mustard seed and leaven, and the human characters are introduced only because seeds do not plant themselves and bread does not leaven itself.

The main "character" in both cases, then, is the small plant—the seed and the yeast—but each is depicted in two contrasting stages. Remarkably small beginnings produce amazingly large results. Unlike the seed growing secretly, there is no emphasis on the period of development; it is mentioned only in passing. Thus, despite their traditional classification with the other parables of growth, they do not really belong in this category. Only one central point seems intended: *The kingdom will eventually attain to significant proportions despite its entirely inauspicious outset.*[77]

In the parable of the mustard seed, all three accounts conclude

---

[76]Caird, *Luke*, p. 179.

[77]Cf. esp. Otto Kuss, "Zum Sinngehalt des Doppelgleichnisses vom Senfkorn und Sauerteig," *Bib* 40 (1959):641-53; Franz Mussner, "1QHodajoth und das Gleichnis vom Senfkorn (Mk. 4, 30-32 Par.)," *BZ* 4 (1960):128-30. Some commentators agree that this was the original meaning of the parable but believe that redactional changes implied a second point about growth. Thus, e.g., Erich Grässer, *Das Problem der Parusieverzögerung in den synoptischen Evangelien und in der Apostelgeschichte* (Berlin: Töpelmann, 1957), p. 142, on Luke; Kingsbury, *Parables*, p. 77, on Matthew. But if the parable can make two points, these distinctions are unnecessary.

with an allusion to Ezekiel 17:23 and related Old Testament passages (esp. Ezek 31:6; Dan 4:12; Ps 104:12), in which the birds of the air come to nest in the branches of the mighty cedar of Lebanon. In that context the birds stand for all the peoples of the earth, that is, predominantly the Gentiles. It is hard to know if such a meaning is intended in Jesus' parable as well. The lowly mustard plant, even though it can occasionally reach heights of ten to twelve feet and be legitimately considered a small shade tree, pales in comparison with the lofty cedar. Nevertheless, there may be deliberate irony in this choice of imagery.[78]

Alternately, Jesus may have chosen the mustard seed simply because it was proverbial for its smallness. He then could hardly avoid the fact that it did not grow up to be as large a tree as the cedar.[79] The striking contrast could still be made, and the allusion to Ezekiel still apply.[80] But whether or not the peoples of the earth are intended as a referent for the birds in the parable, no separate, second point seems to be made here. The allusion simply reinforces the central thrust of emphasizing the surprising size of the final product in light of the tiny beginnings.[81] At any rate, there is no reason to consider this closing purpose clause as a secondary addition. Nor does it introduce allegory into a nonallegorical passage. The one central governing metaphor, with its initial and final stages reflecting the onset and culmination of God's kingdom, has already made the passage a brief allegory.[82]

The fact that the woman "hides" the leaven should not be over-interpreted to mean deliberate concealment of the kingdom. This is just a graphic way of picturing the mixing in of the yeast, according to common baking practice.[83] The variation between the two par-

---

[78]E.g., Robert W. Funk, "The Looking-glass Tree Is for the Birds," *Int* 27 (1973):3-9; Perkins, *Parables,* p. 87.

[79]Supporting the naturalness of the description of the mustard plant without needing to see allegorical overtones cf. Walter W. Wessel, "Mark," in *Expositor's Bible Commentary,* vol. 8, p. 653; Robert H. Mounce, *Matthew* (San Francisco: Harper & Row, 1985), p. 132.

[80]Supporting the presence of the allusion in a subordinate role only, cf., e.g., Hill, *Matthew,* p. 233; Lane, *Mark,* p. 171.

[81]Rightly, Stein, *Parables,* p. 161, n. 31. Cf. Harvey K. McArthur, "The Parable of the Mustard Seed," *CBQ* 33 (1971):198-210.

[82]Contra, respectively, Hans-Josef Klauck, *Allegorie und allegorese in synptischen Gleichnistexten* (Münster: Aschendorff, 1978), p. 217; Pesch, *Markusevangelium,* vol. 1, p. 260.

[83]Contra, e.g., Hill, *Matthew,* p. 234; Stein, *Parables,* p. 161, n. 32.

ables from the man to the woman is appropriate in the culture of the day for the tasks involved and should be given no added significance,[84] except perhaps that Luke liked to balance pairs of parables or stories about men and women (e.g., Lk 15:3-7 and 8-10; 11:5-8 and 18:1-8; or 11:30 and 31). He may be trying to appeal to as wide an audience as possible.

Although the passages do not break the bounds of realism, they at least border on the extravagant.[85] Mustard trees do not usually grow large enough to entice many birds to nest in them, and the "three measures of flour" which the woman leavens have been variously estimated as equalling a quantity of 25-40 liters, capable of feeding over 100 people. There is no promise here that the kingdom will come in such grandeur that Jesus' followers will dominate the earth. But it does appear that the end result will be far greater than what anyone observing Jesus and his band of disciples would have imagined. The remarkable quantity of leaven and surprising size of the mustard plant point to the second level of interpretation, but the parables do not thereby become inauthentic. And, although the number of measures of flour has provided plentiful grist for the mill of allegorizers, it almost certainly has no further significance beyond pointing to this extravagance.[86]

A few commentators have tried to make the yeast retain its typically evil connotations as in earlier Jewish literature as well as elsewhere in Jesus' teaching (e.g., Mk 8:15 pars.). This can be overt, as in one dispensationalist view which takes the parable to be teaching the ever-increasing growth of evil until the last days;[87] or covert, as in the view which sees Jesus as parodying the Jewish leaders' attitude toward the makeup of his followers—tax collectors and sinners—the scum of the earth in their eyes.[88]

---

[84]Contra esp. Elizabeth Waller, "The Parable of the Leaven: A Sectarian Teaching and the Inclusion of Women," USQR 35 (1979-80):99-109.

[85]See esp. Jeremias, Parables, pp. 31, 149. Cf. Jacques Dupont, "Le couple parabolique du sénéve et du levain," in Jesus Christus in Historie und Theologie, ed. Georg Strecker (Tübingen: Mohr, 1975), pp. 331-45.

[86]Rightly, Kistemaker, Parables, pp. 48-49, who notes several of these approaches.

[87]For a survey and thorough rebuttal of this view, see Oswald T. Allis, "The Parable of the Leaven," EQ 19 (1947):254-73.

[88]E.g., Francis W. Beare, The Gospel according to Matthew (San Francisco: Harper & Row; Oxford: Blackwell, 1981), p. 309; Schweizer, Matthew, p. 307. Scott, Hear, pp. 324-26 is subtler still, arguing that Jesus is deliberately challenging the ritual purity laws of Judaism which equate leaven with corruption.

But immediate context must always take priority over background, and the parallel parable of the mustard seed can hardly be taken in such light. The dispensationalist view, further, rests on a one-sided view of Scripture's teaching about the influence of good and evil in the last days (avoiding the force of, e.g., Mk 13:10 pars.), whereas the approach that sees a kind of parody reads in an overly subtle form of irony not characteristic of Jesus' teaching elsewhere. If there is a difference between the point of the mustard seed and of the leaven, it is more likely along the lines suggested by Carson: the former depicts "extensive growth" and the latter "intensive transformation."[89] Yet in light of the minimal role afforded to the process of growth in these parables, even this distinction seems dubious.

8.2.4 Other Passages

Other shorter metaphors occasionally classified as parables no doubt similarly teach only one central lesson. Despite numerous popular expositions of the "salt of the earth" and the "light of the world" (Mt 5:13-16) in terms of modern uses of salt and light (e.g., adding flavor or color), the only demonstrable purpose of these metaphors in a *Sitz im Leben Jesu* would be one which fit the primary uses of salt and light in antiquity. Above all else, Jesus is teaching that disciples must arrest corruption and illuminate darkness.[90]

The "parable" of the physician (Lk 5:32; Mt 9:12-13) compares Christ's ministry of salvation to a doctor's healing, without necessarily implying any further correspondence between their techniques. The metaphor of the bridegroom (Mk 2:19-20 pars.) contrasts the joy of the days of Christ's ministry with the sorrow that would attend his crucifixion, and the adjacent metaphors of garments and wineskins point out the incompatibility of following Jesus with the old ritual of Judaism.[91] Balancing this contrast, the parable of the scribe trained for the kingdom (Mt 13:52) suggests that some continuity between old and new covenants remains as well.

---

[89]Carson, "Matthew," p. 319.

[90]Cf. H. N. Ridderbos, *Matthew* (Grand Rapids: Zondervan, 1987), pp. 94-95.

[91]Cf. Carson, "Matthew," p. 227. On the close relationship between these metaphors and the miracle at Cana see Blomberg, "Miracles," pp. 333-37.

8.3 Conclusions

The lessons of Jesus' dyadic and monadic parables reinforce the themes of the triadic narratives analyzed in chapters six and seven. Contrast parables like the Pharisee and tax collector and the two builders recall the parallel rabbinic form and mirror the messages of triadic texts like the parables of the good Samaritan or ten virgins, but without the third points associated with a master figure. The parables of the unprofitable servant, seed growing secretly, rich fool, and barren fig tree recall, respectively, the parables of the faithful servant, sower, rich man and Lazarus, and wicked tenants, but without the contrast which comes from having two opposite subordinates rather than just one. The unjust judge and friend at midnight form a pair of a fortiori parables, affirming the justice and generosity of God as a stimulus to bold and persistent prayer. The parable of the householder stands out with the most unusual imagery of all for Christ—he resembles a thief! But Jesus is not likening himself to a criminal so much as to one who arrives totally unexpectedly.

The six monadic parables all offer simple comparisons of what the kingdom is like, emphasizing its inestimable value and the need for sacrificial commitment in order to lay hold of its blessings. But even these passages sometimes have partial parallels among the more elaborate parables—compare, for example, the mustard seed and leaven with the sower. Diversity in the number of principal characters in Jesus' parables is therefore more a guide to the number of points intended by each passage than a criterion for distinguishing the nature of those points. The actual structure of the texts and the relationships among their characters offer a more direct indication of the specific content of the lessons that Jesus teaches.

9

The Theology of the Parables: The Kingdom & the Christ

WHAT ESSENTIALLY IS JESUS TRYING TO SAY IN ALL THIS TEACH-
ing in parables? Once we have discerned the messages of individual
texts, it is natural to seek a synthesis of the lessons learned. To do
this we must answer the question of how the principles of the
parables ought to be classified or categorized. A synthesis of the
teaching in parables also invites comparison with Jesus' proclamation throughout the rest of the Gospel tradition. And one of the
most central and controversial aspects of Jesus' overall teaching, as
the evangelists record it, deals with his self-understanding. Thus
one often asks two other questions. What contribution to Jesus'
total message do the parables make? And what do they disclose
about the identity of the one who spoke them? The issue of classification or categorization follows naturally from the observations
of chapters six through eight concerning the structure of the parables and will be dealt with relatively briefly. The other two questions merit more scrutiny.

9.1 Classification

1. Probably the most common approach to classifying the teachings of the parables is to group different passages together topically. For example, A. M. Hunter identifies certain parables which describe "the coming of the kingdom," others which elucidate "the grace of the kingdom," a third group which portrays "the men of the kingdom" and a final collection dealing with "the crisis of the kingdom."[1] Robert Stein proposes a threefold division under the headings of "the kingdom as a present reality," "the kingdom as demand" and "the God of the parables."[2] And Joachim Jeremias divides the parables into nine categories, with such titles as "now is the day of salvation," "the challenge of the hour," "the imminence of catastrophe," "God's mercy for sinners" and the like.[3]

Even when the parables are viewed as making but one point each, these topical classifications do not appear overly helpful. Too many parables can too easily fit under more than one heading. Hunter, for example, includes the parable of the wheat and tares under "the coming of the kingdom," but its focus on the mixture of righteous and wicked individuals could make it just as promising a candidate for inclusion under "the men of the kingdom." So too, its grim picture of the fate of the tares at the final harvest easily qualifies it for consideration as a parable concerning "the crisis of the kingdom." Or again, Hunter groups the parables of the tower builder and warring king together as illustrations of the "men of the kingdom," whereas they might just as easily speak of the kingdom's coming or its crisis.[4] Jeremias's categories, moreover, overlap so much that it is hard even to distinguish one from another. For example, the first three of his chapter titles listed above all seem relatively interchangeable.

If we admit that most of the parables teach two or three lessons each, then such topical categorization breaks down altogether. One

---

[1]A. M. Hunter, *Interpreting the Parables* (London: SCM; Philadelphia: Westminster, 1980).

[2]Robert H. Stein, *An Introduction to the Parables of Jesus* (Philadelphia: Westminster, 1981; Exeter: Paternoster, 1982).

[3]Joachim Jeremias, *The Parables of Jesus* (London: SCM; Philadelphia: Westminster, 1972).

[4]Hunter, *Parables*, pp. 45-46, 65. For similar classifications by topic, cf. A. T. Cadoux, *The Parables of Jesus: Their Art and Use* (London: J. Clarke, 1930; New York: Macmillan, 1931); B. T. D. Smith, *The Parables of the Synoptic Gospels* (Cambridge: Univ. Press, 1937); Peter R. Jones, *The Teaching of the Parables* (Nashville: Broadman, 1982).

individual narrative regularly brings together multiple themes which might otherwise be parceled out under separate headings. The story of the prodigal son, for example, poignantly depicts God's grace and mercy in the actions of the father, but it also reminds prodigals that now is the day of salvation while warning the hard-hearted that their response to Jesus and the outcasts to whom he ministers is equally critical. So, even as Stein rightly includes this passage under "the God of the kingdom" (focusing on the gracious father),[5] the parable's other two points (derived from its other two characters) make it equally appropriate for the "present reality" and the "demand" of the kingdom.

What Hunter, Stein, Jeremias and many others like them rightly recognize, however, is that all of Jesus' parables revolve around one central theme: the kingdom of God. Numerous parables explicitly begin with the formula, "the kingdom of God is like . . ." or some similar introduction (e.g., Mk 4:26; Mt 13:44, 45, 47; Lk 13:18, 20). A few interpreters have argued that only those parables specifically linked with the kingdom should be interpreted as teaching about it,[6] but such a distinction overlooks the structural and thematic similarities of other passages with those which do explicitly refer to the kingdom.

For example, of the four parables of Matthew 24:42-25:30, only the story of the ten virgins actually mentions the kingdom (25:1). But common themes so closely link this parable with the stories of the householder and thief, the faithful and unfaithful servants, and the talents, that they must all be taken as teaching about the same topic. Explicit kingdom parables have appeared in each of the three previous chapters of this study, suggesting that all of the triadic, dyadic and monadic forms discussed above generically parallel one or more narratives indisputably dealing with the kingdom.

2. More progress may be made on the problem of systematizing the teachings of the parables if one follows structural clues. Dan Via helpfully distin-

---

[5]Stein, *Parables*, pp. 115-24.
[6]E.g., T. W. Manson, *The Teaching of Jesus* (Cambridge: Univ. Press, 1935), pp. 70-81; C. Leslie Mitton, *Your Kingdom Come* (London: Mowbray; Grand Rapids: Eerdmans, 1978), p. 52. Robert F. Capon has gone so far as to write two entirely separate books on *The Parables of the Kingdom* (Grand Rapids: Zondervan, 1985) and *The Parables of Grace* (Grand Rapids: Eerdmans, 1988).

guishes between "comic" and "tragic" plots, depending on whether the climax of a narrative focuses on salvation or judgment.[7] An approach which recognizes lessons on *both* eternal life and eternal death in a given parable may nevertheless agree with Via that one of the lessons is more climactic. The parable of the unforgiving servant, for example, teaches about both grace and judgment, but the latter stands out more prominently.

On the other hand, although both themes appear again in the parable of the sower, the "law of end stress" suggests that Jesus' emphasis this time rests with the final, good soil which bears abundant fruit. J. D. Crossan examines the parables' plots in even greater detail, distinguishing three structures, which he labels "advent," "reversal" and "action," depending on the sequence of the three components of "crisis," "response" and "denouement."[8] Crossan's greatest contribution may be his repeated reminder of the frequency with which Jesus' parabolic characters act in entirely unexpected and culturally inappropriate ways, creating shocking reversals of conventional expectation.

3. Notwithstanding these and similar structural observations,[9] the most straightforward and probably most helpful classification simply builds on the triadic and dyadic models elaborated above. Where a parable makes three points, invariably one lesson focuses on the nature of God, one highlights the behavior of those who are truly his people, and a third describes the activity and/or destiny of the unrighteous. Dyadic parables usually offer two of these three foci. John Vincent

---

[7]Dan O. Via, Jr., *The Parables: Their Literary and Existential Dimension* (Philadelphia: Fortress, 1967). Cf. B. B. Scott, *Jesus, Symbol-Maker for the Kingdom* (Philadelphia: Fortress, 1981), pp. 40-47.

[8]J. D. Crossan, *In Parables: The Challenge of the Historical Jesus* (New York and London: Harper & Row, 1973). Cf. Robert W. Funk, *Parables and Presence* (Philadelphia: Fortress, 1982), pp. 35-54. Pheme Perkins, *Hearing the Parables* (New York: Paulist, 1981), pp. 10-13 defines the three subgenres as follows: advent parables emphasize the rule of God as recasting the future, action parables involve crucial situations which require decisive activity, and reversal parables overturn commonly held views concerning status or privilege.

[9]Other categories might include servant parables (e.g., A. Weiser, *Die Knechtsgleichnisse der synoptischen Evangelien* [München: Kösel, 1971]), parousia parables (e.g., Gerhard Schneider, *Parusiegleichnisse im Lukasevangelium* [Stuttgart: Katholisches Bibelwerk, 1975]), and τίς ἐξ ὑμῶν ("which one of you . . . ?") parables (e.g., Heinrich Greeven, " 'Wer unter euch . . . ?' " *Wort und Dienst* 3 [1952]:86-101). In my "Parable," in *International Standard Bible Encyclopedia, Revised,* ed. Geoffrey W. Bromiley, vol. 3 (Grand Rapids: Eerdmans, 1986), p. 658, I have distinguished nature parables (Mk 4:1-9, 26-29, 30-32; Mt 13:33; Lk 13:6-9), discovery parables (Mt 13:44, 45-46, 47-50), a fortiori parables (Lk 11:5-8, 18:1-8, 16:1-13, 17:7-10, 14:28-33, 11:11-13, 14:5) and contrast parables (the bulk of the triadic and dyadic forms which depict two contrasting subordinate figures).

captures this bi- and tripartite thrust admirably, while also introducing a crucial Christological element: "The main aim of the parables is to describe the activity of God in Jesus, more particularly
so that men may trust in it and become disciples, or else be offended
at it."[10]

Most of the characteristics of God and humanity which the parables incarnate do not sound radical to theologically trained Christians, and many of Jesus' teachings, in principle, would not have
raised the ire of first-century Jews. But people of all religious traditions are often much quicker to affirm dogma than to live by it,
especially when it is taken to a radical, though logically consistent,
extreme. So one affirms God's love for sinners, for example, but
remains horror-struck when Christ extends it to those who rank
among the most disgusting and objectionable people in his society.[11]

Systematizing the lessons of the parables is important in order to
avoid the errors of claiming either that the parables teach nothing
that can be stated propositionally or that they yield an unlimited
number of principles of an undefined nature.[12] But the rhetorical
power of the narratives is obviously lost by means of propositional
paraphrase, as is a portion of their meaning. One must therefore
not assume that dogmatic affirmations are adequate substitutes for
narrative theology. Each has its place, and neither may be jettisoned
(cf. further, above, pp. 138-44).

The central theology of the parables, therefore, may be formulated as follows:

1. *Teaching about God.*[13] God is sovereign. He commands his ser-

---

[10]John J. Vincent, *Secular Christ* (Nashville: Abingdon, 1968), p. 113. J. Arthur Baird, *The Justice of God in the Teaching of Jesus* (Philadelphia: Westminster, 1963), pp. 63-64, identifies fifteen Synoptic parables where a main figure can be identified with God. The parables then teach about God's relationships with those who are and are not his people, revealing his attributes of love and wrath. Baird believes that the concept of God's "justice" or fairness best encompasses both of these attributes.

[11]Three recent works which have perhaps best highlighted the parables' original shock value are Frederick H. Borsch, *Many Things in Parables: Extravagant Stories of New Community* (Philadelphia: Fortress, 1988); Tim Schramm and Kathrin Löwenstein, *Unmoralische Helden: Anstössige Gleichnisse Jesu* (Göttingen: Vandenhoeck & Ruprecht, 1986); and Joseph A. Grassi, *God Makes Me Laugh: A New Approach to Luke* (Wilmington: Glazier, 1986).

[12]James P. Mackey, *Jesus the Man and the Myth* (London: SCM; New York: Paulist, 1979), p. 128, elaborates: One must not assume "that the message conveyed by parable could not be communicated in any other form; for if that were the case, all the erudite books written on the parables could be accused of ignoring their own warning and misleading the general public."

[13]For a book-length exposition of this theme, see Kurt Erlemann, *Das Bild Gottes in den Synoptischen Gleichnissen* (Stuttgart: Kohlammer, 1988).

vants as he chooses (Lk 17:7-10) and sows his word in whatever soil he selects (Mk 4:3-9 pars.). God is patient. He delays his punishment of evildoers in the hopes that they will at last bear the fruit of obedience to his commands (Mk 12:1-9 pars.) and that he will find faith on earth at the end of the age (Lk 18:1-8). He takes great pains not to destroy evil where good might be destroyed as well (Mt 13:24-30). God gives generously to those who ask him (Lk 11:5-8; 18:1-8). God is gracious and merciful beyond all expectation. He does not reward on the basis of merit (Mt 20:1-16). He goes to great lengths to seek and to save the lost, extending his concern even to the disenfranchised of society (Lk 15; 7:41-43, 31-35 par.; 14:16-24; Mt 18:23-35). God entrusts all people with tasks of stewardship (Mt 21:28-32; 25:14-30; Lk 16:1-9), and he will judge them in accordance with their faithlessness or faithfulness to his charge (Lk 13:6-9, 16:19-31; Mt 24:43—25:13 pars.; 13:47-50).

2. *Teaching about God's people.* Those who would truly follow Christ must be prepared to abandon whatever might stand in the way of whole-hearted discipleship (Lk 14:28-32; Mt 13:44-46). In so doing they acknowledge their utter unworthiness to earn God's favor (Lk 17:7-10). They commit themselves to a life of stewardship (Mt 25:14-30), obeying God's commands, making concern for society's oppressed and afflicted a priority (Lk 10:25-37; 16:19-31), and as-siduously avoiding the idolatry which invariably comes with the needless accumulation of possessions (Lk 12:13-21; 16:1-9; Mt 18:23-35). They must not presume to know how long a span of time they have in which to exercise this stewardship, but they must remain alert to the possibility that the end could come at any moment (Mt 24:43—25:30).

They bring their needs to God in prayer, boldly and without shame (Lk 11:5-8; 18:1-8). They look forward to seeing the kingdom grow into a powerful force despite its inauspicious beginning and often imperceptible presence (Mk 4:1-34 pars.). They must not begrudge God's generosity to others nor try to box him into molds of predictable behavior (Lk 15:11-32). They must realize that their disobedience and faithlessness can lead to their forfeiting the privileges which should be theirs (Mt 21:28-32; Mk 12:1-9 pars.; Lk 14:16-24; Mt 22:11-14). Those who persevere until the end will ultimately be rewarded with eternal fellowship with God and the company of all believers (Mt 13:24-30, 47-50; Lk 16:19-31; 12:35-48).

3. Teaching about those who are not God's people. Profession of allegiance to God or Christ is inadequate in and of itself. A visible life yielding the "fruits befitting repentance" must follow (Mk 12:1-9; 4:3-9; Mt 21:28-32; 7:24-27). Positions of status in organized religion are no substitute for true repentance and deeds of mercy (Lk 18:9-14, 10:25-37). Now is the day in which to make a full commitment, while judgment is delayed for just a little while longer (Lk 13:6-9; 19:11-27). No sin or state of degradation is so vile that God will refuse to forgive the repentant heart (Lk 15:11-32). Persistent rebellion is ultimately nothing but hypocrisy, since it rejects true happiness and denies human sinfulness (Lk 7:31-35 par.). All excuses for remaining outside the kingdom are remarkably flimsy (Lk 14:16-24). A day will come when it will be too late to repent, and then those who have spurned God will have no further prospect save that of a fearful, eternal judgment in separation from all things good (Mt 13:24-30, 47-50; 18:23-35; 24:45—25:30).

Undoubtedly the most shocking aspect of Jesus' teaching about those who are and are not God's people is his consistent reversal of contemporary expectations. Over and over again he proclaims that the Jewish leaders, the religious elite, have missed the mark, while he embraces with open arms the "scum" of his society— women of ill repute, tax collectors, Samaritans and Gentiles, the poor, lepers and all kinds of ceremonially unclean individuals simply lumped together under the category of "sinners." Today's churches would do well to consider seriously how many of their own members will fail to pass the test of true discipleship on Judgment Day, and how many whom they have glibly written off as outside "the faith" may have a far more genuine relationship with God than they ever suspected.[14]

But how does all this teaching from Jesus' parables relate to the

---

[14]Günther Bornkamm, *Jesus of Nazareth* (London: Hodder & Stoughton; New York: Harper & Bros., 1960), p. 93, expresses the parables' two messages for individuals responding to God in this way: "The future of God is *salvation* to the man who apprehends the present as God's present, and as the hour of salvation. The future of God is *judgment* for the man who does not accept the 'now' of God but clings to his own present, his own past and also to his own dreams of the future." When phrased this way, the teaching of Jesus' parables can easily be seen to reveal that organized religion is often more of a hindrance to true salvation than a help.

central theme of his preaching, the kingdom of God? And how do the parables help one to understand better just what Jesus had in mind when he spoke of this kingdom? At the very least one may conclude that God's kingdom has a king (God) and loyal subjects (God's people), and that both regularly come into contact with another group of individuals who are not citizens of the kingdom (those who are not God's people). Even though certain parables begin with the formula "the kingdom is like a man/woman who . . ." the underlying Aramaic which Jesus would have spoken implies the sense, "It is the case with the kingdom as with a person who . . . [did such and such]." In other words, Jesus never likens the kingdom just to an individual subject or object in a given parable but to the situation described by the entire narrative.[15] Every facet of the parables' plots may thus potentially illuminate Jesus' conception of the kingdom.

9.2 Kingdom Theology

I. Howard Marshall has recently pointed out key areas of agreement among scholars on the kingdom. A widespread consensus affirms that (1) the kingdom of God was Jesus' central theme; (2) a substantial portion of Jesus' teachings on this topic as recorded in the Synoptics is authentic; (3) Jesus believed that the kingdom was in some sense both present and future; (4) the kingdom refers primarily to God's rule or reign rather than to a realm; and (5) the way in which the kingdom was present was through the proclamation and activity of Jesus.[16]

Of these five affirmations, (3) and (5) are the least secure. A significant minority continues to argue that Jesus saw the kingdom as only future, though possibly so imminent that he could speak of the present as if the kingdom had virtually arrived.[17] Issue (4) has

---

[15]See esp. Jeremias, *Parables*, p. 147; Robert M. Johnston and Harvey K. McArthur, *They Also Taught in Parables* (Grand Rapids: Zondervan, forthcoming).

[16]I. Howard Marshall, "The Hope of a New Age: The Kingdom of God in the New Testament," *Themelios* 11 (1985):5-15. The most up-to-date history of modern interpretation of the kingdom is Wendell Willis, ed., *The Kingdom of God in 20th-Century Interpretation* (Peabody, Mass.: Hendrickson, 1987). For an anthology of some of the most significant modern treatments of the subject, see Bruce D. Chilton, ed., *The Kingdom of God in the Teaching of Jesus* (London: SPCK; Philadelphia: Fortress, 1984).

[17]E.g., Dale Moody, *The Hope of Glory* (Grand Rapids: Eerdmans, 1964), pp. 115-42; Richard H. Hiers, *Jesus and the Synoptic Tradition* (Gainesville: Univ. of Florida, 1970), pp. 72-77; A. J. Mattill, Jr., *Luke and Last Things* (Dillsboro, N.C.: Western North Carolina Press, 1979).

also been challenged by a few important dissenters.[18] Most recently, Clayton Sullivan has denied the present aspect of the kingdom, stressing those texts that speak of future entrance into a realm.[19] But Joel Marcus has clearly demonstrated that this language elsewhere in Scripture often refers to human participation in God's already present activity in the world.[20] And the whole question of the relationship between the spiritual and material, the "other-worldly" and "this-worldly" aspects of the kingdom, remains hotly disputed. Related to this last question, finally, is the issue of the relationship between the kingdom, the church and Israel. Jesus' parables shed important light on each of these debates.

9.2.1 Present vs. Future

George Beasley-Murray's voluminous compendium of present and future aspects of the kingdom of God in the teaching of Jesus conclusively supports "inaugurated eschatology."[21] That is to say, Christ inaugurated the kingdom during his lifetime, but its entire consummation awaits his return. Imagery from the parables which supports this two-pronged approach may therefore be summarized quite briefly.

1. *Present aspects of the kingdom in the parables.* Those who respond to Jesus' words in obedience are laying a foundation for their spiritual building (Mt 7:24-27 par.). But the proclamation of the gospel meets with varied response and grows in mysterious ways (Mk 4:3-29 pars.). The beginnings of the kingdom seem insignificant (Lk 13:18-21 pars.), and its citizens often continue to appear virtually indistinguishable from those whose loyalties lie elsewhere (Mt 13:24-30). Nevertheless, God's rule will embrace people of all kinds (Mt 13:47-50) despite hostility and antagonism from those without.

---

[18]See esp. Sverre Aalen, " 'Reign' and 'House' in the Kingdom of God in the Gospels," *NTS* 8 (1961-62):215-40. J. Ramsey Michaels, *Servant and Son: Jesus in Parable and Gospel* (Atlanta: John Knox, 1981), p. 74, argues that both should be given equal stress. George W. Buchanan, *Jesus: The King and His Kingdom* (Macon: Mercer, 1984) takes a highly idiosyncratic approach by arguing that Jesus was laying plans to lead his disciples in a literal nationalistic revolt against Rome. But he simply assumes this view and then shows how the parables can be interpreted in its light far more often than actually pointing to exegetical evidence in support of his hypothesis.

[19]Clayton Sullivan, *Rethinking Realized Eschatology* (Macon: Mercer, 1988).

[20]Joel Marcus, "Entering into the Kingly Power of God," *JBL* 107 (1988): 663-75.

[21]G. R. Beasley-Murray, *Jesus and the Kingdom of God* (Exeter: Paternoster; Grand Rapids: Eerdmans, 1986). For treatment of the parables in particular, see pp. 108-43, 194-218.

The kingdom has inestimable value; it is worth sacrificing every-thing necessary to obtain it (Mt 13:44-46). Entrance into the kingdom requires acknowledging inadequacy before God, and life within the kingdom is based on forgiveness and grace (Lk 7:41-43; 17:7-10; 18:9-14; Mt 18:23-35; 20:1-16). Proper humility and self-renunciation lead naturally to love for one's enemies and a concern to seek and save all of the lost (Lk 10:25-37; 15:1-32; Mt 21:28-32). Citizens of the kingdom must obey their king, acknowledging God's lordship and receiving his messengers, including his Son (Lk 13:6-9; Mt 21:33—22:14 pars.). They must wait expectantly for the end of the age, meanwhile exercising faithful stewardship of the gifts and resources with which God has entrusted them (Mt 24:43—25:30 pars.).

The citizens of the kingdom persevere in prayer, boldly request-ing the speedy completion of God's kingdom-building activity (Lk 11:5-8; 18:1-8). They avoid the idolatry of materialism, while using money shrewdly (Lk 12:13-21; 16:1-31) and counting the cost of discipleship (Lk 14:28-33). Failure to obey key commands of God, finally, may lead to the forfeiture of temporal privileges of leader-ship in the kingdom (Lk 13:6-9; Mk 12:1-9 pars; Lk 14:16-24).

2. Future aspects of the kingdom in the parables. Virtually all of the activity described above has significance for the future Day of the Lord, when the kingdom will be consummated in all its fullness. Then all who have ever lived will be judged on the basis of their response to Jesus' person and message. Those who built on the solid foundation of Christ's words will be preserved; all others will perish (Mt 7:24-27 par.). God's reign, dimly perceived in earlier eras, will now be clearly visible throughout the world as the most influential power with which persons must reckon (Mk 4:1-34).

Those who have borne fruits befitting repentance will enjoy eter-nal presence with God, while everyone else will endure permanent, agonizing separation from him (Mt 13:24-30, 47-50). Forgiveness in that day is contingent on forgiving others in this life (Mt 18:23-35). To state it with greater theological precision, if we have truly expe-rienced God's loving pardon, we will not be able to avoid responding to others in kind (Lk 7:41-43). Right use of money will be another key test case for discerning true discipleship (Lk 12:13-21; Lk 16).

Among God's people there will be no differentiation in reward (Mt 20:1-16); salvation is by grace alone (Lk 17:7-10). Eternal life with Christ is the ultimate perfection to which nothing could be added anyway. On the other hand, unbelievers will experience degrees of severity of judgment, in accordance with the extent of their knowledge of God's will and conscious rebellion (Lk 12:47-48). Professions of faith or disbelief in God do not count for anything unless they continue throughout a person's life; it is our ultimate relationship with God rather than our initial attitude which counts (Mt 21:28-32; Lk 15). The end may arrive sooner than anyone expects, it may be delayed, or it simply may come by surprise, but when it does, there will be no more opportunity for repentance (Mt 24:43-25:13). At that time all injustice will be vindicated (Lk 18:1-8) and all unbelievers condemned.

Of course many interpreters would play down the extent of such teaching about either present or future aspects of the kingdom. But they can do so only by denying the allegorical nature and the authenticity of key portions of the parables. If chapters two through eight prove even partially cogent, that is, if one can accept the parables with their interpretations as they stand in the gospels, then something similar to the above syntheses necessarily follows.

A more radical skepticism, however, denies the temporal nature of the kingdom altogether. Instead of realized (present), thoroughgoing (future) or inaugurated (present and future) eschatology, some recent scholars have described Jesus' teaching in such terms as "permanent eschatology." In Crossan's words, Jesus was not proclaiming the end of *this* world, but

> announcing God as the One who shatters world, this one and any other before or after it. If Jesus forbade calculations of the signs of the end, it was not calculations, nor signs, but end he was attacking. God, in Kingdom, is the One who poses permanent and unceasing challenge to man's ultimate concern and thereby keeps world free from idolatry and open in its uncertainty.[22]

---

[22]Crossan, *In Parables*, p. 27. Cf. Funk, *Parables*, pp. 67-79. A highly idiosyncratic approach to Jesus' teaching appears in James Breech, *The Silence of Jesus* (Philadelphia: Fortress, 1983), who brackets so many texts as not demonstrably authentic that the tiny core with which he is left is almost certainly not representative of Jesus' main emphases. Nevertheless, from this core of twelve parables (themselves reduced and reconstructed tradition-critically), Breech believes that Jesus advocated a hyperindividualism (which paradoxically is committed to "someone or something beyond one's self"—p. 112) in which every person finds his own highly particular way to live with genuineness and integrity. Thus Jesus' purpose in all of these parables is to "communicate to his listeners his own perception of, and attitude toward, human reality." This is what the kingdom of God refers to. It contrasts both with existence as a member of a group and as a solitary individual (p. 213).

In other words, Jesus' teaching offers a new form of authentic human existence rather than describing acts of God at certain unique points in history. To maintain such a perspective, however, requires a rejection of a fairly sizable body of evidence which grounds Jesus' teaching in Jewish apocalyptic thought.[23] Though disagreeing on their answers, Jews of all kinds at the beginning of the Christian era were debating questions about the end of the world and the coming of the Messiah in such a way as to make modern ahistorical, existentialist interpretations of the parables almost certainly anachronistic.[24]

Three additional issues concerning the temporality of the kingdom as expressed in the parables need clarification. First, it is common to speak of parables such as the seed growing secretly, the mustard seed, the leaven, the sower, and the wheat and tares as "parables of growth." Numerous interpreters have assumed that a major emphasis of Jesus' teaching about the kingdom in general, and in these parables in particular, was to describe the steady, sometimes hidden, yet always relentless growth of the kingdom from its unpromising origins to its triumphant culmination.[25] In amillennial and postmillennial circles, these parables are often cited as proof that the age of the kingdom can be equated with the age of the church or at least with one glorious golden era of Christianity prior to the return of the Lord.[26]

Nevertheless, only the seed growing secretly (Mk 4:26-29) and the wheat and tares (Mt 13:24-30) focus any noteworthy attention on the period of growth itself (as over against the times of planting

---

[23]As, e.g., by Marcus J. Borg, *Conflict, Holiness and Politics in the Teachings of Jesus* (New York and Toronto: Edwin Mellen, 1984), pp. 248-63. Pheme Perkins, "The Rejected Jesus and the Kingdom Sayings," *Semeia* 44 (1988): 79-94, argues that kingdom sayings often circulated independently of apocalyptic teaching and could refer to salvation as a recovery of a primordial dimension of reality. But Perkins discusses primarily Gnostic texts which do not represent as early a stage in the tradition as she alleges.

[24]J. Ramsey Michaels, "The Kingdom of God and the Historical Jesus," in *Kingdom of God in 20th-Century Interpretation*, pp. 109-18; for details of that apocalyptic background, see Beasley-Murray, *Jesus*, pp. 39-62.

[25]E.g., Nils A. Dahl, "The Parables of Growth," in *Jesus in the Memory of the Early Church* (Minneapolis: Augsburg, 1976), pp. 141-66; Jack D. Kingsbury, *The Parables of Jesus in Matthew 13* (London: SPCK; Richmond: John Knox, 1969), pp. 81-84; Perkins, *Parables*, pp. 76-89.

[26]E.g., John J. Davis, *Christ's Victorious Kingdom: Postmillennialism Reconsidered* (Grand Rapids: Baker, 1986), p. 52; Loraine Boettner, *The Millennium* (Philadelphia: Presbyterian and Reformed, 1957), pp. 131, 284; Jesse W. Hodges, *Christ's Kingdom and Coming* (Grand Rapids: Eerdmans, 1957), pp. 133-48.

and harvest). Yet these are precisely the two passages in this group of "nature parables" which give no hint of their plants having reached any particular size or level of fruitfulness. So the category of parables of growth and resulting applications probably need to be abandoned.

Second, there is a built-in ambiguity in most of Jesus' parables concerning the time of the judgment referred to here as future. C. H. Dodd so emphasized the crisis nature of Jesus' own ministry that he interpreted Judgment Day to be present whenever people responded to Jesus.[27] Traditional Christianity has often gone to the other extreme and linked judgment exclusively with the Second Coming of Christ.

Probably both poles need to be embraced (as seen clearly in John's Gospel), along with one additional observation. While the early church naturally interpreted the interval of time between the departure and return of the masters in the various servant parables (e.g., Lk 12:35-48 pars.; 19:11-27; Mt 25:1-13) as corresponding to the period between Christ's first and second comings, a Jewish audience listening to Jesus would first of all have thought of the interval initiated centuries earlier with the Old Testament prophets' warnings that "the Day of the Lord was at hand" (e.g., Zeph 1:7; Joel 1:15).[28]

The problem of God's spokesmen proclaiming a near end of the world despite the continuation of epochs of human existence was not a new one for Jesus' followers. Thoughtful Jews had been wrestling with this apparent contradiction for hundreds of years and had even applied the same text from the Psalms (Ps. 90:1) that 2 Peter later would apply in Christian circles (2 Pet 3:8-10) to help explain God's "delay."[29] It is therefore highly unlikely that Jesus' original audience would have automatically associated the imagery of master figures leaving and returning with his own departure and com-

---

[27]C. H. Dodd, *Parables of the Kingdom* (London: Nisbet, 1935; New York: Scribner's, 1936).

[28]Cf. Hans Conzelmann, *The Theology of St. Luke* (New York: Harper & Row; London: Faber & Faber, 1960), pp. 95-136, who believes all the delay motifs refer to the parousia of the Son of man but finds them secondary; with Ernst Fuchs, *Studies of the Historical Jesus* (London: SCM; Naperville: Allenson, 1964), p. 59, who finds them all referring to the parousia but original. More persuasive than either is David Flusser, *Die rabbinischen Gleichnissen und der Gleichniserzähler Jesu*, vol. 1 (Frankfurt a. M. and Las Vegas: Peter Lang, 1981), pp. 89-93, who finds the references all original but first of all referring to God's long-standing delay in bringing the Day of Judgment.

[29]See esp. Richard Bauckham, "The Delay of the Parousia," *TynB* 31 (1980):3-36.

ing again, and it is equally clear that when his followers did make this association later, they were not introducing a new tension (the so-called delay of the parousia) which had not characterized earlier Judaism. It is thus entirely natural that Jesus should have predicted the imminent demise of this world, while at the same time preparing his followers for the possibility that they would have to live in community for a sizable length of time after his death.[30]

Third, while an acceptance of the "whole counsel" of Jesus' teaching in parables demands that one recognize both a present and a future aspect to the kingdom, it was Jesus' teaching about the kingdom's presence which was by far the more distinctive of the two emphases. Jewish thought traditionally looked forward to the kingdom's coming,[31] but had never previously dared to believe that it had arrived.[32] Moreover, most conceptions of the kingdom were more narrowly ethnocentric—nationalistic and sometimes even militaristic. A kingdom which revolved around a defiance of the dietary laws by means of table fellowship with ritually unclean "sinners" was unprecedented. Such a kingdom raises key questions about community, social concern, the Mosaic covenant and Jesus' own identity.

9.2.2 Reign vs. Realm

If the kingdom of God was present in the ministry of Jesus, then clearly it is not a geographical territory to be located on a map somewhere near, say, the kingdom of Jordan or the kingdom of Arabia! Admittedly, George Buchanan has recently tried to suggest that Jesus was actually preparing his followers for revolt against

---

[30]On the outworking of the two poles of this spectrum in the parables, see esp. I. Howard Marshall, *Eschatology and the Parables* (London: Tyndale, 1963).

[31]On the kingdom of God in the Old Testament and intertestamental literature, see esp. Odo Camponovo, *Königtum, Königsherrschaft und Reich Gottes in den Frühjüdischen Schriften* (Freiburg [Switzerland]: Universitätsverlag; Göttingen: Vandenhoeck & Ruprecht, 1984). Cf. John Gray, *The Biblical Doctrine of the Reign of God* (Edinburgh: T. & T. Clark, 1979); John Bright, *The Kingdom of God* (Nashville: Abingdon, 1953).

[32]See esp. John Riches, *Jesus and the Transformation of Judaism* (London: Darton, Longman & Todd, 1980), pp. 87-111. Cf. Gösta Lundström, *The Kingdom of God in the Teaching of Jesus* (Edinburgh and London: Oliver & Boyd, 1963), p. 234. Bruce Chilton, "Kingdom Come, Kingdom Sung," *Forum* 3, no. 1 (1987):51-75, speaks of the transformations of the kingdom in the "performance" of Jesus in a broader sense, not read strictly against Jewish apocalyptic background, but against the Targumic notion of kingdom as "God's definitive intervention on behalf of his people" (p. 54). Chilton thus prefers not to speak of the transformation of Judaism but of Jesus' distinctive "usage of the kingdom in a pressing, public announcement" (p. 55).

Rome in order to establish his own political claim over an earthly empire. But time and again Buchanan simply assumes that certain socio-economic details in the parables are to be taken literally rather than as pointers to a spiritual level of meaning, and in so doing flies in the face of virtually all Gospel criticism without ever seriously challenging more standard interpretations.[33]

At the same time, as Marshall points out, the kingdom of God "is not just the sovereign activity of God; it is also the set-up created by the activity of God, and that set-up consists of people."[34] So, *in addition to conceiving of the kingdom as God's dynamic rule or reign, one should probably compare it to a cluster of concepts such as God's "community," "society" or "house(hold)."*[35] Once one rejects the faulty notion that Jesus could not have envisioned a community of his disciples carrying on his work after his death and resurrection, the obvious realm in which to look for "God's new society" is in that community which has come to be known as the church.

But to place the locus of God's dynamic reign in the fellowship of Christian believers is not to equate the kingdom with the church. Of course, numerous parables depict the life of servants in a household (Lk 12:35-38, 42-48; Mt 18:23-35, 25:14-30) corresponding to God's people presently living in community. And possibly the imagery of plants growing together in a field in the nature parables of Matthew 13 points to the same reality.

But in the interpretation of the parable of the wheat and tares, it is clear that God's reign also incorporates his judgment on unbelievers. The field which is harvested is the world (Mt 13:38), but it can also be referred to as the "kingdom," out of which all of the wicked will be gathered for eternal judgment (v. 41).

More splendid is the picture of the Messianic banquet, the ultimate reunion of all God's people, depicted in terms of table fellowship—one of the most intimate forms of personal communion in ancient society. The parables of the great supper (Lk 14:16-24), the

---

[33]Buchanan, *Jesus*, esp. pp. 102-28, 140-66. To cite just one example, Buchanan finds the treasure hidden in a field an apt comparison for a "geographical territory ruled by a king" (p. 103), but never demonstrates that it is more apt than other interpretations.

[34]Marshall, "New Age," p. 12.

[35]See, respectively, Gerhard Lohfink, *Jesus and Community* (Philadelphia: Fortress, 1984; London: SPCK, 1985), pp. 26-29; John Drane, *Jesus and the Four Gospels* (San Francisco and London: Harper & Row, 1979), pp. 90-92; Aalen, " 'Reign' and 'House.' "

wedding banquet (Mt 22:1-14) and the marriage feast attended to by the five wise bridesmaids (Mt 25:1-13) all depict a future celebration by those who will spend eternity with God in a setting which cannot easily be equated with the church as it now exists or with what the church could hope to create apart from God's supernatural intervention at the return of Christ.

To use the categories of systematic theology, the imagery of these parables supports a premillennialist eschatology.[36] That is to say, God's ultimate community on earth with his people from all ages (the millennium of Revelation 20) will not take shape until after Jesus' Second Coming. The kingdom is therefore neither just God's rule in the lives of Christians today nor simply his coming millennial reign on earth, but his dynamic activity in history, powerfully displayed in the ministry of Jesus, then present in the church which he founded, and ultimately climaxed by Christ's coming earthly kingship.[37]

This climactic manifestation of the kingdom will bring together those who have truly served God in every epoch of human history, not merely to worship him and to experience unending bliss, but to do so in the context of the intimate fellowship of all believers one with another. To the extent that the church today creates meaningful spiritual unity among its members, it experiences the reality of the already-present kingdom and foreshadows that coming perfect community which is the goal of history.[38] Second- and third-world Christianity frequently offers such fellowship among the less

---

[36]By far the best defender of this claim, with detailed reference to the parables, is George E. Ladd; see his *The Gospel of the Kingdom* (Exeter: Paternoster; Grand Rapids: Eerdmans, 1959), pp. 52-65; *The Presence of the Future* (Grand Rapids: Eerdmans, 1974; London: SPCK, 1980), pp. 218-42; and *A Theology of the New Testament* (Grand Rapids: Eerdmans, 1974; Guildford: Lutterworth, 1975), pp. 91-104.

[37]Bruce D. Chilton, *God in Strength* (Freistadt: F. Plöchl, 1979; Sheffield: JSOT, 1987), rightly emphasizes that aspect of the kingdom which focuses on God's personal and powerful self-revelation, though perhaps focusing on it too exclusively and thus neglecting other legitimate aspects. Cf. also Norman Perrin, *Jesus and the Language of the Kingdom* (Philadelphia: Fortress; London: SCM, 1976); Helmut Merklein, *Jesu Botschaft von der Gottesherrschaft* (Stuttgart: Katholisches Bibelwerk, 1983).

[38]It is arguable that the creation of such visible (though not necessarily institutional) unity among Christians is the single most important task of the church in any age. Cf., e.g., Eph. 3:6 (speaking of the Jew-Gentile unity in the church) which when manifest to the hostile powers makes fully clear the eternal, inscrutable purposes of God (vv. 9-11). On what the church should look like today in order to testify publicly to the presence of God's reign, see esp. Howard A. Snyder, *A Kingdom Manifesto* (Downers Grove: IVP, 1985 [= *Kingdom Lifestyle* (London: Marshall, Morgan & Scott, 1986)]).

well-to-do, in the context of worship and Bible study, in a way that puts many affluent Westerners to shame. All Christians must strive for the delicate balance between solely focusing on God as father and exclusively concentrating on neighbor as brother.[39]

9.2.3 Personal Transformation vs. Social Reform

God's people clearly have a mandate to witness to those outside the kingdom as well as to fellowship with those within. But the nature of that witness is vigorously debated. Should Christians call exclusively for unbelievers to repent and experience the personal transformation that comes with conversion? Or is spiritual freedom wholly summed up by modern liberation movements which seek to redress the social and economic inequities of various oppressed and disenfranchised classes of individuals? Again, although one can easily find supporters of each extreme,[40] the truth probably lies somewhere in between. At least four propositions can be defended from the parables.

1. *God's kingdom is not fully at work unless people are first of all in right relation with him, but true discipleship goes beyond private piety, seeking to combat evil in all forms in which it appears in this world—personal, social and institutional.*

The parables poignantly illustrate this bipolar nature of the kingdom. The tax collector prays the classic prayer of personal repentance ("God be merciful to me a sinner"—Lk 18:12), but the Pharisee in the same narrative is condemned for his prejudicial attitude toward those he deems "beneath" him. The prodigal, too, is prepared to confess his sins, but his father's welcome never gives him time to finish his confession. And the climax of the story focuses not at all on the need for the blatantly wicked to convert but on the re-

---

[39]Jon Sobrino, writing out of the Latin American context, splendidly captures this balance, in *Christology at the Crossroads* (Maryknoll: Orbis; London: SCM, 1978), p. 45: "Brotherhood without filiation can indeed end up in atheism; but filiation without brotherhood can end up in mere theism, not in the God contemplated by Jesus. The essence of God as embodied in the notion of God's reign does not allow us to choose between the two aspects; both are of equal and primary importance." Somewhat in tension with this balance, however, is Sobrino's subsequent claim that "orthopraxis must take priority over orthodoxy."

[40]On the former, see, e.g., James H. Cone, *A Black Theology of Liberation* (Maryknoll: Orbis, 1986), p. 128: the kingdom is seeing the oppressed "rise up against its oppressors, demanding that justice become a reality now, not tomorrow." On the latter, see, e.g., Robert L. Saucy, "The Presence of the Kingdom and the Life of the Church," *BSac* 145 (1988):44: "the blessings of the kingdom today focus on the spiritual aspect of life and not the material."

sponsibility of the "righteous" not to categorize certain individuals as inferior.

In the parable of the two sons, Jesus makes plain that it is performance rather than promise which counts; professions of faith are meaningless without accompanying works of obedience (Mt 21:28-32). In fact, most of the shock value of individual parables comes from their positive acceptance of the outcasts of Israel's society. God sides with the poor (Lk 16:19-31), the widow (Lk 18:1-8), the tax collector (Lk 18:9-14) and the prostitute (Lk 7:41-43) against the religious elite who think they can safely neglect such categories of individuals.

Jesus, furthermore, at least hints at the inclusion of the Gentiles in God's kingdom (Mt 21:43; Mk 4:32; Mt 13:37). He uses despised characters such as women and shepherds as the heroes of his stories (Lk 15:1-10). And in the parable of the good Samaritan, in addition to having that most hated of all individuals as a hero, he offers a model for compassionate outreach to people's physical needs which dare not be neglected in any full-orbed exposition of the kingdom.[41] Marshall concludes that Jesus' teaching on the kingdom begins with personal transformation but leads necessarily to social action. "In this way the [Kingdom of God] clearly becomes a symbol of hope for the downtrodden in society."[42]

What kind of support should God's people then show for society's powerless?

2. On the one hand, there is no support in Jesus' parables, and little if any in his teaching overall, for violent, revolutionary attacks on injustice, which at best replace one type of evil with another.[43] Jesus clearly rejects the "Zealot option" and instead commands his followers to pray that God might redress injustice (Lk 18:1-8). Vengeance is the Lord's, and to try to take justice into one's own hands is to usurp the authority of God. Over and over the parables make clear that ultimate redress for the wrongs of this world will not come until Judgment Day. The intro-

---

[41]Cf. Jon Sobrino, *Jesus in Latin America* (Maryknoll: Orbis, 1987), p. 93. This parable "admirably illustrates that true love is measured by the objectivity of what is done, not by the intention or a priori quality of the doer."

[42]Marshall, "New Age," p. 8.

[43]Cf. esp. Richard J. Cassidy, *Jesus, Politics, and Society* (Maryknoll: Orbis, 1978); John H. Yoder, *The Politics of Jesus* (Grand Rapids: Eerdmans, 1972); J. Massyngbaerde Ford, *My Enemy Is My Guest: Jesus and Violence in Luke* (Maryknoll: Orbis, 1984).

duction to the parable of the rich fool ("Man, who made me a judge or a divider over you?"—Lk 12:14) suggests that even Jesus himself refused to enter into worldly struggles over power and possessions.[44]

3. *On the other hand, the importunate widow persists in her pleas with an assertiveness which eventually leads a corrupt judge to grant her justice. To the extent that all human authorities are ordained by God (Rom 13:1), it is appropriate for God's people to use nonviolent means which do not involve them in some sinful compromise to try to right the inequities of society.*

Jesus' own ministry provides a paradigm for helping the helpless which all Christians should emulate. But Jesus went beyond offering personal aid to the needy; he prophetically denounced the sins of the powerful in his world. Christians should feel an obligation to speak out in similar fashion today on behalf of the oppressed and exploited, calling this world's power brokers to behave more compassionately. While God's people cannot expect that the life of the kingdom's community can be reproduced outside the fellowship of those who worship the Lord, they may certainly model that community for others and then seek to implement policies and create structures in the public arena which reflect God's concern for social justice.

Choan-Seng Song offers well-balanced insight from the perspective of suffering Christians in Asia. In the context of his discussion of the parable of the laborers in the vineyard (Mt 20:1-16), Song explains that God's kingdom "is to be characterized as the power that does good, manifests mercy, and embodies love." Because the poor have special needs here they occupy a special place in the reign of God:

> He stands on their side, identifies with them, and defends their rights. In word and in deed he shows that the transformation of the power that oppresses and exploits the poor and the powerless into the power that protects and cares for them is central to his ministry. It is at this point that Jesus inevitably comes into conflict with the institutions and structures of political power in the world.[45]

---

[44]Timothy Gorringe, "A Zealot Option Rejected? Luke 12:13-14," *ExpT* 98 (1987):267-70.

[45]Choan-Seng Song, *Third-Eye Theology* (Maryknoll: Orbis, 1979; Guildford: Lutterworth, 1980), p. 234.

Or from a corresponding African perspective, "The regime [i.e., kingdom] Jesus describes does not enjoy only an ethereal existence in the clouds, but takes the form of a life and a society that are being built here and now in freedom, justice, and brotherhood." Nor can this regime be limited to the church. "The reign of God is therefore really present among us, wherever human beings allow the Spirit of God to rule their lives and wherever the peacemakers and those hungry and thirsty for justice are at work in God's name."[46]

4. *Perhaps the most specific lesson which emerges from the parables concerning the type of social justice for which Christians must struggle is that problems of financial and economic inequity are preeminent on God's agenda.* While it is clear that the rich fool and the rich man who fails to help Lazarus are not condemned for their riches per se, it is equally evident that it is their refusal to use their abundant resources to help others which most directly demonstrates their lack of a right relationship with God (Lk 12:16-21; 16:19-31).

Conversely, the unjust steward is commended for his shrewd use of finances to help others (and, in so doing, to help himself!), even at a purely material level (Lk 16:8). Jesus then laments that his followers are not equally wise in the compassionate use of their material resources for spiritual purposes (v. 9). In fact, if they cannot handle their money well, there is little hope of their being able to manage spiritual treasures (vv. 10-12). Ultimately money is the single greatest competitor with God for human affection (v. 13).

No particular economic system arises out of these texts. The servants entrusted with various talents elicit praise from their master because of their profitable investments (Mt 25:14-30; cf. Lk 19:11-27), whereas the parables discussed above suggest that the proper thing to do with wealth in other situations is to give some of it away. Both those who try to mine Scripture in order to prove that God is fundamentally pro-capitalist and those who find prooftexts to label him pro-socialist are equally misguided.[47] Nor is Jesus trying to call into question the work ethic of his peasant audiences

[46]Bakole wa Ilunga, *Paths of Liberation: A Third World Spirituality* (Maryknoll: Orbis, 1984), pp. 80-81.

[47]Contrast, e.g., Ronald H. Nash, *Poverty and Wealth* (Westchester, Ill.: Crossway, 1986); and Brian Griffiths, *The Creation of Wealth* (London: Hodder & Stoughton; Downers Grove: IVP, 1984); with José P. Miranda, *Marx and the Bible* (Maryknoll: Orbis, 1974; London: SCM, 1977); and Jacques Ellul, *Money and Power* (Downers Grove: IVP, 1984).

as too little cognizant of God's sovereignty.[48] Christians can live with integrity under virtually any economic system, but they can do so only by using their personal resources in accordance with scriptural principles.

Alleviating physical need is a crucial aspect of God's reign, but it is not all that his rule entails. Andrew Kirk articulates a comprehensive formulation of kingdom priorities:

> The kingdom sums up God's plan to create a new human life by making possible a new kind of community among people, families and groups. [It combines] the possibility of a personal relationship to Jesus with man's responsibility to manage wisely the whole of nature; the expectation that real change is possible here and now; a realistic assessment of the strength of opposition to God's intentions; the creation of new human relationships and the eventual liberation by God of the whole of nature from corruption.[49]

Thus to advance God's kingdom today includes the struggle for social justice, an item often bypassed on Christians' agendas, but such advancement is by no means limited to that struggle as some sloganeering might suggest.[50]

9.2.4 The Kingdom and Israel

Reflection on the relationship between the kingdom and the church suggested that Jesus' parables support premillennialism. For many, however, premillennialism is directly equated with dispensationalism, even though the historic or classic premillennial position boasts a far more ancient pedigree.[51] But one of the crucial tenets of dis-

---

[48]Contra Douglas E. Oakman, *Jesus and the Economic Questions of His Day* (Lewiston, N.Y., and Queenston, Ont.: Edwin Mellen, 1986). The most balanced study of Jesus' parables which impinge on economic questions is found in David P. Seccombe, *Possessions and the Poor in Luke-Acts* (Linz: Studien zum Neuen Testament und seiner Umwelt, 1982).

[49]Andrew Kirk, *A New World Coming* (London: Marshall, Morgan & Scott [= *The Good News of the Kingdom Coming* (Downers Grove: IVP)], 1983), p. 47. Cf. John Gladwin, *God's People in God's World* (Leicester: IVP, 1979; Downers Grove: IVP, 1980), p. 132.

[50]R. T. France, "The Church and the Kingdom of God: Some Hermeneutical Issues," in *Biblical Interpretation and the Church*, ed. D. A. Carson (Exeter: Paternoster, 1984; Nashville: Thomas Nelson, 1985), pp. 30-44.

[51]For a clear presentation of the distinction between historic and dispensational premillennialism, along with a comparison with amillennialism and postmillennialism, see Robert Clouse, ed., *The Meaning of the Millennium* (Downers Grove: IVP, 1977). One of the standard introductions to modern dispensationalism from an insider's perspective (Charles C. Ryrie, *Dispensationalism Today* [Chicago: Moody, 1965], pp. 66-67) readily admits that the movement in several of its key distinctives dates only from the nineteenth century.

pensationalism is that Israel *as a nation* rejected Jesus' offer of God's kingdom, and that only then did Jesus begin to teach about the church, often by means of parables which expounded a "mystery" (the church age) never previously revealed.

The Gospel of Matthew, many dispensationalists allege, demonstrates this sequence most clearly: Israel decisively rejects the kingdom by the end of chapter 12, and in chapter 13 Jesus begins to speak of the mysteries of the kingdom in parables.[52] *To be sure, Matthew does depict a progressively more hostile response by the Jewish leaders to God's message, but a careful study of all of Jesus' teaching makes most of the traditional dispensationalist distinctives difficult to sustain.*

To begin with, it is impossible to find any text prior to Jesus' arrest and execution which decisively shows that the entire nation of Israel (or even her leaders in any demonstrably official action representing the entire nation) ever rejected Christ's teachings. Matthew 11-12 contain strong words from individuals and groups of Jews, and Jesus' replies are often equally harsh. But large numbers of Jews are also following Christ as late in his ministry as the triumphal entry (Mt 21:1-11).

Even Matthew's distinctive addition to the parable of the wicked tenants, in which Jesus declares that "the kingdom of God shall be taken from you, and given to an ἔθνει ["people"] bringing forth the fruits of it" (Mt 21:43) is specifically addressed to the chief priests and Pharisees (cf. vv. 23 and 45). And the disputed term ἔθνει (often translated "Gentiles" when it is in the plural, not, as here, in the singular) makes no sense if taken politically or geographically, inasmuch as the people to whom Jesus transferred the kingdom did not form a geo-political entity.[53]

---

[52]Cf. Stanley D. Toussaint, *Behold the King: A Study of Matthew* (Portland: Multnomah, 1980), pp. 147-76; John Walvoord, *Matthew: Thy Kingdom Come* (Chicago: Moody, 1974), pp. 95-108; J. Dwight Pentecost, *Things to Come* (Grand Rapids: Dunham, 1958), pp. 138-49. Recently, however, many dispensationalists have moved away from this traditional approach; the following critique does not have them in view. A highly nuanced and generally compelling dispensationalist interpretation appears in Donald Verseput, *The Rejection of the Humble Messianic King* (Frankfurt a. M. and New York: Peter Lang, 1986). Verseput concludes that "it is only with violence that an actual periodization can be inserted into Matthew's reflection. More in keeping with the Evangelist's interest would be to speak in terms of a series of new beginnings" (p. 303).

[53]Alva J. McClain, *The Greatness of the Kingdom* (Grand Rapids: Zondervan, 1959), p. 296, recognizes this fact but nevertheless concludes that "the nation as represented by its then existing rulers had rejected the King; therefore, the Kingdom is taken from *them*." But this conclusion is logically inconsistent. If the punishment for the Jews was primarily in political categories, then the reward for Gentiles should have been political as well.

With the vineyard a stock metaphor for Israel, moreover, the wicked tenants must almost certainly be limited to Israel's leaders, so that the parable itself does not specify whether the new tenants will be Jewish or Gentile. By the time the Gospels were written, however, both are possible, so that for the evangelists the transfer of ownership of the vineyard to tenants of any possible ethnic background makes it clear that "true Israel" after the death of God's Son is to be identifed with the sum total of all Christians.

No divergent conclusions emerge from a survey of the other parables. Those who refuse the invitations to the great supper and wedding banquet need refer to no more than individual Jews who rejected Jesus. The invitees who replace them, like the eleventh-hour laborers in the vineyard, need not refer to the Gentiles (though they *may*) but may merely describe those Jews who responded more positively. The barren fig tree (Lk 13:6-9) may stand for the nation of Israel or for her leaders, but even if it be the former, the predicted destruction (in light of vv. 1-5) is more likely to refer to the Roman suppression of the Jewish revolt in A.D. 70 than to any judgment of God upon the political state of Israel dating from the Christ's lifetime onward.

The parable of the children in the marketplace laments the attitude of "this generation" (Mt 11:16), but presumably Jesus is not also condemning his Jewish disciples. A few verses later he makes clear that he is distinguishing rather between the worldly-wise and the spiritually humble (11:25). The parable of the two sons (Mt 21:28-32) offers perhaps the best disproof of the notion that God judged the nation as a whole while still holding out hope to particular Israelites who accepted Jesus as Messiah. Both those who accept and those who reject are depicted as parallel groups of Jewish individuals (the Jewish leaders vs. the tax collectors and harlots). To take one to refer to the entire nation and the other simply to lone individuals is to destroy the careful symmetry of the narrative.

In addition, dispensationalists have usually overestimated the rupture between Matthew 12 and 13.[54] Jesus does not first speak

---

[54]An overestimation, paradoxically, found even in Frederick D. Bruner, *The Christbook* (Waco: Word, 1987); idem, *The Churchbook* (Waco: Word, forthcoming). In this two-volume commentary on Matthew, Bruner strongly denounces dispensationalism but nevertheless himself regularly imposes foreign categories of systematic theology on Matthew's text, not least in seeing a sharp disjunction between the primary focus on Christology in chaps. 1-12 and on ecclesiology in 13-28.

in parables in Matthew 13 (cf. Mt 7:24-27 par.; 11:16-19 par.), nor can it be argued that only his later parables are about the kingdom or the church or that the kingdom of heaven and kingdom of God are distinct.[55] The story of the wise and foolish builders, which climaxes the Sermon on the Mount, is addressed specifically to disciples (5:1) and deals with the way in which they are to build on the foundation of Jesus' teaching.

Jesus uses parables to teach disciples about the the kingdom as often as he uses them to conceal truth from outsiders. In fact, Matthew offers almost no teaching in parables to Jesus' opponents outside of chapter 13, so it is impossible to sustain the claim that this chapter marks a major shift in strategy or style. There is simply not enough comparable material elsewhere to enable one to know. The new element which Matthew 13 does identify as a mystery is not the establishment of the church or the postponement of the kingdom but the fact that the kingdom of God is present but not with irresistible power.[56] Even some of the Jewish religious leaders (Joseph of Arimathea and Nicodemus) respond positively to Christ both before and after this proclamation.

Furthermore, the fact that dispensationalists themselves debate at what point the kingdom offer was finally withdrawn from Israel (if not at the end of Matthew 12, how about Acts 2 or 13 or 18 or 28?) suggests that none of these texts clearly delineates the end of an era after which God retracted his offer of the kingdom to the Jews.

Ironically, dispensationalists today often boast of better Jewish-Christian relations than do many other Christians because of their belief in the restoration of the state of Israel as part of their eschatology. What is often overlooked is that their interpretations of the events of the first century are actually more anti-Semitic than those of many other Christian traditions, because they insist that God judged the entire nation rather than simply treating individuals along the lines of their personal responses to Jesus. Of course today

---

[55]See esp. George E. Ladd, *Crucial Questions about the Kingdom of God* (Grand Rapids: Eerdmans, 1952), pp. 101-17, who also expounds and refutes the "postponed kingdom" theory more generally.

[56]Ladd, *Gospel*, p. 56. Contra, e.g., Ray E. Baugham, *The Kingdom of God Visualized* (Chicago: Moody, 1972), p. 88.

virtually all forms of Christianity must face charges of anti-Semitism from various quarters.

The picture of Jesus' kingdom teaching which emerges from the parables, however, presents him as no more (though no less) radical than the Old Testament prophets with respect to his denunciation of the leadership of Israel.[57] More radical claims emerge only when one turns to the final question which this chapter must address: what does Jesus' teaching in parables imply about his own self-understanding and identity?

9.3 Christology

If virtually every study of the kingdom deals with Jesus' parabolic discourse, the same is decidedly not the case for studies of Christology. A sizable number of treatments of the person and work of Christ have nothing at all to say about Jesus' parables. Apparently they have no bearing in the eyes of many scholars on an understanding of who Jesus was or who he thought he was. Another group of studies makes this presumption explicit. Gustav Aulén speaks for an impressive array of modern interpreters when he explains that at best Jesus believed that God was working through him:

> When Jesus in the parables wants to defend *his* conduct, he speaks, as we have said before, of how *God* acts. This does not imply that he is putting himself in God's place, but it undoubtedly means that he views himself as the chosen instrument of God's new deal.[58]

In this case, the parables may disclose Jesus as a great teacher or prophet, perhaps even as the greatest in Israel's history, but he remains simply a faithful Jew allowing the Spirit to use him for God's service.

Throughout the history of Christian interpretation, however, this

---

[57]Most Jewish studies of Jesus say little about the parables. What is often noted is the parables' understanding and unusual illustrations of grace. Some find this emphasis too antinomian; others take it as a sign of diversity in first-century Judaism. See Donald A. Hagner, *The Jewish Reclamation of Jesus* (Grand Rapids: Zondervan, 1984), pp.196-198, and on the kingdom more generally, pp. 133-70.

[58]Gustaf Aulén, *Jesus in Contemporary Historical Research* (Philadelphia: Fortress, 1976), p. 143. Cf. Etienne Trocmé, *Jesus as Seen by His Contemporaries* (London: SCM; Philadelphia: Westminster, 1973), p. 96. Breech, *Silence*, p. 217, goes so far as to affirm that "one of the most striking characteristics of Jesus' core sayings and parables is that he remained basically silent about himself."

view has appealed only to a minority of commentators. The vast majority in earlier ages have seen explicit Christology in much of the parabolic imagery. And even today a few interpreters believe that Jesus was directly depicting himself by means of some of the characters in his stories. A more substantial number reject this opinion but admit implicit Christology of one form or another. The rest of this chapter will distinguish and assess three different groups of perspectives across the spectrum of interpretation which range from seeing only the barest hints of Messianic consciousness in Jesus' parables to finding it plainly taught in many places. The two ends of this continuum will be examined first, and then a mediating view will be presented.

9.3.1 Explicit Christology?

Pre-critical exegesis not only regularly understood the parables as allegories but consistently assumed that key characters in the various narratives unambiguously stood for Jesus himself.[59] Common equations included linking Christ with the good Samaritan, the shepherd searching for the lost sheep, the sower scattering seed, and the bridegroom in the parable of the ten virgins. Some commentators have also seen references to Jesus behind the figures of the treasure hidden in the field,[60] the pearl of great price,[61] one of the unnamed individuals who sorts through the fish caught by the dragnet,[62] and the man who gave the great supper.[63] In these latter instances, it seems clear that devotion for Christ has replaced level-headed exegesis.

The treasure and pearl more naturally stand for the kingdom, and while Christians believe that Jesus is at the center of the kingdom, he is not the sum total of it. In the case of the dragnet, Matthew 13:49 explicitly identifies the fish sorters as angels. And to the extent that Matthew's wedding banquet is modeled on Luke's great supper, even if the two passages reflect distinct utterances from separate occasions in Christ's ministry, then the banquet giver in

---

[59]For the earliest (i.e., ante-Nicene) period of parable interpretation, see esp. Maurice F. Wiles, "Early Exegesis of the Parables," *SJT* 11 (1958):287-301. For a defense of this ancient Christologizing, see Leslie W. Barnard, "To Allegorize or not to Allegorize?" *ST* 36 (1982): 1-10.

[60]Irenaeus *Adv. Haer.* IV, xxvi, 1.

[61]Clement of Alexandria *Fragments from the Nicetas* V.

[62]Origen *Commentary on Matthew* X, 11-12.

[63]Augustine *Sermons on New Testament Lessons* 62.

each case must be God. If Christ appears at all he would be the king's son—a character who appears only incidentally in Matthew 22:1 and not at all in the Lukan account.

The former equations of Jesus with Samaritan, shepherd, sower or bridegroom still occur occasionally in scholarly treatments.[64] The latter three identifications are fairly natural, for in each instance they match Jesus with the master figures in the parables. But according to the interpretations developed in this book, these characters symbolize God first of all, rather than Jesus. There may well be Christology here, but it does not seem explicit. As for the Samaritan, he is not a master figure at all, though he does offer help for the wounded man, much as Jesus showed compassion on many with varying ailments. But the most incisive thrust of the parable— redefining "neighbor" to include even one's hated enemy—is often masked when the Samaritan is read as a cipher for Christ, so it is doubtful if interpreters should warm to this approach.

Other modern commentators have proposed different allegorical equations. Jesus has been found in such unlikely places as behind the tower builder and warring king, the men who discovered the hidden treasure and precious pearl, and even the prodigal son and the man left for dead in the ditch![65] In the first two pairs of parables, the correspondence is understandable; Jesus did count the cost before embarking on his mission of redemption, and he was willing to give up all for the valuable people he came to save. But the contexts of each of these parables suggests rather that Jesus is teaching *his disciples* both *what* they must sacrifice and *for what* they must sacrifice in order truly to follow him.

Karl Barth's famous view of Jesus as the prodigal compensates for the oft-noted lack of any imagery for atonement in the parables. But it is inappropriate to expect every theological topic to emerge from any limited cross-section of Jesus' teaching, and Barth's under-

---

[64]So, respectively, Birger Gerhardsson, *The Good Samaritan—The Good Shepherd?* (Lund: Gleerup, 1958); Jacques Dupont, "La parabole de la brebis perdue," *Greg* 49 (1968):265-87; Rudolf Schnackenburg, *God's Rule and Kingdom* (New York: Herder & Herder, 1963), p. 151; Fred L. Fisher, *Jesus and His Teachings* (Nashville: Broadman, 1972), p. 89.

[65]See, respectively, J. D. M. Derrett, "Nisi Dominus Aedificaverit Domum: Towers and Wars (Lk XIV 28-32)," *NovT* 19 (1977):249-58; Jeffrey A. Gibbs, "Parables of Atonement and Assurance: Matthew 13:44-46," *CTQ* 51 (1987):19-43; Karl Barth, *Christian Dogmatics*, vol. 4.2 (Edinburgh: T. & T. Clark, 1958):21-25; Hermann Binder, "Das Gleichnis vom barmherzigen Samariter," *TZ* 15 (1959):176-94.

standing of Jesus' humanity involves certain questionable assumptions about Christ's having a sinful nature.[66] Jesus parallels the man in the ditch, finally, only in that he too was rejected by the Jewish leaders and embraced by unlikely adherents. But his disciples do not rescue or nurse him; the parallels break down too quickly to prove very convincing. In sum, it would seem best not to claim that Jesus intended any of the characters or objects in his parables to stand *solely* for himself. As consistently noted, they first of all point rather to God, God's people and God's enemies.

9.3.2 Implicit Christology Indirectly Expressed?

A significant minority of scholars agree that it is improper to equate any given parabolic character with Jesus but nevertheless believe that Jesus was implicitly teaching about his own mission and identity through the imagery of the parables more generally. For many in this camp, the precise nature of that identity is not clear, since Jesus only drops hints about it. Thus one reads that the parables are "an expression of Jesus' self-understanding" that the "saving relationship" which his teaching implies is "to him,"[67] that Jesus is the one who "uniquely brings [the kingdom] to expression . . . through his words and deeds and so makes it happen,"[68] or that his Messianic character lies not in any titles or explicit claims but in the "unmediatedness of his historic appearance."[69]

Authors of such statements make it clear from their writings overall that they do not believe Jesus understood himself to be the Messiah with anything like the clarity which historic Christianity has assigned to him, but they are equally clear that they believe Jesus was more than just a great religious teacher. Still, it is often difficult to pinpoint just what precisely they do believe about Jesus in between these two poles.

At least three claims do seem to emerge, however, among those writers who may be described as supporting implicit Christology

---

[66]Dale Moody, *The Word of Truth* (Grand Rapids: Eerdmans, 1981), p. 419, declares: "Karl Barth asserted that Jesus had a 'fallen human nature' and that is what Paul meant when he said the Son of God came in the likeness of human flesh. D. M. Baillie is not too severe when he identifies this with . . . adoptionism." For Moody on the other hand, "it was the sinless humanity of Jesus that made him the only true man who ever lived."

[67]Edward Schillebeeckx, *Jesus: An Experiment in Christology* (London: Collins; New York: Seabury, 1979), pp. 170-71.

[68]Michael L. Cook, *The Jesus of Faith: A Study in Christology* (New York: Paulist, 1981), p. 47.

[69]Bornkamm, *Jesus*, p. 178.

indirectly expressed. *First is the audacity with which Jesus justifies his seemingly scandalous actions by referring to God's similar behavior.* The parables of Luke 15 supply the classic examples of this practice. Jesus has been criticized for eating with tax collectors and sinners, and he replies with three stories about God's unrelenting efforts to seek and to save the lost. Eduard Schweizer concludes forcefully:

> Does Jesus then appear in this parable? Certainly not—and yet the joy that the parable seeks to have us share is found only where Jesus imparts the presence of God to men. . . .
>
> Those who nailed him to the cross because they found blasphemy in his parables—which proclaimed such scandalous conduct on the part of God—understood his parables better than those who saw in them nothing but the obvious message which should be self-evident to all, of the fatherhood and kindness of God, meant to replace superstitious belief in a God of wrath.[70]

Similar claims surface when one considers the implications of the parable of the two debtors (Lk 7:41-43), the children in the marketplace (Lk 7:31-35 par.) and the wicked tenants (Mk 12:1-9 pars.). In the last of these passages especially, it becomes obvious that Jesus' parables do not merely illustrate spiritual truths, but attack his opponents for failing to recognize the unique presence of salvation which his person and ministry represented ("And they sought to lay hold on him, but feared the people; for they knew that he had spoken the parable against them"—Mk 12:12).[71]

Second, the parables themselves bring a division among Jesus' audience. Some persons are attracted and others repelled. To borrow from the terminology of the new hermeneutic, the parables create "language events" which bring about the very situation they describe—the inbreaking reign of God—and thereby supply salvation for some and pronounce judgment on others.

Martin Petzoldt's detailed study of the parables and Christian doctrine demonstrates how a given narrative repeatedly teaches both about the ways of God with men and the ways of men before God. For Petzoldt, Jesus' parables act as a linguistic mediation between

---

[70]Eduard Schweizer, *Jesus* (London: SCM; Richmond: John Knox, 1971), pp. 28-29.

[71]Others who stress the radical nature and Christological implications of Jesus' self-defense in light of God's behavior include Jeremias, *Parables*, p. 230; Eta Linnemann, *Parables of Jesus: Introduction and Exposition* (London: SPCK, 1966 [= *Jesus of the Parables: Introduction and Exposition* (New York: Harper & Row, 1967)]), p. 87; and Fuchs, *Studies*, p. 21.

the divine and the mortal, with the unique ability actually to bring about the type of transformation which Jesus discloses God as requiring of every human life.[72] More generally, in Beasley-Murray's words, "the mission of the one who proclaims the kingdom and bears its grace is none other than the mission of God acting in sovereign graciousness towards men."[73] Not only does Jesus have the audacity to justify his behavior by talking about God's activity, but he also claims to be the unique bearer of the kingdom's presence, the one who is inaugurating God's reign through his speech and his actions.

Third, Jesus' parabolic discourse involves extraordinary self-referential claims. In using parables to justify his table fellowship with the ceremonially unclean, Jesus is implicitly setting himself above the Mosaic dietary laws no less than in the more explicit debates with the Pharisees over cleanliness ritual (cf. esp. Mk 7:1-23 pars., esp. v. 19b). Yet who can set aside God's law but God himself? Or again, in pronouncing forgiveness of sins for the woman of ill repute (Lk 7:36-50) and for the tax collector rather than the Pharisee (18:9-14), Jesus implicitly claims for himself a prerogative reserved exclusively for God. No less than in the controversy engendered by the healing of the paralytic (Mk 2:1-2 pars.), Jesus raises the question of who has the right to forgive sins if not God alone.

Royce Gruenler thoroughly examines similar examples, even while limiting his study to sayings and parables deemed authentic by Norman Perrin's fairly minimalist core of Gospel tradition. In some instances Gruenler would appear to overstate his case, but enough solid evidence nevertheless remains to justify his conclusion: "The overall effect is quite convincing that Jesus was conscious of a divine authority in claiming the power to forgive sins and inviting sinners and outcasts to the messianic banquet table."[74] So

---

[72]Martin Petzoldt, *Gleichnisse Jesu und christliche Dogmatik* (Göttingen: Vandenhoeck & Ruprecht, 1984). Cf. Hans Weder, *Die Gleichnisse Jesu als Metaphern* (Göttingen: Vandenhoeck & Ruprecht, 1978); Merklein, *Jesu Botschaft.*

[73]Beasley-Murray, *Jesus*, p. 129. Cf. A. Ambrozic, *The Hidden Kingdom* (Washington, D.C.: Catholic Biblical Association of America, 1972), p. 132; Jürgen Roloff, *Das Kerygma und der irdische Jesu* (Göttingen: Vandenhoeck & Ruprecht, 1970), p. 227.

[74]Royce G. Gruenler, *New Approaches to Jesus and the Gospels* (Grand Rapids: Baker, 1982), p. 32. Similarly, John B. Cobb, Jr., *Christ in a Pluralistic Age* (Philadelphia: Westminster, 1975), p. 134, observes "in Perrin's account that Jesus associated himself and his ministry with the present reigning of God in a way that implicitly claims an authority that goes far beyond that of the prophets." The work on which Gruenler and Cobb primarily rely is Norman Perrin, *Rediscovering the Teaching of Jesus* (New York: Harper & Row; London: SCM, 1967).

too, as Leonhard Goppelt remarks in connection with Luke 15, "wherever Jesus bestowed his fellowship on sinners—be it through table fellowship, through healing the infirm, or through the summons to follow in discipleship—here was where forgiveness coming from God took place, even though this was not expressly stated."[75]

9.3.3 Implicit Christology Directly Expressed

Perhaps the best approach to the parables accepts all of the insights of those scholars who perceive implicit Christology as just discussed, but then goes one step further. *Without denying that God the Father is the primary referent behind all of the master figures in Jesus' narratives, we may argue that Jesus frequently intended his audiences to associate him with the Father in some respect.* In other words, the meaning of a stock metaphor may point above all to God, but its use in the contexts of the parables may suggest a derivative application to Jesus.

Unlike the *explicitly* Christological view, this approach does not see Jesus as the only or primary referent behind various parabolic characters, but it does go beyond the type of implicitly Christological interpretations discussed above to grant that Jesus did intend a direct (one could even say allegorical)[76] application of certain imagery to himself at the level of second-order meaning or significance.

Probably the best exposition of this "implicit Christology *directly expressed*" appears in a little-known article by Philip Payne. Since Payne uses the term "Christology" in the narrower sense of that which points to Jesus as Christ or Messiah rather than the more common, broader sense of *any* teaching about the person of Jesus, he prefers to speak of "Jesus' implicit claim to *deity* in his parables."[77]

Payne surveys ten images, commonly found in the parables, which regularly refer to God in the Old Testament. These include sower, director of the harvest, rock, shepherd, bridegroom, father, giver of forgiveness, vineyard owner, Lord and King. In several

---

[75]Leonhard Goppelt, *Theology of the New Testament*, vol. 1 (Grand Rapids: Eerdmans; London: SPCK, 1981), p. 131.

[76]As in E. J. Tinsley, "Parables and the Self-Awareness of Jesus," *ChQ* 4 (1971):18-26.

[77]Philip B. Payne, "Jesus' Implicit Claim to Deity in His Parables," *TrinJ* n.s. 2 (1981):3-23, italics mine. Cf. Jacques Dupont, *Pourquoi des paraboles?* (Paris: Cerf, 1977), pp. 35-40, who identifies fifteen parables which interpret Jesus' mercy, judgment and patience in light of God's corresponding behavior, as represented by specific characters in the various narratives. Søren Ruager, *Das Reich Gottes und die Person Jesu* (Frankfurt a. M. and Cirencester, UK: Peter Lang, 1979), believes the parables directly disclose Jesus' *Messianic* self-understanding.

instances such language does not require a view of Christ any different from Aulén's, noted above: Jesus was acting as God's representative. Payne admits as much, but then goes on to stress that the overall impact of such imagery goes far beyond that of any of God's previous prophets or spokesmen.

Never did such individuals apply symbols for God to themselves so consistently as did Jesus, and none ever claimed that he was doing precisely what the Scriptures said God himself would do. Yet in the parables Jesus claims to forgive sin, usher in the kingdom, sow his word in human hearts, graciously welcome undeserving sinners into God's presence, seek out and rescue his lost sheep, oversee the final judgment, and distinguish those who will from those who will not enter the kingdom. Finally, many of the images of Jesus' parables focus not simply on what Jesus does but on who he is: the bridegroom, the good shepherd, the returning king, the lord of the vineyard who may do whatever he wants with what is his, or the master with authority to reward the faithful and punish the wicked. Payne appropriately concludes, "The very fact that Jesus so consistently applies to himself images and symbols for God reinforces the case that he sees himself, in some sense at least, as God."[78]

J. Ramsey Michaels also envisions Jesus putting himself in the place of various characters in the parables. Michaels admits that a Christological interpretation of the parables is usually seen as a later development in Christian reflection. But he goes on to argue that the reverse is also possible—that Jesus originally identified himself with a given individual in his stories and told the parables in order to invite others to make a similar identification.[79] Examples include the good shepherd, the woman with the lost coin, the sower, the harvester of the wheat and tares, the owner of the vineyard, and the bridegroom.

But Michaels goes one step further and considers that Jesus may also often have identified with subordinate characters in various parables. Clearly in the wedding banquet or great supper, the wicked tenants, and the householder and thief, if Jesus is to be linked with any of the stories' individuals, it must be with a son,

---

[78]Payne, "Jesus' Implicit Claim," p. 20.

[79]Michaels, *Servant and Son*, p. 105.

servant or burglar rather than with the master/owner figures. May one generalize from this and see Jesus behind some of the servant figures elsewhere?

It was certainly central to his teaching that Jesus came as one who would serve rather than be served (Mk 10:45 pars.) Thus Michaels speculates that Jesus might have identified, in turn, with more than one character in a given parable. For example, in the wheat and tares, his original point of self-identification might well have been with the servants who asked their master about the field, even though by the end of the story Jesus is ready to identify the one who sows the good seed with "the Son of man" (Mt 13:37).

Or in the story of the prodigal, Christ "can share the perspective of the waiting father only by first putting himself in the place of the aggrieved older son."[80] Again, like the servants who risked investing their master's money in the parables of the talents and pounds, Jesus knew that his mission "meant risking all for the 'lost sheep of Israel,' for the tax collectors and prostitutes to whom he was sent."[81] In some places Michaels seems to push this interpretive perspective too far, but in principle it underscores an important truth. If the parables implicitly point to Jesus' deity, they equally carefully underline his full humanity.

Additional details further highlight how the parables focus attention not merely on God but on Jesus' claiming extraordinary authority. In the parable of the two builders, the criterion of judgment is whether or not people put into practice "these words of mine" (Mt 7:24). The Old Testament prophet might make the same claim, but it would be clear that he was speaking not his own words but the Lord's. Jesus' pronouncement points to a more direct connection between himself and God.

So also the vindication promised by the conclusion to the children in the marketplace is based on people's responses to Jesus as the Son of man (Mt 11:19). The Son of man in the parable of the wheat and tares, however, is no mere human being, but one who exercises authority over the angels, sending them to judge humanity (Mt

---

[80]Ibid., p. 218.
[81]Ibid., p. 296.

13:37).[82] The conclusion to the parable of the unjust judge depicts the Son of man exercising a similar judicial role (Lk 18:8).

If the sower in the parable so-named is a natural image for Jesus, at least derivatively, then the same must be said about the farmer of the seed growing secretly, the man who plants the mustard seed, and the woman who leavens her bread.[83] At least in its current context, the parable of the laborers in the vineyard is a direct response to the question of Jesus' disciples about what reward they will receive for following him (Mt 19:27). The warring king and tower builder similarly describe what it takes not just to be part of God's family but to be one of Jesus' disciples (Lk 14:33).

Of course, most of these interpretations are commonly assigned to a later stage of the Gospel tradition, but I have argued in part one of this book that such assignments are unwarranted. And even when one adopts a rigorous traditio-historical method of analyzing the Gospels, so that only that which is demonstrably pre-Markan in origin and Semitic in style may even be considered as possibly authentic, solid support emerges for a Christological interpretation of the parables at the earliest stages of the tradition.[84]

In fact, the type of implicit Christology for which this chapter has argued stands as strong a chance as any of representing what the historical Jesus actually intended to communicate. For, on the one hand, it remains sufficiently muted and ambiguous that it would not likely have arisen in the early church. A post-Easter desire to exalt Jesus would have almost certainly done so more explicitly.[85]

---

[82]The meaning and authenticity of the various Son of man sayings is an area of vast research and controversy. I have dealt with it briefly in *The Historical Reliability of the Gospels* (Leicester and Downers Grove: IVP, 1987), pp. 249-51. I do not find the arguments persuasive which attempt to overthrow a fair consensus of interpreters who hold that the majority of the Son of man sayings fall into the core of the more demonstrably authentic Gospel tradition, and that at least some of them require an interpretation of the Son of man, with whom Jesus identified himself, as an exalted heavenly figure comparable to that of Daniel 7:13. See esp. Chrys C. Caragounis, *The Son of Man* (Tübingen: Mohr, 1986); Seyoon Kim, *"The 'Son of Man' " as the Son of God* (Tübingen: Mohr, 1983; Grand Rapids: Eerdmans, 1985); William Horbury, "The Messianic Associations of 'The Son of Man,' " *JTS* 36 (1985):34-55.

[83]Dahl, "Parables of Growth," pp. 162, 166.

[84]Hubert Frankemölle, "Hat Jesus sich selbst verkündet? Christologische Implikationen in den vormarkinischen Parablen," *Bibel und Leben* 13 (1972):184-207.

[85]Cf. Payne, "Jesus' Implicit Claims," p. 18: "These symbols for God applied by Jesus to himself in the parables are not interpreted in the gospels as divine claims. In the light of these factors, we can be confident that they were not later theologically-motivated insertions." The same logic is applied to other aspects of Synoptic Christology in F. F. Bruce, "The Background to the Son of Man Sayings," in *Christ the Lord*, ed. H. H. Rowdon (Leicester and Downers Grove: IVP, 1982), pp. 50-70; and D. A. Carson, "Christological Ambiguities in the Gospel of Matthew," in ibid., pp. 97-114.

Yet, on the other hand, such a striking and substantial conjunction of images for God applied to the person and work of Jesus, however implicitly, is not likely coincidental. Jesus himself must have intended to hint at his heavenly origin by means of these metaphors, even if he never explained them as such in so many words.[86]

9.4 Conclusions

Although many scholars shortchange the doctrinal value of the parables, these passages actually disclose a rich treasure of theological insights. They illuminate the nature of God and of discipleship, and they warn of an inescapable future judgment for all humanity. The concept which best encapsulates all this teaching is the kingdom of God: God's dynamic, personal rule throughout the universe which fashions a community of faithful followers to model his mandates for creation.

Jesus inaugurated the kingdom with his ministry, but its culmination remains still future. It includes both reign and realm, personal transformation and social reform. The kingdom is larger than the church, but it does embrace all who are truly God's people. There is no evidence that Jesus offered the kingdom to Israel *as a political entity;* instead he invited all *individuals* of various ethnic backgrounds who heard him (first Jews, then Gentiles) to respond by becoming his followers.

In doing so, he raised the question of his own identity and self-understanding. Who is this one who points people not merely to the Lord but to himself? Who is he who claims to be able to forgive sins, to supersede the Mosaic ceremonies and to judge who will be condemned and who will be justified on the Last Day? Jesus' parables raise the Christological question in a more veiled fashion than do other portions of the Gospel tradition, but they raise it nevertheless. By consistently utilizing stock metaphors for God to justify his own actions, Jesus does not explicitly link himself with his parables' characters by direct allegorical equation. But he does invite his audiences to consider that if various figures in his narratives stand for

---

[86]Again such ambiguity is consistent with Jesus' teaching throughout most of the Gospel tradition. See esp. the thorough study by Joachim Jeremias, *New Testament Theology*, vol. 1 (London: SCM; Philadelphia: Westminster, 1971). Cf. also I. Howard Marshall, *The Origins of New Testament Christology* (Leicester and Downers Grove: IVP, 1976).

God, and if Jesus acts as God does, then in some sense Jesus must be claiming divine prerogatives.

Nothing anywhere close to full-blown Chalcedonian Christology emerges. At the same time, it seems impossible to account fully for Jesus' words without assuming that he understood himself to be more than just a man. It remains for audiences then and now to decide for themselves how to interpret such self-understanding. Was Jesus mad or deliberately deceptive? Or could he actually have been the Son of God? This last option seems far more probable than the former two.[87] If his teachings about judgment are true, then the single most important decision anyone who listens to the parables can make is to follow Jesus in discipleship.

---

[87]The argument here, of course, relies on C. S. Lewis's famous trilemma which I have developed at greater length in my *Historical Reliability;* see esp. pp. xx, 257-58. The discussions of authenticity in part one of this book forestall the fourth possible option which I considered in my earlier book, namely, that Jesus' claims were legendary.

Conclusions to
Part Two

As AT THE END OF PART ONE, THE CONCLUSIONS TO THIS SECtion of the book will be listed in serial fashion. First are conclusions concerning the interpretation of individual parables, then those that arise from a synthesis of Jesus' parabolic teaching.

Individual Parables

1. Eleven parables exhibit simple three-point form. They have three principal characters each, from whom three main lessons may be derived. In each case, the three characters include a master and two contrasting subordinates who symbolize God, his people and those who reject him. These passages include Matthew 11:16-19 par.; 13:24-30, 36-43; 13:47-50; 21:28-32; 24:45-51 pars.; 25:1-13; Luke 7:41-43; 15:4-7 par.; 15:8-10; 15:11-32; and 16:19-31.

2. Ten of Jesus' parables exhibit a complex three-point form. Though at first glance they seem to have additional characters or a more complicated structure than the simple three-point form, they ultimately disclose three main points based on the actions of

three main characters or groups of characters. These passages include Matthew 18:23-35; 20:1-16; 22:1-14; 25:14-30; Mark 4:3-9, 13-20 pars.; 12:1-12 pars.; Luke 10:25-37; 14:15-24; 16:1-13; and 19:11-27.

3. Nine parables are two-pointed. They have only two main characters or elements and teach only two lessons. Two of these parables offer pure contrasts. They resemble the simple three-point form with the master figure removed. These include Matthew 7:24-27 pars. and Luke 18:9-14. Six of these parables depict a master and only one subordinate. They resemble the simple three-point form with the second subordinate removed. These include Mark 4:26-29; Luke 11:5-8; 12:16-21; 13:6-9; 17:7-10; and 18:1-8. One of these parables fits into neither of these two categories. It still contains two characters from whom two distinguishable lessons may be discerned, but it is so brief that it is tempting to try to collapse these into one central truth. This text is Matthew 24:43-44 par.

4. Six parables have only one central character and make only one main point. These include Matthew 13:44; 13:45-46; Luke 13:18-19 pars.; 13:20-21 par.; 14:28-30; and 14:30-32. Many shorter passages, usually not classified as parables, resemble these brief texts too.

Synthesis of Parables

1. Jesus clearly has three main topics of interest: the graciousness of God, the demands of discipleship and the dangers of disobedience. Many insights concerning each emerge when the parables are analyzed in the fashion described above.

2. The central theme uniting all of the lessons of the parables is the kingdom of God. It is both present and future. It includes both a reign and a realm. It involves both personal transformation and social reform. It is not to be equated either with Israel or the church, but is the dynamic power of God's personal revelation of himself in creating a human community of those who serve Jesus in every area of their lives.

3. The teaching of the parables raises the question of Jesus' identity. Who is this one who, by his teaching, can claim to forgive sins, pronounce God's blessing on social outcasts and declare that final judgment will be based on the responses people make to him?

Christological claims are concealed in the parables. They are not as direct as in some other strands of the Gospel tradition, but they are present nevertheless. The restraint of the claims reinforces the case for their authenticity.

4. Jesus' parables include implicit claims to deity. Jesus associates himself with authority figures in his parables which obviously stand for the God of the Hebrew Scriptures. His audiences must decide whether to accept these claims and worship him or reject them as misguided or even blasphemous. But Jesus' parables leave no neutral ground for casual interest or idle curiosity. They sharply divided their original audiences into disciples and opponents. They must continue to function in the same way today.

Author Index

Scripture Index

N.B.: references alluded to only tangentially are not included in this index; main exegetical treatments of specific parables appear in boldface type.

Deuteronomy
20:5-9—*85, 234*
20:19—*269*
21:15-21—*85*

2 Samuel
12:1-10—*48, 184*

Psalms
90:1-4—*89, 301*
118:22—*80, 249*

Isaiah
5:1-7—*248*
6:9—*40*

Ezekiel
17:23—*284*
34:1-31—*180*

Joel
3:13—*264*

Matthew
5:13-16—*287*
7:24-27—*61, 81,* **258-60,** *295, 297-98, 312, 321*
9:12-13—*106, 287*
11:16-19—*60, 109-10,* **208-10,** *311-12, 321*
12:7—*106*
12:11—*118*
12:29—*118*
13:1-52—*90, 111-15, 287, 310*
13:1-23—*40,* **226-29**
13:24-30, 36-43—*17, 30,* **197-200,** *294-95, 297-98, 300, 303, 306, 321-22*
13:31-35—**284-87**
13:44-46—**278-81,** *294, 298*
13:47-50—**201-3,** *294-95, 297-98, 314*
18:12-14—*83, 117,* **183-84**
18:23-35—*60, 117,* **240-43,** *294-95, 298, 303*
19:27-30—*223, 322*
20:1-16—*31, 35, 45, 66, 91, 117, 137,* **221-25,** *294, 298, 307*
21:28-32—*117,* **186-90,** *294-95, 298-99, 306, 311*
21:33-46—*108-9, 123, 189,* **247-51,** *298, 306, 310*
22:1-14—*64, 83, 117, 120-21,* **237-40,** *294, 298, 304, 315*
22:34-40—*230*
24:32—25:46—*90, 117-18, 127, 291, 294-95, 298-99*
24:43-44—**277-78**
24:45-51—*123-26, 128,* **190-93**
25:1-13—*64, 128,* **193-97,** *301, 304*
25:14-30—*32, 83, 142,* **214-17,** *294, 303, 308*
25:31-46—*202*

Mark
2:1—3:6—*41, 90, 106, 318*
2:17—*105-6*
2:18-22—*124-25, 287*
4:1-35—*90, 111-15, 294, 298*
4:3-9, 13-20—*17, 30-31, 80, 107,* **226-29,** *294-95, 297*
4:11-12—*20, 30, 33, 40, 53-55*
4:26-29—*77,* **263-66,** *297, 300*
4:30-32—*45, 73, 90, 122,* **284-87,** *306*
4:35—6:6—*90*
11:12-14, 20-25—*270*
12:1-12—*17, 41, 55, 63, 79-80, 107-8, 123,* **247-51,** *294-95, 298, 317*
12:28-34—*230*
13:28-31—*89, 97, 126, 270*
13:33-37—*83, 126, 190-91*
14:3-9—*184*

Luke
4:23—*46*
5:31-32—*105,287*
5:33-39—*124-25*
6:20-26—*258*
6:47-49—*61, 81,* **258-60**
7:29-30—*187*
7:31-35—*109-10,* **208-10,** *294-95, 317*
7:36-50—**184-86,** *294, 298, 306, 317-18*

8:4-8, 11-15—*107, 111,* **226-29**
9:51—18:14—*86, 116-17*
10:25-37—*31, 35, 73, 75-76, 138-39, 143,* **229-33,** *294-95, 298*
11:5-13—*60,* **274-77,** *294, 298*
11:21-22—*118*
12:13-21—**266-68,** *294, 298, 307-8*
12:35-38—*67, 83, 190-91, 262, 295, 301, 303*
12:39-40—**277-78,** *301*
12:41-48—*123-24, 125-26, 141,* **190-93,** *222, 299, 301, 303*
13:1-9—*31,* **268-71,** *294-95, 298, 311*
13:18-21—*81, 90, 122,* **284-87,** *297*
14:5—*118*
14:15-24—*45, 83, 127,* **233-37,** *294-95, 298, 303*
14:28-33—*92, 142,* **281-84,** *294, 298, 322*
15:1-7—*35, 83, 142, 151-52,* **179-83,** *294, 298-99, 306, 317*
15:8-10—*60, 141,* **179-83,** *294, 298-99, 306, 317*
15:11-32—*15-17, 63, 73, 76-77, 152, 154, 159-60,* **172-79,** *294-95, 298-99, 317*
16:1-13—*32, 60, 93, 219,* **243-47,** *294, 308*
16:19-31—*32-33, 77, 86, 149-50, 152,* **203-8,** *294-95, 298, 306, 308*
17:7-10—**260-63,** *294, 298*
18:1-8—*46, 93,* **271-74,** *275, 294, 298-99, 306*
18:9-14—*141,* **256-58,** *295, 298, 305-6, 318*
19:11-27—*67, 83, 88, 127,* **217-21,** *271, 295, 301, 308*
20:9-19—*79, 88, 107, 123,* **247-51**
21:31—*126*

Romans
13:1—*307*

2 Peter
3:8-10—*89, 301*